Council for Standards in Human Service Education (CSHSE) Standards Covered in This Text

The Council for Standards in Human Service Education (CSHSE) developed ten national standards that guide Human Services departments and help students understand the knowledge, values, and skills as developing Human Services practitioners. These guidelines reflect the interdisciplinary nature of Human Services.

STANDARD	CHAPTER
Professional History	
Understanding and Mastery...	
Historical roots of Human Services	2
Creation of Human Services profession	2
Historical and current legislation affecting services delivery	1–3, 8
How public and private attitudes influence legislation and the interpretation of policies related to Human Services	1, 8
Differences between systems of governance and economics	3
Exposure to a spectrum of political ideologies	
Skills to analyze and interpret historical data application in advocacy and social changes	3
Human Systems	
Understanding and Mastery...	
Theories of human development	2, 8, 9
How small groups are utilized, theories of group dynamics, and group facilitation skills	9
Changing family structures and roles	6, 9
Organizational structures of communities	
An understanding of capacities, limitations, and resiliency of human systems	8
Emphasis on context and the role of diversity in determining and meeting human needs	11
Processes to effect social change through advocacy (e.g., community development, community and grassroots organizing, local and global activism)	3, 8, 10
Processes to analyze, interpret, and effect policies and laws at local, state, and national levels	3, 10
Human Services Delivery Systems	
Understanding and Mastery...	
Range and characteristics of Human Services delivery systems and organizations	1, 3, 10
Range of populations served and needs addressed by Human Services professionals	10
Major models used to conceptualize and integrate prevention, maintenance, intervention, rehabilitation, and healthy functioning	4
Economic and social class systems including systemic causes of poverty	8
Political and ideological aspects of Human Services	
International and global influences on services delivery	2, 3
Skills to effect and influence social policy	

Adapted from the October 2010 Revised CSHSE National Standards

Council for Standards in Human Service Education (CSHSE) Standards Covered in This Text

STANDARD	CHAPTER
Information Management	
Understanding and Mastery...	
Obtaining information through interviewing, active listening, consultation with others, library or other research, and the observation of clients and systems	9
Recording, organizing, and assessing the relevance, adequacy, accuracy, and validity of information provided by others	
Compiling, synthesizing, and categorizing information	
Disseminating routine and critical information to clients, colleagues or other members of the related services system that is provided in written or oral form and in a timely manner	
Maintaining client confidentiality and appropriate use of client data	
Using technology for word processing, sending e-mail, and locating and evaluating information	10
Performing elementary community-needs assessment	
Conducting basic program evaluation	
Utilizing research findings and other information for community education and public relations and using technology to create and manage spreadsheets and databases	10
Planning & Evaluating	
Understanding and Mastery...	
Analysis and assessment of the needs of clients or client groups	6, 8
Skills to develop goals and design and implement a plan of action	6, 8
Skills to evaluate the outcomes of the plan and the impact on the client or client group	6
Program design, implementation, and evaluation	9
Interventions & Direct Services	
Understanding and Mastery...	
Theory and knowledge bases of prevention, intervention, and maintenance strategies to achieve maximum autonomy and functioning	8, 10
Skills to facilitate appropriate direct services and interventions related to specific client or client group goals	3, 5, 8, 10
Knowledge and skill development in: case management, intake interviewing, individual counseling, group facilitation, and counseling, location and use of appropriate resources and referrals, use of consultation	2, 5, 6
Interpersonal Communication	
Understanding and Mastery...	
Clarifying expectations	5, 6, 12
Dealing effectively with conflict	5, 6, 12
Establishing rapport with clients	5, 6, 12
Developing and sustaining behaviors that are congruent with the values and ethics of the profession	4–6

Council for Standards in Human Service Education (CSHSE) Standards Covered in This Text

STANDARD	CHAPTER
Administration	
Understanding and Mastery...	
Managing organizations through leadership and strategic planning	7
Supervision and human resource management	7, 12
Planning and evaluating programs, services, and operational functions	7
Developing budgets and monitoring expenditures	7
Grant and contract negotiation	7
Legal and regulatory issues and risk management	7
Managing professional development of staff	7
Recruiting and managing volunteers	7
Constituency building and other advocacy techniques such as lobbying, grassroots movements, and community development and organizing	7
Client-Related Values & Attitudes	
Understanding and Mastery...	
The least intrusive intervention in the least restrictive environment	8
Client self-determination	8
Confidentiality of information	8
The worth and uniqueness of individuals including: ethnicity, culture, gender, sexual orientation, and other expressions of diversity	1, 11
Belief that individuals, services systems, and society change	8
Interdisciplinary team approaches to problem solving	
Appropriate professional boundaries	
Integration of the ethical standards outlined by the National Organization for Human Services and Council for Standards in Human Service Education	4, 8
Self-Development	
Understanding and Mastery...	
Conscious use of self	6, 11, 12
Clarification of personal and professional values	4, 6, 11, 12
Awareness of diversity	11, 12
Strategies for self-care	11, 12
Reflection on professional self (e.g., journaling, development of a portfolio, project demonstrating competency)	6

STANDARDS FOR EXCELLENCE SERIES

Designed to help students advance their knowledge, values, and skills, the Standards for Excellence Series assists students in associating the Council for Standards in Human Service Education (CSHSE) National Standards to all levels of human services practice.

FEATURES INCLUDE

- **Standards for Excellence grid**—highlighting chapters where various standards are addressed.
- **Standards for Excellence critical thinking questions**—challenges students to think critically about the standards in relation to chapter content.
- **Multimedia links**—correlates content to multimedia assets throughout the text, including video, additional readings, and more.
- **Self-study quizzes**—found throughout the text, self-study quizzes test student knowledge and comprehension of key chapter topics.
- **Chapter review**—link to a scenario-based chapter review including short answer discussion questions.

Human Services

. . . .

A Student-Centered Approach

Susan Kinsella
Saint Leo University

PEARSON

Boston Columbus Indianapolis New York San Francisco Upper Saddle River
Amsterdam Cape Town Dubai London Madrid Milan Munich Paris Montréal Toronto
Delhi Mexico City São Paulo Sydney Hong Kong Seoul Singapore Taipei Tokyo

Editor in Chief: Ashley Dodge
Editorial Assistant: Amandria Guadalupe
Managing Editor: Denise Forlow
Program Manager: Carly Czech
Project Manager: Doug Bell,
    PreMediaGlobal
Development Editor: Angela Mallowes
Executive Marketing Manager: Kelly May
Marketing Coordinator: Jessica Warren
Procurement Manager: Mary Fisher
Procurement Specialist: Eileen Collaro
Art Director: Jayne Conte

Cover Designer: Suzanne Behnke
Interior Designer: Joyce Weston Design
Cover Art: Shutterstock/yellowj
Digital Media Director: Brian Hyland
Digital Media Project Manager: Tina
    Gagliostro
Full-Service Project Management:
    Sudip Sinha/PreMediaGlobal
Composition: PreMediaGlobal
Printer/Binder: LSC Communications
Cover Printer: LSC Communications

Credits and acknowledgments borrowed from other sources and reproduced, with permission, in this textbook appear on appropriate page within text.

Many of the designations by manufacturers and seller to distinguish their products are claimed as trademarks. Where those designations appear in this book, and the publisher was aware of a trademark claim, the designations have been printed in initial caps or all caps.

Library of Congress Cataloging-in-Publication Data
Kinsella, Susan.
    Human services: a student-centered approach/Susan Kinsella, Saint Leo University.—
First edition.
        pages   cm
    Includes bibliographical references and index.
    ISBN-13: 978-0-205-87927-4
    ISBN-10: 0-205-87927-6
    1. Human services—Textbooks.   I. Title.
    HV40.K456 2013
    361—dc23
                                                            2013035634

9   17

ISBN-10: 0-205-87927-6
ISBN-13: 978-0-205-87927-4

Contents

· ·

3. The Early History of Helping Others   38

. . . .

4. Developing Competence with Diverse Cultures   70

. . . .

7. Strategies of Intervention with Communities and Organizations   129

8. Current Social Issues   146

Preface

To my husband, Kevin, and my sons, Matthew and Patrick, who are the source of my inspiration.

Human Services: A Student Centered Approach is based on ideas students have given me over the last 30 years. I have taught both social work and Human Services classes for many years and the challenge has been to get students to actually read the book! As I was developing this textbook, my main goal was to make sure students would want to read this text and engage in its features.

Features

There are many features in this text to enhance your experience; however, they are only as useful as you make them. By engaging with this text and its resources, you'll gain a sense of professional development and opportunities including:

- **History of Professional Helping**—engages students to review each area, on their own, of the country's historical account of significant people and the popular programs and services they created in their region of the United States.
- **Exercises and Practice-related case studies**—engages students to read, review, and practice knowledge, values, and skills in case management; prepares for interviewing, assessing, and developing treatment plans; and assess their own skill level and competencies.
- **Research and Data**—current details about what's happening with children, adolescents, adults, and the elderly worldwide.
- **Career Opportunities**—including the job outlook for Human Services, where to find jobs, and how to prepare yourself for such a rewarding career.
- **Multimedia Resources**—including links to national organizations, conferences, and videos for skill development.

As you learn about the Human Services profession, you will develop insight into your own personal style of working with people and develop knowledge, values, and skills that will enhance you both personally and professionally.

Learning Outcomes

Students will be able to achieve a variety of learning outcomes by using this text and its resources, including:

- **Critical Thinking Skills**—students can develop their critical thinking skills by reviewing the standards boxes (indicated by the National Standards series band) and engaging with the multimedia resources highlighted in boxes throughout the chapter.

- **Oral Communication Skills**—students can develop their oral communication skills by engaging with others in and out of class to discuss their comprehension of the chapter based on the chapter's learning objectives.
- **Assessment and Writing Skills**—students can develop their assessment and writing skills in preparation for future certification exams by completing topic-based and chapter review assessments for each chapter.
- **CSHSE's National Standards**—students can develop their comprehension and application of CSHSE's national standards by discussing the standards box critical thinking questions.

You are sure to read, watch, or learn something interesting as you practice the exercises and develop your professional skills in each chapter. I have also added plenty of information on career opportunities, the job outlook for Human Services, where to find jobs, and how to prepare yourself for such a rewarding career. You are about to enter on a journey like no other. As you learn about the Human Services profession, you will also develop insight into your own personal style of working with people and develop knowledge, values, and skills that will enhance you both personally and professionally.

I would love to hear from you as you read this book. Send me an e-mail and let me know what you think. I'm at susan.kinsella@saintleo.edu

Acknowledgments

I would like to thank my colleagues from the National Organization of Human Services, the Southern Organization of Human Services, the Council on Standards in Human Services Education, and the faculty, staff and administration of Saint Leo University. So much of who I have become has evolved over the years with my professional and personal associations with peers who have inspired me to think out of the box, develop new ideas, be persistent, and forge ahead in this profession of Human Services. I have been fortunate to have wonderful mentors along the way and a family that supports my work and the love of helping others.

Many thanks to the reviewers of this book, Maureen Donohue-Smith, Elmira College; Alice Lun, Borough of Manhattan Community College; Lori Gardinier, Northeastern University; Kelly Felice, Metropolitan State University of Denver; Brenda Forster, Elmhurst College; Brian Flynn, Binghamton University; David Cousert, University of Southern Indiana; Maria Ortega, Washtenaw Community College; and Justine Pawlukewicz, New York City College of Technology, who have taken the time to read the text and offered me ideas and kept me motivated to finish the book. Pearson and PreMediaGlobal have been wonderful, specifically Carly Czech, Angela Mallowes, and Doug Bell, who have provided valuable assistance to this first-time author and novice at publishing. Nazveena Begum found the beautiful photos you see in this book and Mark Schaefer checked on the technical permissions. Sudip Sinha oversaw the copyediting as the project manager, a tedious but necessary job. Many other people were involved in the publishing of this book, but these are the people I worked with the most. What a learning experience this has been for me! I could not have written this book without the team. Saint Leo University has provided a photo for one Chapter 11, which was helpful in painting a visual picture of a Christmas crèche. My sons, Matthew and Patrick, spent their Christmas holiday creating drawings for several chapters, and my husband, Kevin, read each chapter and offered critical advice. He also spent many evenings over the last year preparing dinner while I worked on the book. Thank you everyone.

Susan Kinsella

This text is available in two formats—digital and print.
To learn more about our programs, pricing options, and customization,
visit **www.pearsonhighered.com**

CHAPTER 1

Introduction to Human Services

. . . .

What Are Human Services and Service Delivery Systems? Why Are They Needed?

Jim West/Alamy

The chapter-opening photo shows professional workers and volunteers assisting people after Hurricane Sandy struck the Northeastern seaboard from New Jersey through New York and parts of New England in October of 2012. Thousands of people were stranded in shelters for days without enough food or drinking water or proper sanitary restroom facilities, and then became hostages in buildings that were flooded and dangerous. People, mostly those who were poor, sick, mentally ill, and disabled, were at the mercy of volunteers, police officers, Red Cross workers, or others who toiled for days to move people out of the decaying conditions. Millions of people were without power to light or heat their homes, or to charge their cell phones, so they were completely cut off from the help they needed. Hospitals had to move patients after generators shut down. The main transportation system in New York, the underground subway, was flooded and closed, preventing people from moving in or out of the city. Staten Island was one borough that workers could not reach for days and were not aware that help was so desperately needed until residents were finally able to notify people that they needed immediate assistance. Workers had to bring food, water, and supplies to stranded residents across several states, get transportation to move people both in and out of the city, and provide medical help for many who suffered with illnesses, diabetes, heart problems, and other life-threatening medical problems. The coast of New Jersey was obliterated with many communities disappearing under a deluge of sand. The destruction was massive, the worst in American history for a storm of that magnitude, with billions of dollars in estimated damages across several states.

This brings back memories for me. In 1972, another hurricane of historic proportions, Hurricane Agnes, hit the northeastern part of the country. In Pennsylvania where I lived, people were forced to evacuate and move to higher ground. The international airport was the site chosen as the emergency shelter. Along with a group of friends, I made my way to the airport to help those families whose lives had been turned upside down. I remember working with the Red Cross and many local churches to serve food, hand out blankets, and often just to sit and reassure people that things would turn out all right. I was 16 at the time, and although the situation was dire, I was enjoying myself. It felt so natural to be helping others, and I found that no job was too menial. I prepared food, cleaned sleeping areas, helped with child care, made telephone calls for people, sat with elderly residents, and handed out clothes, blankets, and so on. Whatever was needed, I did it. It was easy to be helpful and a bit exciting to be up all night as busloads of people arrived from the flooded areas. Afterward, many people wanted to know why I stayed so long to help. I was there over 48 hours, and after going home to rest and change clothes, I wanted to go back. I knew then I had found my calling. I didn't know there was a name for helping others and I didn't know that professional helping skills could be learned to become more effective. I only knew that it was challenging, fast paced, and very rewarding to help people with services they needed. The strange thing is that after I wrote this first chapter, another flood, named Irene, struck northeastern Pennsylvania in September of 2011 in the exact same spot where it had flooded over 39 years ago. Then in October of 2012, Hurricane Sandy hit the Northeastern seaboard and did even more destruction than anyone could have ever imagined to the coastal areas of several states.

Human services practitioners help adults, the elderly, and the disabled in hospitals, nursing homes, or senior centers.

Matthew Kinsella

After my experience with the Red Cross, I volunteered at summer fund-raising festivals and auctions to help the mentally challenged, worked with autistic children at a residential facility, received paid employment as a child care worker at a day care center, and then became a counselor at a Girl Scout camp. I loved it all. When I enrolled in college, however, I was not sure what I wanted to study. It never occurred to me that my love of helping others could actually be a field of study.

It's all about helping others and enjoying what you do, knowing that your work could make a tremendous difference to someone. It's not a job; it's a choice. If you have never volunteered in an agency or if you feel that you need to spend some time helping others, go to your local United Way agency. It usually will have a list of local agencies that need volunteers. Take time to volunteer now and see if you enjoy helping others before you make a commitment to the Human Services major.

> **Explore the Disaster Response – U.S. section of the Red Cross website to learn more about disaster efforts.**

What's It All About?

What Are Human Services? Who Needs Help? What Is Available?

So you think you want to be a Human Services worker, and you are wondering what exactly that means? This may be the career for you if you like helping children, adolescents, adults, or the elderly meet their needs, or make a necessary life change. Have you ever had a difficult situation at some time in your life and a family member, friend, or some concerned individual came to your aid? You may feel the need to help someone else now. This compassion is what draws thousands of students across the country to the field of Human Services each year. They are determined to make a difference in someone's life.

Perhaps someone told you that you are a people person. Can you remember listening to a friend and helping that person work through a problem? Maybe you are the "go to" person when anyone in your family has an issue. Do you *take time to help others* and actually enjoy doing it? Maybe you are a *good listener* or are *resourceful in finding the services people need*. If so, you are what we call a *natural helper*. These are good qualities that lay the foundation for developing a more *professional* set of *knowledge, values,* and *skills* known as Human Services. Now you need to think about what specific area of Human Services interests you the most. You may like working with adults with disabilities, the elderly with mental health issues, the developing child, or adolescents with substance abuse issues.

In Human Services, you will learn to become competent in certain skill areas that will help you to *assess client needs* and then *select interventions that will help people* work toward achieving their goals (Council for Standards in Human Services Education, 2010). You may find it challenging but productive to learn *interviewing skills* to work with individuals, *facilitation techniques* to work with groups and families, and *public speaking skills* to work with communities. Human Services workers learn about stages of human development so they become knowledgeable about early childhood, adolescence, adulthood, and aging (Neukrug, 2002). People at all stages of life may suffer from physical illnesses, disabilities, drug and alcohol issues, crime, violence, juvenile delinquency, and poverty. These are the kinds of issues that we study in our classes so that Human Services students become comfortable handling these types of problems.

> ### Client-Related Values and Attitudes
>
> *Understanding and Mastery: The worth and uniqueness of individuals including culture, ethnicity, race, class, gender, religion, ability, sexual orientation, and other expressions of diversity*
>
> **Critical Thinking Question:** In providing Human Services to people, there is a professional belief that everyone is entitled to equal treatment. Why are values so important in Human Services? What are some examples of values that we use in our everyday work with clients?

According to the National Organization for Human Services (NOHS), the profession of Human Services is very broad and involves services to meet human needs through a variety of programs ranging from prevention to remediation of problems to improving the quality of life for many populations. The training is *interdisciplinary* and includes learning a *knowledge base* infused with *ethical values* and focusing on *interpersonal skills*. Human Services professionals advocate for improving the quality of care provided in direct service delivery systems as well as increasing the accessibility, accountability, and coordination of services among professionals in a community (NOHS, 2009). In other words, Human Services workers try to prevent problems from happening as well as working to help clients solve problems if they do occur.

You may choose to work *directly* with people in agencies that provide counseling, assist with resources like SNAP, which is the new acronym for the food stamp program, or health care, teach parenting classes, help people find jobs, supervise youth in group homes, or assist women in domestic violence situations. The types of agencies that provide services for life needs are endless. So are the descriptions of jobs that are available for Human Services workers.

You may also choose to work *indirectly* with people by becoming an agency administrator. There are many jobs where you will be more involved in operating an agency than in working with the clients.

There are multiple areas of practice to consider in Human Services. If you like working with children, you may choose a group home for adolescents, a school, or even a day care center for your employment. For those who like working with adults better, agencies like a homeless shelter, women's counseling agency, or mental health center may be a better fit. Some programs have a spiritual emphasis and they may appeal to workers who see themselves helping in a hospice agency or cancer clinic. If you have a religious interest, many churches hire youth counselors to establish programs for adolescents. Most offer some type of counseling to their adult members, a food pantry for families, or even an emergency shelter. Large faith-based organizations also offer international opportunities for mission trips to serve impoverished areas of the world where they bring food and resources as well as religious information. For people with professional degrees in Human Services, there are international opportunities with many religious and professional organizations (Martin, 2014).

Watch the video from the Human Services Council of New York to get a better idea of Human Services work in an urban area.

Watch the HSC video by Pro-Media on the <u>Human Services Council</u> website to learn the value of Human Services organizations.

Understanding Human Services Delivery Systems

Private, Proprietary, Non-Profit, and Government Services

An integrated system of Human Services *through government, private for-profit, and private non-profit agencies* is necessary to provide for the needs of our citizens (Kinsella, 2010). Human Services graduates may choose to work in a variety of different agencies that may be funded through the local, state, or federal government. They may also work for a private agency that may be organized as either a profit-making or a not-for-profit agency. An example of a **government agency** could be each state's Department of Family and Children's Services. These state agencies are responsible under the law to protect children from neglect and abuse. They hire professionals as **caseworkers** to investigate cases of suspected abuse, often place children in foster care, and also teach parents better interpersonal and disciplinary skills that can be used to raise their children. Workers may also recruit and train foster parents or seek adoptive parents for children who are no longer able to live with their biological parents. You may be trained to protect children by removing them from dangerous homes where drugs, alcohol, or violence may threaten their lives. Additional training is often provided by these agencies to assist workers in the decisions they have to make regarding foster home placement (Martin, 2014).

Human Services graduates may also work with government agencies in their state or with the federal government like the Department of Health and Human Services, the Department of Agriculture, the Department of Labor, the Department of Housing and Urban Development (HUD), the Department of Justice, the Social Security Administration, or the Economic Opportunity Authority. You may become an **intake worker** and learn how to determine a person's **eligibility** for *food stamps, rental assistance,* or *unemployment benefits.* You may be working to help someone provide a better life for themselves and their families by getting *disability benefits* or finding *training or employment.* You may be working with a senior who is retiring and applying for *social security benefits and Medicare.*

All branches of the U.S. military also offer many social services to the enlisted members. Programs in **Military Community Services** provide care for military members as well as their families. Some jobs require a master's degree or professional licensing, but bachelor level jobs are also available. Workers provide *education and training* to families as well as *offer resources and counseling* (Kinsella, 2009).

Private non-profit agencies are another type of agency where Human Services workers may be employed. These agencies are considered *charitable and can collect donations* from individuals and businesses in order to meet their annual budgets. They are *exempt from federal or state taxes* and can also benefit from *grants* that are available. Private non-profit agencies provide a vast amount of the Human Services that are available in the United States. Not only do Human Services workers in these agencies provide services directly to clients, but they often learn how to do *annual fund-raising, write grants,* and *participate in administrative activities* of the program. **Direct service workers** do *case management, intake, do counseling, make home visits,* and may also assist consumers with life issues like *disaster assistance* or *homelessness.* Sometimes the workers organize and supervise local educational and recreational programs for children and adolescents. Agencies in this category include programs like the Red Cross, Salvation Army, the YMCA, Goodwill, Boy Scouts, Girl Scouts, United Cerebral Palsy, and religious organizations. Most churches offer social services such as a food bank, counseling, cash assistance, shelter, senior companion, or youth programming. If you belong to a church, what does it offer? Do you ever assist with the activities for children, adults, or the elderly? You can read more about the interesting history and current services of some of the above-mentioned non-profit organizations in Chapter 3.

Administrative jobs often appeal to Human Services workers who want to work *indirectly* with people. They may be more interested in working in agencies *developing programs, writing grants, recruiting volunteers,* or *advocating for a change* in social policy. They do not see themselves working directly with the clients. These jobs are important in Human Services since we need people who are interested in operating programs. *Skills in management, budgeting, grant writing, public speaking,* and *program planning* are necessary if you think you would enjoy this type of work. Interpersonal skills are still necessary in this job since workers need to *build relationships* with staff, other community members, and also *work with a board of directors.*

Many **proprietary or private for-profit agencies** also offer Human Services. They are the newest addition to our helping profession. Unlike non-profit agencies, they *cannot solicit donations* and usually are *not eligible for government grants*. They *are not dependent upon annual fund-raising* and *are not tax exempt*. However, many services are now offered that are private for-profit and operate as franchisees or chains. Programs like Le Petite Day Care or Kinder Care are good examples. There are also many proprietary counseling agencies nationwide, recreational programs for children like Chuck-E-Cheese, and even some private prisons. Jobs in these agencies can be attained with your Human Services degree. The same skills are required as for jobs in other sectors. You may also consider operating your own agency if you see a need that is not being met for some service in your local community.

Regardless of where Human Services practitioners are employed, they may offer a variety of services to families that are unable to provide all of the basic necessities of daily living like food, shelter, and clothing. The recent downturn in the American economy has affected many people who did not require services in the past. Often these families have dropped in their social status from middle to lower income, and so they are not accustomed to asking for assistance. Many do not even know where to acquire social services, and barriers like *pride, shame, fear,* and *embarrassment* prevent many people from asking for help. Often they are *not even aware* that they are eligible for assistance. Sometimes people can't connect with the services they need because they don't have the transportation to get there. So they may find it difficult to obtain the free lunch or get to the homeless shelter, or apply for food stamps, unemployment benefits, Medicaid, or disability benefits. It is hard to imagine what people have to endure when they are unemployed, have no money, lose their

Human Services Delivery Systems

Understanding and Mastery: The range and characteristics of Human Services delivery systems and organizations

Critical Thinking Question: Do you think that higher taxes would increase our ability to provide more and better services for our children, seniors, disabled, mentally ill, and those in poverty? Do you think that private proprietary services (those that are privately owned and make a profit) are ethical when it comes to offering a service like day care, counseling, or prisons? Why or why not?

Human Services caregivers work in day care centers with young children.

jo unruh/E+/Getty Images

home, or suffer with substance abuse, or have other physical or mental disabilities. When we try to put ourselves in their position, we call this **empathy**. Workers who are empathic can understand the hardships of living and try to provide the quality of service they would like others to give to them if they were in the same situation.

> **Assess your comprehension of <u>Understanding Human Services Delivery</u> by completing this quiz.**

Around the Globe

The American Red Cross Offers National and International Aid.

In January of 2010, a 7.0 magnitude earthquake hit the country of Haiti, the poorest nation in the Western Hemisphere. The city of Port-au-Prince sustained the greatest damage with reconstruction of major buildings and homes yet to begin. Over 200,000 people were killed and over 300,000 were injured. One million people still live in homes in tent cities, and chronic illnesses like cholera have been spreading with over 5,000 reported deaths so far. It is hard to imagine something so devastating as these details. Human Services workers from organizations like the Red Cross and Habitat for Humanity have worked non-stop for three years to help people rebuild their lives.

Explore the International Services provided by the <u>Red Cross</u>. Learn about the progress made in Haiti.

The American Red Cross is a U.S. national emergency organization. It provides a variety of services from disaster relief at home and abroad to health and safety training, which includes first aid and Cardio Pulmonary Resuscitation classes. The Red Cross is also America's go-to agency for blood, and it both collects and distributes this lifesaving fluid. It also supports military families by providing an

Stefan Trappe/Alamy

Red Cross workers help an injured child unto a stretcher in Haiti.

information and referral service, linking families to necessary services both in the United States and in foreign countries. When an emergency strikes, the Red Cross uses its communication network to notify military members and their families of the problem. The American Red Cross also works on an international level with the Global Red Cross and the Red Crescent to offer services to vulnerable countries around the world.

Interested in becoming an International Red Cross worker? Explore <u>Career Opportunities</u> to learn more.

The American Red Cross also helped to vaccinate over 1 billion children for measles from 2001 to 2008. It is still educating people worldwide about how to prevent HIV/AIDS, and between 2004 and 2011 it has taught 1.7 million people these prevention measures.

Putting Theories to Work

The Human Services Model

Human Services practitioners must consider what problems their clients bring to the agency. The concern is for the individual and that person's *interaction* with the environment. Is the interaction *functional* or *dysfunctional*? The environment may be the family, neighborhood, work community, or other institutions like a school, church, or criminal justice system. The **Human Services Model** allows the practitioner to *assess* both the client and the environment and consider the *balance* between the two. The focus of treatment is to provide services that will allow the clients to help themselves. Unlike other theoretical models, the Human Services Model understands that problems in living are normal and expected (Woodside and McClam, 2011). How people choose to handle those problems is the concern. Adolescents who reject the rules of their parents and who consider them to be out of date and too controlling are actually normal in their teenage perspectives. Most teens think their parents are out of touch. As long as teens continue to attend school, pass their classes, and come home by a certain time,

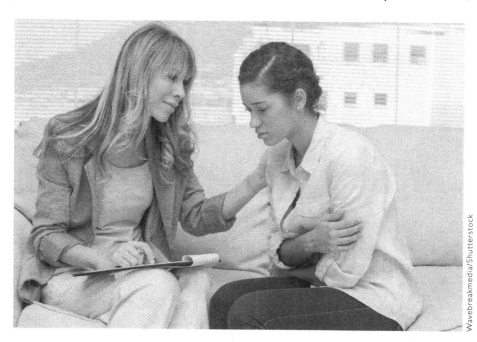

A human services practitioner counsels a troubled adolescent.

Wavebreakmedia/Shutterstock

their interaction with their parents is *functional*, although it may be strained. However, when the teen refuses to follow the house rules, skips school, begins to fail classes, and starts to ignore weekend curfews, then the interaction becomes *dysfunctional* and problems in the balance of the relationship develop. This is when teens run away, get arrested for drugs and alcohol issues, or get pregnant. At this point, parents and students look for assistance with family problems and may enter a counseling agency, guidance office, or mental health center. The Human Services Model offers the practitioner the opportunity to assess both the client situation and the environment and to use a **problem solving approach**. This includes *identifying the problem area, looking at the strengths of the client and the environmental system, and then choosing an intervention that will bring the client and the environment back into balance*. It is important to remember that the work must be *mutual*, indicating that the client must be invested in the intervention as much as the worker is invested, if change is to occur. In this manner clients are taught the problem solving approach so they can begin to solve their own issues. It is important for Human Services practitioners to build on the client's strengths, who must be actively involved in this process. Clients learn from the Human Services worker how to choose interventions and make appropriate decisions, which will guide the change process. In this way they are taught how to apply the Human Services Model in future situations when hopefully they will be able to solve their own issues.

Assess your comprehension of <u>Putting Theories to Work</u> by <u>completing this quiz</u>.

Think Human Services

What Philosophy Best Describes How Americans Feel about Providing Social Services to U.S. Citizens?

Have you ever had to apply for food stamps or some other social service in your lifetime? How did it make you feel? Were others aware that you were receiving this type of benefit? Did you tell them or were you embarrassed to admit that you needed assistance? Sometimes people feel inadequate if they admit to others that they need social services. Why do you think this is the case?

In some countries people receive a **family allowance**, a set amount of money paid for each child in the family. This is provided for all citizens of that country when they have children. It protects children from falling into poverty, even if the parents lose their employment. Every industrialized nation on earth provides this benefit *except for the United States*. All other industrialized countries also provide national health insurance except for the United States (Mandell and Schram, 2009). These countries have an **institutional philosophy** or understanding that all people should have equal access to these **universal services**. In other words, people in those countries agree to pay higher taxes in exchange for public benefits like family allowances, health care, public education, free or subsidized day care, and pension or retirement plans.

The United States is often called the *Reluctant Welfare State*, because of its reluctance to offer universal social services. The philosophy here is clearly not that every one should receive the same services. In fact, admitting that you collect food stamps or some other benefit is more stigmatized here. People are unwilling to pay higher taxes for more benefits. President Obama's health care plan, **the Patient Protection and Affordable Care Act** (2010), also known as "Obama Care," requires everyone to have some type of insurance. This new law was met with intense resistance. People don't want to be told they have to purchase insurance, and yet without it, the costs of health care cannot be controlled. Those who use the emergency room or other services of a hospital and then have no insurance to cover the cost, and no money to pay the bills, drive up the cost of health care for everyone. Who will pay their bills? Other citizens will, because those with health care plans will have higher premiums to cover the costs of those with no insurance. Is this a fair system? Under this new law, everyone must purchase some form of insurance. The U.S. government has offered affordable plans for low- and moderate-income families. States must make insurance available for children of low-income parents. Medicare has been strengthened under this new law, young adults are allowed to stay on their parent's health care family plan until they are 26 years of age, and no insurance company can deny coverage to a child with a disability or anyone with a pre-existing condition. Seniors will receive more money for their prescriptions (APHA, 2012). What exactly do people not like about those benefits? President Obama's reelection seems to have solidified those health care reforms in the United States despite those who disagree with the law.

Search the ABC News website for the article "With Obama's Win, Affordable Care Act Lives" and compare it to recent news reports about Obamacare.

Obviously the philosophy toward social welfare benefits in the United States is not an institutional philosophy with universal benefits given equally to everyone as in other industrialized countries. Instead, the United States is fiercely independent and believes strongly in the work ethic. It maintains a **residual philosophy**, meaning that Americans believe that only those who are most deserving should receive benefits. As a result, there is an established system of *eligibility requirements* for most social services here. In order to receive food stamps, Temporary Assistance to Needy Families (TANF), housing rental assistance, energy assistance, or other benefits, you must prove that you fall below income guidelines. We refer to these as **means-tested services**. You do this by presenting your intake worker with pay stubs from your employment and declaring all income that you receive in a month's time. In this way, only those people who truly need services receive them. We call this maintaining a safety net for those who must have services in this country. Do you think Americans are providing enough care for all the people who need assistance in their country? What philosophy do you think is more equitable for a country, the institutional philosophy or the residual philosophy?

Assess your comprehension of Think Human Services by completing this quiz.

Linking Theory to Practice

Are Health Care Services Offered Equitably to All People?

Now that you realize what Human Services are all about, how programs are delivered, and what philosophies one encounters in the United States, you will understand the importance of volunteering. People may not be eligible for the services they need, so it is necessary to find programs that offer benefits to people without eligibility requirements. As Human Services workers, we are the people who know what is

Explore the St. Joseph's – Candler website to learn more about the Good Samaritan Clinic.

On Wednesday evenings, the local Catholic hospital, called the Good Samaritan Health Care Clinic, sponsors a free health care clinic for anyone who does not have insurance. Most of the patients who come to the clinic are low-income minority people in the community. Mexicans who work in the agriculture industry in the state are among those who wait in long lines for services on Wednesday evenings. They pick onions, fruits, and tobacco for little pay and no benefits. Most are legal immigrants now because employers are fined heavily when Immigration and Customs Enforcement officers from the state monitoring agencies randomly visit the farms and discover illegal workers. In fact, illegal workers are not eligible for any health services or emergency room visits at hospitals in some states due to new legislation. They are denied any benefits regardless of their situation. In some states, illegal, immigrant women who are pregnant or illegal children who need immunizations can receive emergency room services. Despite their legal status, Mexican workers and their families with working visas may receive no help from American social welfare programs. The Personal Responsibility and Work Opportunity Reconciliation Act of 1996 created a block grant known as Temporary Assistance to Needy Families (TANF) for cash assistance for those who are eligible. This legislation changed the way services are offered to the poor in the United States, especially women and children (DiNitto, 2011). Under this new law, families are eligible for cash assistance if they earn less than minimum wage and are American citizens. A three- to five-year lifetime limit is also imposed on the benefits, depending on the state where you live. This means that any American family that earns less than minimum wage would be eligible for a small cash benefit each month, but only for most likely three years or five years maximum in their lifetime. However, in order to receive the benefit, the parents must begin to work at least part time or volunteer at a local community service where they live. As soon as they earn full-time, minimum wages, they are often denied benefits because they may be above the eligibility guidelines for cash assistance. As a result, many of the people previously on the program became ineligible due to the time limit of three years, or as a result of earning minimum wage with their jobs. Many more people were denied benefits because they were not citizens (Mehr & Kanwischer 2011). Depending on when they arrived to the United States, legal Mexican immigrants who previously received benefits to supplement their meager wages were perhaps no longer eligible for services. So, legal workers with visas who arrive with their families and work in dangerous jobs that no one wants, cannot afford health care in emergency situations. As a result, religious organizations, churches, and other non-profit groups offer the services that many of these families need. Physicians, dentists, nurses, and Human Services workers donate their time on Wednesday evenings to care for the crowds of uninsured people who arrive hours early to stand in line, waiting for a chance to receive health care, a benefit that is provided free to people of other industrialized nations in the world.

available in our community. We may even advocate for free services for people who need care but who are not eligible for benefits because they are a few dollars over the guidelines.

Did You Know?

Churches and Religious Organizations Are One of the Largest Providers of Human Services in the United States.

Most people don't realize that churches and religious organizations are one of the largest providers of Human Services in the United States. **Catholic Charities USA** is the second largest provider of services to vulnerable populations across the United States,

including children, the elderly, sick and disabled, substance abusers, those who need rehabilitation services, those who require job training, or those who live in group homes. Second only to the federal government in terms of the services they offer, they also provide disaster response and recovery services. With more than 1,700 agencies across the country, they served more than 8 million people in 2008 with a network of charities that crisscrosses every state. Catholic Charities is headquartered in Alexandria, Virginia, and operates with an annual budget of over $4.6 billion in revenues. Approximately 2 billion of those dollars come from the federal government in Faith-Based Initiatives dollars, with 90 cents of every dollar going directly to services for people.

Many people would be surprised to know that the U.S. government and the country's religious organizations are working together to provide services to those most in need. In fact, other religious organizations, like the Salvation Army, Lutheran Welfare Services, and Jewish Family Services, are also government contractors. This collaboration between the federal government and religious organizations allows the United States to offer a variety of services directly to people in its communities rather than through federal or state services. Funding for religious organizations to offer services was not always available and it was becoming increasingly difficult for churches and religious organizations to continue offering services to clients in their communities without some aid. The White House Office of Faith-Based and Community Initiatives was started in 2001 under President Bush and continues today under President Obama as the White House Office of Faith-Based and Neighborhood Partnerships. The purpose of the program is to strengthen faith-based programs as well as meet the needs of low-income, sick, elderly, and disabled members of American communities through direct grants to religious organizations. In order to protect the separation of church and state, funds cannot be used for religious purposes, prayer, worship, or religious instruction.

Many churches provide help to their members without any direct funding from the federal government. If we consider all the services offered through the churches and

Explore the <u>Catholic Charities – USA</u> and the <u>White House</u> websites to learn more about faith-based programs.

religious organizations in the United States, it is understandable that we provide more services through this private, non-profit sector in the country than through any other type of delivery system. The United States could not provide services to all the people of its country who need help without these faith-based services.

What Would You Do?

Have You Ever Considered Creating a Human Services Program?

Now that you know something about Human Services, where do you see yourself working? Are you interested in a job with children, adolescents, adults, or the elderly? Consider the different types of agencies where you can work in your community. Make a list of all of the agencies that interest you. You may want to find out if they have volunteer opportunities so that you can offer your services and find out if you like the work.

Do you see yourself providing a program that currently does not exist? What type of program could be developed? Would it be a private for-profit or private non-profit agency? Write down your thoughts about the kind of services that should be provided, where it could be offered, and how much you would charge for services. You will read more about these different types of agencies and the skills that are required in other chapters.

Now put yourself into groups of two and work with another partner. Share your answers. What do they see themselves doing in Human Services? Have either of you ever had any experience in Human Services or working with people?

Recall what you learned in this chapter by completing the <u>Chapter Review</u>.

CHAPTER 2

TV Land/AP Images

Human Services Becomes a Profession

. . . .

It Is Expected That more Human Services Professionals Will Be Needed As World Populations Age Upward

If you enjoy watching situational comedies, you may have already seen *Hot in Cleveland*, the television comedy that debuted in 2010, starring Betty White. Although she plays alongside three younger actresses, it is Betty who steals the show with her perfect timing, wit, and wisecracks about her roomies. I often wonder how she can remember all of her lines. She doesn't miss a beat. The show was an instant hit and has been renewed for several seasons already. It makes us think about how we stereotype our seniors. Betty looks great and obviously is doing well at 90! As she says on the show, "90 is the new 70." White is still a comedic powerhouse and successful actress with a long career in television and film. She has upset possible traditional beliefs that seniors need to wind down and their skills are no longer viable. She is a great example of how many seniors are not slowing down and instead continue to work and do the things they enjoy and are still good at doing.

The reality is that demographics in the United States are changing. According to Gillon (2004), post World War II, population rates began changing as 7.6 million babies were born between 1946 and 1964. Known as baby boomers, they make up 40% of America's population. At no time in the history of the United States have birthrates spiked as high as during these decades. After 1964, birthrates leveled off in the United States. These demographic changes have a significant impact on the population today. As the baby boomers age, America will continue to see increases in the senior population and less growth in younger age groups. As this trend continues, Americans will face numerous challenges. Human Services workers will be needed to provide services for this growing age group. Recreational and retirement programs, independent living centers, group homes, nursing home care, day care centers for seniors, Meals on Wheels programs, senior companion programs, health care programs, and mental health services are just a few of the services that will continue to expand as the aging population increases. In addition, Americans will need trained professionals to deal not only with their seniors but also with their children, adolescents, and adults as well. It is antici- pated that the Human Services profession will grow by 28% by the year 2020.

Watch Betty White in *Hot in Cleveland* clips on the TV Land website.

What's It All About?

There Are Many Helping Professions but Human Services Is among the Newest, Having Come on the Scene in the 1960s

A century ago, there were few organized programs or government-provided services for people. It is amazing what has occurred in the United States in such a short period of time regarding new legislation and reforms such as the following:

- Labor laws
- Cash benefits for low-income families
- An organized system of food distribution through the food stamp program
- Social security benefits
- Medicare for aging seniors
- Cash assistance for those with disabilities
- Educational services for those with physical and mental disabilities
- Counseling services and medications for those with mental illness
- Unemployment benefits for those who lose their jobs
- Prevention and crisis programs for child abuse and neglect
- State-mandated foster care and adoption programs for all children under the age of 18

It is hard to imagine not living with the many services that exist today. In Chapter 3, you will learn about the numerous people who stepped forward to develop some of the most useful and creative social service programs that we still have in the United States today. You will be surprised how many of the organizations that we know of were started by just one person with an idea. Many people were involved in devel- oping programs and policies to shape the services that were needed for immigrants to the United States, working women, those with physical disabilities, and mental illness, homeless children, juvenile delinquents, and aging adults who had no pen- sions or retirement benefits.

Social work, psychology, and sociology are all fields of study that began over 100 years ago. While psychology and sociology were more academic degrees based upon research of the individual (psychology) or of groups and communities (sociology), social work was the degree that was more focused on applied skills. The idea of a **helping professional** came about during this time as well. Social work taught a systematic set of skills to enhance the theories of psychology and sociology, which could be used directly with the individual.

The Mental Health Movement in America

As the country moved from the idea that poverty was the result of an individual's fail- ures to understanding that social and economic conditions contributed to a person's success, the concept of how it should be treated changed as well (Kinsella, 2010). People became socially active, women gained the right to vote, and legislation became more progressive in allowing people certain rights in employment, housing, and education, and finally in obtaining social services. More and more people required mental health services, and by the 1950s, it was a national concern. However, with the development of antipsychotic medications, even severely mentally ill people could return home to live in their communities as long as they took their daily dose of medicine. By 1955, the policy of deinstitutionalization began, which meant that patients could begin leaving the mental hospitals and return home. It also meant that once patients were released, those departments of the mental hospital could be shut down and closed forever. Some 400,000 people were returned to their communities with the development of the **Community Mental Health Act**, which called for treatment centers to be built in each community and staffed with professional mental health workers (Woodside & McClam, 2011). At the time, mental health workers referred to psychiatrists, psychologists, social workers, and nurses.

Read "Deinstitutionalization: A Psychiatric Titanic" on the <u>PBS</u> website to learn more about the deinstitutionalization movement in the United States.

The Human Services Movement in America

Historical roots of the Human Services profession are found in the mental health movement, which gained momentum during the 1960s. Since more community services were needed for those returning home to live, there was a need for more advanced workers to assist in these mental health centers. Grants were made available to assist in educating, training, and staffing these programs. The **Scheuer Subprofessional Career Act of 1966** supported the idea that low-income people and minority group members, if trained properly, could become effective mental health aides. Programs were quickly developed in two-year schools to train these people to also become child care workers, correctional officers, and teachers' aides. It was felt that these programs could also help end poverty by assisting underprivileged people to receive job training that would lead to employment.

Read "<u>So You Want to Be a Human Services Worker: What Exactly Does That Mean?</u>" for a better understanding of the Human Services profession.

Since the 1960s, Human Services as a profession and movement has grown exponentially. As a result of their training, Human Services workers increased the number of clients who were served in the mental health system during the 1970s. These workers are known to have provided more direct service care to a large number of clients, allowing those with more difficult issues to be seen by the more advanced practitioners (Kinsella, 2010).

During the late 1970s, the Department of Health and Human Services was created, separating education from health and welfare. This gave Human Services an opportunity to grow beyond mental health and for four-year schools and universities to expand their programs. It was during this time that the National Organization for Human Services and the Council for Standards in Human Services Education were created to help develop the professionalism in the degree.

Many people are credited for moving the profession of Human Services forward. Harold McPheeters, Audrey Cohen, Joann Chenault, and Fran Burnford are four of those people. In *Human Services Professional Education: Future Directions* (1978), Chenault and Burnford describe this process. They believed that education along with field placement experience would help professionalize workers. Human Services organizations would assist students in developing a professional identity and the Council on Standards would assist programs in creating relevant curriculum. McPheeters was a practicing psychiatrist and member of the Southern Regional Education Board (SREB), who realized that additional professionals were needed in the mental health community centers. He received a grant from the National Institute of Mental Health (NIMH) to establish educational programs for mental health workers. This grant allowed community colleges in the southern region of the country to develop associate degree programs in mental health. This training led to direct service jobs as paraprofessionals in the community mental health centers. Later this was changed to an associate's degree in Human Services so that training could be expanded beyond mental health to include all areas of the helping professions. This was the beginning of the associate's degree in Human Services in the United States (Neukrug, 1994). Perhaps you will get to watch a video sponsored by the Council for Standards in Human Services Education entitled, "A Conversation with Dr. Harold L. McPheeters: Founder of Human Services Education in the United States." Ask your instructor about obtaining this video from the Council for Standards in Human Services Education. This is an interesting video, which gives a greater insight into the life and ideas of Dr. McPheeters. As a result of his efforts, today Human Services degree programs have expanded across the country and include bachelor's, master's, and doctoral level degrees.

Other professionals helped to advance the profession of Human Services in their area of the country. Audrey Cohen is considered a champion of women's rights and worked especially hard with economically disadvantaged women in New York. In her work as a women's rights leader, she saw that many women were economically challenged and that social improvements were needed to advance their careers. She worked with women who were on public assistance and developed the Women's Talent Corps, where new paraprofessional positions could be created. Starting with a group of ten students, she went on to create employment for hundreds of thousands of people and inspired the development of Metropolitan College of New York. The Women's Talent Corps went on to become the College for Human Services, indicating its inclusion of all people. Cohen believed in students becoming involved in their education and studying what was meaningful to them. She was indeed an educational reformer who developed the idea of a transdisciplinary curriculum that would include knowledge, values, and skills from many different disciplines. These ideas have become the hallmark of the Human Services degree.

> ## History
>
> *Understanding and Mastery: The historical roots of Human Services; the creation of the Human Services profession; historical and current legislation affecting service delivery*
>
> **Critical Thinking Question:** When social policy changes and new legislation are implemented, they often create the need for programs to adapt to these changes. How did the passage of the Community Mental Health Act lead to the need for a new profession called Human Services? How did community agencies respond to the new law? Who were some of the people who advanced the profession of Human Services forward?

Read about Audrey Cohen, Metropolitan College of New York's founder, to learn more about her contribution to the Human Services profession.

The idea of a multidisciplinary curriculum is what sets Human Services apart from other helping professions like social work, psychology, or sociology. The Human Services curriculum allows students to focus on meeting competencies in certain areas, which can include other disciplines. Coursework may include sociology, social work, psychology, criminal justice, anthropology, political science, economics, or other disciplines. This collaboration allows Human Services students to understand perspectives from various professions and to acquire the knowledge, values, and skills they need to promote economic justice, advocate for community change, and understand and appreciate the need for community partnerships.

Assess your comprehension of What's It All About? by completing this quiz.

Monkey Business Images/the Agency Collection/Getty Images

A Human Services practitioner conducts a group meeting for Downs Syndrome families.

Becoming a Generalist

The Roles of the Human Services Practitioner

Human Services is a broad field where you focus on developing competencies in the specific areas of *interpersonal relationship building, theoretical content knowledge, ethical value enhancement, and professional skill development* (Mandell & Schram, 2012). You learn strategies and techniques that can be used with a range of different problems in order to work with a vast array of populations like children, adolescents, adults, and the elderly. This *generalist* training allows you to develop a proficiency in working in many different settings. Other helping professions like psychology, counseling, or social work are more specialized and require different training. Human Services practitioners are more generalized and their training more inclusive of many different social science perspectives so they understand psychology, sociology, social work, and Human Services viewpoints. This flexibility makes a Human Services degree conducive to social service agencies that hire a mix of social science undergraduate and graduate majors who are flexible in their thinking and maintain a variety of theoretical perspectives in their work. Human Services workers seek to make changes in society by identifying problems and barriers to services and then working to promote social change (Martin, 2013). They are solution-focused and work as change agents to organize and change systems. Since their training is interdisciplinary, the courses they take in a variety of disciplines broaden a student's perspective on issues. This rigorous academic program is an example of how Human Services education is unique in incorporating a range of disciplines into its curriculum, allowing students to link knowledge from many academic areas into practice. Interdisciplinary education is what sets Human Services apart from other helping professions that focus on only one academic area. Human Services education by

Read "Educational Training" to learn more about Human Services' educational development.

contrast includes several areas in the social sciences in addition to its own Human Services curriculum. Coursework may include sociology, psychology, criminal justice, social work, anthropology, political science, or other specialized areas. This collaboration among disciplines allows Human Services students to learn the knowledge, skills, and values they need to promote social and economic justice, understand the importance of community partnerships, and appreciate the need for including and evaluating multiple perspectives when they deal with social issues (Kinsella, 2010).

Cultural competence is necessary in Human Services because we work with such a *diverse* group of people in so many different types of agencies. It is important to understand something about the cultural background of the populations we work with such as children with Attention Deficit Disorder, delinquent adolescents, immigrant adults, elderly patients with mental illness, or the single-parent victim of domestic violence. Cultural competence involves having the ability to use your *knowledge, values,* and *skills* to assess client issues in relation to characteristics such as *race* and *ethnicity* as well as *religion, age, sexual orientation, physical disability, mental ability,* and *gender*. Human Services workers use their skills to develop interpersonal relationships with people of all backgrounds in an effort to assist them with their life issues. We will learn more about cultural competence in Chapter 4.

A "Human Services professional" is a general term for people with professional and paraprofessional jobs according to the National Organization for Human Services (NOHS) website (2013). Human Services workers may be employed in settings such as child and adult residential group homes and treatment facilities, child and family service agencies like the department of family and children's services or the department of juvenile justice, or juvenile probation and parole, correctional and halfway houses for juveniles and adults, mental health centers, drug and alcohol programs, domestic violence shelters, homeless shelters, and senior centers for aging adults. Human Services practitioners work with a variety of clients, ages, and problems in a number of different settings. Your roles and responsibilities will vary depending on the agency.

> **Read the article "Helping those in need: Human service workers" by Colleen Teixeira Moffat from _Occupational Outlook Quarterly_. Learn about the growing demand for Human Services practitioners. Are there any jobs that interest you?**

There are many *occupational titles* for those with degrees in Human Services according to the NOHS (2013). See Table 2.1 for a partial listing.

The U.S. Bureau of Labor Statistics ranked Human Services as an occupation that is growing rapidly in the country today. Job opportunities are expected to increase by 28% between 2010 and 2020 due to expanding aging population and people with health care needs. The broad base of education along with an internship helps graduates move into a multitude of jobs as direct or indirect service workers. The job title and description may differ depending on where you are employed. You can get a better idea of a job in Human Services by checking out the following website.

Watch the Behavioral Health – Human Services Worker video from the AHEC Health Occupations & Technology Guide.

Table 2.1	Examples of Occupational Titles of Human Services Workers	
case worker	family support worker	youth worker
client advocate	social service liaison	counselor
eligibility counselor	behavioral management aide	child advocate
case management aide	alcohol counselor	day care worker
adult day care worker	drug abuse counselor	probation officer
life skills instructor	neighborhood worker	intake worker
social service aide	group activities aide	group worker
social service technician	therapeutic assistant	case monitor
gerontology aide	juvenile court liaison	parole officer
child abuse worker	home health aide	mental health aide
crisis intervention counselor	community organizer	outreach worker
social work assistant	community action worker	psychological aide
halfway house counselor	assistant case manager	case manager
rehab case worker	residential manager	Human Services

Case Manager

A local department of child welfare has just hired you as a **case manager**. You are excited about your new job, working with families with children under the age of 18 but wonder exactly what you will be doing. Case managers, or anyone working directly with people for that matter, must first use good interpersonal skills to develop a relationship with their clients, based upon mutual trust. When you have a good *rapport*, or a working relationship, then you can proceed with an *assessment of the problem* and *develop a plan of action* with necessary goals and objectives. Case managers coordinate client services and make sure that all the client's needs are met. Sometimes our clients are not aware of what services are available to them in their community, and sometimes they are afraid to ask for services. As a case manager, you will be doing the following:

- Interview the client
- Gather necessary information to assess the situation
- Think about what your clients need to be successful in meeting their goals and objectives
- Develop a plan of action or contract to proceed with the necessary changes

In order to develop your mastery in these direct interventions, let's consider some case examples. We will begin with the case that you will read on the next page of Claudia. First of all imagine yourself in this situation. What would it be like to be single and try to make ends meet. If you did not have enough money to pay your bills you would become homeless, have your utilities cut off, and not have enough to eat or feed your children. Once you put yourself in Claudia's shoes then you can begin to think about what you would need as a parent in this situation. As a case manager, what services can you help her find? As the case manager, you will be not only working within your agency, the department of family and children's services, but also coordinating services with other agencies that

In your first case, a single-parent mother, Claudia, has been reported to the child welfare agency by a neighbor, for leaving her two young children alone in her home while she works in the evening. Upon investigating the situation, the mother does not deny the allegations. Instead she reports that she must work two jobs in order to support her family. She receives no child support, and while her children attend day care, she works. She picks them up from day care at 5 p.m., gives them supper, plays with them for a short time, and then gives them a bath and gets them ready for bed. When they are asleep, she locks the door and heads out to her second job in the evening around 9 p.m. She works as a waitress at an all-night restaurant and returns home around 3:30 a.m. You can see that she is exhausted from this routine. Although she knows this is unsafe for her children, she believes that there is no other way to pay her bills. Your job is to develop an intervention plan with her and monitor her progress to make sure she's following it. Claudia will need to appear in court to defend her right to keep her children, so it is important that the intervention plan be prepared in anticipation of her court date. She must demonstrate her ability to follow the plan; otherwise her children will be placed in foster care.

Since the children are minors, under the age of 18 in most states, it is necessary to get informed consent documents signed from the mother. This permission allows you to seek services for the children and to offer her the opportunity to enroll her children in any programs or services that you feel are beneficial. You would also want to include the mother in any decision-making regarding other services for the children or parenting sessions for her. Then when her court date approaches, you will be prepared with a plan of action, services that are in place, and a report to the judge indicating your efforts to coordinate services for the family and the results of those efforts.

could be helpful to your client. You may refer her to a housing program to see if she is eligible for rental assistance. This could help her with monthly bills. You will be talking with Claudia to make sure she has an adequate plan of supervision for her children when she is not at home. Are there parents, neighbors, or friends who can help? Is she a member of a local church? How can they be helpful? What about child support payments? You will need to work on getting the biological father to provide support for his children. If goals for your client include educational achievements like a GED (General Educational Development), then you will be working with the school to make sure she can attend a program to attain her diploma. This may help her get a better job and can also help her in the long run. You may also connect your client with a local YMCA or Boys' and Girls' Club to offer appropriate adolescent and adult role models for the children in this family. These agencies may offer recreational opportunities for the children, which currently don't exist. You will need to work with them to determine if your client is eligible for services. They may also provide some child supervision at times when her day care is closed.

Interventions and Direct Services

Understanding and Mastery: Knowledge and skill development in the following areas: case management, intake interviewing, individual counseling, group facilitation and counseling, location and use of appropriate resources and referrals, and use of consultation

Critical Thinking Question: What community groups or programs would offer services to assist Claudia with housing, food, utilities, training or better employment, supportive parenting classes, or child care?

Do you think you would like a job as a case manager? It is a very important job that graduates of Human Services programs can attain. This position can be found in a variety of agencies. Good coordination skills and knowledge of local resources are important in case management. Some agencies will hire a graduate with an associate's degree in Human Services, if the person has some experience. Those with a bachelor's degree in Human Services are eligible for the position. You may want to consider a Human Services internship in case management to strengthen your application. These jobs may also be listed as **case coordinators** or **caseworkers**.

> Explore the <u>Case Management Society of America</u>.

Intake Worker

When clients come to agencies for assistance, the **intake worker** is usually the first person they meet. It is important that the intake worker be friendly, empathic, objective, and professional. Intake workers must have good interviewing and interpersonal helping skills so they are able to collect all the client data in an effective and efficient manner. If the clients feel that the worker is not interested in helping them or too bureaucratic to understand their problem, they may decide not to accept the service. Even though the intake worker is usually a beginning level position, it is a very important job within the agency. Human Services workers with an associate's level degree and some experience or a bachelor's level degree are eligible for these positions. These jobs are offered in schools, hospitals, mental health centers, counseling agencies, and many state offices that provide social services.

> Read <u>Community and Social Services Occupation</u> profiles and research available job opportunities.

Child Care Worker

A **child care worker** provides professional care for children in a variety of settings from birth through age 12. You may be asked to supervise the play of children in a day care center or Head Start Program, or you may be working with developmentally or physically challenged children in a school or therapeutic setting. Some children are in the protective custody of the state and live in residential group homes or treatment facilities (Crosson-Tower, 2013) Your role in these facilities may be to supervise their daily activities, teach them skills to live in a group setting, or manage their behavior using some management techniques. You may be asked to live at a facility for a few days a week as a house parent or member of a team that works in shifts. You will need to be knowledgeable about child growth and development, psychological theories of behavior management, and interpersonal skills in relationship building. Knowing how to develop a curriculum of activities that includes art, music, dramatic play, outdoor athletic games, reading, science, cooking, circle time, field trips, or other activities for children of different ages would be necessary. If you are asked to facilitate a group for children, it will be important for you to know how to develop a group and how to lead or colead it. So, a course in group dynamics would be essential. Those with associate's or bachelor's degrees are eligible for these positions. An internship working with children could increase your competence and experience, which would better prepare you for a job with this population. Working with children requires a lot of energy, patience, creativity, and a positive attitude.

> Watch Child Care Best Practices at <u>ChildCare Aware</u>.

> Watch the video from <u>The Home of Little Wanderers Agency</u> to learn about therapeutic child care.

Education or Prevention Specialist

Some workers are called **education or prevention specialists**. These jobs allow practitioners to work with voluntary or high-risk groups of children, adolescents, adults, and the elderly to teach them about a particular issue. Sometimes the consumers have been chosen to attend the program due to the nature of their problem. For instance, teen parents may be asked to attend a program on childbirth, early childhood development, or disciplining a young child. Prevention programs offer an opportunity to identify those who are at high risk for social problems such as child abuse, alcoholism, high school dropouts, or teen pregnancy, to name just a few. By offering educational programs and establishing relationships with the members, Human Services workers can prevent high-risk behaviors from turning into crisis events. Education and prevention specialists work in schools, mental health centers, counseling agencies, and other nonprofit and state agencies where they can provide information either to the general public or to a targeted audience. Practitioners who offer these programs have received the specialized training themselves, are often certified in a specific topic, and are now ready to share their knowledge with others. Programs like training for foster parents, information on HIV/AIDS, drug awareness in schools, good touch/bad touch that teaches about sexual abuse to children, and the First Steps Program for parents of newborns are all examples of this type of programming. Those with a two- or four-year degree in Human Services and specialized training and certification in the subject area are eligible for these jobs.

Watch Human Service videos at CareerOneStop to learn more about a variety of jobs.

Counselor

A **counselor** is a trained professional who works with people who want to change the way they think, feel, or behave. Sometimes people suffer with conscious issues like marital or relationship issues that can be resolved with several sessions of interpersonal interventions that include psychotherapeutic techniques. Other times people with chronic mental illness suffer with cognitive and emotional issues that require medication as well as psychotherapeutic interventions. Counselors are skilled in identifying and diagnosing mental health issues and can use the counseling techniques and personality theories they have learned to help their clients. Work includes developing a trusting, interpersonal relationship with the consumer and then collecting enough information to make a thorough assessment of the client's issues, which includes accurate background and historical information. The client's issues are then prioritized and work begins with the development of a treatment plan that includes measurable goals and objectives (Mehr & Kanwischer, 2011). Oftentimes, referrals to psychiatrists or medical doctors may be necessary if patients need medication that counselors cannot prescribe. The patient may be asked to attend individual, group, couples, or family counseling as part of the treatment plan (Toseland & Rivas, 2011).

Counseling requires very specific training and a license to practice in the state where you work. It is necessary to understand all types of treatment modalities and techniques so these positions usually require a master's or doctoral degree (Kinsella, 2010). Those with master's degrees in Human Services and a special concentration in mental health counseling with extensive internship hours can sit for licensing examinations in some states, called a licensed mental health counselor (Springfield College, 2010).

Certified Addictions Professional

Some schools offer a bachelor's or master's degree in Human Services with a special concentration in addictions studies. After completing the Human Services degree and required number of classes in addictions studies and an extensive internship, students can become certified addictions professional in some states. This training allows you to work in substance abuse treatment facilities, doing individual or group work with patients under the supervision of a licensed professional, like a doctor, psychiatrist, psychologist, or social worker.

The role of a **Human Services mental health counselor** or an **addictions counselor** varies from state to state with regard to licensing requirements, certifications, education, and internship hours.

Watch the Mental Health and Substance Abuse Social Workers videos from the Human Services videos at CareerOneStop.

Administrator

An agency **administrator** is responsible for managing Human Services programs. Agency administrators spend their days developing budgets, writing grants, working with their boards of directors, creating fund-raising events for their agencies, supervising staff, hiring personnel, expanding services to clients, and conducting research and program evaluations to ensure quality services in their agencies. Unless it is a private for-profit agency, agency administrators are employed by the organization and are supervised by their boards of trustees or a local, state, or federal entity. Courses in Human Services administration, business administration, or public administration would benefit people in these positions. Human Services practitioners with education and experience are eligible for these jobs. In most areas, a master's or doctoral level degree is required.

Assess your comprehension of <u>Becoming a Generalist: by completing this quiz.</u>

Human Services administrators manage agencies, facilitate board meetings, and share new information.

©Franz Pfluegl/ShutterStock.com

| Table 2.2 | Generic Human Services Professional Competencies | 25 |

The following six statements describe the major generic knowledge, skills, and attitudes that appear to be required in all Human Services work. The training and preparation of the individual worker within this framework will change depending on the function of the work setting, the specific client population served, and the level of organizational work.

1. Understanding the nature of human systems: individual, group, organization, community and society, and their major interactions. All workers will have preparation that will help them understand human development, group dynamics, organizational structure, how communities are organized, how national policy is set, and how social systems interact in producing human problems.

2. Understanding the conditions, which promote or limit optimal functioning, and classes of deviations from desired functioning in the major human systems. Workers will have understanding of the major models of causation that are concerned with both the promotion of healthy functioning and treatment-rehabilitation. This includes medically oriented, socially oriented, psychologically and behaviorally oriented, and educationally oriented models.

3. Skill in identifying and selecting interventions, which promote growth and goal attainment. The worker will be able to conduct a competent problem analysis and to select those strategies, services, or interventions that are appropriate to helping clients attain a desired outcome. Interventions may include assistance, referral, advocacy, or direct counseling.

4. Skill in planning, implementing, and evaluating interventions. The worker will be able to design a plan of action for an identified problem and implement the plan in a systematic way. This requires an understanding of problem analysis, decision analysis, and design of work plans. This generic skill can be used with all social systems and adapted for use with individual clients or organizations. Skill in evaluating the interventions is essential.

5. Consistent behavior in selecting interventions, which are congruent with the values of one's self, clients, the employing organization, and the Human Services profession. This cluster requires awareness of one's own value orientation, an understanding of organizational values as expressed in the mandate or goal statement of the organization, Human Services ethics, and an appreciation of the client's values, lifestyle, and goals.

6. Process skills, which are required to plan and implement services. This cluster is based on the assumption that the worker uses himself as the main tool for responding to service needs. The worker must be skillful in verbal and oral communication, interpersonal relationships, and other related personal skills, such as self-discipline and time management. It requires that the worker be interested in and motivated to conduct the role that he has agreed to fulfill and to apply himself to all aspects of the work that the role requires.

Source: National Organization for Human Services. http://www.nationalhumanservices.org/

Professional Knowledge, Values, and Skills

The Heart of the Curriculum in Human Services

According to the **National Organization for Human Services (NOHS)**, there are knowledge, values, and skills that students need to master if they are to be successful practitioners. The NOHS describes these duties and functions based on six points that it calls <u>Generic Human Services Professional Competencies</u> (Table 2.2).

Around the Globe

Why Is Sweden One of the Best Places in the World to Be a Child?

Human Services in the Scandinavian countries, especially Sweden, are considered to be the best in the world. Attention is given to services for all people, regardless of age.

Niklas Larsson/AP Images

At a playground in Sweden fathers watch their children play and enjoy the day. Parental leave allows both parents to split the time equally so both can care for their children. Henrik Holgersson says, "Spending time with my son, Arvid, has been the best time of my life."

Although personal tax rates are high, people are in agreement that Human Services need to be excellent, and they are willing to pay for such quality.

When we study Human Services, we learn from our psychology courses that the early years of a human's life are critical to that person's future growth and development. Both Erikson and Piaget, who studied the early years, have emphasized the importance of a *stable environment, nurturing caregivers,* and *the freedom for a child to learn from in his or her environment by experiencing the world around them.* Maslow's theory indicated that an individual's basic needs like *food, shelter, safety,* and *love* had to be met in order for an individual to reach higher levels of human potential (Baird, 2012). Sweden then is one place where all of these needs can be met. According to UNICEF, Sweden is one of the best places in the world to be a child (UNICEF Report, 2009). Swedish laws provide for the protection of all children, and in 1979, Sweden became the first country in the world to make *beating or spanking a child a criminal offense* (Freden, 2009). The government, as well as many organizations, oversees the well-being of children. In a country with 9.4 million people, about 2 million are children under the age of 18. Unlike the United States, where many children live in single-parent families, 70% of Swedish children under the age of 18 live with their biological parents, and almost a third of children live with a biological parent and stepparent (Fact Sheet, 2012). Although the divorce rate is high in Sweden, it rises with the age of the child. By the time a child reaches age 17, he or she is more likely to be living with the mother. The stress of raising young children is reduced by *universal* governmental supports that ensure a child care place for every Swedish child (Korpi, 2007). All families receive *monthly allowances* based upon their number of children. *Health care* is provided for all residents with free or very affordable preventive services, prenatal and postnatal education programs, and regular medical care. Sweden's **parental insurance system** is known worldwide for its generous benefits, which supports the equal rights of both men and women while they combine employment with parenthood. This insurance provides for either the mother or the father to stay at home for up to *360 days after the birth of a child with 80% of their compensation* (Fact Sheet, 2012). Parents can share in the benefit by each choosing to stay at home for some time with their child. This bonding in the early years is important for the child as well as the parent. *It is unusual for a child under the age of one year to be placed in a child care facility because of this benefit.* Children who are ill do not attend child care either. Parents receive a benefit of *60 days total per year for each child* under the age of 12. Either parent can use the benefit, which pays 80% of their compensation for days missed at work due to child sickness or school conferences. Swedish labor laws protect the rights of parents who use their benefits due to child sickness, pregnancy, or school needs. Although more women than men use the parental benefits, men do share in child care responsibilities. All parents receive *480 paid days of leave per child*, which *must* be used before the child turns eight. This encourages both men and women to care for their own children, take paid leave when their children are babies, or take time for school conferences, which are covered by the policy. It is not unusual for Swedish women to work full time through their child's preschool years, with 80% of the women in the labor force. This is possible because they have affordable, quality child care with paid parental time off for child sickness. Swedish men use about 20% of the annual child care leave to care for their children (Freden, 2009).

Since the early 1970s, Sweden has had a *national social policy that combined parenthood and employment* with generous parental leave policies and quality early childhood educational programs (Lagerberg, 2012). The goal is to blend early education and kindergarten with child care. This new publicly funded program is known as **forskola** and

---

Case Study ▷ **Attending a Forskola**

Imagine your child attending a forskola where she will become familiar with a small group of 12 children and two professionally trained adult preschool teachers. Her group will have its own rooms in a pleasant and relaxing atmosphere. Her learning or personal development will not be assessed, and so there is no challenge or requirement to meet certain educational milestones each year. She will learn about the world through play and activities that center around themes like the seasons, holidays, or the environment. Programs are under the National Ministry of Education and Research that publishes the *Curriculum for Preschool*, which is the beginning level for education in Sweden. Compulsory education starts at age seven with preschool at age six. School is free and required for nine years. The government subsidizes the early care and higher education. Students can decide to go on to senior high if they choose. All children between the ages of six and nine are offered before and after school care at *leisure centers*. Approximately 76% of Sweden's children attend these programs. When children attend school and parent meetings are scheduled with the teaching staff, both mothers and fathers have paid leave from their employment, which can be used to attend these conferences since these meetings are seen as important.

Children are Sweden's top priority and this country has the lowest rate of child mortality in the world. It is the safest place for children to be born and has the distinction of being a country where fewer children die under the age of five than in any other country on earth.

works to provide families with the services they need. *Every child is guaranteed a child care place* and it is the responsibility of the municipality to ensure that spot. Services for all families integrate early childhood education, kindergarten, and child day care no matter where the families live and what language they speak, with little or no expense to them.

Since 2002, limits have been established on maximum child care fees. Families can pay 3% of their monthly income up to a cap of 1,260 kronor or approximately $193.00 for the first child, 2% for the second child with a cap of $129.00, and 1% for the third child with a cap of approximately $64. There is no charge for a fourth child. Statistics show that 85% of two- to three-year-olds were enrolled in care, 97% of all four- and five-year-olds were enrolled in programs, and 76% of six- to nine-year-olds were enrolled. Only 30 babies under the age of one year were in care. In addition, in 2003, a policy was passed entitling children ages four and five to *525 free hours of care a year* (Fredan, 2009).

> ## Human Services Delivery Systems
>
> *Understanding and Mastery: International and global influences on service delivery*
>
> ---
>
> Critical Thinking Question: Do you think that the U.S. government should provide family services like universal health care, monthly allowances, and child care like other industrialized countries do, even if it means that taxes will go up for everyone in order to pay for these kinds of services?

Explore the <u>Sweden</u> website to learn more about its policies on children.

Putting Theories to Work

Using an Interdisciplinary Approach to Develop Knowledge, Values, and Skills

Since Human Services is a program with an interdisciplinary curriculum, students will most likely take coursework in psychology, sociology, social work, criminal justice, political science, and Human Services. The purpose of interdisciplinary work is to engage students in courses that will challenge their thinking. Human Services students learn to look at issues from many different perspectives and learn theories and schools of thought from other disciplines. This is important to the Human Services worker who upon graduation may be working in a setting with a team composed of psychologists, social workers, nurses, psychiatrists, or law enforcement officers. There is no standardized curriculum for Human Services in the United States, but programs must meet standard competencies. It is considered to be a social and behavioral science.

A career in Human Services ensures that you have acquired a broad liberal arts education that includes *interdisciplinary* coursework in psychology, sociology, social work, political science, and criminal justice, as well as specific courses in Human Services. It can lead to an associate of arts degree found in community colleges or a bachelor of arts degree found in a four-year college or university. It is considered a fairly new profession with its inception sometime around the mid 1960s. In that short period of time, Human Services programs have become popular in schools across the United States. Some schools are now offering graduate as well as doctoral degrees in Human Services.

The accrediting body for Human Services is known as the **Council for Standards in Human Services Education (CSHSE)**, which was established in 1979. Since then it has worked to support and guide schools and encouraged them to move toward *accreditation* of their Human Services programs. It has developed national standards for the Human Services curriculum and competencies for each subject area and now provides accreditation for all Human Services degrees at colleges and universities (Martin, 2013).

Both an associate's and a bachelor's degree in Human Services will require students to take a number of foundation or core curricula established by the educational accrediting body of the region. Classes such as English, math, communication, business, sciences, arts and humanities, foreign language, economics, political science, history, anthropology, physical education, and general electives fall in this category. Most two-year programs require 60 credits for graduation and four-year programs require 120 credits. The CSHSE requires that Human Services programs cover standard content areas. Although the curriculum is not standardized, schools must document how students are mastering competencies through the coursework, which must cover theory, skills, and values of the profession. Each school may develop an individual curriculum but must include courses in the history of the profession, the depth and breadth of the Human Services profession, human systems, clinical interventions that cover individual, group, family, and community techniques, planning and evaluation methods, and self-development exercises. Students are expected to complete required hours in a field experience with appropriate, guided supervision (Martin, 2013). Schools must meet these standards with an interdisciplinary approach using a variety of disciplines to meet the competencies.

> Review the **Council for Standards in Human Services Education** website for more information.

Courses in the curriculum include *Introduction to Human Services*, a beginning level course that focuses on the history of the profession, qualities of workers, employment settings, and issues that affect Human Services workers (Mandell & Schram, 2012). Sometimes this course is offered with an opportunity for service learning or a volunteer component so that students can begin to test out their special interests. Other introductory courses include psychology and sociology, where students begin to learn about theories in human growth and development, and human behavior and society (Wade & Tavris, 2011).

Advanced classes in Human Services are offered after students complete the introductory classes for Human Services, psychology, and sociology. Students learn how to integrate theory and practice by incorporating the knowledge and research content from their classes into real practice cases. They study ethical values and apply the code of conduct for Human Services to real agency issues. Finally they practice the skills they have learned in their interpersonal helping skills and group classes. These skills can be applied to agency cases, class role-plays, and actual field placement situations. Specific classes in Human Services may include the following:

- *Interpersonal Skills*—This class gives students practice in role-playing scenarios where they learn how to develop relationships with clients, conduct interviews, do assessments and treatment plans, and evaluate those plans. They also learn how to work as a treatment team (Mehr & Kanwischer, 2011). Along with their classes, students often visit local agencies to observe how professionals conduct interviews with various groups of people.
- *Group Dynamics*—Students learn how to facilitate groups for children, adults, or the elderly in local settings (Toseland & Rivas, 2011). They learn how to initiate activities with different groups in settings like hospitals, schools, mental health centers, or day care centers.
- *Social Policy*—Students learn how legislation is passed and implemented for social service programs. They might get to observe how local elected representatives work to pass new bills. Some students become politically active and learn how to advocate for effective social policy (DiNitto & Cummins, 2011).

- *Ethical Issues*—Human Services students can begin to understand professional values by studying the *Human Services Code of Professional Ethics*. Some cases involving issues of life and death, moral codes of conduct, or ethical violations require students to think about the decisions they make when working with clients. This class presents a model for students to follow regarding decision-making with clients (NOHS, 2013).
- *Internship or Field Experience*—This is probably the last course that Human Services students will take before they graduate. They complete a required number of hours in an agency setting where they can practice the skills they have learned working with children, adolescents, adults, or the elderly.

Other courses may be added as electives to the curriculum and include interdisciplinary classes such as the following:

- Abnormal psychology
- Social issues
- Marriage and family
- Juvenile delinquency
- Human sexuality
- Cultural competence
- Race and ethnic relations
- Fields of child welfare
- Aging issues
- Criminology
- Drugs and society
- Grantsmanship
- Human Services administration
- Program planning
- Child and/or adolescent psychology

The interdisciplinary nature of Human Services means that our students are learning to look at theories and models from the viewpoints of many different disciplines. This is an advantage to our field as we work to collaborate with others. As we master the competencies in knowledge, values, and skills, we learn that professionalism can be accomplished through research, testing, observation, and field instruction.

Think Human Services

Psychological and Sociological Theories

Psychological theories like **Maslow's Hierarchy of Needs** (Figure 2.1) are basic to our understanding of what humans need in order to survive. Abraham Maslow (1971) believed that all humans struggled to develop their potential to the fullest, which he called **self-actualization**. In order for this to occur, a series of needs had to be met first. He believed those who had physiological needs satisfied, along with safety, love, and self-esteem needs, could more easily work toward self-actualization than those who were stuck on the bottom level trying to meet their basic needs. Once this series of needs could be attained, then people could more easily move ahead to the next level. He believed that self-actualization was a lifelong struggle and that certain needs

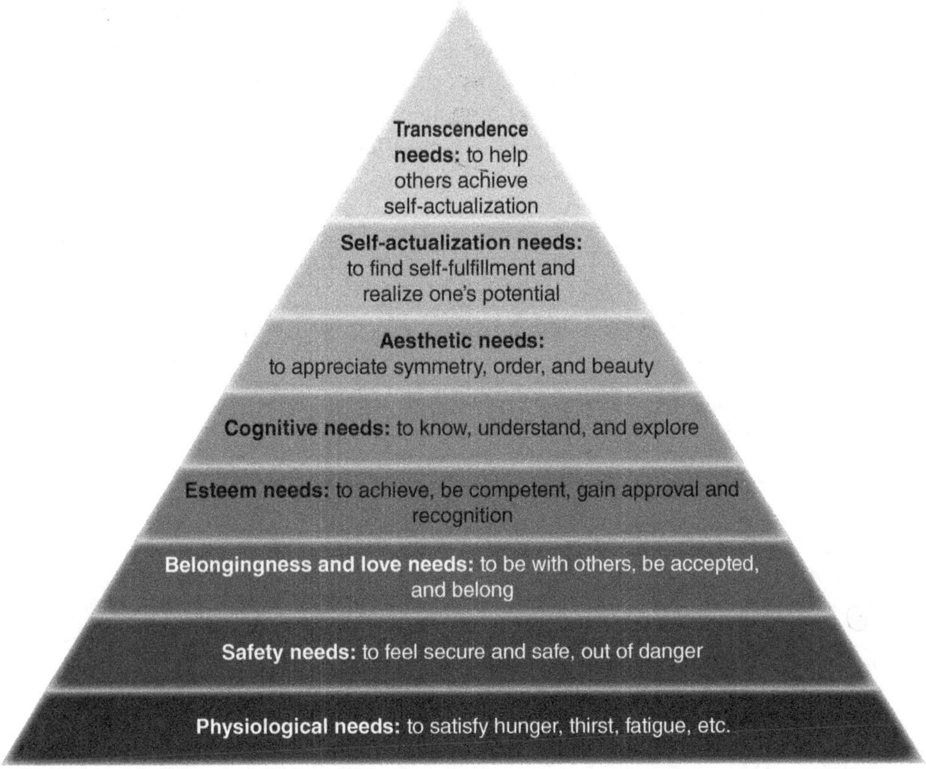

Transcendence needs: to help others achieve self-actualization

Self-actualization needs: to find self-fulfillment and realize one's potential

Aesthetic needs: to appreciate symmetry, order, and beauty

Cognitive needs: to know, understand, and explore

Esteem needs: to achieve, be competent, gain approval and recognition

Belongingness and love needs: to be with others, be accepted, and belong

Safety needs: to feel secure and safe, out of danger

Physiological needs: to satisfy hunger, thirst, fatigue, etc.

Figure 2.1 Maslow's Hierarchy of Needs

were more important at different stages of life. He felt that self-actualization led to happy, healthy individuals who benefit society. Characteristics of a self-actualized person included acceptance of self and others, is self-directed, seeks truth and justice, has problem solving abilities, is creative, and has satisfying relationships with others (Henslin, 2012).

In Human Services, we often work with clients who are at the bottom of Maslow's hierarchy, and our job is to secure items like food (from food banks or SNAP, the food stamp program), clothing (from Salvation Army, Goodwill, or local churches), or shelter (housing assistance programs or local homeless shelters). We work with single mothers who need some assistance to provide basic care for their children, who need some encouragement and support to continue being a strong parent, and who often go on to develop their potential through education or job training programs.

Erikson's Eight Stages of Psychosocial Development (Table 2.3) provide us with the milestones we need to assess individuals' development so we can determine what life stages they have mastered and where they still struggle. According to Erikson (1963), in Stage 1, or the early part of life, infants learn to trust others and know who they can depend on. The caregiver who provides consistent food at mealtimes, changes wet diapers, and holds them when they cry helps babies to develop the trust they need in others. In Stage 2, toddlers learn to become independent and they must try to dress, feed themselves, and use the toilet. A sense of accomplishment is earned when the child is able to do these things for himself. Students who want to work with young children and their parents have to understand this concept so they are better equipped to deal with the difficult toddler who refuses to let anyone dress him or who uses "no" or "mine" continuously. If children are punished often, restricted, or not encouraged to become independent, then shame or self-doubt occurs.

Table 2.3	Erikson's Eight Stages of Development		
	Erikson's Psychosocial Stages of Development		
Stage	**Developmental Crisis**	**Successful Dealing with Crisis**	**Unsuccessful Dealing with Crisis**
1. Infant Birth to 1 year old	Trust Versus Mistrust Babies learn to trust or mistrust others based on whether or not their needs—such as food and comfort—are met.	If babies' needs are met, they learn to trust people and expect life to be pleasant.	If babies' needs are not met, they learn not to trust.
2. Toddler 1 to 3 years old	Autonomy Versus Shame and Doubt Toddlers realize that they can direct their own behavior.	If toddlers are successful in directing their own behavior, they learn to be independent.	If toddlers' attempts at being independent are blocked, they learn self-doubt and shame for being unsuccessful.
3. Preschool Age 3 to 5 years old	Initiative Versus Guilt Preschoolers are challenged to control their own behavior, such as controlling their exuberance when they are in a restaurant.	If preschoolers succeed in taking responsibility, they feel capable and develop initiative.	If preschoolers fail in taking responsibility, they feel irresponsible, anxious, and guilty.
4. Elementary School Age 5 to 12 years old	Industry Versus Inferiority When children succeed in learning new skills and obtaining new knowledge, they develop a sense of industry, a feeling of competence arising from their work and effort.	When children succeed at learning new skills, they develop a sense of industry, a feeling of competence and self-esteem arising from their work and effort.	If children fail to develop new abilities, they feel incompetent, inadequate, and inferior.
5. Adolescence 13 to early twenties	Identity Versus Role Confusion Adolescents are faced with deciding who or what they want to be in terms of occupation, beliefs, attitudes, and behavior patterns.	Adolescents who succeed in defining who they are and finding a role for themselves develop a strong sense of identity.	Adolescents who fail to define their identity become confused and withdraw or want to inconspicuously blend in with the crowd.
6. Early Adulthood Twenties and thirties	Intimacy Versus Isolation The task facing those in early adulthood is to be able to share who they are with another person in a close, committed relationship.	People who succeed in this task will have satisfying intimate relationships.	Adults who fail at this task will be isolated from other people and may suffer from loneliness.
7. Middle Adulthood Forties and fifties	Generativity Versus Stagnation The challenge is to be creative, productive, and nurturant of the next generation.	Adults who succeed in this challenge will be creative, productive, and nurturant, thereby benefiting themselves, their family, community, country, and future generations.	Adults who fail will be passive, and self-centered, feel that they have done nothing for the next generation, and feel that the world is no better off for their being alive.
8. Late Adulthood Sixties and beyond	Ego Integrity Versus Despair The issue is whether a person will reach wisdom, spiritual tranquility, a sense of wholeness, and acceptance of his or her life.	Elderly people who succeed in addressing this issue will enjoy life and not fear death.	Elderly people who fail will feel that their life is empty and will fear death.

In Stage 3, preschoolers must step out and begin to explore the world. Those who are punished or not allowed to experience new relationships or experiences will have more guilt and are more likely in future years to become passive observers.

By age six, in Stage 4, children need to begin to feel productive. They need to succeed in play, school activities, and relationships with others. Often they compare themselves with others, and feeling less productive or having fewer skills to master activities may make them develop a sense of inferiority. Human Services workers who are employed in school use this theory to better understand the importance placed on student accomplishment. All students need to feel that they do something well. Children who are passive, introverted, have difficulty with others, or have behavior issues are often children who need to have their self-esteem raised.

Interested in working with children? Review the sociological theory: <u>Parten's Model of Social Play</u>.

Everyone is good at something. Finding out what makes a child smile is an important lesson for a worker. In Stage 5, adolescents begin to learn more about themselves and the roles they play as a student, athlete, son or daughter, friend, artist, or musician. It is important at this stage that appropriate adult role models guide the child toward successful career or adult activities. Human Services workers who choose to work with adolescents in this stage are often challenged by juveniles who commit crimes or run away or students who drop out of school or become pregnant. Workers are often the appropriate role models these youth need to help guide them through a difficult stage of life. Counseling families and teaching parenting classes are important skills for workers.

In Stage 6, young adults are often faced with relationship difficulties that may go unresolved, leaving a person to follow one bad relationship after another. Human Services workers who are employed with young adults often teach communication skills or conflict resolution to couples.

As people age, they reach the next stage of maturity, Stage 7, where adults guide the younger generation. They aim to be productive and think of others in a non-selfish way. Those who are unable to think of others become self-absorbed and fixated on their own issues. They lose their productivity and become stagnated.

During the last stage of life, Stage 8, people tend to reflect over their life experiences. Those who feel good about what they have done and given to others develop ego integrity. Others who have failed to cope with past events successfully, eventually feel despair (Kunz, 2011). As Human Services workers, we deal with people in all eight stages of life. Understanding the issues and tasks associated with each stage is helpful to our work.

Human Systems

Understanding and Mastery: Theories of human development

Critical Thinking Question: Integrating a variety of interdisciplinary theories requires an understanding of different perspectives in the social and behavioral sciences. Do you think this focus on several viewpoints is necessary in our work in Human Services? Why or why not?

Explore the <u>Sweden</u> website. Review why Sweden is One of the Best Places in the World to Be a Child. Why do you think Sweden doesn't use testing to determine if its preschoolers are developing adequate educational goals like reading and writing?

Figure 2.2
Parten's Model
of Social Play
Source: Santrock, J. W.
(2007). Parten's classic
study of play. In *A topical
approach to life-span development* (3rd ed., p. 573).
New York: McGraw Hill
(original work published
2002).

Parten's Model of Social Play	
Unoccupied behavior	*Child displays no activity*
Onlooker play	*Child observes other child at play*
Solitary play	*Child plays independently*
Parallel play	*Child plays independently alongside other children*
Associative play	*Children play together but the play is not organized; they share toys and talk*
Cooperative play	*This play involves organized interaction; children have a similar goal; they make something together or play on teams, follow rules, and are part of a group*

Parten's Model of Social Play

Have you ever observed children in a day care center or school? Some children are very social and play easily with others. Not all children are comfortable with group interaction. According to **Parten's Model of Social Play** (Figure 2.2), as children age they begin to develop the social skills they need to interact with others. Young babies may demonstrate no activity with any children at all. They are at the stage of unoccupied play. Gradually they become interested in what others are doing and begin to observe others in what Parten calls onlooker play. As young children learn how to play, they develop a set of skills through solitary play that allows them to become independent. In parallel play, a child moves alongside another and plays independently but with others nearby. As children's skills and developmental stages advance, they move into associative play, where they begin to share toys and games with others but still there is no organized goal. In the most developed stage of play, children begin cooperative play as they interact and become part of a group or team. As you observe, a child's play will tell you a lot about where he or she is developmentally.

Put yourselves into groups of three or four and discuss the sociological importance of Parten's Model of Play. Why do Human Services workers need to understand this model?

Assess your comprehension of <u>Think Human Services</u> by completing this quiz.

Linking Theory to Practice

Why Is Service Learning Important?

Field Experience

*Understanding and Mastery: Demonstrate that
students are exposed to Human Services agencies
and clients early in the program*

Imagine you are going with your class to a local
homeless shelter to do a service learning project.
What theories have you learned that would apply
to this agency? What would these clients need?
How would you provide this service? What would
you need to keep in mind about these clients?

Have you ever heard the term **service learning**? It refers to using the knowledge and skills you learn in a classroom setting and applying them to a real practice setting in your community. Service learning can involve any discipline and makes learning more active and meaningful for students. For instance in a biology class, you might learn how to use a microscope and test water samples for organisms that pollute the water. Then your class may actually work with a local environmental group to help test water samples from a local river or waterway where fishing is allowed. This would certainly make the class more interesting, and you may study harder and earn better grades because you are really interested in learning about how water becomes polluted, especially if you fish in nearby waters. Well, now think about all the things that we learn in Human Services from our classes. Where would you like to try out the theories and models you are learning? All Human Services students will complete a professional internship at some point in the academic program. Until then perhaps your class could do volunteer work at a shelter, or use the assessment skills you will be learning to help out at a Red Cross center. Maybe you could use your group work skills to run a group for adolescents at a youth center or group home. Service learning is done as a class and applies the knowledge, values, or skills you have learned to a real community setting.

Did You Know?

How To Earn Your Associate or Bachelor's Degree in Human Services

How to Earn Your Associate's Degree in Human Services?

Many community colleges and technical schools offer a two-year degree in Human Services. The curriculum may include some general education courses in English, math, and the sciences. However, a large part of the coursework will be in your major and include classes specific to Human Services. You may even participate in an internship that allows you to apply the theory you have learned to practice situations in an agency setting. Most associate or two-year programs are about 60 credits in length. You can usually obtain financial aid for these programs. Even if you are working you can attend school since most programs are now offered at night and weekends in addition to the day classes. Contact your local community colleges to see if they offer Human Services, or go online and search for associate degree programs in Human Services.

What Can You Do With It?

Read the list of employment opportunities in this chapter for a complete idea of how to use your degree in Human Services. Since the curriculum teaches a set of competencies, you will be trained to be a generalist. This means that you will learn how to use a body of knowledge, values, and skills to work with individuals, groups, and families in your community. You will work in a variety of settings like schools, hospitals, aging programs, Head Start centers, recreational programs, mental health centers, residential facilities, or agencies like juvenile probation or child welfare to name just a few. You will work with different age groups doing a variety of tasks. As an associate degree graduate you may be hired to assist a professional Human Services worker who has an advanced degree. You may be considered a paraprofessional depending on the agency you work for, and your pay scale may be less than that of a worker who has more experience or advanced training.

How to Earn Your Bachelor's Degree in Human Services?

A bachelor's degree is a four-year degree with about 120 credit hours, depending on your school. You usually have a general education curriculum of about 60 credit hours in English, math, science, some social sciences, humanities, or even computer science. Some religiously oriented schools will require coursework in religious education in the general curriculum as well. The last two years will require rigorous work in the Human Services major with upper level coursework that may teach you interpersonal helping skills, group work, administration, research, and some psychology or sociology coursework. Financial aid is usually available for students who want to pursue a bachelor's degree from an institution of higher learning. As with the associate's degree, check with your local schools or online for programs that are offered to meet your needs such as day, night, or online programs.

What Can You Do With It?

You can work with a variety of people in distinctly different settings. If you like helping children, adolescents, adults, or the elderly doing various tasks like working in a Head Start center, doing case management with an elderly adult so she can remain in her home instead of going to live in a nursing home, or counseling a runaway teen, then you have found the right profession in Human Services. See the list of employment opportunities in this chapter. An Associate's or Bachelor's degree in Human Services will allow you to sit for the accrediting exam known as the Human Services Board Certified Practitioner Examination, which leads to the HS-BCP designation.

What Would You Do?

Recommend a Human Services Worker or Career Path in Human Services

After reading through this chapter, you should have an understanding of the different roles Human Services workers play. Using this knowledge, consider the following cases and decide what type of Human Services worker you would suggest these clients see.

Case Study	Recommend a Human Services Worker

ERIC

Eric is a 16-year-old high school student who has become increasingly dependent on alcohol. It started out as Friday night partying, but Eric soon found that he not only liked the taste of beer and whiskey but felt more relaxed and carefree when he was drinking with his friends. He talked more, everyone thought he was more social, and it was easier to talk to girls. Lately though, Eric finds that he wants a drink in the morning before school, just to take the edge off the day. He hides beer in his backpack for his lunch break, and he has alcohol stashed in the trunk of his car.

What kind of worker does Eric need to see and why?

JOHN

John lives alone with his 83-year-old mother. His new job as a sales representative is taking him away from home for longer periods each day. He is concerned that his mother is spending too much time by herself in their home, and he is worried she may slip or fall while he is at work.

What type of worker can help John with his mother's daily needs?

DANIELLE

Danielle and her boyfriend James have just separated. As a single mom, she now has responsibility for her 2-year-old daughter. She is not sure if James is returning to the area or if he has any interest in supporting his daughter. Several of her friends are encouraging her to get assistance. She has never received any public benefits before.

What type of worker should she see to assist her with her financial issues?

GEORGE

George has just been arrested for a DUI. Since this was his first offense he was released on bail and has a court hearing in one week. He lost his license, and he will have fines to pay as well.

He is very sure he will be expected to see this type of worker monthly.

Case Study ▷ **Recommend a Career Path in Human Services**

The following people are interested in pursuing a career in Human Services. Based on their interests and strengths, which career path would you suggest for each of them?

FELICIA

Felicia loves psychology. She can't get enough of learning about personality theories and effective psychotherapies, using the *Diagnostic and Statistical Manual of Mental Disorders*, published by the American Psychiatric Association.

When she graduates with her Human Services degree this year, where should she start to look for a job?

TALITHA

Talitha loves to work with her hands. She has made beautiful arts and crafts projects from scraps of material, wood, and old jewelry. She also loves to cook and sew. People enjoy being around her because she is pleasant and always has some idea for a new project that she is willing to share with others. Talitha will graduate in May with her degree in Human Services.

What type of job should she consider with her professional training and her personal interests?

MARTHA

Martha is the president of the Human Services club at her school. She always has ideas for fund-raising and thinks that the students could earn enough this year to pay for their travel to the NOHS conference. She is a natural leader and always gets her club involved in community service during the holidays.

What type of Human Services job should she consider when she graduates?

Recall what you learned in this chapter by completing the Chapter Review.

OLIVER TWIST PRODUCTIONS LLP/
FERRANDIS, GUY/Album/Newscom

The Early History of Helping Others

. . . .

Who Created Some of Our Current Day Programs?

Chapter Outline

- What's It All About? 39
- Regional Influences in America 44
- Around the Globe 61
- Putting Theories to Work 63
- Think Human Services 66
- Linking Theory to Practice 66
- Did You Know? 67
- What Would You Do? 68

If you want to know what it was like to live in an almshouse or a poorhouse, watch the classic movie *Oliver Twist*. This tale, by Charles Dickens, is about life in old England in centuries past. It describes the life of Oliver Twist, who was born to an unmarried, aristocratic mother. She was forced to deliver her son in the county poorhouse since she was not married, and her death upon childbirth sealed Oliver's fate. He had to spend his young life in the county poorhouse, where other orphans, the sick, and the elderly reside. He had a hard life of work and no play in this institution. Rules were inflexible and punishment was swift and severe for disobedience. Many of the older residents bullied the younger ones, and the living environment was dingy and sterile. Gruel or porridge, a thick mush-like grain, was the staple food for residents in these institutions. A bowl of gruel along with hard bread completed the meal. Food was rationed and regulations prohibited asking for seconds. When Oliver asks for "more please," it creates a ruckus in the dining hall. He is thrown out of the poorhouse for disobeying the rules.

The movie is an accurate description of what life was like for children during Elizabethan times in London. An orphan would either live in these residential poorhouses or live on the streets, falling in with bands of criminals. Before we understood human development, it was believed that children were like small adults and were expected to work, often earning dangerous jobs like chimney sweeps because their small bodies could easily squeeze into tight spaces (Crosson-Tower, 2013). Homeless children were plentiful, and thieves and pickpockets were eager to teach their trade to youngsters. The movie, *Oliver Twist*, does a good job of portraying street children as well as those who lived in poorhouses and describes the lives those children endured during this period in history. Many people were concerned for Oliver's welfare in the movie and make concerted efforts to help him. As you read through this chapter, you will find that several people during this period in history were concerned about the poor, the disabled, the mentally challenged, and others who were treated unfairly. Many of the services we have today were started by caring people during this era.

When you learn about the history of social services, what does it teach us about helping those in need today, especially children and the poor? What kinds of services are currently available for children who have no parents? Compare these services with the poorhouse Oliver lived in during the 1800s. How do we help those who are poor now? In this chapter we will look at how children, the poor, and other groups of people were treated during Elizabethan times in Europe and compare it with services in the United States today. We will look at the beginning of social policies that created formal systems of helping for those in need.

Watch the *Oliver Twist* clip at IMDb.

What's It All About?

Historically, Who Was Responsible for Helping the Poor?

Have you ever been asked to help someone—a friend, sibling, or classmate? Chances are you said "yes" and listened to what the person needed. Sometimes a problem can seem monumental to one person, but someone else can look at the problem in a different way and come up with a new solution. As they say, "two heads are better than one." You may have been asked to lend money, provide advice, help with some basic need like food, or even just listen to a friend. First you had to decide that you wanted to help, then you listened to the problem, and finally, you had to make sure you had access to the resources that were needed. You probably developed a plan with the person to help solve the problem. This process of helping has been in existence for thousands of years. Sometimes it is easier to ask for help from our families and friends. We call these our **informal systems** of helping. When these systems are not able to help us, more **formal systems** of helping need to be used. This chapter is all about the beginning of formal systems of helping in the United States. To understand this, we need to go back in time to early civilizations that existed before the United States became a nation.

If we were to travel back in time, we would see many people who needed help due to sickness, lack of money, jobs, or shelter. In Europe, during *feudal* times, the king assumed responsibility for the people who lived on his land. A sense of **mutual obligation** developed where the King allowed peasants or serfs who lived in his kingdom to farm the land four days a week for him and three days a week for themselves. In this way people were allowed to keep what came off the land to help them survive. A few times a year the king would hold a feast in the castle, and everyone in the kingdom was allowed to partake in the food and social activities. In this way the king and feudal lords assumed much of the responsibility for everyone who lived on their land, including those who were poor and sick. It was not considered a burden to assist those who needed help but rather it was seen as the king's duty. The quality of life for those in the kingdom was varied. Knights and Lords and church officials, who assisted the king, had greater wealth than the serfs. The serfs were the lowest residents of the kingdom who farmed the land

A sense of mutual obligation existed in feudal times; serfs farmed the land for the king four days a week and three days a week for themselves.

Patrick Kinsella

and lived a very meager existence. It was the belief of the Church that those with wealth and resources had a responsibility to help those who were poor. The Catholic Church, the primary religious organization at the time, provided Human Services like legal assistance, counseling, and spiritual help until later in the Middle Ages when social policies were established and town governments stepped in to provide assistance. Religious leaders like St. Thomas Aquinas and St. Francis of Assisi were the first to help establish institutions for the poor, orphans, the elderly, and those with disabilities. Asylums for the mentally ill were developed in the 15th and 16th centuries. However treatments were often ineffective, and the quality of services in the asylums was poor.

As feudalism declined in Europe and commerce began to spread with the beginning of capitalism and later industrialization, the growth of those in need began to spread as well. The idea of mutual obligation gave way to a more definite plan of assisting those who were poor, sick, unemployed, homeless, dependent, or mentally ill. Often those in need roamed around with nowhere to go and no feudal lord to help them. The cities became havens for orphaned children who, like Oliver in the movie, fell into the hands of criminal street thieves, who took them in and educated them on delinquent survival skills. As a result of the problems in large cities, social policies were developed to help those in need and to protect society from those who committed crimes. Although the church continued to help those who were poor, by the 16th century, the state assumed control over many of the services previously provided by the church, among these were Human Services (Day, 2012).

The Elizabethan Poor Laws of 1601

In 1601, the **Elizabethan Poor Laws** were established in England to provide a policy for caring for those who could not care for themselves. Many provisions were set forth in this new law, the first of which stated it was the *responsibility of the family to care for its members*. If for some reason a family could not care for its members, then it was the *responsibility of the state to provide services* in the person's local community. **Residency requirements** were established for those needing help, indicating that services would only be provided in the county of their birth. This eliminated the possibility of people traveling around the countryside becoming a burden to other communities. It also prevented people from moving too far away from their county of origin. This served as a means of social control over people, allowing the state to maintain a sense of order over communities that suffered with disease, famine, and poverty. The new law provided a tax, which raised funds to help those in need. Local community governments created a system for administering the funds. People were classified according to their ability to work. This included children, the able-bodied poor, and those unable to work. It became the responsibility of the community agency to determine who was eligible for services. In some communities, children, the disabled, and the elderly were considered "worthy" of help even though they could not work. They were offered *outdoor relief* in the form of food baskets, or other services in their home. More often, however, institutional services were provided for those unable to work by sending them to live at the local poorhouse. Children became wards of the state and were apprenticed at a young age if their parents were unable to care for them. Boys were apprenticed to learn a skill until age 24 and girls until age 21. Those able to work were provided a job at the county workhouse, which was much like the county poorhouse. Services in these institutions, known as *indoor relief*, were often substandard as can be seen in the movie *Oliver Twist*. These institutions often served as hospitals, workhouses for the poor, and orphanages. The Elizabethan Poor Laws also set forth the idea of *philanthropy*, encouraging those who could afford to donate money to local charities like the poorhouse/workhouse or relief baskets to do so. In return they were given tax relief, the beginning of the idea of tax donations to help the poor. In Elizabethan times, people often believed that helping the poor and donating money would secure a place for them in the afterlife in heaven, a concept endorsed by the church (Trattner, 1998).

Social Policies in Colonial America

When the English colonists first arrived in America they had great plans. In this new land they could start over, secure property, and work hard to make their lives better and more prosperous than it had been in England. Their familiarity with the English Poor Laws allowed them to naturally adopt some similar policies in this new land. However, colonists saw this land as providing new opportunities for everyone, and the need for many charities and laws to help the poor was seen as unnecessary in a capitalist society. It was believed that anyone who wanted a job could have one, and indeed the economy in early America was robust. Skilled craftsmen could earn more money for their products here than they could in Europe since fewer artisans and craftsmen allowed for bigger profits. As in England, orphaned or poor children were apprenticed to tradesmen to learn an employable skill. Records in many American cities show children, as young as age four, who were apprenticed as blacksmiths, housekeepers, silversmiths, and so on during colonial times. However, unlike England, it was not seen as the responsibility of the colonies to provide services for the poor or to tax residents for services they saw as unneeded in America.

As the colonies prospered one by one, and residents became tired of paying what were seen as unnecessary and increasing taxes to the king, revolution occurred. After the Revolutionary War and the independence from England and the king, the Declaration of Independence allowed the new America to consider social policies that would make the country separate and distinct from the oppressive policies of England. As a result of their experiences, early Americans were not in favor of undue taxation. They also believed separating the powers of the church and the state was in their best interest, so as to limit the power of either institution. It was felt that a capitalistic society would allow everyone to own property, work hard, earn a profit, and keep their own resources. Unlike the Elizabethan Poor Laws of England, America did not develop a federal policy to take responsibility for its most vulnerable citizens. Instead those who were poor, disabled, or in need were dependent upon the generosity of their family, friends, neighbors, and church for necessary resources. Early records in America show that many services were provided by the church or through philanthropic organizations, where donations by wealthy individuals could be used for tax purposes. From the very beginning, American colonists used the model of community collaboration, rather than taxation, when providing services for the poor. Eventually, each colony developed its own programs to address the needs of its residents, as we will see in the section on the growth of regional Human Services in America.

The development of almshouse was not as prevalent in the United States as it was in England. There are records for four early facilities that provided for the poor or sick. In 1713, the **Friends Almshouse** was developed by Quakers in Philadelphia to help poor members of the Society of Friends, a local Quaker organization. This was the first almshouse in America to care for poor citizens, and it was a combination poorhouse/workhouse. It provided food, housing, work, and modest health care for the poor. Then in 1731, Pennsylvania established the first government-sponsored care for the poor in America by opening the **Blockley Almshouse**. By 1835, it had four buildings and became a hospital for the sick, an insane asylum, a poorhouse, and an orphanage. Conditions were dismal, and in 1864 the "female lunatic asylum" was destroyed by fire when workers tried to install heaters. Eighteen women died and twenty were injured. Such were the conditions of the poor and the sick at that time. Historic writings describe the almshouses as old, unsanitary facilities with beds of straw for sleeping. Children who lived in these facilities often suffered from eye infections due to congenital diseases. By the end of the 1700s mortality rates for children in almshouses were quite high, and records show that by 1868 conditions had not improved that much. Foundlings Hospital in New York had 1,527 children in 1868 but one year later, all but 80 were dead. The 20th century saw improvements in medical and psychiatric care. In 1903, the Blockley Almshouse was turned over to the Bureau of Hospitals, and in 1906, the mentally ill were moved to its own facility at the Byberry Mental Hospital. Today the site is occupied by parts of Children's Hospital of Philadelphia, the University of Pennsylvania Health System, and the Veterans Health Administration.

Other almshouses existed in different parts of the country. Carrollton, Illinois, was also the site of another almshouse called the **Green County Almshouse**. It is now listed as a National Historic Site on a township road and was probably used for poor immigrants who traveled west to Illinois. Massachusetts ventured into caring for its poor in May of 1854 with the opening of the **Tewksbury Almshouse**. By December of that year, 2,193 European immigrants were admitted. At the time, 14 people were employed by the facility, and it cost the state 94.5 cents per resident per week. Compare that to the residential cost of housing children today in group homes or adults in prisons, which could be hundreds of dollars a day.

The history of the United States provides a rich and unique picture of the creation of services for its people. As colonies progressed into states and the territory expanded from the Atlantic to the Pacific, new ways of helping people and meeting needs were created. The development of the Constitution of the United States allowed for the creation of the nonprofit sector in American society, which was thought to be the instrument through which all needy, disabled, and dependent members of society could be helped. Although eventually some states did institute taxes and provided better services for their residents, it was not until the passage of the Social Security Act in 1935, during President Franklin D. Roosevelt's administration, that the federal government began to offer services to America's needy through a system of individual taxation. It was the federal government's first step into providing services for its U.S. residents.

History teaches us that American Human Services evolved over time as a partnership among our *social, economic, and public institutions.* These three institutions are the social or **nonprofit sector**, the economic or **private sector**, and the government or **public sector**. Informal assistance provided by family and friends was the first help offered to early Americans, but as the needs increased, even with the resources of our religious organizations, it was difficult to provide all the help that was needed. The development of the nonprofit sector allowed more charities to provide services to the sick, elderly, orphaned children, and the mentally ill. These not-for-profit businesses, which are today organized under Section 501(c)3 of the Internal Revenue Service, were allowed to raise funds and solicit tax deductible donations for services. By the late 1800s, they would become exempt from paying state, local, or federal taxes. Wealthy individuals and businesses, our private sector, were encouraged to donate money to these charities in their local community. It was seen as one's civic duty, and so for many years, both the private sector and nonprofit organizations were the primary source of local Human Services. As we discuss the beginning of early social services in America, you will also see the significant impact the religious communities have had on the development of programs for people of all ages. However, with the increasing assistance of the federal government in the 20th century, with the passage of the 1935 Social Security Act, American Human Services developed into a triangle of partnerships among the government, business and the private sector, and our nonprofit organizations. This partnership is unique to the United States and allows each of the institutions to contribute resources for the health and well-being of all Americans. As Human Services professionals, it is often difficult but necessary for us to encourage all three partnerships to continue their contributions in an equitable manner so as to ensure the array of services we have today.

History

Understanding and Mastery: Historical and current legislation affecting service delivery; differences between systems of governance and economics

Critical Thinking Question: How does this historic legislation affect current delivery of Human Services? Do you think the unique partnership of private for-profit businesses, nonprofit agencies, and government services is working effectively?

Assess your comprehension of <u>What's It All About?</u> by completing this quiz.

Regional Influences in America

The Key Americans Who Helped to Develop Early Human Services

If you think one person can't make a difference, then read this section and think again. Many of the services that we have in the United States today came about because of the persistence of an individual who felt strongly about assisting homeless children, helping the sick, changing attitudes toward the poor or the mentally ill, or finding a way to change their community. Human Services professionals can make a difference. Let's look at how some people helped to shape the social services available in America today. Maybe one day you will be the person in your community who starts a special program to help others. Let's look at some significant Americans who developed early Human Services in the *southern, mid-Atlantic, northeastern, midwestern, and western* regions of the country. This is by no means an exhaustive list of all the services that were developed. We will continue to read about early pioneers in Human Services around the United States in all of our chapters and learn how they made changes that affected services for children, the mentally ill, workers' rights, and the elderly. I hope you enjoy reading this section as much as I did researching these organizations. I encourage you to take the time to go to the websites that I have given to check out the history, read more about the founders, and participate in the interactive activities that some of the websites offer. Do you know who started some of the early Human Services programs?

> ### History

Understanding and Mastery: Skills to analyze and interpret historical data for application in advocacy and social change

Critical Thinking Question: As you read through all of the following services that were developed around the United States, can you identify the Human Services values and skills demonstrated when individuals step forward to advocate for another, more vulnerable population like children, the elderly, the mentally ill, those with disabilities, or those who live in poverty?

Is there a significant person or program in your community that should be listed?

Send me an email!

Southern Region

Watch *Annie* to gain a better understanding of what life was like inside an orphanage.

An **orphanage** was the name given to describe a facility where children were cared for due to the death of their parents, or their parent's inability to care for them. Today orphanages may also be called **residential facilities** or **group homes**. They take the place of foster care and adoption and can be good places for children without families to grow and learn. However, the unregulated orphanages of the past were often dangerous, abusive places for children.

Let's look at some early orphanages in the United States and some other programs for youth as well.

URSULINE NUNS In 1727, probably the first orphanage to be developed in North America was opened by the Ursuline nuns in New Orleans to provide homes to children whose parents had died of disease or disaster. In 1729, they opened another orphanage in Natchez, Mississippi, after many adult settlers were killed in clashes with Native Americans in that area. The name of the orphanage is unconfirmed, and the facility no longer is in operation. It may have been originally designed as a religious school for poor girls but quickly became a facility for the growing numbers of orphaned and neglected children.

THE NEW EBENEZER ORPHANAGE   In 1731, 20,000 Protestants were expelled from the Province of Salzburg, now known as Austria, because they followed the teachings of Martin Luther. After receiving an invitation from the trustees of the colony of Georgia, 300 Salzburgs came to America to begin a new life without religious persecution. Arriving in 1734, they established their first site many miles inland of Savannah, Georgia, but disease, death, and infertile soil left them sick and destitute after a short time. They petitioned General Oglethorpe to allow them to move closer to the banks of the Savannah River in Effingham County, where they developed New Ebenezer. Here they built a church, a rice and grist mill, and one of the first orphanages for children in this country, the **New Ebenezer Orphanage**. The community remained until 1752 when it was burned by the British during the Revolutionary War.

> **Explore the Georgia Salzburg Society website, which is devoted to the early history of this group.**

THE BETHESDA HOME   The oldest operating orphanage to be developed in the United States was established in the colony of Georgia in 1740. When the outbreak of cholera killed many immigrant parents in Savannah, many young children were left without a family. **George Whitefield**, a 25-year-old evangelical Methodist preacher, and **James Habersham**, a prominent founding father of Savannah, created the **Bethesda Home for Children** in Savannah, Georgia, on a 500-acre king's land grant, given by the Royal Charter of 1732. Bethesda, which means "House of Mercy," was the name given by Whitefield who had great plans for the facility, and who hoped great acts of mercy would take place there. Whitefield believed in the religious awakening of America and was often nontraditional in his preaching, often speaking out of doors and not in churches. He was moved by Georgia's poor orphans and solicited donations to open an orphanage, an academy, and eventually a college. It was founded as a nonprofit organization with funds coming from Whitefield, who donated $2,539 of his own wealth and raised

Andrea B. Dove/Bethesda Academy

Original entrance to the Bethesda Academy, in Savannah, GA., the oldest continuously operating children's facility in the country. What used to called an orphanage is now an educational academy for residential and nonresidential boys.

funds from other wealthy English and American donors. He had plans for the facility to be self-sustaining. The house was two stories high with 20 rooms and two smaller buildings for an infirmary and a workhouse. The name was changed to the *Bethesda Home for Boys*, reflecting the greater need for a boys' home at the time. The children were to learn a trade so they could earn a living as adults. They provided their own food through a small farm they operated with livestock and gardens. A strong religious influence permeated the facility where children learned spinning, carding, mechanics, and agriculture. Whitefield had plans for expanding the orphanage into a university, but funding setbacks and a fire in 1773 almost closed the facility. Despite its challenges, the Bethesda Home for Boys still operates today as a Christian educational facility for boys. It is now known as *Bethesda Academy*. It has been through many changes but still offers a residential program for boys who are in need of supervised care and an excellent educational program for both residential and nonresidential boys. The farm is still operable, and the residents are active in both learning and working with plant and animal life. The boys operate a fresh, organic produce market weekly from their own gardens. They learn the financial end of running a business and are allowed to keep the money they earn in savings for themselves as well. A technology program has been added to the school so the boys can learn media production, which they also operate as a small community enterprise. Although plans for a university on site were never realized, children growing up at Bethesda are educated and offered a variety of training options as young adults through local vocational colleges, academic colleges, or military training (Cashin, 2001).

> **Explore the Bethesda Academy website for more information.**

CHARLESTON ORPHAN HOUSE   The *first publicly supported orphanage* in the United States was in Charleston, South Carolina. A city ordinance was passed in 1790 to use public funds for the **Charleston Orphan House**. It was located in downtown Charleston and over the years served hundreds of children. It became an independent, nonprofit organization in 1978. The mission also changed to include treating the emotionally disturbed child. Still operating today, it is known as the Carolina Youth Development Center and serves 600 children and their families each year in two emergency shelters, a career center, and other outreach programs that include a *Big Brothers and Big Sisters* program.

THE JENKINS ORPHANAGE   In 1866, a year after the end of the Civil War, **Reverend Anthony Porter**, a Confederate Army chaplain, asked President Andrew Johnson for federal assistance to help the African American children who were orphaned after the war. President Johnson was touched by this concern for black children from a Southern, white minister. He then donated $1,000 of his own money to start the first African American orphanage in Charleston, for the orphaned children of the freed slaves. With the money, Porter purchased the old mariner's hospital next to the prison in Charleston and proceeded to solicit donations to build his program. Reverend Porter preached at churches in the northeast and often collected donations at his sermons in Philadelphia, Boston, and New York for his Charleston orphanage. The program lasted from 1866 until 1870 when funds ran dry, and the orphanage then became affiliated with St. Mark's Church in Charleston. It wasn't until 1890 that the orphanage again came to life under the directorship of **Reverend Daniel Jenkins**. In 1891, Reverend Jenkins, pastor of

> **Explore South Carolina's Information Highway to learn more about Jenkins' Orphanage.**

this small African American church in South Carolina, took in four orphans under the age of 12 years whom he found in an old abandoned building in Charleston. Having been a slave himself, Reverend Jenkins understood the plight of the African American children and quickly took the children under his care. He knew without shelter the children would be placed in a reform school or hard work as farm hands. Within a year he had 360 boys in the **Jenkins Orphanage**, which is still one of the oldest operating African American residential facilities in the United States.

Many of the orphans were sick and suffered with tuberculosis. He had even less success than Reverend Porter with soliciting funding for his school and decided that donations were not going to support his program. Instead he had another creative idea to raise money. He was going to start a school band, which would play on street corners in Charleston for donations. His hope was that by playing brass instruments the ailing health of his boys would improve. Instead of money, Reverend Jenkins solicited help from the local community for instruments and band uniforms. He was successful in getting the Citadel Cadets, a military college in Charleston, to donate their old uniforms and a local music store to donate some brass instruments to the boys. This was the start of the **Jenkins Orphanage Brass Band**. Although he was not a musician, Reverend Jenkins encouraged the help of local musicians to teach his boys to play. Not only did the trumpets, trombones, saxophones, and other instruments improve the breathing and lung ailments of his orphans but also the band developed a following up and down the coast of the United States. The orphanage became known for the excellent musical instruction it provided, teaching the boys how to read music and how to understand musical theory. The band became famous for its musical numbers, playing both Souza marches and a type of music known as "rag" or jazzy notes. The band also engaged the crowds with fancy steps the boys had learned from a group of native island people known as the Gullah in South Carolina. People in New York, Philadelphia, and Boston loved to hear the boys play and later the Jenkins Orphanage Band was credited with creating the early sounds of both ragtime and perhaps even some early jazz. The dance the band made famous became known as the "Charleston" and could be seen in all the northern cities by the 1920s. By this time, the Jenkins Orphanage Band was well known and played in Harlem, Europe, all the northern cities, the Midwest, the St. Louis World's Fair, and even at President Theodore Roosevelt's and President Taft's inaugural parades. Several boys from the Jenkins Orphanage Band went on to play in Count Basie's Orchestra as well as with Duke Ellington. What started out as a need to help youngsters find a place to live turned into an excellent school of music as well as a home (Sigalas, 2009). The Jenkins Orphanage is still operating today in South Carolina as the Jenkins Institute for Children.

Listen to the music of the Jenkins Orphanage Band.

GIRLS SCOUTS OF AMERICA   When you were a youngster, did you ever belong to the Girl Scouts or Boy Scouts? Both of these social organizations were started during the Youth Movement of the early 1900s and can be traced back to the initiative of one or more individuals. Robert Baden-Powell, a war hero in England, applied the army scouting techniques he had learned to develop a program for young boys in Britain in 1908. In 1911, **Juliette Gordon Low**, a native of Savannah, Georgia, and wife of a young English businessman, met Robert Baden-Powell and became interested in the youth movement that was taking place at the time. She returned to Georgia with a renewed enthusiasm, telling friends and family she finally found something useful to do with her life. Her love of the outdoors, art, music, poetry, plays, and animals were funneled into her new creation called the Girl Scouts. This program for all girls was developed with the initiation of 18 girl guides in Savannah in 1912. The next year the name was changed to **Girl Scouts of America**. Juliette, or Daisy as her friends called her, believed that all girls should be given an opportunity to develop self-reliance and self-resourcefulness. The Girl Scouts prepared them not only for traditional roles as a homemaker but also for roles outside the home in business, science, and the arts. It was one of the first organizations to welcome girls with disabilities, which Daisy thought was the most natural policy of all. Juliette herself became deaf during her lifetime and suffered with back problems and cancer. This *nonjudgmental attitude* is one of the values we recognize in the Human Services profession today.

> **Review *The Story of Juliette Gordon Low* on the <u>Girl Scout</u> website.**

The Girl Scouts today is the largest educational and social organization for girls in the world and has over 3.7 million members in the United States, Puerto Rico, and the Virgin Islands. The birthplace of Juliette Gordon Low, in Savannah, Georgia, is the national headquarters for the Girl Scouts and the home of the archives of this organization. Juliette Gordon Low is considered an American Woman of Achievement, and in 2005, she became part of the new national monument in Washington, D.C., **The Extra Mile—Points of Light Volunteer Pathway**, which is dedicated to those Americans who realized their dreams by creating movements that have had a lasting impact in America. Many of the people that you will read about in this section are honored on this pathway.

> **View the <u>Points of Light</u> website to read about the new monument, *The Extra Mile—Points of Light Volunteer Pathway*, in Washington, D.C.**

Mid-Atlantic Region

Did you ever think that someone else had a good idea and so you tried to do the same thing? Well that is exactly what happened with many of our Human Services in this country. As U.S. citizens traveled abroad and saw what other countries were doing for their residents, they came back to the United States with plans of replicating those same services here.

THE AMERICAN RED CROSS   Did you ever feel you were too young or too old to do something? Well, age or gender never let Clara Barton stop her from doing anything. She became a teacher at a time when most teachers were men, and she became one of the first women to gain federal employment. She was working in the U.S. Patent office in Washington, D.C., during the Civil War and felt that she could be more useful to the soldiers if she was bringing needed supplies to them. She was around 40 years of age when she ventured to the battlefields and brought clothing, food, and supplies to the wounded soldiers. She often traveled by wagon at night to reach the field hospitals with the necessary supplies. She became known as the "Angel of the Battlefield," not only bringing supplies but offering personal support by listening to the men, reading to them, writing letters for them, and praying with them. She learned how to collect needed items, appeal to the public for support, and then store her items and distribute them when needed. This is a skill that today we call *mobilizing resources*. After the war Clara was in Europe when she met **Henry Dunant**, the founder of the **International Red Cross**, a Swiss organization that provided domestic and overseas relief efforts and aided the military in many countries.

At age 60, Clara actively campaigned for the development of an **American Red Cross**, which was organized in 1881. Due to her efforts, the United States ratified the

Geneva Convention in 1882 to protect those who were injured in war. She became the head of the American Red Cross for the next 23 years and developed the Red Cross into a program that assisted the military in the United States and abroad, giving relief and serving as the communication between the armed forces and their families. She also worked with the International Red Cross during peacetime to assist with disasters and relief efforts worldwide. She implemented the Red Cross tracing services, finding missing soldiers for families and initiated the idea of a national cemetery for military soldiers and for memorializing those who could not be identified. This was the idea behind the Tomb of the Unknown Soldier.

A Congressional Charter in 1900 and again in 1905 authorized the American Red Cross to give relief and serve as the medium of communication between members of the Armed Forces and their families and to provide national and international disaster relief efforts. Additional services continued to be added including first aid, water safety, public health and nursing programs, training for civil defense, CPR, HIV/AIDS, and emotional care for victims of disaster. The Red Cross helped to develop the Federal Emergency Management Administration (FEMA), and today, the Red Cross serves as the principle supplier of mass care in federally declared disasters. Even though it works closely with the government, the Red Cross is an independent, nonprofit organization that is volunteer-led and is funded through contributions and cost-reimbursement charges. The president of the United States serves as the honorary chairman of the board and appoints eight governors and the chairman of the board who nominates the president of the Red Cross. The 50-member volunteer board then elects the president who is responsible for carrying out the policies of the Red Cross board. The American Red Cross works closely with the International Committee of the Red Cross on international conflicts of a political, military, or social nature, often bringing relief services to victims of war and unrest. The American Red Cross also works with 175 other national relief societies to bring disaster assistance to countries worldwide.

> **Assess your comprehension of <u>Regional Influences:</u> (Part 1) by completing this quiz.**

BOYS SCOUTS OF AMERICA   **Robert Baden-Powell** is considered the founder of the Boy Scouts in England. After returning from the Boer War, he found that youth were interested in many of the military activities he had learned. He reorganized a program for boys by utilizing information from his military training manual. He collected information on other youth programs that were already operating in other parts of the world and then added the idea of earning badges for work done on citizenship, moral codes, secret signs, woodcraft, rituals, and uniforms among other things. He added these concepts to a program in England in 1908 called the Boys Brigade, and the new program became a success in Britain. He called his new program the Boy Scouts. Other similar programs for youth were started about this same time in other countries so others often claim to be the original founder of the Boy Scout Movement. In 1910, the **Boy Scouts of America** program was brought to the United States by **William Boyce**. The first program was organized in Washington, D.C.

> **Read to learn more about the history of the <u>Boy Scouts of America</u>.**

CATHOLIC CHARITIES   By now you have probably realized how important religion has been to the development of many of our Human Services. Many people who initiated these programs had a strong belief system and faith in a higher being. They believed morally and ethically that helping others was an obligation. Many of our Human Services today are still offered by our faith-based organizations and our churches. One of these organizations, **Catholic Charities**, can trace its roots back to the **French Ursuline nuns** who developed the first orphanage for children back in 1727 in New Orleans. As more children needed services, additional Catholic institutions were established along the East Coast. Based in Alexandria, Virginia, Catholic Charities is one of the largest social service networks in the country today providing social work, health care, and advocating for the poor. As a nonprofit organization, Catholic Charities has been in existence for over 280 years, and although each local program develops its own services based upon community needs, it continues to offer such necessities as food, shelter, supportive housing, clothing, financial assistance, counseling, immigration and refugee services, adoption, disaster response, child care, employment training, and supports for seniors.

As a nonprofit organization, it can accept donations for its mission. It is proud to report that 90 cents of every dollar donated goes directly to service, making Catholic Charities one of the most cost-effective social services. It believes that every human being is worthy of *dignity and respect*, and its mission is to *empower people, strengthen families, and communities* and work to *eliminate oppression* and build a compassionate society. These are the same values that we teach in Human Services.

Northeastern Region

Imagine the courage and determination it must take to convince other people that your ideas are good ones. Even in the face of danger, many Americans stepped forth to help others and in the process started some very dynamic programs that still exist today. In Human Services we teach students about the importance of morals, beliefs, and values. We discuss qualities like *acceptance of others, being honest, having integrity, being non-judgmental, promoting social justice, maintaining confidentiality, and respecting yourself and others*. As you read about the beginning of many programs, think about the people who first had an idea and then started building these ideas into real programs for others.

From the middle of the 19th century to around the turn of the century, a youth movement was occurring worldwide as more people were becoming aware of the needs of children with such issues as poverty, homelessness, child labor, lack of education, and crime. Those interested in helping to create changes were known as *progressives*. Both men and women answered the call to help the youth. You will recognize these programs, many of which are alive and well today.

THE YMCA   Did you ever have a great idea about something but thought no one would listen to you because you were too young or inexperienced? Well, in 1844, **George Williams** was a 22-year-old farmer-turned department store worker in London, England. He observed many problems as people moved from rural farm life into the cities, with housing becoming a critical issue. He witnessed firsthand the dangerous temptations of the city with its bars and nightlife and the cramped quarters of the tenement apartments. Along with 11 of his friends, he started the **Young Men's Christian Association (YMCA)**, an organization devoted to housing, Bible study and prayer for those moving to the city.

Locate the YMCA closest to you.

The Rancho Family YMCA in Rancho Penasquitos conducts the final stretching exercise for its step aerobics class. YMCAs are family friendly centers with lots of activities, exercise, and child care.

ZUMA Press, Inc./Alamy

Thomas Valentine Sullivan, a retired sea captain and marine missionary, learned of this program, and in 1851, it became a reality on this side of the Atlantic. At the site of the Old South Church in Boston, it became a safe house for sailors and merchants with volunteers running the early programs. Facilities in the early YMCAs included affordable housing in hotel-like rooms, gyms, and auditoriums. At an exercise class in Boston, the term "body building" was used to explain the necessity for regular and consistent exercise. The programs flourished, and in 1853, the first black YMCA was opened by a freed slave, **Anthony Bowen**, in Washington, D.C. The YMCA became synonymous with welcoming newcomers and immigrants, and in 1856, the nation's first *English as a Second Language (ESOL)* class was held for German immigrants at the Cincinnati YMCA. Also in 1856, Cumberland University, in Lebanon, Tennessee, had the first YMCA in the country for college students. Their program focused on leadership issues. The YMCA is a good example of an organization that *meets community needs* and continues to change over time as local communities define what services they must provide. Today there are over 1,200 YMCA associations nationwide. In 2010, First Lady Michelle Obama chose the YMCA to launch her "Let's Move" campaign to fight childhood obesity (Hinding, 2001).

THE YWCA Did you ever wonder who supported outspoken, intelligent women during the 19th century? During the 19th century, it must have been difficult for these women to stifle their voices and conform to the standards of the times. Children were "to be seen and not heard," and men were expected to control their wives and children. Did you ever hear of "the rule of thumb?" That term meant that a man could beat his wife and children, when necessary, with a board no thicker than his thumb. This was the acceptable standard of the day.

Explore the **YWCA: USA** website to learn what different states are doing.

One organization was a supporter of women, beginning in 1855. **Emma Robarts** and **Mrs. Arthur Kinnaird** of London opened the first **Young Women's Christian Association (YWCA)**, which is the oldest and largest multicultural women's organization in the world. By 1858, both New York City and Boston had programs, but in 1860 New York City had the first boarding house for female students, teachers, and factory workers. The mission of the YWCA has always been to *eliminate racism and empower women.*

YWCAs have been involved in many movements over the past century including women's rights, the labor movement, and race relations. Although each program is unique to the needs of the community of which it is a part, the YWCAs may provide safe havens for victims of domestic violence and women in rape crisis, counseling for women, child care, job training, and health and fitness. They were one of the first organizations to provide bilingual instruction for immigrants, and in the 1940s they adopted an interracial charter denouncing segregation years before the Supreme Court decision. Did you know that in the 1960s, the Atlanta YWCA was the first desegregated dining facility in the city? There are over 300 YWCA associations in the United States and can be found in over 100 countries worldwide.

BOYS AND GIRLS CLUBS OF AMERICA   Have you ever been concerned about something that was happening in your neighborhood or your local school? Well, back in 1860, several women in Hartford, Connecticut, were concerned about the young boys who roamed their streets, committing acts of vandalism and petty theft. As the number of immigrants increased and families moved from rural areas to the cities to gain employment, children were often left unsupervised while parents worked or hunted for employment. Children often worked alongside their parents before child labor laws and education laws required them to be in school. If children were unemployed or lost a job, they often wandered the streets or joined gangs for protection. The development of the **Boys Clubs** offered these children a chance to participate in meaningful activities. In 1906, the Boys Clubs began to affiliate and 53 member organizations formed the Federation of Boys Clubs in Boston. The name was changed to the Boys Clubs of America in 1931, and a U.S. Congressional Charter was given in 1956.

Explore "The Scoop" on the **Boys and Girls Club** website.

John Collins, the first club professional, believed in character development and instituted a curriculum of informal guidance to improve behavior and increase personal goals. **Aaron Fahringer**, the regional director for the West Coast in the 1950s, scripted the Code of the Boys Club, which includes a belief in God, the Constitution, and the Bill of Rights. It also states an adherence to fair play, honesty, and sportsmanship. The organization was renamed the **Boys and Girls Clubs of America** in 1990 to acknowledge the importance of activities for girls. Research continues to demonstrate that Boys and Girls Clubs have positive outcomes for youth. Currently 4 million kids attend 4,000 clubs across America. The Annual Report of the Boys and Girls Club (2011) indicates that their programs are effective at improving school performance and dropout rates and furthering postsecondary education. Their activities are goal-oriented and are designed for academic enrichment and school engagement, dropout prevention, and intensive intervention and case management. In a Harris survey in 2010, 90% of club alumni indicated they graduated on time, and 80% felt the club was responsible for their positive attitude toward fitness.

The national committee on community-level programs for youth concluded in its research that community programs promote youth development. At-risk youth are considered those with too much free, unsupervised time during nonschool hours, youth with disabilities, and those from troubled families. Although many adolescents from affluent areas are doing well, minority youth from inner cities and rural areas tend to have the lowest scores on achievement tests and the highest dropout rates. Youth programs in these areas would be welcome additions to a community (Eccles & Appleton-Gootman, 2002).

BIG BROTHERS BIG SISTERS OF AMERICA   In 1904, in New York City, **Ernest Kent Coulter** helped to organize the first children's court. As a court clerk, Ernest saw that the number of young, delinquent boys coming through his courtroom was increasing. He solicited the help of 39 adult volunteers to mentor these youth and started the first program known as Big Brothers and Big Sisters of New York City. It was so successful that by 1916 the Big Brothers Program was replicated in 96 other cities in the United States. To better assist the girls, the Ladies of Charity befriended the girls in the children's court and started Catholic Big Sisters, which grew into Big Sisters International. Although both groups developed independently, in 1977 they merged to become **Big Brothers Big Sisters of America**. This organization now operates in all 50 states, and by 1995 scholarly research indicated that positive gains were realized for youth who had relationships with a mentor from the Big Brothers Big Sisters program. In 2004, New York City celebrated its centennial anniversary for this effective program.

GOODWILL INDUSTRIES   Have you ever cleaned out your closet and donated clothes or other items to the **Goodwill Industries** in your community? Did you know it was an organization started by one individual with an idea to help the poor? Iowa-born **Edgar Helms** had moved to Boston to attend theology school. As a Methodist minister he worked at a church in the south end of Boston, known for its poor, immigrant parishioners. Helms was a social innovator who had the idea of collecting used clothing and household items from the wealthier side of town; he then trained and hired people who were poor, to repair and sell the used goods. The term "a hand up, not a hand out" was born, and the first Goodwill organization was opened in 1902. Helms believed that everyone had the potential to work and that work provided dignity and empowerment for all individuals. The nonprofit organization was successful and was replicated in many cities across the country with each Goodwill independent, incorporated, and governed by a local board of directors. The mission of Goodwill is still to help others achieve economic stability, build strong families and communities by providing employment, training, and vocational rehabilitation for people of limited employability.

Goodwill Industries became a global entity in the 1920s, assisting countries worldwide. By the 1930s, it began serving not only the poor but the disabled as well. In 1940, Jacksonville, Florida, had the first collection box for community drop-offs, a well-known symbol of Goodwill today. By 2007, Goodwill Industries had served over 100 million people with its services and programs. What started out as a small idea to help the poor has grown into a $3.2 billion a year industry. The goal by 2020 is for Goodwill Industries to improve self-sufficiency of 20 million people and their families.

Read the "Community Programs to Promote Youth Development" study from The National Academies Press.

Explore the Big Brothers Big Sisters website to learn more about this organization.

Explore the Goodwill Industries International, Inc. website to learn more.

THE NATIONAL JEWISH WELFARE BOARD   In many communities today you may be familiar with Jewish Community Centers (JCCs) where recreational, social, and educational activities take place. Back in 1913, the Council of Young Men's Hebrew and Kindred Associations was organized to coordinate various programs that were offered throughout the United States by Jewish associations such as JCCs and Young Men's Hebrew Associations. In 1916, this Council developed a military committee to meet the religious and welfare needs of Jewish soldiers who were engaged in warfare on the Mexican border. By World War I, services had expanded to include assisting rabbis serving near military posts. By 1917, representatives of five major Jewish religious bodies joined with the Council to create the Jewish Board for Welfare Work in the United States Army and Navy.

Search the <u>Center for Jewish History</u> database to learn more about American Jewish history.

The name was changed to the **Jewish Welfare Board (JWB)** in 1919 and became the official organization to serve American Jewish servicemen in the military. They developed an abridged prayer book, which they distributed to Jewish soldiers along with prayer shawls, mezuzah scrolls, Jewish calendars, and other religious and nonreligious items. They provided kosher food for the soldiers and sponsored musical entertainment and dances, literary clubs, and English and history classes. They offered social services in the form of hospital visits for those wounded and home visits for family members of servicemen. Over time the JWB evolved into a national federation of local agencies whose mission was to meet the social, cultural, intellectual, physical, and religious needs of the American Jewish community.

Midwestern Region

As new services continued to be developed for people, an energy was growing in the country that encouraged people of all backgrounds—rich and poor, religious, or secular—to reach out and help others. Many people risked their lives and left personal fortunes to create new services where none existed. You will read about the beginning of programs for immigrants, Native Americans, African Americans, the elderly, the sick, and the disabled.

HULL HOUSE   Have you ever had a desire to help those less fortunate than you? Then you will enjoy reading about **Jane Addams**, the first American woman to receive the Nobel Peace Prize in 1931. She came from a large family of privilege in Illinois. Her father, an agricultural businessman and later Illinois state senator, was a friend of Abraham Lincoln. Jane was devoted to her father, having lost her mother during childbirth when she was two years old. She had many health problems during her life as a result of tuberculosis of the spine, which left her deformed. She attended college in Illinois, was an avid reader, and was inspired by religion. She was baptized as a Presbyterian at age 26 and felt strongly that Christians should be more engaged with the world. After traveling to Europe to visit the first **settlement house** in London at Toynbee Hall in 1888, she was motivated to return to America to initiate the settlement movement here. In discussions with Samuel and Henrietta Barnett of Toynbee Hall, she agreed that the poor could be helped in such a facility if the social classes were allowed to mingle for mutual benefit. Along with her college friend and intimate life partner, Ellen Gates Starr, she cofounded **Hull House** in 1889 in the near west side of Chicago. Initially she used her personal finances to update the estate home of Henry Hull, but wealthy friends and women who supported her cause were generous in their annual donations, so large contributions on her part did not continue to be necessary (Addams, 1981).

Hull House was in a neighborhood of European immigrants who suffered from poverty, unemployment, and language barriers. Ethnic groups represented included Germans, Jews, Greeks, Polish, Irish, Canadian, French, and Italians. As the first settlement house in America, Hull House was a model for the provision of services. Around 2,000 people visited the house each week for services, which included a night school for adults, kindergarten classes, clubs for older children, a public kitchen, an art gallery, a coffeehouse, a gym, a girls' club, a bathhouse, a book bindery, music school, drama group, language classes, reading groups, library, college extension courses, and many labor-related activities, cultural events, and social services. The residence itself grew into a dormitory for 25 female volunteers who worked and taught there. Later it would become a complex of 13 buildings with the addition of a playground and a summer camp (Jane Addams Hull House Museum, 2009).

Explore Jane Addams' Hull-House Museum website to learn more.

Jane continued to campaign for labor reform, juvenile court laws, tenement house regulations, 8-hour workdays, workers' compensation, justice for immigrants and blacks, women's rights, and she became a charter member of the **National Association for the Advancement of Colored People (NAACP)**. She helped develop the first factory laws and is remembered as a sociologist, author, leader in the women's suffrage movement, and advocate of world peace. She was a leader of the Progressive Era and was concerned about issues effecting mothers, needs of children, and public health. She spoke out against the war, advocating peaceful measures instead. She believed that women had a responsibility to clean up their communities, but that they needed the right to vote to do so.

As a social and political activist and community organizer, she worked to keep families safe and improve community and societal conditions. Jane fought for better housing for the poor, improvements in public welfare, stricter child labor laws, and protections for working women. She fostered the Play Movement in America believing that children should not be involved in work at young ages. She became the founder of the National Playground Association and advocated for playgrounds across the country. She supported research and the service fields of leisure, youth and Human Services. She also brought the idea of **social justice** and reform to the social work profession, and her idea of the Neighborhood Settlement House became a movement that was replicated in many cities resulting in over 500 settlement houses nationwide. It is amazing what this one woman accomplished in her lifetime!

Read "As Chicago's Hull House Closes Its Doors, Time to Revive the Settlement Model?" from The Nation.

Although most of the complex is now gone, the Hull House main building is a museum at the University of Illinois, Chicago campus. Until recently, the Jane Addams Hull House Association was one of the largest nonprofit social welfare organizations in Chicago with 50 programs at over 40 sites serving 60,000 individuals, families, and community members each year. In 2012, the Hull House Association closed its doors after declaring bankruptcy. The financial problems it suffered were related to a dependence on federal money that was decreasing with each passing year.

LUTHERAN SERVICES IN AMERICA The history of Lutherans in America goes back hundreds of years, and its ministry to the poor, sick, and immigrants goes back nearly as far. With congregations and synods across the country, the early Lutherans— mostly German, Dutch, and Scandinavian—provided for the needs of their community members from the northeast to the western regions of the United States. In 1849,

Sister Louisa Marthens was the first deaconess to the United States to work in an infirmary, which is now the Passavant Hospital in Pittsburgh. She established hospitals and orphan homes from Philadelphia to the west of Chicago. The Silver Springs-Martin Luther School for Orphans was opened in Plymouth Meeting, Pennsylvania, in 1859. The Lutheran Home at Germantown, Philadelphia, was the first residential program to open for older and infirm adults. In 1888, **Sister Elizabeth Fedde** established Lutheran Homes and Hospitals in Minneapolis and more in Chicago by 1896. By the late 1800s, many Lutheran church groups came together to become the American Lutheran Church.

Lutheran Social Services in Minnesota can trace its history back to 1865 when **Eric Norelius** of the Vasa Lutheran Church near Red Wing opened the church basement to care for four orphan children whose parents had been from Sweden. This was the beginning of the Vasa Children's Home, Minnesota's first and oldest orphanage. Lutheran Social Services in Minnesota continued to provide for its most vulnerable citizens over the years including children, the elderly, and the disabled with services like orphanages, day care, inner-city missions, employment programs for women, kindergartens, boys programs, services for refugees, homeless facilities, financial counseling, and residential care for unwed mothers, those with developmental disabilities, and boys with behavioral issues. It continues to operate safe houses for homeless youth, transitional housing, Camp Noah, and assisted with the Phillips Park initiative. Services have been offered in Saint Paul, Duluth and surrounding areas.

In other areas of the country, the Lutherans continued to move west and in the 1890s served at Immanuel Institute, a large health care facility in Omaha, Nebraska. The Lutherans continued to provide services for children through orphanages, family finding agencies, health care for the aged and sick, and care for the mentally ill.

After the Trail of Tears, when Native Americans were forced to move from their southeast homes to lands west of the Mississippi River, President Grant developed a "peace policy" and assigned various Christian denominations to work with 71 Indian agencies. In 1871, the Lutherans were assigned the Sac and Fox Reservations near Tama, Iowa. Their work with the Cherokee people in the 1890s also took them to the Oaks Indian Center in Oaks, Oklahoma. By 1893, **John Plocher** moved from Wisconsin to work with the Apache in Arizona. As Lutheran churches were expanded across the country, services to meet the needs of their communities grew as well. From the 1930s on, they developed domestic programs including refugee and chaplaincy work, town and country ministries, student services, and public relations.

Explore the Lutheran Services in America to learn more.

In 1997, Lutheran Services in America became an alliance of Evangelical Lutheran Church, which consisted of 9 regions, 65 synods, and 10,500 congregations and the Lutheran Church—Missouri Synod. The Lutheran social ministry today is served through **Lutheran Services in America** with over 300 independent Health and Human Services agencies, which serve over 6 million people.

In 2003, the state budget of Minnesota cut services so drastically that provisions for children, the elderly, the disabled, the homeless, and others were affected. A capital campaign launched by Lutheran Social Services of Minnesota in 2008 yielded $27 million and restored many Human Services to the area.

BENJAMIN ROSE INSTITUTE ON AGING Do you like working with older people? If you do, then you will like the fact that the population of the United States is shifting, with the number of our older folks increasing as improvements in health care make our life expectancy longer and more fulfilling. Many Human Services programs have courses that focus on older Americans and the needs they face as they age. Over 100 years ago, **Benjamin Rose**, a successful Ohio businessman in his later years, was approached by a former associate who had outlived his resources and needed assistance. The man's only options were the city infirmary or the poorhouse, both undesirable choices. Ben thought that others who were lucky enough to enjoy good health into their golden years may be faced with the same fate. In his will he left his fortune to those who needed other options late in life. Before his death he developed a nonprofit organization and picked the all-female board of directors, believing women to be compassionate and able to continue his vision and goals. The organization began operating in 1908, and originally recipients were selected for service based upon their economic need. Many received monthly stipends of less than $20.00, but often this amount was all that stood between their issues of life and death. By the 1930s, the **Benjamin Rose Institute** added the services of social work and medical care. The passage of the Social Security Act in 1935 allowed it to serve additional people. During the 1940s the institute established three homes in Cleveland, Ohio, for those unable to live alone. It began to develop community partnerships with University Hospitals and by 1953 opened the Benjamin Rose Hospital, which was the *first rehabilitation hospital in the country specifically for elders*. For 16 years the hospital provided services to patients in transition between the hospital and home after debilitating illnesses. The Benjamin Rose Institute opened the Margaret Wagner Nursing Home in 1961, which became a model for the nation on institutional elder care with a homelike approach. Its research department opened that same year with significant studies on elder abuse prevention, and the use of home health aides. The research led the way to the creation of the Benjamin Rose Library, which opened in 1971 and contained an extensive collection on geriatrics and gerontology. The Institute continued to develop partnerships with community organizations to develop more and better services for its population. In 1997, it opened the skilled nursing home care facility, which in 2006 was leased to Kindred Hospital for Long Term Acute Care. The upper floors of the facility serve as the administrative headquarters for their nonprofit organization. It continued to develop *community collaborations* and in 2007 created the Katz Policy Institute to expand its presence in the advocacy and public policy arena. The Benjamin Rose Institute still provides for the vision of its donor who wanted to help those who can't afford care as well as to help those who can. For over 100 years it has been a national and Ohio state leader in services, research, and advocacy for older adults.

THE MAYO CLINIC   Known as one of the top U.S. hospitals for the past 20 years, the **Mayo Clinic** was started in 1889 by **Dr. William Worrall Mayo**, an immigrant from the United Kingdom who came to Rochester, Minnesota, in 1846. As a community doctor, he started a single outpatient program that later became the first medical practice in America to integrate the group practices of more than 1,700 doctors. Along with his two sons, Dr. William James and Dr. Charles Horace, and a team of highly qualified medical professionals, Dr. William Worrall Mayo evolved his practice into a medical and research entity that provides innovative and effective treatments for patients with hard to treat illnesses that have gone undetected or untreated for some time. Dr. Mayo and his other partners Dr. Stinchfield, Dr. Graham, Dr. Plummer, Dr. Millet, Dr. Judd, and Dr. Balfour all shared in the profits of the early

Locate a doctor in your area from the Mayo Clinic by asking a health-related question.

medical practice, but were good businessmen and soon realized there were better models for delivering quality health care. During the early 20th century, Dr. Henry Plummer developed the innovative idea of using and sharing individual dossier-type medical records and an interconnected telephone system, which became universally accepted. He went on to create the diagnostic and clinical aspects of the program, and then in 1907, Dr. Wilson was hired to develop a research program. Doctors Will and Charlie Mayo founded the medical school at the University of Minnesota in 1917 with a $2 million gift. In 1919, the Mayo Clinic partners created a nonprofit medical practice, and the Mayo brothers gave their share of the practice to this newly formed entity. The Mayo model involves paying doctors fixed salaries based upon a market rate paid to doctors in comparable group practices, thus eliminating the need for doctors to treat large numbers of patients to increase their earnings. Doctors then spend more time with patients since they are not motivated to see large groups of people. The Mayo model was expanded during the 1900s with other large facilities opening in Scottsdale/Phoenix, Arizona, and Jacksonville, Florida, as well as satellites in other areas. In 1972, the Mayo Clinic initiated its own medical school where innovative medical practices and research were integrated. The Mayo Clinic became a model of high-quality, low-cost medical care and is continually named as one of America's best medical facilities. In 2010, the Mayo Clinic in Rochester was named the #2 overall hospital in the United States. Many Human Services professionals work in medical settings in a variety of roles assisting individuals, groups, and families with health issues. It is continually used as a model for excellent and affordable health care when new initiatives are discussed in Washington.

Western Region

Services in California and the far western region of the country developed slowly as citizens moved west. A review of early charitable and nonprofit agencies in the western region yields fewer resources than in other parts of the country in the 19th century. Perhaps one explanation is that the development of this part of the country took place after the eastern and southern sections were already developed, so many of the national and regional organizations were already created. However, as it became clear that additional services were needed, many individuals and communities created new and innovative programs for its residents.

UNITED WAY In 1887, the religious leaders of Denver, Colorado, realized the needs of their community called for collaborative action. Together **Frances Wisebart Jacobs**, founder of the Hebrew Ladies Benevolent Society, Msgr. William O'Ryan a Catholic Priest, two ministers **Reverend Myron Reed and Dean Martyn Hart**, and one Jewish Rabbi, **William Friedman**, planned the first United Way campaign for ten health and welfare organizations. Their goal was to collect funds for the local charities, coordinate relief services, counsel and refer clients when needed, and make emergency assistance grants available. Their efforts yielded $21,700 and created the beginning of the United Way Movement. They were known as the Charity Organization Society and would continue to plan and organize a single fund-raising event, known as "the United Way," each year for more than 22 agencies. By 1894 charitable institutions became exempt from the federal tax that was imposed on private for-profit corporations. This exemption from Section 501(c)3 of the Internal Revenue Service Code allowed nonprofit organizations to collect tax deductible donations from individuals and businesses and funnel the money back into services for the most vulnerable residents of their communities. By 1913, both the United States and Canada were continuing to think of ways to fund services for its most needy people without raising taxes. In Cleveland, Ohio, the **Community Chest** was created as a fund-raising organization that collected money from local businesses and workers and then distributed those funds to community projects. Similar to the Charity Organization Society of Denver, it was the first community fund developed by the Federation for Charity and Philanthropy. By 1918, executives of 12 fund-raising federations met in Chicago to form the American Association for Community Organizations, the predecessor of the United Way of America. The number of these United Way–type organizations increased from 39 to 353 from 1919 to 1929 and reached 1,000 by 1948.

The national office for the **United Way of America** was moved from New York to Alexandria, Virginia, in 1971 and by 1973 a unique collaboration was formed between the United Way of America and the National Football League (NFL). This innovative connection allowed the United Way to reach millions of Americans through NFL commercials and also encouraged the players to volunteer their time and talent in local United Way agencies during their off-season. The collection of over $1 billion in 1974 convinced both the United Way and the NFL that they had a winning combination. Later that year, the United Way International was formed to help nations around the world develop the same United Way–type agencies in their communities. The United Way continues to be the umbrella agency in most communities for the collection and distribution of funds for social services. It is the nation's largest charity and in 2007 developed its Financial Stability Partnership with a goal of cutting the number of financially unstable families in America by half by the year 2018. The objectives include helping low-income families become independent through employment, affordable housing, savings, manageable expenses, and income supports.

Locate a United Way agency near you.

MONTANA CHILDREN'S HOME AND HOSPITAL   In 1896, the Children's Home Society was organized in Helena, Montana, to care for its homeless children. From 1854 until 1929, orphaned children from the eastern United States were sent by trains to the western part of the country to be placed with families or to live in group homes. Despite the fact that Helena residents had no relationship to these children, they felt it was their duty to help the homeless children. The **Montana Children's Home** was built for this purpose. Many of the children arrived with health problems and so in 1930 a children's hospital was constructed in Helena as well. In 1937, a wealthy businessman, Louis W. Shodair, donated $200,000 to the Montana Children's Home and Hospital for the purpose of building a wing on the hospital for children with disabilities. The hospital was completed in 1938 and was the only hospital equipped to deal with polio patients when the virus hit in the 1940s. The state song "Montana" was written in 1910, but in 1941 the author, Joseph Howard, gave the copyright to the Montana Children's Home and Shodair Hospital so proceeds from the song could benefit the agency.

Read about the bigger dining room at St. Anthony's San Francisco.

ST. ANTHONY'S DINING ROOM   During the late 19th and early 20th century, the population in the western region of the United States was increasing, although it was not as dense as the eastern region. The fierce independence of the frontiersmen and their families often created a barrier to asking for help. Services were usually provided by churches and religious organizations when needed. One of them was St. Anthony's Dining Room in the Tenderloin area of San Francisco. Developed by a Franciscan Friar named **Father Alfred Boeddeker**, St. Anthony's Dining Room provides free meals to the poor in a restaurant-like setting. This was a predecessor of the soup kitchens we have today. Friar Alfred insisted that two values be instituted by all volunteers working in the restaurant. All clients must be served with *acceptance and respect*. Those are the same values we teach in Human Services today. St. Anthony's Dining Room has served over 50 million meals since it opened.

ST. ANTHONY'S FREE MEDICAL CLINIC FRIAR   Alfred also developed **St. Anthony's Free Medical Clinic** in the San Francisco Tenderloin Area. Much like the Good Samaritan Clinic you read about in Chapter 1, it serves homeless and indigent people between the ages of birth and 60 years. The clinic provides primary and urgent care, testing, diagnostics, laboratory and radiology services, and a dispensary. It is the only pediatric clinic in the area and provides free medicine as well. As a *multicultural* facility, it serves all residents and offers multilingual services in English as well as Cantonese, Vietnamese, Thai, Lao, Mien, Mongolian, Mandarin, Portuguese, Spanish, and Russian. There is obviously a *respect for diversity* in this facility.

COMPASS FAMILY SERVICES   Located in California, **Compass Family Services** was known as Travelers Aid and was developed in 1914 to provide assistance to newcomers, women, and girls. As the needs of the community have changed over the years, so have their services. Today they offer child care, serve the homeless through shelters, provide counseling, offer supportive housing programs, and complete intakes and assessments. The number of services they offer keeps growing as do their locations where services are provided.

ALAMEDA HEALTH SYSTEMS   In 1864, the first patient was admitted to the Alameda County Infirmary in California and within a few years the facility would grow into a hospital that would provide acute, long-term care and house tuberculosis patients. By the 1920s, care for indigent residents in Oakland would force the community to continue developing integrated services. Highland Hospital would begin offering comprehensive services in 1927 in a teaching environment. The Fairmont Hospital would provide the first public rehabilitation center in the United States west

Human Services Delivery Systems

Understanding and Mastery: The range and characteristics of Human Services delivery systems and organizations; international and global influences on service delivery

Critical Thinking Question: Why is learning about the history and development of early Human Services important to our work today?

• •

of the Mississippi in the 1920s. It would also be the first hospital to offer AIDS services to patients in the East Bay area in the 1980s. A chain of neighborhood health care clinics would be initiated in the 1960s. Today the integrated health care system is known as the **Alameda Health Systems** and includes Fairmont Hospital, Highland Hospital & Highland Wellness, and the John George Psychiatric Pavilion Hospital, as well as three area clinics. The psychiatric facility is named in honor of John George, a county supervisor who was a champion for the mentally ill. In addition to their health care services, they are unique in offering language interpretation in person, by phone, and with video technology in two dozen languages. A Human Services worker in this environment would have professional characteristics of *knowledge, values, and skills.*

Can You See How Important Nonprofit and Faith-Based Organizations Are to Human Services?

Assess your comprehension of <u>Regional Influences: (Part II)</u> <u>by completing</u> <u>this quiz</u>.

Around the Globe

How Did European Social Services Influence American Programs?

As you were reading the descriptions of the beginning of many social services in America, you may have been surprised to learn that several programs had actually started in Europe and were brought to the United States by Americans who learned of these services. The Boy Scouts, Girl Scouts, YMCA, American Red Cross, settlement houses, and others were actually developed in England or other European countries. **The Salvation Army** is another example of a leading American social service agency that was brought here in 1880. Active in over 100 countries, the Salvation Army is an international movement that was started in East London in 1865 by a Methodist minister and his wife, William and Catherine Booth. Known as a traveling, independent evangelist, Booth held his first meeting in an improvised tent in East London. The couple's original idea was to bring Christianity to the poor and destitute by performing evangelical, social, and charitable work. Their first converts were street people and criminals, gamblers, prostitutes, and alcoholics, a population not encouraged to attend neighboring churches. Booth believed that redemption started here. Along with Catherine, he developed a program of the three Ss to serve the poor: soup, soap, and salvation.

Review one of the featured stories on <u>The</u> <u>Salvation</u> <u>Army</u> website.

The Booths organized their ministry around a loose military style with William as the "General" who recruited "soldiers" to help their efforts. Catherine solicited the wealthy for money to continue the efforts. The organization grew and developed its own flag, uniforms, and music, despite ridicule from many who rejected the idea that the poor and unstable homeless could be saved, since they were seen as "unworthy." The brass band became an important part of the ministry, and the members were soon recognizable for their ribbon-laden tambourines. The music symbolized cheerful religion and the joy of the Salvationists. They began preaching and singing in the streets and became known as the "Hallelujah Army."

Commissioned as a Lieutenant in the Salvation Army, **Eliza Shirley**, joined her parents when they left England to find work in America. She held the first meeting in 1879 in the Kensington district of Philadelphia and later notified General Booth that America was ready for its own Army. However, when Commissioner George Scott Railton and seven women officers arrived in Battery Park, New York in 1880, they were met with ridicule, attacked, and arrested. They persevered and found several Salvationists willing to join them in their work. Together they developed an American based program, which served alcoholics, morphine addicts, prostitutes, and other destitute individuals. Services included free rehabilitation for drug and alcohol abuse, but members were asked to stop drinking, gambling, and smoking. Within three years they expanded their operation into California, Connecticut, Indiana, Kentucky, Maryland, Massachusetts, Michigan, Missouri, New Jersey, New York, Ohio, and Pennsylvania.

In the United States, the Salvation Army became a symbol of hope and help, and its reputation swelled as a result of the disaster relief services it provided. By 1886 President Grover Cleveland became the first federal official to endorse the activities of the group. The Galveston Hurricane of 1900 and the San Francisco Earthquake of 1906 were two of the biggest disasters to hit the United States, and the Salvation Army was there to provide assistance in the form of food, pastoral counseling, and social services. The Salvation Army is known as the first to arrive with help after a natural or man-made disaster. More recently, in the wake of Hurricane Katrina, it served more than 5.7 million hot meals and 8.3 million sandwiches, snacks, and drinks, and contributed more than 900,000 hours of service. It was also one of the first on the scene after the 9/11 attacks in New York. It is estimated that it serves more than 32 million people in the United States alone each year through its community centers, disaster relief, and refugee camps. It is also one of the largest organizations to work with the displaced people of Africa.

Well known for the diverse services it offers, Salvation Army receives charitable donations from wealthy individuals with philanthropic tendencies, as well as from people in every other income bracket. In 2004, it received the largest gift ever given to a single organization when Joan Kroc, wife of McDonald's CEO, Ray Kroc, donated $1.6 billion in her will. Nye Lavalle and Associates (1996) found that the Salvation Army was the fourth most popular charity/nonprofit organization in America of over 100 charities that were researched. People trust this organization to use their donations wisely in the delivery of services. In 2007, their donations totaled almost $2 billion.

In addition to donations, the Salvation Army raises funds by operating thrift stores where they sell donated items at a low cost. The thrift stores provide the money for the Adult Rehabilitation Centers or ARCs as they are known. Another source of funds are the Victorian Bell Ringers, a traditional American scene at Christmas, raising funds for the support of local Salvation Army programs through their Red Kettle campaign. However, opposition to the bell ringers over the past few years has forced the Army to create new and modern ways of raising funds.

Some communities and department stores have banned the bell ringers from collecting donations at Christmas saying they are too noisy or that they disrupt traffic flow and annoy shoppers. In some malls the bell ringers have been allowed to stand and collect funds but not ring bells. Instead they hold signs that say "ding dong." Despite these changes, Salvation Army reports that $139 million were collected in holiday donations. In 2011, the Salvation Army began an online collection asking holiday shoppers to remember the poor at Christmas by donating online. You may have seen the bell ringers icon if you shopped online last holiday season. The Salvation Army has been touted as having one of the world's best nonprofit blogs. You can reach them on Facebook, Twitter, and YouTube.

Human Systems

Understanding and Mastery: Processes to effect social change through advocacy work at all levels of society including community development, community and grassroots organizing, and local and global activism; processes to analyze, interpret, and effect policies and laws at local, state, and national levels that influence service delivery systems

Critical Thinking Question: Do you think that people get annoyed when they are asked to help the poor? Should new methods involving social media, like Facebook or Twitter, be used to solicit funds for organizations that help the poor, elderly, disabled, or other vulnerable groups rather than traditional methods?

Putting Theories to Work
Sociological Theories of Helping, Social Philosophies, and Social Reformers

What exactly are Human Services and why do theories help us understand them? Well, our idea of what humans need has changed over time. If you read through all the programs that were just described, you see that early services in the United States were provided for those who were ill, poor, delinquent, alcoholic, addicted, or dependent. Early pioneers of Human Services programs were called *progressives* because of their liberal and progressive ideas or philosophies of helping others. Citizens who wanted to help others or their community often started programs when they saw a need like child abuse or neglect, lack of recreational programs for youth, or poor medical care. Programs like the Boy Scouts or Girls Scouts, the YMCA, orphanages for children, or affordable health care programs such as the Mayo Clinic were all started by private individuals. These services were often designed to help people who could not help themselves. The idea of Human Services has grown to include preventative programs like drug education programs, parent training, job creation, and financial information. Today we think of Human Services as this broad, multidisciplinary, holistic, and multifaceted approach to helping a variety of age groups with various needs. (Kanel, 2008) As a result, we study Human Services from many different perspectives.

Unlike other disciplines that have only one theoretical or disciplinary focus, Human Services looks at problems and possible solutions from the perspective of many different theories and disciplines. For example, when we look at social issues like poverty, juvenile delinquency, or aging, we study psychological and sociological theories. When we look at solutions to poverty, we may study business concepts or apply management principles to our Human Services agencies. This is what we mean by Human Services being a multidisciplinary major.

How can we apply theories to Human Services? Well, if we were to study some traditional *sociological theories* we would discover different ways of looking at the same problem. Some theories look at the big picture, studying society and the causes and effects of social problems on communities and large groups. We call these **macro level** theories. Others theories look at small-scale patterns of social interaction, focusing instead on people's relationships and how that affects social issues. These are called **micro level** theories.

Functional Analysis is a sociological theory that states society is a whole unit made up of interrelated parts that work together. If everyone does their part then society operates smoothly. However, society ceases to function when all the parts do not work together harmoniously. **Herbert Spencer** is considered a functionalist who believed that societies were changing and could be studied without interference from sociologists. He applied Darwin's theory of evolution to society believing that society's most intelligent and resourceful people were survivors (the fittest), while those with less capabilities were destined to die out (Henslin, 2013). In this way societies would advance unless "do-gooders" (that's us in Human Services!) interfere and help the less fortunate survive. Obviously he did not believe in helping the poor.

He coined this concept the *survival of the fittest*. This philosophy is known as **Social Darwinism**.

Early female sociologists in America considered that the study of sociology could lead to changing society. Some academics used their knowledge to do objective research, but other sociologists used their knowledge to make improvements for people. They became known as *social reformers* because they believed that the conditions of the poor, mentally ill, orphaned children, and immigrants needed to change. They focused on how to assist African Americans, integrate the new wave of immigrants, or provide homes for orphaned children. Noteworthy are women like **Grace Abbott** who became the *first chief of the United States Children's Bureau*, or **Frances Perkins** who was the first woman to hold a cabinet position. Frances was the *secretary of labor for 12 years under President Franklin Roosevelt* and helped develop the first federal work programs during the depression. **Jane Addams**, famous for her work with the poor, the sick, the aged, and immigrants at Hull House in Chicago, was very knowledgeable of *social class and structure*. She was keenly aware of how poor and rural immigrants were exploited in the work place by the powerful upper classes. Her knowledge allowed her to work diligently to develop services and advocate for the powerless and vulnerable in our society. Along with her professional colleague, **W. E. B. DuBois** and others, she founded the NAACP. DuBois, the first African American to graduate from Harvard in 1895, studied and wrote extensively about racism in American society. He is considered both a sociologist and a social reformer of his day (Henslin, 2013). Most social reformers were soon called *social workers* rather than sociologists, because their work did not involve scientific research nor did they hold university positions.

Social reform involves understanding both macro and micro theories of sociology since advocacy involves teaching those who are oppressed how to use the laws to improve their lives. Professional qualities of social reformers include *assertiveness, knowledge, patience*, and the *ability to interact and build relationships* with a variety of people of all *social classes and racial and ethnic backgrounds*. They must have **cultural competence**. Social reform can be risky since it is often considered too radical and liberal to change the status quo. However, as we work to promote social justice in Human Services, it is necessary to understand the principles of social reform.

Conflict Theory is another macro sociological perspective that focuses on the composition of society. Unlike *functionalism*, which *looks at society as one whole with interrelated parts that must work together cooperatively*, the *conflict* theorists believe that society is composed of *groups that are competing for scarce resources*. **Karl Marx**, the founder of this theory, studied society during revolutionary periods in Europe and came to believe that in every society small groups gain control of the means of production and exploit those who are not in control. The weak, vulnerable, and poor are those exploited by others. Those in power control the political and legal systems. He called this **class conflict**. Sociologists today have expanded Marx's Conflict Theory beyond the worker and employer scenario to include such struggles as the modern balance of power in relationships, family, and the constant battles that occur when individuals or groups try to decide who has authority or influence over others (Leeson, 2006; Piven, 2008).

Another sociological theory that became popular in the 19th century was **Symbolic Interactionism**. This is a micro theory that focuses on the individual and those symbols to which we attach meaning. These symbols help us understand how we view the world around us and make sense of our relationships. Symbolic interactionists study face-to-face interactions and determine how people view life. **Charles Horton Cooley** (1864–1929) was an American sociologist and Symbolic interactionist who taught at the University of Michigan. Cooley believed that people developed their sense of self by interacting with others and he called this process *the looking glass self.* (Henslin, 2013) This concept of the self involved three elements that included:

1. We imagine how we appear to others—are we seen as intelligent, attractive, or boring?
2. We interpret others' reactions—do people like us because we are intelligent or dislike us because they think we are boring?
3. We develop a self-concept—how we perceive others' reactions to us determines how we feel about ourselves; this leads to either a positive or negative self-concept (Ferrante, 2011)

Another Symbolic interactionist was George Herbert Mead (1863–1931) who taught at the University of Chicago. He believed that play was very important to the development of our concept of self. When we play with others, we learn to put ourselves in someone else's place and begin to understand how the other person thinks and feels. This idea of learning to take the part of another person is important as we grow and become members of groups like family, friends, and workers. In the last chapter we studied Parten's Model of Social Play and learned that as children develop, they move through stages of solitary play to more types of organized group play. Mildred Parten, like Mead, also believed that play was an important part of social development. In her five stages of play, Parten noticed that younger children play differently than older children. (Parten, 1932) In his studies, Mead researched the stages that humans go through in learning to play and to assume the character of another person. He concluded that young children first learn to imitate by observing other people in their environment. This might be their family, television actors, or movie characters. Usually around preschool age they begin to role-play and can often be seen dressing up in their favorite play clothes. My son loved his cowboy boots and wore them everyday when he was about four. At this age children imagine themselves as superheroes, firemen, Cinderella, or whatever fantasy they can dream up or have observed. They begin to role-play as they dress up and put themselves in the place of the other person. As they age, children move beyond role-play to more organized games. School age children, for instance, join teams or play sports and can take on multiple roles and work with others in their group without needing to pretend (Henslin, 2013). Spend some time observing small children and see if you can identify what stage of play you are watching.

Think Human Services

What Theories Guided Social Reform in America?

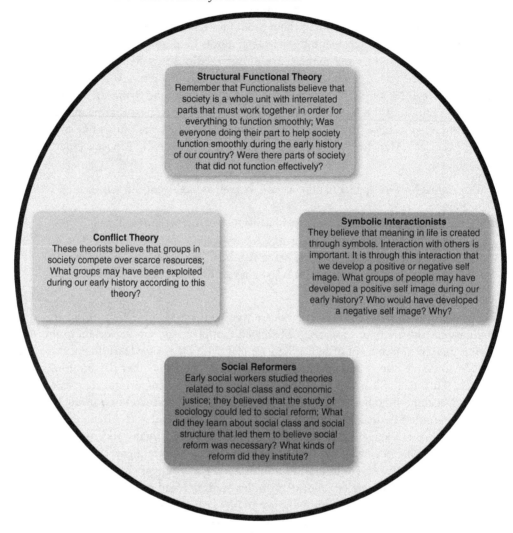

Structural Functional Theory
Remember that Functionalists believe that society is a whole unit with interrelated parts that must work together in order for everything to function smoothly; Was everyone doing their part to help society function smoothly during the early history of our country? Were there parts of society that did not function effectively?

Conflict Theory
These theorists believe that groups in society compete over scarce resources; What groups may have been exploited during our early history according to this theory?

Symbolic Interactionists
They believe that meaning in life is created through symbols. Interaction with others is important. It is through this interaction that we develop a positive or negative self image. What groups of people may have developed a positive self image during our early history? Who would have developed a negative self image? Why?

Social Reformers
Early social workers studied theories related to social class and economic justice; they believed that the study of sociology could led to social reform; What did they learn about social class and social structure that led them to believe social reform was necessary? What kinds of reform did they institute?

Linking Theory to Practice

The Development of Social Casework

During the early part of the 20th century, it was an exciting time to be in the helping profession. Many changes were taking place, among them the development of a new profession. Social reformers who developed the Settlement House Movement and the Charity Organization Society became known as social workers. This new profession was seen as the beginning of necessary help for vulnerable populations like the poor, immigrants, children, the sick, the mentally ill, and the disabled. It was believed that a specific set of skills, knowledge and understanding was needed to work with these populations (Woodside & McClam, 2011). *Social Casework* became the method of practice. Mary Richmond of New York wrote *Social Diagnosis*, a handbook describing casework as a process that involved investigation, diagnosis, prognosis, and treatment. This was the first book ever written about social casework theory and method (Zimbalist, 1977). This idea of a specialized profession called social work to deal with the poor and destitute was unique and historically significant because it established the framework for future related programs like Human Services.

Social casework is still used today and the knowledge and skills required are taught in Human Services programs in classes like interpersonal skills. A new addition to the original method of social casework is called case management. It is used to assess the needs of an individual and then to apply a variety of community resources to the problem area. Other helping methods of intervention include group work and community organizing.

Did You Know?

Child Welfare Services Began in 1874 with the Case of Mary Ellen Wilson

Interventions and Direct Services

Understanding and Mastery: Skills to facilitate appropriate direct services and interventions related to specific client or client group goals

Critical Thinking Question: According to Mary Richmond's book *Social Diagnosis*, case work includes investigation, diagnosis, prognosis, and treatment. If you were the case worker, what would you have included in the investigation of Mary Ellen Wilson? What do you think would be an effective course of treatment?

. . . .

Case Study ▶ Brief Case History of Mary Ellen Wilson

We started the chapter by telling you a story of a boy named Oliver Twist who had a miserable existence living in a county poorhouse in England in the 1800s. Although the story was fiction, I did tell you that children were often mistreated, abused, or neglected during this period of history. They were seen as expendable and treated as small adults who needed to work to support themselves, their families, or the institution they lived in. There were no mandatory requirements for school attendance, no child welfare laws to protect them from harm, and often no adults willing to step up and offer assistance if they needed food, clothing, or shelter. Children were considered the property of their parents, and so harsh discipline and hard work were expected. During the Victorian times, "children were to be seen and not heard," meaning disobedience was not tolerated. The "rule of thumb" meant that a man could beat his wife and children with a board no wider than his thumb. Anything wider would be unacceptable. Men were taught to keep their families in line and so spankings, whippings, or even what we would consider physical abuse today, were unfortunately common. Police were not involved in any private family matter since these were domestic issues. Now that you can imagine what life would be like for many children at this time, read the case of Mary Ellen, a true occurrence and not a fiction story.

Eight-year-old Mary Ellen Wilson lived with Francis and Mary Connelly, but was the daughter of Mary Connelly's first husband. The neighbors often saw the child in a New York neighborhood poorly dressed in cold weather and often locked out of her house in the middle of winter. She was beaten regularly with a leather strap and her cries could be heard around the block. One neighbor, particularly upset by the cries, called a church worker, Etta Wheeler, for help. Ms. Wheeler tried summoning the police but at that time police were not involved in domestic disputes. Ms. Wheeler turned to the Society for the Prevention of Cruelty to Animals (SPCA) for help, insisting that children had more rights than animals. The director of the

SPCA, Henry Burgh, did intervene and asked his good friend, attorney Elbridge Gerry, to act on Mary Ellen's behalf. Gerry successfully prosecuted the case, which became a controversial trial. In 1875, the Society for the Prevention of Cruelty to Children, the SPCC, was established in New York City as the first agency created to intervene on behalf of abused and neglected children (Crosson-Tower, 2013). Soon the SPCC spread to other major cities and by 1881 was given the authority to make investigations and give magistrates the power to protect the rights of children. By that time society was becoming concerned about protecting children and prosecuting abusive parents.

Today we study psychology and sociology to understand more about the causes of abuse and we learn interventions in Human Services to protect children and prevent both neglect and abuse. If abuse has occurred, we work to rehabilitate and teach parents new methods of child discipline and anger management for them. We work to keep the family intact whenever possible.

What Would You Do?

Think Like a Social Reformer

Recall the early reformers and the innovative ideas they had for developing new services for people. Then put yourselves into student groups of four to six with others who have the same interest. Can you think of any services that people in your community need but are not provided? How would you go about setting up a program for people who need services? Brainstorm ways of providing new services. Remember there is no one way of doing something. Be creative. Maybe you will come up with a totally new way of providing a service to people that has not been done before. Think about the following:

Rationale—Think about what service(s) are currently needed and why? Do you have a large rate of poverty, aging residents, increasing child health issues, high dropout rates, and other issues? Think about the age group you will serve and the type of service needed.

Goals—What do you want to achieve? Do you want to *reduce* the dropout rate, or *increase* the number of children receiving health care, or *prevent* teen suicide, and so on? Keep your goals measurable. You want to be able to evaluate later whether you have reached your goal.

Basic Plans—How many people will you serve? Where will the program be located? Do you have a facility or do you need one? What would be the hours of operation? Number and qualifications of staff involved? How much will your program cost? Where will funding come from? What kinds of supplies and equipment do you need to start your program?

Program Planning—What service(s) will you provide and how will you do it? Example: mental health counseling will be provided daily for teens; individual counseling will be offered from 3 p.m. to 8 p.m. Monday through Friday, teen groups will operate every Wednesday night from 7 p.m. to 8 p.m. and on Saturday from 2 p.m. to 4 p.m. Be specific when you think of what service(s) you will provide and how you will do it.

Evaluation—Did you reach your goal? Did you achieve what you wanted to do? How will you evaluate the program? Think about surveying those using the service, or keeping track of statistics. Did you *reduce, increase,* or *prevent* the problem from occurring as you said you planned?

Consider each key person who was an early social reformer listed here. What personal and professional qualities did they possess which helped them develop innovative ideas to assist others? What programs did they develop? Where are they located?

Now think about yourself. What personal and professional qualities do you have that would make you a good Human Services worker? Spend time reviewing the websites for the agencies that you have read about. Not only will you find out more about the programs, but you will enjoy the stories about the people. I have spent hundreds of very entertaining hours learning about these early Human Services workers. Watch the old footage of the Jenkins Orphanage Band. It is a classic. Have a class discussion about some of the early Human Services in your area. Who started them? What early reformers were most interesting to you? What Human Services competencies did early reformers demonstrate?

Social Reformer	Personal Qualities	Professional Qualities
Jane Addams		
Clara Barton		
Fr. Alfred Boeddeker		
William & Catherine Booth		
Anthony Bowen		
William Boyce		
Ernest Kent Coulter		
W. E. B. DuBois		
Edgar Helms		
Reverend Daniel Jenkins		
Juliette Gordon Low		
Sister Louisa Marthens		
Emma Robarts		
Benjamin Rose		
The Ursuline nuns		
Thomas Sullivan		
George Williams		

Recall what you learned in this chapter by completing the Chapter Review.

CHAPTER 4

Lions Gate/Everett Collection

Developing Competence with Diverse Cultures

··

What Knowledge, Values, and Skills Do We Need to Help People from Different Cultures?

Did you ever see the movie *Crash*, which is about a group of unrelated people from various cultures who reside in the United States? At one point in the movie many of these people's lives intersect "crashing" into each other. It is a poignant dramatization of how our multicultural society interacts and develops relationships with one another. When I show this movie in my cultural diversity class, I have to warn my students about the violence, cursing, and disrespectful language they will hear. If they haven't seen the movie, at first they are shocked by the frankness with which people address one another. In anger the characters lash out with derogatory remarks using cultural slang and ethnic stereotypes. They have no patience with one another, lack trust in their fellow man, and believe the worst about their neighbors. When we analyze the movie later, my students often say the movie is real in depicting how strangers may react to one another and how people familiar with one another may feel but who often keep their racial comments to themselves. We are prone to stereotyping groups of people and thus deny ourselves the opportunity to learn more about who they really are and what unique strengths and talents they offer.

Watch a trailer for *Crash* on IMDb.

What's It All About

*How Can We Apply the Ethical Standards of the CSHSE
in Our Professional Practice?*

Have you ever had a friend from another culture? I was lucky enough to grow up in an ethnic area of northeastern Pennsylvania. The history of that area reveals that 150 years ago or so immigrants from Eastern Europe started arriving on the eastern seaboard. As these families moved from New York City looking for work and places to live, they often ended up in small communities living in neighborhoods with relatives or other people from their homelands. Many areas of the northeast developed into ethnic neighborhoods of Italian, Irish, Polish, Russian, Lithuanian, Greek, Jewish, or German descent. As time went on, the boundaries between neighborhoods became blurred, but the traditions and culture of each ethnic group remained firm. As a child I grew up in an Irish family but lived in an Italian neighborhood. Thursday night was Rigatoni night at my friend's home where I was a weekly guest. I learned to make marinara sauce at an early age, shared Passover with my Jewish friend, and learned to appreciate the Russian Orthodox mass on holiday visits to another friend's home. When I married my high school sweetheart, I enjoyed his Lithuanian tradition of making homemade pierogies at Christmas. It was also interesting to watch how families spoke to one another, how they treated their grandparents, and how their particular religion played a major part in their lives. This was the beginning of my interest in cultures and **sociology**, the study of people and society.

In Human Services, our ability to understand ourselves and to develop our competence in working with people from other cultures is very important. As professionals, we strive to become competent in dealing with people from cultures different than our own. Of course, it is understandable that we will probably be the most comfortable in dealing with our own culture since that is where our experience lies. However, we are always limited by our own experiences and perceptions as well. We work to become sensitive and to increase our awareness of another's culture by *studying their history, learning their language, eating their food, observing their traditions, and meeting their people* (Rothman, 2008).

When we speak about cultural diversity, it is important that we understand what we are talking about. A **culture** can be *a group with shared beliefs and traditions* so we need to understand that we are not necessarily referring to ethnic groups (Rothman, 2008). A group of disabled veterans that shares distinct beliefs and traditions with the military and a history that is unique to it, is a culture. So people who share a culture may come from the same geographic area, religion, ethnicity, or life experience. Culture can include religious ideals, values, language, history, institutions, customs, and beliefs (Lum, 2004). When we speak of **diversity** within cultures, think of differences in gender, race, ethnic groups, nationality, skin color, language, size and appearance, sexual orientation, age, social class, religion, ability/disability, immigration status, and/or region of the country.

Prejudice and Discrimination

Do you know the difference between prejudice and discrimination? In the movie *Crash*, the Syrian storeowner is sure the Hispanic locksmith is cheating him. The storeowner's experience of living in the United States has taught him that prejudice exists and certain people are discriminated against. As a Middle Eastern man, he doesn't trust the Hispanic man to fix his door, and he keeps yelling at the locksmith to "just fix the lock." The locksmith tries to explain that the door is broken and a lock won't fix the problem. The storeowner needs a new door. Still, the storeowner is convinced the man is cheating him. If this were the case, it would be an example of discrimination.

Prejudice and discrimination are two different forms of oppression. **Prejudice** refers to a belief or feeling you have about a particular person or group. **Discrimination** refers to unfair actions or behaviors you take against an individual or a group (Henslin, 2011). So you can be prejudiced in your beliefs about someone or about a group of people, but you may not act on that prejudice. You may keep your opinions to yourself but believe, based upon your own experiences, that you are right in your prejudices. On the other hand, if you deliberately take action against a person or a group to cause them harm in some way, then you are a discriminator. In Human Services, we try not be either a prejudiced or a discriminating person. This is part of our professional attitudes and values that are clarified in our Ethical Standards (Council for Standards in Human Services Education, 2011).

Are we aware that not all clients celebrate the same holidays? Do we offer good wishes for Hanukkah or Passover? Ramadan?

Knowledge, Values, and Skills

As mentioned earlier, it is important that we have the ability to work with and respect people from various cultural backgrounds. Developing **cultural competence** involves both the *process of building our knowledge base, understanding values, and practicing skills* to work with *diverse populations*. This means that we will learn about different cultures by studying their history, reading about current issues that affect their group, becoming aware of their traditions, and learning from the clients about their culture. It also involves actually working with and applying these knowledge, values, and skills with others. Cultural competence involves working "respectfully and effectively" with "people of all cultures, languages, classes, races, ethnic backgrounds, religions, ages, genders, sexual orientation, or any other 'diverse background'" in a way that values their worth as individuals, families, and communities (NASW, Standards for Cultural Competence in Social Work Practice, 2001).

Specifically, Human Services workers must demonstrate competency in several areas (Pierce & Pierce, 1996). According to Mehr & Kanwischer (2011), workers must be able to do the following:

1. Value diversity—Human Services workers need to understand that although everyone has basic needs, each culture has distinct values, behaviors, and ways of interacting.
2. Complete a self-assessment—Human Services workers should understand their own culture and family history so they can better understand their own cultural values, beliefs, and preconceptions.
3. Be conscious of dynamics when cultures interact—Human Services workers must be sensitive to the relationships between and among cultures of different backgrounds; workers need to be aware of power differentials, prejudices, and stereotyping.
4. Develop cultural knowledge—Human Services workers must be able to understand diverse cultures and their belief system regarding family, health, community, and acceptance of services.
5. Adapt to diversity—Human Services workers need to understand and value all cultures and create a fit between the available services and the needs of the culture (Mehr & Kanwischer, 2011).

In addition to knowledge, Human Services workers must demonstrate an understanding of the professional values in the code of ethics.

We use the professional values in our code of ethics to develop relationships with all people based on a *nonjudgmental attitude* and a feeling of *acceptance*. If we were not raised this way, it can take some effort to overcome our prejudices. In our discipline this is very important since it is at the root of all that we believe in and all that we do for people. We cannot pick and choose the type of clients we want to work with, nor can we be sure that we will never have a client who is a drug addict, a convicted felon, or a child abuser. This means that as Human Services workers, we often come into conflict with our own personal values and ethics. When we believe that our own ethnic background is superior to others and that our culture is the best, we are practicing **ethnocentrism**. According to Neukrug (2008), when we assume that everyone has the same worldview as we do, we are often incorrect in our assessments of people and are not effective during the helping relationship. We may perceive clients as being weird, emotionally disturbed, or wrong if they perceive events differently than we do. Many of our minority clients may not have had the same opportunities, and their experiences with acquiring education, health care, and social services may have been difficult, expensive, and not worthwhile. We need to practice seeing the world from another's worldview to get a better understanding of how events are perceived by others. Clients are entitled to *respect, acceptance, and dignity*. Workers must protect their clients' **right to privacy**, maintain **confidentiality**, and allow clients the **right to self-determination**.

According to Taylor, Bradley, & Warren (1996), Human Services workers use skills in competency areas to fulfill their job functions. Some of these skills and competency areas include:

- *Empowerment*—The Human Services worker helps raise the self-esteem and assertiveness of clients and supports them in their decision-making.
- *Communication*—The Human Services worker tries to establish a collaborative working relationship with clients.
- *Assessment*—The Human Services worker needs to understand formal and informal assessment systems.
- *Community and Service Networking*—The Human Services worker needs to understand the community service system and be able to assist the client in accessing services.
- *Facilitation of Services*—The Human Services worker understands the planning process and uses techniques to implement collaborative plans within the community.
- *Community Living Skills and Supports*—The Human Services worker understands how to identify supports and interventions and can match them with client needs; the Human Services worker knows how to use friends, family, and community relationships.
- *Education, Training, and Self-Development*—Human Services workers should be able to identify areas for self-improvement and find necessary education and training and share resources with others.
- *Advocacy*—The Human Services worker should be able to identify the diverse challenges facing the client and use effective strategies to advocate for change.
- *Vocational, Educational, and Career Support*—The Human Services worker should be able to assist clients in reaching their goals through educational and career resources.

- *Crisis Intervention*—The Human Services worker should be knowledgeable about crisis prevention, intervention, and resolution and match techniques to the needs of the client.

- *Organizational Participation*—Human Services workers support the mission of the organization they work for.
- *Documentation*—The Human Services worker maintains proper documentation.

Self-Development

Understanding and Mastery: Clarification of personal and professional values

Critical Thinking Question: Take a minute and think about yourself. Is the Human Services code of ethics consistent with your own personal values? Do you respect, accept, and treat all others equally? Are these the values that you could uphold in your work with all people?

As Human Services workers, we use our professional knowledge, values, and skills in working with individuals, groups, families, and the community. We must be proficient at assessment and treatment skills, writing reports, and communicating with other workers, our clients, and local agencies. In our practice, it is necessary that we respect cultural diversity and continually develop our competence in working with others.

Test your comprehension of <u>Prejudice and Discrimination</u> <u>and</u> <u>Knowledge, Values, and Skills</u> by completing this quiz.

Around the Globe

How Important Is Learning a Language to the Development of Cultural Competence?

Culturally competent practitioners value the differences in their clients. They understand their own family history and background and welcome the beliefs, values, behaviors, and customs of other groups. What we want to practice is **cultural relativism**, a belief and value in our own culture with openness to learning about other cultures. When we practice cultural relativity, we learn to build our knowledge base by exploring the differences that our clients bring to the professional relationship. We are sincere in wanting to understand what experiences have shaped their belief system, what traditions are important to them, and what they value. This means that in building our knowledge, values, and skills in cultural competence, we learn about another's language, racial and ethnic heritage, and customs as they relate to their country of origin.

Some people would say Americans are **ethnocentric** because they expect other cultures to learn English. This has become a topic of debate in some areas of the country where languages other than English are widely spoken. For example, if you travel to Miami, you will hear Spanish spoken often. If you visit New York City, you will hear a mix of international languages spoken everywhere.

How do we compare with other countries in our knowledge of other languages?

Read "EU Pupils are Learning Foreign Languages at an Earlier Age" on <u>Europa</u>.

In a study of 19 countries and 22 educators, researchers found that 7 countries began teaching a second language to students before age eight. In Belgium, children begin learning another language at age three! In eight other countries, students started learning a second language by upper elementary school. In some countries, children start learning two languages, other than their native language, in elementary school. By contrast the United States begins language education around age 14 in most schools (Pufahl, Rhodes, & Christian, 2001). There is also an indication that European countries are beginning to teach foreign languages at an earlier age since children seem more interested and are better able to grasp new languages when they are young. Some countries are even teaching children two foreign languages in the primary grades (Europa Press Releases, 2008).

It is true that most European countries that study a second language learn English as a requirement. If other countries are learning English then why do Americans need to learn a different language? You may be surprised to learn that in addition to English, 311 other languages are spoken in the United States. Of these, 162 are indigenous to the United States, and 149 can be considered immigrant languages.

What happens when children study languages at an early age? Educators are developing curricula that include the study of other countries and the languages spoken there. When children become interested in another culture and learn their customs and traditions, they develop an early respect for their differences. Education is a way to encourage children to learn about others in the world to reduce stereotyping and prejudice. When students learn about other cultures at an early age, they grow up to *appreciate differences* rather than developing an ethnocentric perspective. So learning a language can be a first step in developing your cultural competence.

Did you know that there are currently 14 million households in the United States where English is not the primary language? Read <u>How Many Languages are Spoken in a US Household Exactly?</u> on Gadling to learn more.

Explore <u>You Can Teach Children About Other Countries and Cultures in Fun Ways</u> to learn about great ideas for teaching children about other countries and cultures.

Test your comprehension of <u>Around the Globe: How Important Is Learning a Language</u> to the Development of <u>Cultural Competence?</u> by completing this quiz.

Putting Theories to Work

What Professional Theories or Models Would Help You to Work with People from Various Cultures?

In the helping professions there is a **model of client empowerment**, which is used in many countries to assist those people who by no fault of their own, experience powerlessness through poverty, lack of education, unemployment, homelessness, violence, and lack of resources. Professional helpers who work with those who are not empowered learn to *encourage* and *support* clients and *assist* them in developing a plan of action to change their situation. This plan includes education so that oppressed individuals learn how to understand their situation and then proceed to make the necessary changes, both economically and politically, to become active in their cultural community (Woodside & McClam, 2011). In Human Services, we also believe that every individual has values and strengths that can be used to solve personal conflicts.

Human Services Delivery Systems

Understanding and Mastery: The major models used to conceptualize and integrate prevention, maintenance, intervention, rehabilitation, and healthy functioning

Critical Thinking Question: How would understanding the model of client empowerment as well as the strengths perspective help in developing a relationship with clients, as well as assessing and treating their problem?

The Model of Client Empowerment	The Strengths Perspective
Clients have a sense of powerlessness	Workers build on clients' strengths
Workers value clients	Strengths exist in individuals and in families, groups, and communities
Workers demonstrate client respect	Workers must understand the culture of the client to utilize all possible resources
Workers teach clients about their oppressive situation and develop a course of action	Work is best when collaboration is done with clients
Change efforts include education and political information so clients gain control over their own lives and can work to change oppressive situations	The worker and client relationship is important since a belief in clients can help them overcome painful or difficult past experiences

The strengths perspective is another practice framework useful in developing cultural competence. Rather than telling people what they should do, Human Services workers first assess what strengths the individual, group, family, or community already possesses and then decide how to build on those strengths. For instance, a homeless mother and her child may come to you for help. In working with the mother, you find that she has college credits that she earned some years before, which can help her land a better job. Perhaps she is a candidate for continuing her degree so that her earning potential may be greater in the future. It is important in culturally competent work that we use the strengths perspective to understand clients and their environment and community before we decide what resources to use (Rothman, 2008).

Think Human Services

Can the Model of Client Empowerment and the Strengths Perspective Be Useful Tools When We Deal with Xenophobia?

When people feel threatened by strangers and afraid that they are going to lose something because of this new person or group, discrimination often results. Sociologists call this phenomenon xenophobia. The model of client empowerment and the strengths perspective model indicate how Human Services workers can employ their skills in working with oppressed populations by utilizing the professional code of conduct in Human Services. The model of client empowerment teaches us to respect and value all human beings. We educate oppressed people about their situation and teach them how

In this scene from Hotel Rwanda, a Hutus man hides Tutsis in his hotel to protect them from the conflict which killed over 800,000 African Tutsis in 1994.

Splash News/Newscom

to develop a plan that may include political action. The strengths perspective considers the available resources the clients have in their family or community, and the worker builds on that strength. The culture of the client is considered before any work is initiated. In real life, people don't always realize they are discriminating against someone and might not change their behavior. In fact, sometimes laws are developed that prevent groups of people from realizing their human rights or living their life in a nonthreatening manner.

The mass murder of over 800,000 African Tutsis in Rwanda by the majority Hutus in 1994 is an example of how xenophobia can lead to prejudice and discrimination. During the Rwanda conflict, which lasted just 100 days, Hutus raped Tutsi women and beat their men and children to death. While the media in Rwanda encouraged the killings of the Tutsis, several Hutu sympathizers tried to help but most were killed as well. The Hutus justified their murder as ethnic cleansing. View other examples of xenophobia throughout world history.

Interpersonal Communication

Understanding and Mastery: Developing and sustaining behaviors that are congruent with the values and ethics of the profession

Critical Thinking Question: Can you think of any current examples of xenophobia in the United States? In your state? In your community? In your family? What can you do to change this behavior?

. . . .

Test your comprehension of Think Human Services by completing this quiz.

Linking Theory to Practice

How Is Micro-lending an Effective Tool for Ending Global Poverty?

Micro-lending is a very good example of utilizing both the strengths perspective and the model of client empowerment when we work with diverse populations. Micro-lending involves lending small amounts of money to the poorest of the poor in countries where poverty exists. The money is used to start small businesses where people can begin to develop a living for themselves and their families. Organizations like the *Grameen Foundation* work to bring micro-financing and technology together to end global poverty. What a great way to value people, show them dignity and respect, and work to strengthen and empower their lives both economically and politically.

Practice *micro-lending* by pooling the resources of your class and making a donation to a country that practices this technique to help the poorest people on the globe. You can donate as little as $20 to some people in some countries.

Did You Know?

How Familiar Are You with Continents, Countries, and the Cultures They Represent?

In Human Services, we need to know where continents are located, what countries are on those continents, and what cultures live there in order to be culturally competent. The United States is the one country in the world with more

Review this World Atlas as a reference to follow along with me.

people from other parts of the globe than any other country. Do you know anything about your ancestors or early family traditions? In order to understand other cultures it is important that we know our own history first. In my own family, I can remember my grandmother speaking a few words of Gallic, the language of my Irish ancestors. However, the language was not often spoken in my home nor was it shared or taught. **Genealogy** is the study of our ancestry and family history. I wish I had spent more time learning about my genealogy and the traditions and culture in Ireland. I am probably not alone in my quest to discover what interesting traditions previously existed in my family. As a *multicultural* or **pluralistic society**, we need to be knowledgeable about all the cultures that reside in the United States.

Asia

Countries in Asia include China, Japan, Vietnam, Korea, and India for a start. Do you think these countries are the same because they are on the same continent? Of course not, they are all very different countries with various languages, customs, family traditions, values, beliefs, and even food choices. The United States has seen an increase in the number of immigrants from Asia over the past century. Let's take a look at some of the distinct differences.

CHINA   Did you know China, located in southeast Asia, is the third largest country after Russia and Canada? Fourteen countries border China, and it has the world's largest

Human Services professionals need to be culturally competent. Embracing diversity, learning languages, and accepting the traditions of others is all a part of our cultural competence.

Patrick Kinsella

population of 1.3 billion. There are 56 ethnic groups with the Han people making up 93% of the population. The earliest humans came from China, and the country's contributions to the world include art, calligraphy, opera, music, and of course their unique cuisine.

Many Chinese American families have resided in the United States for generations. Some still practice ancient family traditions, but many Chinese Americans, like so many families that have lived in America for a century or more, no longer practice any traditional Chinese customs.

Learn more about China's history and traditions at Travel China Guide.

Read about the Traditional Lifestyle on Cultural China.

JAPAN   Japan is a country of contrasts steeped in history and traditions on the one hand and at the forefront of the latest fads and technology on the other. A land of about 126 million people who mostly live in the urban areas, only 1% of the population is non-Japanese with most of those being Koreans. There are strict codes of behavior, although they do appreciate the Westerners' attempt to use their language. Japan is slowly recovering from the devastating earthquake in 2011. It is a country of great pride and resiliency.

Explore Inside Japan to learn more about Japanese culture, traditions, and people.

VIETNAM   There are over 54 distinct ethnic groups in Vietnam, each with its own culture and traditions. However, the official language of all groups is Vietnamese. Basic to all groups is the belief in four tenets: allegiance to the family, yearning for a good name, love of learning, and respect for other people. The ethics of Confucius and the strong value in family are followed. Harmony between the self and others is a goal to be attained. Nonverbal communication is important. Elders are respected, and children are taught that they owe everything to their parents and grandparents. Ancestor worship is practiced. After the war in Vietnam ended, the United States saw a surge of immigrants from that country coming to America for a better life, freedom, and educational opportunities. How much do you know about Vietnam?

Listen to the History of Korea podcasts by Dr. Charles Armstrong, Columbia University, at The Korean Society.

KOREA   Located in East Asia, Korea is a medium-sized country divided between the North (The Democratic People's Republic of Korea) and the South (Republic of Korea). South Korea has strong ties to the United States and has become an important global player. Family ties are strong with male dominance a factor in family life.

INDIA   India is a diverse country in Asia with many indigenous groups and tribes, religions, and languages. Despite its effort to outlaw the caste system, the country is still heavily dictated by the inherited social class. **Endogamy**, the practice of marrying within your same social class or ethnic group, is still followed today. Indian society, rather than the government, dictates this social standard of maintaining inherited social standing. The father is still seen as the patriarch of the family, and parents and relatives arrange many of the marriages for their children. Since divorce is not advocated, the rate of divorce is low, with brides and grooms agreeing to submit to arranged marriages. Consent of the bride and groom is a must before the wedding can proceed. Family life is respected above all else, and generations of family members live together in one household. As Indian families emigrate to the United States, can you see any cultural conflicts that may occur?

Read Indian Culture: Traditions and Customs of India to learn more about the culture, history, traditions, and food of India.

Africa

Africa as a continent has 54 countries or states, terms that are used interchangeably. Forty-eight of the countries are on the continent and six are island nations. The countries of Africa are diverse with hundreds of different religions and languages, with people living in a variety of houses from urban townhomes to rural dwellings for indigent tribes. Cultural activities center around the family. The continent is rich in art, music, oral literature, and dance. Many immigrants to the United States come from such countries as Ghana, Kenya, Senegal, Uganda, Tanzania, Algeria, or Zimbabwe, to name just a few of the countries. Some come for educational opportunities, but many come for freedom and safety, leaving areas where violence, AIDS, poverty, and ethnic dominance prevail. How much do you know about the 54 African countries?

Explore more information about Ghana's matrilineal society at The Africa Guide.

GHANA   If you would like more information about specific countries, try reading about Ghana, one of the few matrilineal societies on the west coast of Africa. A matrilineal society refers to the individual's line of descent. In a few west African countries, the line of descent is traced through the mother and maternal ancestors. Land rights, inheritance of property, offices, and titles would be determined by this system. Kinship ties are traced to the mother's side of the family. This is a social system that focuses on interactions between matrilineal relatives.

KENYA   Kenya is located on the east coast of Africa between Somalia and Tanzania. It is another interesting country with 62 languages spoken, 13 ethnic groups evident with 27 smaller groups scattered around the area. Most Kenyans belong to the Bantu tribes and are group rather than individual oriented. The extended family is the center of cultural life with many family members living together. Explore interesting facts about the Kenyan people at Kwintessential.

SENEGAL   Senegal is a country on the western side of Africa. Predominantly a Muslim area, it is also a country known to have other religious beliefs. Only 20% of women work outside the home, and men are considered the heads of the household. Unions are mostly **polygynous** with women having few rights. Discrimination and violence against women exist. Economic problems and unemployment affect the population.

Read about Senegal to gain an overview of information on the customs and 12 ethnic groups.

UGANDA   Uganda is a unique country in Africa with a strong cultural heritage. Many areas of Uganda are united as kingdoms. They maintain a culture of art, music, and dance with each area having dances specific to its region. The main instrument, the drum, is crafted and played there.

North America

Countries in North America include the United States, Canada, and Mexico. The United States as a multicultural society has 50 states with many ethnic groups and religions across the country. English is the primary language spoken, although many families are bilingual, speaking another language at home. Spanish is most likely the second language spoken. Puerto Rico, although not officially a state, is recognized as a territory of the United States with rights and privileges for its citizens allowing them to travel back and forth to their island freely. If we are to work with many cultures in the United States, we have to understand what rights are afforded people from other nations. Many ethnic groups are prevalent in the United States, having arrived with the influx of European immigrants in the 19th century. These families now represent second- and third-generation Italian, German, Polish, Russian, Irish, Swedish, and Jewish ethnic groups. Native Americans are also part of the landscape.

> **Review the Exploredia website for statistics and more about various ethnic groups in America.**

> **Explore Kwintessential to learn more about the language and customs of Canadian people.**

CANADA   The country to the direct north of the United States is Canada. Culturally diverse, with an immigration policy that has always encouraged people to come to Canada but to retain their own culture, it is a tolerant country. There are many different regions or provinces with a variety of languages. The culture places a great deal of emphasis on individuals' responsibility to their community. Although they can be considered individualistic, they are equally community oriented.

MEXICO   The country to the direct south of the United States is Mexico. A land of many indigenous peoples, it has one of the largest populations who **immigrate** to the United States, both legally and illegally each year. This is not a new phenomenon. In 1942, with the passage of the Bracero program, the United States created a labor contract with Mexico allowing it to fill labor shortages in agriculture. Those who participated in the program were granted temporary working visas. This helped to reduce the number of illegal immigrants from Mexico. Today the problem of illegal immigration still exists with the majority of undocumented immigrants arriving here with the hopes of finding employment. The combined gross income of all Latin American workers in the United States was $450 billion in 2004 with 93% of that money staying in the United States (Rothman, 2008).

The history of the United States and Mexico is an intricate one dotted with battles, wars, and treaties. The relationship of the United States with the Mexican people is constantly shifting with positive economic agreements like NAFTA, the North American Free Trade Agreement, and negative legislative actions such as Arizona's state policy on illegal immigrants. Attitudes

> **Read the article, The Relationship of the United States with Mexico to gain a better understanding of the relationship of the U.S. with Mexico.**

and prejudices about this population are changing as Americans come to realize that Mexicans are a hard working, family-oriented culture with a sincere interest in becoming citizens of the United States. Understanding the relationship of the United States with Mexico helps us to understand the immigrants who come to this country looking for work and who at some point may need the services we offer in Human Services. Watch the film *The Gatekeeper* to get a better idea of what life is like for undocumented immigrants in the United States.

Central America

Several countries lie between North America and South America and offer a variety of cultures rich in history, language, and traditions. Some of these people emigrate from their country to come to the United States each year, so it is useful to understand their history and customs. Even though they share a peninsula, these countries are unique in their history, cultures, and relationship with the United States. Costa Rica, Nicaragua, and Panama are three examples of such countries.

COSTA RICA   With a population of just over 4 million, Costa Rica, a country between Nicaragua and Panama, is a beautiful vacation spot for Americans. It is surrounded by volcanic mountains and suffers periodic earthquakes. Read about the progress the country has made in providing its citizens with free access to health care, education, and social welfare services.

> **Read about <u>Costa Rica</u> to learn more about the socialization, religion, family traditions, history and economics.**

NICARAGUA   Nicaragua is the largest and poorest of the Central American countries with a population of somewhere around 4 million. Since it has been decades since a census has been taken, this is only an estimate. Although a beautiful country surrounded by volcanic mountains and tropical vegetation, it is not a vacation paradise like parts of Costa Rica. Nicaragua's tumultuous history and 1979 Sandinistas' revolution allows for current day concerns about this country's economic and political stability. The family is of utmost importance in this culture with personal dignity held in high regard. It is still an agricultural country with little urban industry. Rice and beans are main staples.

Review more about <u>Nicaraguan culture</u>.

PANAMA   Panama serves as the bridge between South and Central America and has enjoyed good relationship with America for decades. A country of many cultures, including Spanish, Greek, Chinese, Italian, Portuguese, and Jewish, it remains a democracy with a woman who has served as its president. Its industry is primarily agribusiness with sugar and bananas a major export. Read about <u>Panama</u> to learn more on this history, people, food and customs.

South America

South America is a continent rich in its people and resources. It is the fourth largest continent with 12 countries and three territories. It was influenced by the early Mayan civilization and has also been impacted by European settlers, Portuguese sailors, and the African slave trade. Half of all the world's cultures reside somewhere in South America. Each country has its own colorful history of invaders, immigrants, and settlers. You have probably heard about countries like Argentina, Brazil, Bolivia, Chile, Colombia, Ecuador, French Guiana, Guyana, Surinam, Paraguay, Uruguay, Venezuela, Peru, Anguilla, and Falkland. Many immigrants come from South America to the United States, and although they can be found in any state, they are more likely to be found in places like New York City or Miami, Florida. Many restaurants now feature foods from countries in South America with specialties like Arroz con Pollo (chicken and rice) or Paella.

> **Explore the <u>Maps of the World</u> to learn more about the history and culture of some South American countries.**

ARGENTINA   If you like music, you would enjoy visiting countries in South America. European settlers, Spanish conquistadors, and African slaves all contributed to the beat that is distinctive of South American music. Originating from the Andes mountains, music is part of the daily lives of every South American. Instruments are specific to the region and include pan flutes, rattles, guitars, and drums. Argentina, on the southern-most part of South America, is famous for its history of the gaucho, the Argentine cowboy, as well as for its beautiful, modern city of Buenos Aires. Read to learn more about <u>Argentina</u>, including the contribution of the dance known as tango.

PERU   Do you like Ceviche? Then you can thank Peru for this delicious seafood dish. The northeastern part of the country is home to the famous Amazon tropical forest. A country with vast geographical differences from deserts to tropical forests to urban areas in Lima, Peru is an historical treasure of the Inca civilization. Read more about <u>Peru</u> and its history, family traditions, and religion.

BRAZIL   You may recognize Brazil from scenes of its *carnival* in the movies. What an interesting and exotic country. Although Brazil has one of the world's largest economies, it also has the largest disparities in wealth between the rich and the poor. A blend of many cultures, the country strives to provide for all of its citizens.

> **Read more about <u>Brazil</u>, as well as the social stratification and how social welfare programs are developed and distributed to the poor.**

You may remember the movie *Evita*, about the wife of President Juan Peron (played by Madonna). She was characterized as the champion of the poor and loved by some of her people. Many immigrants to the United States come from Brazil looking for a more equal distribution of income and opportunity. Do you think they will find it in America? Learn more at the <u>Evita Perón website</u> about her work with the poor and her love of social work.

COLOMBIA   Colombia is another South American country that has become more familiar to Americans now that actress Sophia Vergara (Gloria) is making weekly references to her country in the Emmy Award–winning television show *Modern Family*. Many Colombians reside in the United States in places like southeastern Florida. With a population of 42.3 million people, 75% of their people share a mixed race heritage with European, Indian, and African ancestry. Read more about <u>Colombian traditions and family life</u>.

Europe

There are 47 countries in the continent of Europe each with its own distinct culture, traditions, and language. Many of the citizens of the United States share their ancestry with one or more of these countries; although after **assimilating** into American culture, many families have lost the traditions of their ancestors.

GERMANY   Let's take a look at some of the countries where the early immigrants to the United States had previously lived. We can start with Germany since that was one of the countries with early immigrants to the United States. You can read about <u>Germany's social welfare programs</u> by scrolling down to the Social Welfare and Change Programs section of the website. Germany has some of the oldest programs for its citizens, having passed legislation in 1881 for health and accident insurance as well pensions for its older members. Germans in the United States were supportive of early attempts at legislation for Social Security here. Some of Germany's concerns today focus on its low birthrate.

UNITED KINGDOM   The United Kingdom is one country with its history linked to the early history of the United States. As a country, it accepts responsibility for its citizens and uses the majority of tax dollars for universal services. Programs like health care, education, maternity and paternity leaves, and retirement plans are available for all UK citizens. Do you think we should have higher taxes to support universal services for everyone in the United States? Read more about <u>British history, culture, and traditions</u>.

FRANCE   France is a country whose early explorers and traders came to North America and settled in areas around Louisiana as well as in parts of Canada. The French are known for their passion for food and wine and still go to great lengths in preparing daily family meals as well as traditional holiday meals. Read about

Read about the country of <u>France</u>, its history, culture, and traditions.

how the French are opposed to engineered and prepackaged foods and instead prefer fresh, whole foods. Go to the website (see marginal box) and scroll down to the section on social welfare to read about their social insurance system, which is funded solely by employers and workers. It includes family allowances, payments for pregnant women, and supplements for single parents. Payments for disability and sickness are also provided.

IRELAND   Another country with early links to the United States is Ireland. Irish immigrants have flocked to both the northern and southern coasts of the eastern seaboard of the United States for the past 200 years, hoping to escape the famines, wars, and poverty of their island nation. When discrimination and prejudice prevented them from advancing in the United States, the Irish developed their own system of political patronage in many of the northern cities and began to help their own. They have historically been a religious people with many traditions tied to the Christian church.

ITALY   Situated in southern Europe, Italy has a history rich in culture and tradition both in Europe and abroad. Many Italian descendants live in cities across America and have helped to create the American landscape by incorporating their food, music, and art into American culture. You probably can't think of an area, urban or rural, that doesn't have an Italian restaurant, or a major city that doesn't offer an Italian opera. The family is pivotal to the Italian culture. Italian women are considered to be the most liberated in Europe.

Read more about **Irish history,** **traditions, and** **culture.**

Read more about gender roles, socialization of children, and traditions in Italian culture.

There are 47 countries in Europe but I have just mentioned 5 that had early immigrants to America. Read about various other cultures represented in the United States from countries like Spain, Poland, Russia, Sweden, or Portugal, to name just a few. You can pull up websites for any European country and read about its customs. If your heritage is European, I encourage you to check it out. Go to the website (see marginal box) to learn about family traditions, history of the country, social stratification or their economy. Having an understanding of a culture is the first step to learning more about how a person is affected by issues like marriage, divorce, death, or even parenting.

Review the European Union National Institutes for Culture for an explanation of what is acceptable in Europe today regarding cultural tolerance.

Australia

Australia is the second smallest continent and home to six states, Western Australia, Southern Australia, Victoria, Tasmania, New South Wales, and Queensland. Inhabited originally by native Aborigines, later the Chinese, then outcasts that were sent from England, and finally settlers from other lands, the continent has grown into a vibrant Mecca of urban cities, tourism, and eco-tourism. It distinguishes itself by its attitude of equalitarianism, offering equal access to services to all citizens. It was the first to give women the right to vote and the first to offer a 40-hour workweek to its people. Issues today include growing unemployment with concerns about poverty, the ability to pay for social services, an aging population, and care for its youth.

Explore more about Australia's history, social welfare services, and culture.

Antarctica

Antarctica is the smallest continent with a climate so severe that few can live on it, except for scientists who study its environment. Some eco tours explore its landmass.

Since people don't immigrate to the United States from this continent, it is unlikely we would ever work with clients who came from there. However, military personnel and scientists do frequent the continent to study a variety of subjects. <u>Learn more about this interesting, but isolated, continent.</u>

What Would You Do?

What Are Some Practical Ways to Build Your Cultural Competence Now?

Get some hands-on experience! Use your skills to call ahead and ask if you may visit a local synagogue and ask to observe a Sabbath program. Visit a local Muslim mosque and observe how women and men pray. Learn about our multicultural society by eating at a restaurant that serves traditional food from cultures such as India, Russia, Cuba, Vietnam, China, Japan, Germany, Jamaica, Polynesia, Mexico, Thai, France, Spain, or Greece. Practice cultural relativism by taking a field trip with your class to a museum of African art, South American art, Middle Eastern art, or Asian art. Have a discussion on what you saw. How did it build your knowledge base about the culture? Listen to some music from another culture. What sounds did you hear? How was it different from other music you have heard? Practice the skill of empowerment by focusing on someone you know who may be feeling powerless, such as a single parent, a friend who is chronically ill, or a neighbor who may be having a hard time financially. Listen to what they have to say, support them by being attentive and respectful. Encourage them to do something positive and demonstrate **empathy**. Imagine what the person must be feeling—fear, shame, doubt, anger? How did it feel to help someone else?

You will be surprised at how many you can name. Look at the map first so you can identify the areas and then hit Start. If you type in a name and nothing happens, it means that the name is incorrect so delete and put in another name. When you are correct, the name will appear on the map. Have fun and then consider the following questions:

1. How many countries were you able to name out of the 47 countries?
2. Of all the countries in the world that you read about, which ones share the values of the Human Services profession by believing in the dignity and worth of each individual? What countries seem to have issues regarding human rights for individuals?
3. If you could practice Human Services anywhere in the world, where would you like to work? Why? What would you need to know to practice cultural competence in those areas?

Play a game!

After building your knowledge base by spending some time exploring the provided websites for the countries, play <u>Sporcle's geography game</u> to determine *how many European countries you can name in eight minutes.*

Apply what you've learned! Now consider each of the following scenarios and determine what knowledge, values, or skills you would need in order to be effective in each case. What must you consider before you begin to work with each person?

JOSE   Jose is a seven-year-old Mexican boy who recently immigrated to the United States with his family. He is not doing well in his second grade class. You are the school counselor who has been assigned to work with him.

ROBERTO   Roberto is a 12-year-old Colombian boy who lives in a low-income housing project in an urban area. His mother, a single parent, is worried that local gang members are influencing him. You work for a metropolitan Boys and Girls Club and have been contacted by his mother to see if Roberto is eligible for your program.

DAO   Dao is a 30-year-old Vietnamese woman who comes to the local mental health center with symptoms of depression. You are the mental health counselor who has been assigned the case.

Recall what you learned in this chapter by completing the Chapter Review.

ELOISE   You work for a home health agency and have been assigned a new case. Eloise is an elderly, Jewish woman who has diabetes and recently had surgery for a foot amputation. She is now returning home with the prospect of many home health services to assist her daily.

CHAPTER 5

CBS/Landov

Professional Helping Skills

Learn about a Helping Relationship by Developing Skills That Involve Listening, Feeling, and Becoming Actively Involved

The Bob Newhart Show was one of the first television programs to show America the inside of a therapist's office. People were getting comfortable with the idea of seeking treatment for personal problems rather than keeping difficult issues private. Bob's character was in private practice and worked with individuals, groups, and families. In one episode called "Clink Shrink," Bob offers his counseling services to a parolee out on armed robbery. This comedy offers a look at the relationship between a therapist and his client. It's all about trust, and Bob quickly learns this concept as his client divulges all kinds of information that he would rather not have heard. Bob has to use his skills to remain professional and yet develop a bond or *rapport* with his client. In some episodes, Bob's clients try to develop a friendship with him, and they are constantly pushing the boundaries of the relationship. He learns that maintaining personal boundaries is necessary in the helping profession. Through the humor of this television show we begin to see how a working relationship is established, trust is built, and professional skills are used to assist clients in working through their personal difficulties.

> **Watch the episode titled "Clink Shrink" from *The Bob Newhart Show*.**

What's It All About?

The Four Stages of Work, Building Trusting Relationships, and Using both Verbal and Nonverbal Skills

So what is it exactly you are supposed to be doing when you work with individuals, groups, or families? There are four stages of work with a person who needs assistance. Depending on where you work, you may refer to these people as clients, consumers, patients, or students. In some agencies they are simply called by their names. We will refer to the four stages of work as:

Stage 1: Preparing to work
Stage 2: Beginning to work
Stage 3: Continuing to work
Stage 4: Finishing the work

Many authors have written about these stages and the skills needed to be a successful worker in each stage (Cournoyer, 2010). We will cover a combination of these skills and talk about how you can develop your competency using them in each stage of work.

Developing the Helping Relationship

It's All about Building Trust

In the beginning of the helping relationship, it's all about building trust. If there is no trust in a relationship, you can't expect much change to occur. You will feel more inclined to help someone you can trust, who is giving you accurate information, and who is willing to allow you to help. Likewise, people who meet with you must feel that you are sincere, honest, and really interested in helping them, in order to trust you and give you all the information you need to help them. However, if they think you are not honest or sincere about how you will use the information they give you, they may be reluctant to tell you everything you need to know to help them. For example, if a mother is afraid her caseworker from child welfare will remove her children and place them in a foster home, she may not want to reveal that she has no money to buy food or that she is feeling overwhelmed by her new job responsibilities. Instead, she may act like everything is fine and not ask for any help. Believing everything is fine, the worker may leave the home without realizing the mother is severely stressed out and that there is no food in the house to eat. If the relationship had been built on trust, the worker and mother could discuss her new job and the added pressures that came with it. The worker could listen, offer her support, and provide suggestions that may help the mother with her new workload. Perhaps the children could be included in helping their mom by doing some household chores and reduce her burden. Maybe the worker could help find some emergency food for the family from her agency or a local food bank or church. Workers are supposed to be a support and help to their clients, but oftentimes they are seen as a threat by a person who is homeless, unemployed, or ill. This is why trust is such an important ingredient in the helping profession. The more we listen to our clients, learn about their issues, and empathize, the more likely we are to be helpful and to build that trusting relationship.

Using Nonverbal Skills

Why Is What You Do Just as Important as What You Say?

We often meet people by telephone contact, a visit to our agency, or by a referral from another agency. When we have time before we meet our clients, we need to use some nonverbal skills. These include things like reading through a file or contact information to get familiar with their situation. It is important to remember names, dates, and other data that will help us serve them better when we meet them. We try to use empathy by imagining what it must be like for them to come in and ask for assistance. When we prepare for consumers, we also consider things such as what will be needed when we meet the person. Will they come to the interview with children? Do we need to schedule an office or some other space so there is privacy? Will we need to put together an application package or some other materials for this person? We also need to keep records, documenting what we have done so far in the case file. You record things like calls to the consumer, dates set for meetings, arrangements for a meeting room, additional data gathered on the case that you found from reading the file, and goals you would like to discuss during your meeting with the consumer (Howatt, 2000). Sometimes we need to explore how this person is making us feel.

This idea of **self-exploration** helps us to discover our own strengths and areas for improvement. Are we nervous about working with a physically disabled father or a burn victim? How do non-English-speaking people make us feel? Asking ourselves these questions ahead of time will help us think through our own biases and how we might better prepare to deal with new and different people, cultures, and issues. These nonverbal skills are very important and require us to think ahead about developing a *plan for work*, so we know what to do when we meet the client.

Organizational skills are necessary in this stage as you prepare to work, since you must think about all the materials you will need, the arrangement of your environment, your own personal issues, as well as the tasks you need to complete in that first interview. The more experience you acquire, the easier this preparing to work stage will become as you realize what information is needed and how prepared you are to begin your work with the consumer.

Other nonverbal skills can also be used when you are working with clients at any stage of work, not just the preparing to work stage. This includes skills such as *listening* when someone is talking. That means that you are quiet and focusing on what clients say. Pay attention to their story, the details, the feeling behind what they are saying. Did you ever tell a friend some very private or heartfelt experience and he or she hardly listened to you? I remember once telling someone, "I want you to be the first to know

Human service practitioners must thoroughly read and review case files to understand the facts clearly.

Patrick Kinsella

that I made a huge decision to go back to school to get my doctorate." The disappointing response to my announcement was, "Yeah, well they are having a sale on shoes this weekend downtown." As you can imagine, I was crushed for not being recognized for the decision I had made. My friend was not listening or focusing on me at all. It made me feel like my decision was unimportant. If she had used an **encourager** like *nodding her head in agreement* or *making eye contact* when I spoke, I would have felt that she was listening. You can practice maintaining good eye contact by making sure that when you speak you are looking at the person and not down at the ground or around the room somewhere. Also be aware of your *posture*; sit up straight and look professional. Sit or stand in front of a mirror and observe your posture. Stand tall and straight; offer to shake someone's hand during introductions if it is appropriate. When you sit, make sure you don't slouch, put your legs up on a desk, or fold your arms with a closed-off position. All of these nonverbal skills are helpful in developing good rapport with a client (Mandell & Schram, 2010).

> **Test your comprehension of <u>Developing a Helping Relationship and Using Nonverbal Skills</u> by completing this quiz.**

Using Verbal Skills

How We Communicate with Others Is Important

When we use our verbal skills, it requires a different level of training since we need to *evaluate ourselves* as well as get feedback from others about how we are perceived. Good verbal skills take practice. It involves *how we talk—fast or slow*? We may need to practice slowing down our speech or speeding up. *Do we talk too softly? Is* it difficult for people to hear us? On the other hand, are we too loud? I have been accused of being the loudest one in the room, so that is definitely not my problem. But I have learned how to tone it down. I have learned how to be quiet and listen more effectively. Good verbal skills also involve our ability to *listen and focus* on what someone is telling us and then process this information and make an appropriate response (Woodside & McClam, 2011). We use specific skills when we make these responses.

Sometimes we *reflect back to the person the content of what he or she just said*. We call this skill **reflection of content**. This allows the person to hear what was said and think about its meaning. It can be helpful for people who may not have stopped long enough to contemplate what they were saying, how they were feeling, or how they were affecting others.

Human Services worker:	Tell me about what has been happening this week.
Consumer [fidgeting in his seat]:	I lost my job of 20 years since the company is moving its headquarters to China. I have no skills, never finished college, and my son is about to graduate high school.
Human Services worker:	I'm sorry to hear you had such a bad week. It sounds like you have a lot on your plate right now with your job ending, the thoughts of finding a new job, and plans for your son graduating as well.

We can also reflect back the feelings that we are observing. Let's take the same scenario but use a different skill. The whole meaning of the dialogue changes when the Human Services workers use the skill of **reflection of feeling** in their response.

Human Services worker: You seem worried and anxious about this turn of events. I would be too; it's a normal reaction. Are you wondering about what kind of job you can find with no college degree?

We can also add on some additional skills that will help build the relationship. **Self-disclosure** is used when workers want to share something about themselves with their clients that they think will help motivate clients or allow them to think about something in a new way.

Human Services worker: You seem worried and anxious about this turn of events. I would be too; it's a normal reaction. I remember once when I lost my first job as a middle school teacher. The district was cutting back, and I was a new teacher so I was the first to get laid off. I thought I'd never work again; I was so nervous. I wasn't married at the time, but I did have a large car payment. That was eight years ago. I'm glad now it happened because I really love this job. I was able to start as an assistant case manager and then the agency paid for me to go back to school to get my graduate degree in Human Services. Sometimes what seems devastating at one moment can actually turn out ok. You just need to think positively. Maybe we should start there. Let's look at your strengths and see what you would like to do and then see how we can get there.

Other skills that are used in verbal work involve **questioning**. It is important that we feel comfortable asking people questions since that is how we get the information we need in our profession. There are two types of questions—open and closed ended. Closed-ended questions do not leave room for elaboration on the part of the speaker. They require only a yes, no, or very specific answer (Ivey et. al., 2006; Neukrug, 2002). Did you ever meet someone who asks you so many questions at once that you can't answer them all? That person might ask:

"Where do you work?"
"What do you do there?"
"Did you go to college?"
"What is your degree in?"
"Where do you live?"
"How many children do you have?"
"Are you married?"

How does that make you feel? My guess would be that when people ask such questions, it makes you feel uncomfortable. You probably think they are just being nosey and want a lot of personal information. That is because they were not skillful in how they asked you the questions. Their interpersonal skills are rusty. They asked you all closed-ended questions that came across in rapid-fire succession sounding like an interrogation. It probably puts you on the defensive, and you might not want to answer the questions. You might be tempted to say, "that's none of your business." On the other hand, if they interspersed open-ended questions in the conversation it would come across more like a natural flow of information being shared between two people who just met. Questions that are open-ended allow the speaker to elaborate.

Sherry: I noticed you have a Penn State sticker on your car. I'm a Nittany Lion as well. Did you go to school there?

Timetra: No, my brother did. I'm just using his car today. I went to Saint Leo University and got my business degree several years ago. I'm Timetra.

Sherry: Hello Timetra, I'm Sherry. I moved from Pennsylvania a few years ago and thought you might have been from there as well. I was transferred with my company, and I'm really getting to know all of the activities this community has to offer. I have two children, so I'm here on the soccer field a lot on Saturdays, so I may see you again.

Timetra: I have one daughter who plays soccer, and we are here every Saturday as well. I'm from this area, so I'm familiar with all of our state parks and outside activities. Plus my job involves tourism, so I know a lot about what's happening.

Sherry: Where do you work? I'd love to hear about some of those upcoming events. Can you tell me about your job and what I should be aware of that's happening in the area?

This conversation is more natural; it flows. Both open- and closed-ended questions were used in a format that does not sound like an interrogation. The same information was gained as in the closed-ended scenario, but now both people share equally in the conversation. One other skill is used to help build the relationship. Can you identify what it is? If you said self-disclosure, you are correct! Once a person self-discloses, it is easier for the other person to self-disclose as well. Do you think these two women will talk if they meet again on a Saturday morning? Why or why not?

Some other professional skills that we use when we speak are *clarifying, seeking feedback, partializing, summarizing, facilitating, reviewing agency policies,* and *using informed consent*. More advanced skills like *interpreting, confrontation* and *reviewing the work* are also used as we move along in our work with clients (Burger, 2011).

Interventions and Direct Services

Understanding and Mastery: Skills to facilitate appropriate direct services and interventions related to specific client or client group goals

Critical Thinking Question: Why do you think that learning specific, professional skills are important to our work in Human Services? What skills do you do well? What skills do you need to practice?

Practice your <u>communication skills</u> by participating in a group activity.

Clarifying is the professional skill that we use to make sure we understand what the client has said. A worker clarifies when he or she makes a statement about what was just said.

Medical Worker: So, you are saying that you want your mother to come live with you.

Consumer: Yes, that's what I'm saying. I don't want her to go to a nursing home right now. We can talk about that option at another time.

Another use of clarifying is called **clarifying role and purpose**. This is an easy skill to use and can be practiced. It involves giving your introduction to the consumer. You tell them who you are and what you do. For instance, I would say to my student, "Hello, my name is Dr. Susan Kinsella, and I will be your Human Services advisor and one of your major professors. Welcome to Human Services." Now they know who I am and how I will work with them. Clients need to know this as well. It helps them identify the correct people who will work with them in Human Services in an agency.

Seeking feedback is when you ask clients for their thoughts or feelings about what has been said. You want to make sure they understand what has been said so they can make good decisions.

School worker: Now that I have presented you with all the facts about colleges what do you think?

Student: I think I would like to visit a few of the state schools and see if I might be eligible for that scholarship in math that you spoke about. I might like to be a math teacher. I never thought of it before. My family cannot afford college so maybe a scholarship could get me there.

Partializing is another important verbal skill that allows the worker to organize all the issues that are presented by the consumer. Together with the consumer, you rank order those issues that you want to work on first. You prioritize the issues and pick one or two that you want to work on initially. When those issues are successfully resolved, you can then move on to work toward solving other problems. Sometimes clients present so many difficulties that it is overwhelming to both the client and the worker. Imagine if you had as many problems as some of the clients that you work with everyday? I don't think I would cope as well as some of my clients did. When I worked in child welfare some years ago, I was often amazed at the strength my families had in overcoming problems. Many of my cases included single-parent moms with limited resources, two or three part-time, low-paying jobs, and children who suffered from physical or learning disabilities. The issues we dealt with often involved finding resources to help them pay rent, utilities, and food. Often they needed help with parenting, a violent spouse or boyfriend, alcoholism, sexual abuse, poor communication skills, and a lack of hope or belief that anything could change. How do you prioritize those problems? I could understand why a parent could get fed up with everything and walk away, or at least take the weekly pay and spend it all on something unnecessary. That was where my professional skills came in handy. I would work with my families, and together we would decide what they needed the most at that time. Usually it was rent and food. I would help them partialize the issues and start with the most important and work on those. When we reached a satisfactory level with those issues, we would move on to the rest. People feel a sense of pride when they accomplish something, and so the confidence begins to build as you work at solving problems together. Partializing is also a wonderful life skill for all of us to master. Keep that in mind, students, when you are trying to balance work, school, and family life.

Summarizing is another skill that allows the worker to think about all that was completed in the session and to then give a review of this back to the client. It is a brief recapturing of what both the worker and the client have done together. It gives the client a chance to think about all that has been accomplished so far. Sometimes people are amazed by how much has been completed in a short period of time, and that builds their hope that things will change. It also focuses on what still needs to be done so that work can continue.

Facilitating is the skill workers use when they move the sessions along. They ask open-ended questions, allowing the client to do most of the talking. When they work with couples, groups, or families, workers make sure that everyone participates. They use skills that involve the whole group, exercises to get everyone interested, and they ask questions that get people to work on their goals. Facilitating is a process that requires some time and experience to get the skill just right. Workers who facilitate meetings or group sessions know how to keep the group focused and the questions or presentations flowing so the work gets done. If you get an opportunity to watch an agency board meeting or a counseling session, pay attention to the facilitator's skills. Is the facilitator able to move the meeting along or does the meeting get stuck and conversations get off track?

> ### Intervention and Direct Services
>
> *Understanding and Mastery: Knowledge and skill development in group facilitation and counseling*
>
> **Critical Thinking Question:** Many services in our agencies are offered through groups. Are you prepared to facilitate a group if you work in a mental health setting, residential group home, or day care center for children or seniors?

Engage in a role-play exercise to practice your <u>facilitation skills.</u>

Did you ever have an issue that you shared with someone and he or she immediately told you what your problem was and what you needed to do to fix it? It might have irked you that the other person was so matter-of-fact. That person might have come off like a know-it-all, an expert. Well, in the helping professions, we don't do that. We don't tell people what to do. Think about it. When someone tells you what to do, do you listen? Probably not, and it's the same in the helping professions. If we went around telling people what we thought about them and their problems, we probably wouldn't have jobs very long. Do you think our clients would like it if we were to say: "I agree with you,

Design Pics/Don Hammond/Getty Images

This Human Services practitioner facilitates a group for children. It may involve some teaching, counseling, or organizing activities.

your husband is a bum. Get a divorce, you'll be better off." or "I can't believe you left your children, got involved with drugs, and became a dealer. What kind of mother are you anyway? They'd be better off if you were still in jail or if you just left them alone." As you read in other chapters we use our professional values to help understand where a client is coming from. We try to be accepting and nonjudgmental. When it comes to helping them understand how their situation may have gotten so bad, we try to help them look at things from a different perspective. We call this **interpreting**. Clients may not realize their behavior is a direct result of something that happened a while ago. They may also not realize how they are feeling about something because they are not honest with themselves and others, or they have not admitted it out loud to themselves. For instance:

Drug and alcohol worker:	I know you are pleased your husband is no longer drinking and that his new job is working out ok. How are things going with your son?
Client:	Great, he finished school, and he is home now. He isn't like his father. He can drink beer and not get nasty or violent. He just started working at a business near our home.
Drug and alcohol worker:	So, your son is home from college and working now. Is he drinking a lot?
Client:	Well, he drinks at home so it isn't a problem. He doesn't drink and drive, and he starts drinking only after his work is over. Then he just falls asleep. So it's fine.
Drug and alcohol worker:	I must tell you that behavior concerns me. You know that alcoholism is hereditary and your husband is an alcoholic. Your son has picked up some unhealthy behavior that could very well lead to the same condition your husband suffered. It sounds to me like your son may have an alcohol problem as well. You could have some serious issues with him if this is true. Would you consider this?
Client:	I don't want to consider this, but I think you may be right. He is drinking a lot of beer every night, and I find his empty cans in the morning. I'm not sure what to do because I don't really want to deal with this right now. We just got finished with my husband. I think I'm going to need your help again.

Do you see how the client would not have thought this was a problem unless the worker brought it to her attention? She did not want to admit this to herself. Interpreting is a powerful skill, but we must be certain of something before we interpret an issue, a behavior, or the consequences of an action.

Another skill that is important in Human Services refers to our work in agencies. We must be knowledgeable about the policies and procedures under which we work. We then need to make sure our consumers are knowledgeable about these policies as well. Do they understand what financial documents they need to become eligible for student loans, food stamps, housing assistance, or health care programs like Medicaid? What if they give us false information on an application? What does that mean in terms

of termination of the service, possible dismissal from a program, or even criminal pros-
ecution? We need to be very clear with our clients about the consequences of their actions. We call this skill **reviewing agency policies**. Sometimes people are not aware that
if they tell us something that reveals they are about to harm themselves or others, we are
legally responsible to report these facts. Consider this scenario:

You have been working with a female victim of domestic violence for some months.
Against your recommendations, she left the shelter and returned home to her abusive
spouse. She believed that she could control him and that he agreed not to hit her anymore. She was also financially dependent upon him and was tired of living in the shelter program that was not anything like her beautiful home in the suburbs. So, she and
her two small children, ages four and eight, returned home on a Thursday evening. On
Saturday there was a domestic disturbance at the home. She contacted you to say she
was on her way back to the shelter with her children as soon as she could get away. You
contacted the police right away on her behalf, and they were dispatched to her home.
She arrived to the shelter within the hour, and her husband was arrested by the police
shortly afterward. As she brought the children in from the car, you immediately saw
the bruises, black eyes, and her twisted arm. You told her they all needed medical care
and you would accompany them to the hospital. She was livid, saying that he was drunk
and went after the eight-year-old son who tried to protect his mother. She said, "He has
never done this before, never gone after the children. I will kill the *******. As soon as
he gets out of jail tomorrow and the children leave for school on Monday, I am going
back to the house, and I am going to finish him for good." Now what would you do? She
is obviously in a state of distress. Discuss this in a group of three or four. What do you
think your professional responsibility is to her husband?

If you said that you are professionally responsible to find out if she has a plan of
action that she could carry out, you are correct. If you ask her how she would kill her
husband and she has a specific plan of how she will carry out the task, you must report
this incident. For instance, if she has a weapon or access to one, and you believe that
she has all intentions of carrying out her plan, you must notify your agency and her
husband that you have a client who intends to harm him. If a client tells you that he or
she intends to harm himself/herself or others, and you believe this to be true, you must
report this information to your supervisor, the agency where you work, and directly to
the intended victim as well. Human Services is a very accountable profession, and you
must be knowledgeable about all the policies that regulate the profession in your state.
On the other hand people get upset and say things they do not mean. You must question your client in a way that allows you to make a decision as to whether or not you
believe your client has the intention and the means to carry out an act of harm against
himself/herself or others. Then you must make an informed decision and determine if
you must report this situation or believe the person has no intention or plan to carry
out such an act.

This legal responsibility in the United States comes about as the result of a Supreme
Court decision, _Tarasoff vs. the California Board of Regents_. A student at a California
University reported to his counselor that he was upset because of a breakup with his
girlfriend and that he intended to kill her if he could not be with her. The counselor believed him and reported to the school campus security that the man was a danger. Campus security checked into the man's background and searched his apartment. Finding
no weapons and no criminal background history, they believed the man to be no risk.

However, he did indeed kill his girlfriend. The case went to the state courts in California that upheld the decision of the lower court stating that both the counselor and the university were not at fault because they did report the incident to the authorities who did check out the student. However, the case was appealed and made its way to the Supreme Court in the United States with a different result. It was ruled that both the university and the counselor were liable because they did not notify the intended victim. At no time did Ms. Tarasoff realize she was in danger, so she was not prepared to protect herself (Kagle & Kopels, 1994). This decision has strong implications for those in the helping professions in America. We cannot take lightly our responsibility to protect our clients as well as society in general.

When clients come for service, we must tell them initially that if they tell us they plan on harming themselves or someone else, we must report this information. We must also tell clients about all other policies of the agency. We also cannot use clients for research purposes without their consent. We cannot give them service without a consent, we cannot give juveniles service without parental consent, we cannot do anything without clients' consent. This is for their protection. So, as workers we must be constantly vigilant about what we can and cannot do with our clients.

When we inform clients of their rights and give them information in writing, we give them the right to say yes or no to service. This is called **informed consent**. The more familiar you become with your agency, the easier it will be to become proficient at informed consent.

> **Watch the video, "Engagement", based on interviewing skills. Which skills is the worker using?**

> **Test your comprehension of Using Verbal Skills by completing this quiz.**

Around the Globe

Building Interpersonal Relationships by Studying Abroad

Have you ever had the chance to study abroad? Does your school have an international study abroad program? What country would you be interested in visiting? What are some of the concerns that you would have regarding living and studying in a foreign country? Would it be the language, culture, food, or customs? Have you considered the environment? Is it very hot or cold there? Meeting new people and learning about new cultures can be very exciting, but it can also be stressful because you may worry about meeting people, making friends, and developing relationships with others. What are some of the skills that you learned about in this chapter that could help you with an adventure like study abroad? Even though it's not a helping relationship, would the development of trust and rapport be necessary with new people you might meet along the way? Learn about Study Abroad by exploring the Study Abroad with AIFS website.

> **Go to Study Abroad with AIFS to "Change the Way You See Your World."**

Putting Skills to Work

What Skills Are Important for Each of the Stages of Work?

Now that you are aware of both verbal and nonverbal skills, it's time to take a closer look at how we can use these skills as we work with people in the different stages. It is clear

Photo courtesy of Saint Leo University's S.E.R.V.E. Program

Students from Saint Leo University participate in service learning and study abroad activities. Here they are volunteering their services through S.E.R.V.E. at the Father English Community Center.

that nonverbal skills are important in the **preparing to work stage**. Before you even see a client, you need to take time to *review files*, get familiar with the case, learn significant names and dates, *self-explore*, *use empathy*, and imagine yourself in the client's position. *Develop a plan* for your first meeting, make any necessary *arrangements* like scheduling an appointment with the client, or send a letter to notify your client of the meeting. Use your *organizational skills* to be prepared when the client arrives. You may need to use some verbal skills in the preparing to work stage since you might have to consult with your supervisor about the case, meet with another agency professional who referred the case, or ask questions of a previous worker.

Interpersonal Communication

Understanding and Mastery: Clarifying expectations, dealing effectively with conflict, establishing rapport with clients, and developing and sustaining behaviors that are congruent with the values and ethics of the profession

Critical Thinking Question: Read the case studies and imagine what skills you would need to consider before you begin and as you continue to work with the consumer.

Case Study ▶ Maria Valdez

You are an intake worker for a county child welfare department. You received a call from Maria Valdez. Her husband was recently hospitalized for an agricultural accident. She is a legal resident with a green card and has been working part-time in the local chicken factory. She must now work full-time, and her two young children, ages one and four, who are American citizens, need full-time day care. It is difficult to understand all of her requests and her situation because her English is not good. You will meet her in two days at 10 a.m.

What are some of your considerations during the preparing to work stage? What skills in the preparing to work stage would you use?

Now let's review what you learned. In the case of Maria Valdez, if you said that empathy was important to building a good relationship, you are on the right track. Imagine how Maria must feel as the parent with sole responsibility for her two young children in a country that is not the home of her birth. In addition, her husband's condition is an added stress both emotionally and financially.

If you then chose to *read her file* so you could be certain about specific details like her age, her legal status, and her finances, that would be appropriate. You may want to *review any data* or information the agency already has on her and the family. If she ever applied for services before, or if you are working in a county system, sometimes databases are used by several agencies where services are coordinated. Does it appear that she may be eligible for services that she has not requested? The children may be eligible for health care through Medicaid or a state-sponsored health care program. The family may be eligible for supplemental food through SNAP as well.

Before Maria comes for the interview, have you thought about how this case is affecting you? Do you speak any Spanish? Are you comfortable conversing with someone who does not understand English well? Would you feel more confident if you reviewed some basic Spanish phrases so you could at least welcome her and introduce yourself? *Self-exploration* makes us become better workers because we try to strengthen our skills rather than ignoring any areas that need improvement.

Next you need to prepare for the consumer. When she visits the agency, did you think about the fact that her children may be with her? Do you have an area where they can play so you can interview her without interruption? Is this area close by so that both Maria and the children are comfortable with the arrangement? Do you have age-appropriate toys for both one- and four-year-olds? Do you have a movie they can watch? Snacks? Do you need an interpreter in the meeting so communication is clear and understandable? Is the meeting space private so that you can ask for financial information or any other confidential data?

Have you thought about a *plan for work*? If you discuss child care programs, can you take Maria and her children to visit the center of their choice? If not, can arrangements be made so that she and her children can visit on their own time? What is her method of transportation? Does she walk? Take the bus? Drive a car? Is this a reliable source of transportation? Since she does not speak English well, perhaps a course in English as a second language would be helpful to her. How many services are available to legal immigrants who are not citizens? The more information you can acquire, the more helpful you will be. The fact that her children are citizens makes them eligible for services even if she is not.

Once a plan for services is in place, you will need to *record* your meeting, fill out applications, have contracts for service signed, or referrals made to other agencies like health care, child care, food stamps, or any other appropriate services. You can see that writing in Human Services is very important. Since writing is a large part of all Human Services jobs, make sure that your grammar is excellent, that you use spell-check in your word processing, and that you know how to use programs like Microsoft Word, PowerPoint, and Excel. Get personal help with any limitations you may have regarding grammar, spelling, or use of technology.

How did you do? Did you cover all the skills in the preparing to work stage? Did you think of the same or different issues than I presented? How about your partners, did they have the same or different answers?

You are working in an elementary school setting as a Human Services worker. John is a nine-year-old student who has been acting out and getting progressively more problematic as the school year continues. His teacher has asked for your assistance in observing his behavior, meeting with his parents, and working with the other teachers to develop an educational plan for him.

What are some of your considerations during the preparing to work stage? What skills in the preparing to work stage would you use?

In this situation, you will need to consider how to work with both individuals and families since the student, John, along with his family is your client. If you said that *building trust* was essential to this case, good for you. You need to think about using your skill of *empathy* to build a relationship with John so that he will share with you some of his problem areas. At this time, we are unaware of his academic ability, his home life, or his medical condition. Any of these areas could pose a problem for a nine-year-old child. Using some nonverbal skills like good eye contact, focusing, and listening will help you develop the relationship you need to get John to talk with you.

Since the teacher has shared with you that John is getting progressively more problematic, your next step would be to *read the file*. In reviewing his information, you will gain more insight into when his behavior started to become difficult for the teacher. You may learn more about the family and their history. Are his parents living together or divorced? Is there any indication of drugs or alcohol in the home? Family violence? Unemployment? Have they recently moved? Had a death in the immediate family? You can also learn something about John's academic performance. Have his grades recently taken a dive or has he always had difficulty with reading, math, or comprehension? Perhaps John needs to be tested for a learning disability or Attention Deficit Hyperactivity Disorder.

When you have the information you need to *prepare to meet both John and his family*, you will need to be skillful. Observing John in the classroom setting will tell you exactly what the behavior is that the teacher feels is problematic. This is important because you may not see the situation in the same way. Many years ago I was a school social worker, and I had many requests from teachers to observe a problem child. Sometimes what appears as a behavior problem may be something else. I remember one first grader who sat in the back row and was unable to see the teacher or the activities in the front of the room. In fact he was bored in the classroom of 28 children, so he misbehaved, getting the boys around him to engage in games in the corner of the room. After a few class observations, a meeting with his parents and the teacher, and a visit to the eye doctor, it was determined that the child needed glasses. The recommendation was for him to move to the front of the class and wear his glasses, which he cheerfully did. The problematic behavior ended, and he became the best math student in the class. So, it is important to get all the facts before you meet the consumer or make any plans.

Patrick Kinsella

Sometimes the problem is right in front of our eyes. We need to make sure we consider the facts of each case individually. This child was misbehaving in class, not because he had ADD, but because he needed glasses.

If you then said it is important to keep records of any meetings, notes, or results of testing completed on John, you would be correct. Remember that *organizational skills and record keeping* are professional skills in Human Services.

What are some of your considerations during the beginning stage of work with John and his family? What skills in this stage would you use?

In a **beginning to work stage**, we are meeting the consumer for the first time so your interpersonal skills are important. After *reviewing the file* in the preparing stage, you now have an idea of the client's problem and his or her personal data. First impressions are very important. Remember to use good *verbal skills*, smile, and if you feel comfortable and it is appropriate, shake the person's hand upon entering when introductions begin. I remember one of my professors saying that in his opinion, you could tell a lot about people by their handshake. He felt that people who were confident and self-assured shook hands eagerly and with a solid shake. People with a limp shake or a short hand pass were often those with low self-esteem or afraid of engaging in a relationship with others. I have also found that people who have been exploited in relationships with others like victims of violence or abuse may not want to be touched so even a handshake may be intimidating to them. Do use the person's name, remember important information from the case file review, and ask *open- and closed-ended questions*. Encourage them to enter your office or work area. Some workers even have water or other beverages available to offer consumers. It is important to make the person feel comfortable in this stage of work, since you are trying to *develop rapport* and build a feeling of trust between you and the client. Use good *listening* skills *focusing* on what the person is saying and *build the trust* that is important for the continuance of the relationship. In the beginning, it is important to *clarify your role and purpose* in the introduction so people know who you are and what you do in the agency. Non-verbal skills are still important so make eye contact, sit up straight, speak at a normal pace and tone...not too fast or slow, or loud or soft. You can tell when a relationship is developing because both you and the client will become more relaxed. The conversation becomes easier and questions and answers flow without tension or apprehension. The client may start to ask more questions or provide you with information that wasn't asked.

What are some of your considerations as you continue to work with John and his family? What skills in this continuing to work stage would you use?

As you move to the continuing to work stage, you will feel more comfortable with each other. At this stage you are probably moving into a mutual agreement as to what the problem is and how you can work together to help solve the issue. We call this *case assessment* that involves gathering the facts and determining what the problem is all about. You will learn all about this strategy in Chapter 6. Together with the client, you must then develop a plan for work often called a *treatment plan*. You will learn about this strategy in Chapter 6 as well. It is important to note that without a good relationship with the client, it is difficult to do an accurate case assessment and make a treatment plan since it involves *mutual trust* between the worker and the client. So refining your skills so that you are effective and efficient at developing interpersonal relationships is the first professional competency that you must learn.

When you are continuing to work, you will use all of the same skills as in the beginning stage and then add some new ones as well. Using both open- and closed-ended questions allows the person to expand on an issue. A combination of both open- and closed-ended questions will enhance your interview because closed-ended questions can get you information you need quickly while open-ended questions allow you to gather more specific data on a client situation. If you aren't sure about something that has been said, ask consumers if they could explain by clarifying what they mean. Always make certain that your understanding of the situation is the same as the client's. When we *listen*, we observe what the client is saying as well as how the client is behaving. We can then use these observations to *reflect both the feeling as well as reflect the content* of the interview back to the client. This allows the client to think about what they said as well as the emotion behind it.

When you continue to work, you will also do more *facilitating* of the interview especially if you work with couples, families, groups, or even community members. You need to continually *focus* on what is being said and consider how the interview should be moving along. You will have goals and objectives that you will be working toward with your client. You will want to stay focused and keep the conversation on track rather than getting off on a subject like current events or issues that have nothing to do with why the person came for service.

In this stage you may also use some *interpreting* so clients can begin to see a new perspective of what may be happening in the situation. You share any professional knowledge you have on a subject matter with clients so they can make informed decisions based upon fact.

Another skill used during this stage may be *confrontation*. This skill identifies a discrepancy between what clients say they want to accomplish and their actions. For instance, the student who claims he wants to pass math, and yet he never comes to the weekly tutoring session. Confrontation as a skill must always be used with *empathy*. Together they are used to help clients see how their goals and actions are not aligned.

However, confrontation used without empathy comes across like an attack. Compare these two examples:

EXAMPLE A

Teacher: I have been offering tutoring for those students interested in increasing their math score. I haven't seen you there Tom, even though you are failing. I guess you want to fail.

Tom: No, I want to pass, but I've been busy and I can't do math anyway.

EXAMPLE B

Teacher: I know how difficult math is for you Tom. I have been tutoring several students after school, and they think it is helping. They have all increased their math scores. Would you like for me to work with you as well? I think together we can work toward a better result for you in math. You say you want to pass math, and I am willing to help, but you must meet me halfway. Coming to the tutoring would show that you really mean it. Would you come on Monday?

Tom: I'm not good at Math, and I don't know if coming to the tutoring would help or be a waste of my time.

Teacher: Do you want to pass math?

Tom: Yes, I don't want to take this class again.

Teacher: Then let's try on Monday and see where we get after one class, and then you can evaluate whether or not you want to stay in after that session.

Tom: ok, I can do that.

Can you see how empathy makes a difference? When we put ourselves in someone else's situation, we can begin to imagine how the other person might feel. This helps us to reach out to people in a different way. When the teacher indicated that she knew math was difficult for Tom, but yet she felt the tutoring could help him, she was giving him hope that she knew he could change. He opened up by sharing his fear that even if he came to tutoring it might not help. The teacher indicated that it has helped other students and if he wanted to pass he should give it a try. She gave him a chance to come to one class and check it out. She indicated that she was willing to work with him, but he must meet her halfway. She negotiated an agreement with Tom. They are going to work together in order for him to pass math. She agreed to tutor him on Monday, and he agreed to come to one session and then evaluate its effectiveness. By using empathy, the teacher showed Tom that she did care and understood his concerns, but together they might work toward a successful completion of the math course.

What are some of your considerations as you get to the end of your work with John and his family? What skills in this finishing the work stage would you use?

When we get to the end of our work with clients, it is usually because we have finished what we started. I prefer to call this **finishing the work stage** because our intent is to help the client resolve an issue. Some people might call this the ending stage, but if your work is not done, I hope you aren't ending. Too many times our work in Human Services comes to an abrupt end because clients no longer have any money for service, their insurance ran out, clients became frustrated and stopped coming for service, or the worker left the agency for employment elsewhere and there is no one in the agency to temporarily handle the case. In those situations the work did end, but it was not necessarily finished. In Human Services, we want to prepare, begin, continue to work, and then help our clients finish up the work that we have agreed to do with them. This process may take a few days if you work in a setting that moves quickly like a hospital, or it may last a few weeks, months, or even years.

I have a niece who is a social worker, and she has worked with the same developmentally disabled adults in a residential group home for years. Obviously, she knows her clients very well as compared to the worker who may only see her clients once or twice. Nevertheless, professionals who work in a hospital setting have to prepare to finish their work with patients. In those types of settings, assessments and treatment plans are developed quickly, paperwork is still essential, and a plan to finish the work must be in place when the patients leave the hospital. Patients may be released and go home, finish their treatment at a rehab facility, head to a nursing home, or plans are made for them to return home with a relative.

When we are in this stage, we continue to use all of the skills previously used, but we add some new ones like **review of the work**. Workers and clients have to begin to prepare for the last session before they get to this point. It is helpful for clients to know how long they will be receiving the service. If they know they will have four weeks to make a change, attend a group, receive emergency food, or attend parenting classes, they can make the necessary plans required for transportation, child care, or changing a work schedule. They are also more likely to move toward a goal if they recognize that it is time-limited. A skill helpful to both the client and the worker is called review of the work. It allows clients to see all that has been accomplished in the time they have been at the agency. This review can also help them see what positive changes have been made and what still needs to be accomplished before the work is finished. It is a good idea to allow several sessions for the client and the worker to finish their tasks and evaluate if they have achieved the goals they had originally established. It is very rewarding for clients to see that their work has been successful and that goals were achieved, like gaining employment, using new parenting techniques, passing a GED exam, or communicating on a better level with a spouse. The skill of reviewing the work can help clients see exactly what was done, so if they have a similar problem in the future they will know how to handle it themselves.

Test your comprehension of <u>Putting Skills to Work</u> by completing this quiz.

Think Human Services

Why Is It Important to Understand Ourselves before We Begin to Work with Others?

If you had a problem whom would you go to for help? Would you consider a family member or a friend? Would you rather talk with a professional who could help you and does not know you or the issue? Would you just talk with anyone who would listen because you really want to vent and not really get professional help? Sometimes it's hard for people to ask for help and then accept it. As a result, when they finally do go for professional help, they often feel like that person should solve their problem, have all the answers, or tell them what to do. In Human Services, we don't do any of those things. Helping professionals *help people to help themselves*. It is important that we develop a good relationship with our consumers because we work *with* them to help them look at solutions to their problems. We do not tell them what to do or give advice as to what they should do. It is important that the people who train to be workers are knowledgeable about this process and are not attempting to be the expert who tells people what to do. Human Services is a profession that helps and guides others so we begin by learning how to become self-aware of our own personal qualities.

Think carefully about the following questions and type your answers in a Word document.

- What do you like about yourself?
- What do you think other people like about you?
- What would you like to change about yourself? Is this possible to do?
- Would you think or feel any differently about yourself if you could do this?
- What prevents you from making the change?

Now share your answers with another person in your class as you work in dyads. What was this discussion like for you? What did it seem like for your partner? Remember that you are learning skills so even if you are a timid, uncomfortable, soft-spoken person or a loud, aggressive, fast-talker who doesn't listen very well, you can change. That is why you are in this class learning about what strengths you have and how you can improve to become more professional. Unlike other fields of study where you may learn about a process and then take a test, Human Services requires you to become self-aware. That might mean that some of the interpersonal classes are difficult because your personal characteristics might be challenged. If you are interested in staying in this field, be prepared to study yourself and your values as well as give and receive feedback from your classmates and your instructor. You will learn how your behavior affects others and how you can develop your skills to build trusting relationships. These are also life skills and are useful for more that just your professional career.

Be open to the feedback you get from others and use the information to consider how you can improve upon a skill. Becoming defensive or protective of your classmates when feedback is given is not helpful. Your instructor will set the guidelines as to how to give and receive feedback. Always start with a person's strengths. What did they do well? Give specific examples. What could they have improved and how could it have been done differently or better? Give specific examples. If you expect your clients to change their behavior, you must be willing to learn how to change yours as well if necessary.

We must also consider in training Human Services students that certain standards be met. You must be in good physical and mental health in order to help others. If you want to stop smoking would you spend time smoking with your friend on the back porch, or would you attend a smokeout program at your local health department? In Human Services, we need to make sure that our students take the challenge of helping others seriously. If students have a substance abuse problem, are victims of domestic violence, are incest survivors, or attend mental health programs, they can be the most empathic workers because they have experienced life's difficulties. However, it is important that the person has already recovered before they attempt to help someone else. If you were drowning, it wouldn't help to grab another drowning person. So, if you are struggling with a personal issue, get the help you need so that you can become the best worker possible. Be aware that the exercises and feedback you receive in your classes are for your own personal growth and development. It should be challenging. Don't be offended, be introspective and allow yourself to grow.

A study I did in Florida some years ago demonstrated that students in social work and human services programs across the state chose the two majors primarily because of some life event. Experiences like divorce, death of a loved one, a sickness, or being a victim of a crime were some reasons that people who wanted to study the helping professions indicated. They felt strongly that once they recovered from their life event they wanted to help others who may be experiencing the same ordeal (Kinsella, 1997). This type of life experience makes people very empathic, and they can then become excellent motivators who can help others.

Linking Skills to Practice

Memories of the Food Stamp Office

Did you ever have to ask anyone for help? What did they do to make it easy for you? What made it uncomfortable? I remember my own situation many years ago when I was trying to put myself through college. My single-parent mother was unable to offer me financial assistance so I worked hard to get state and federal grants and scholarships. The rest was paid through many hours of employment. After learning about some social service programs, my roommates encouraged me to apply for food stamps to supplement my meager income. I vividly remember bringing in my pay stubs and other documentation to a county office where my eligibility could be determined. This was a new experience for me since my mother had never applied for any kind of social services, although she may very well have been eligible. She was probably unaware of what she could receive after my father left the family, and no doubt her pride would have prevented her from asking for help. At any rate, I did ask for food stamps, but the worker who did the interview thought that I was not revealing all of my income. She could not believe I was able to live in a college setting on such a meager sum! As a result I was determined ineligible. She was convinced I was not telling the truth. This was a very embarrassing situation for me, a 20-year-old student. I also felt betrayed by the system I was being trained to represent and that should have helped me. Later that day, I also felt angry at not being believed and at the doubtful nature by which I was questioned. This worker was obviously not using good practice techniques. I certainly did not trust her or even like her. It is unlikely that I would have developed any rapport with her.

Later in the semester, I received a letter from the county eligibility office that had rereviewed my case. I was finally offered food stamps for the last few months I was in college. Although they did help me tremendously by allowing my income to go for rent instead of food, I was left feeling that I somehow received this benefit but was not worthy to get it. This is not the way social services should make people feel. Workers need to use their skills to assist people in strengthening their coping skills, help them find resources, and to make decisions that will improve their daily living.

What skills could this worker have used to develop a better working relationship? Give specific examples of what she could have said or done differently. If the worker was suspicious that the information I was giving was not accurate, what could she have done to get a better picture of my situation?

Did You Know?

Why an Intake Worker at an Agency Is One of the Most Important Jobs?

One of the first workers you meet in a Human Services agency is an intake worker. They take your information and often refer you to another person in the agency that you will work with like a counselor, a case manager, a group facilitator, or a social worker. Many of the skills that we have described for you so far need to be utilized by the intake worker. Since they are the first professional to meet the consumer, they will begin to build rapport first. They need to be knowledgeable about the agency's services as well as be proficient at interviewing skills. If the consumers feel good about the intake worker and what was discussed, they will return for more service. However, if the consumers feel that the intake worker is not interested in their problem, that they were treated unfairly, or even that they waited too long for service, they may not return.

An intake worker is a type of job that a beginning level Human Services graduate can obtain. Even though it is a beginning level position, it is one of the most important jobs in the agency. Intake workers must obtain all of the background demographic information on the client, their developmental history, medical and psychiatric history, as well as the presenting problem. Many agencies use intake workers, for example, county and state agencies, child welfare agencies, mental health agencies, and counseling type agencies. Students should be proficient at interviewing and the beginning level verbal and nonverbal skills that were discussed in order to qualify for an intake worker's position.

What Would You Do?

What Skills Are You Good At and What Skills Do You Need to Improve?

Think about all of the skills you have learned in this chapter. What skills do you think you are good at and what skills need improving? Then answer the questions in the Skill Survey box.

Skills Survey

1. I think I am a very good listener.
   agree _____ disagree _____ not sure _____
2. I probably need to talk less and listen more to others.
   agree _____ disagree _____ not sure _____
3. I can stay focused on a subject until I come to a resolution.
   agree _____ disagree _____ not sure _____
4. I feel very comfortable speaking and looking someone in the eye while I'm talking.
   agree _____ disagree _____ not sure _____
5. My professional appearance, including how I look and how I sit or stand, is fine.
   agree _____ disagree _____ not sure _____
6. I have a hard time staying focused on just one thing. I usually start out talking about one issue and then get sidetracked and start talking about something else.
   agree _____ disagree _____ not sure _____
7. I can't understand how people get themselves into such difficult situations, and I can't even imagine having the same problem.
   agree _____ disagree _____ not sure _____
8. When people say something I'm not sure about, I usually ask them to repeat it or clarify the issue so that it makes sense to me.
   agree _____ disagree _____ not sure _____
9. I can easily put myself into someone else's shoes and imagine how their problem could affect me.
   agree _____ disagree _____ not sure _____
10. I don't feel comfortable asking people questions. It seems nosey.
    agree _____ disagree _____ not sure _____
11. I will have no trouble asking people questions to help me gather the information I need.
    agree _____ disagree _____ not sure _____
12. I speak too fast, and it's hard for me to slow down.
    agree _____ disagree _____ not sure _____

13. I speak too slow, but it's hard for me to speak any faster.
agree _____ disagree _____ not sure _____
14. People tell me that I am loud.
agree _____ disagree _____ not sure _____
15. I know I speak softly, but I can't help it.
agree _____ disagree _____ not sure _____
16. If I listen to what someone is saying and observe how they may be feeling, I think I can learn to use the skill of reflection.
agree _____ disagree _____ not sure _____
17. I have no idea how to use confrontation so I will need to practice a lot.
agree _____disagree _____ not sure _____
18. I think I am already competent at using basic interviewing skills.
agree _____disagree _____ not sure _____
19. I think I will be good at reviewing agency policies because I am well organized and know how to explain policies clearly.
agree _____disagree _____ not sure _____
20. I will be good at facilitating because I can keep the conversation focused and moving toward the goal when I am in a group.
agree _____disagree _____ not sure _____

Now go back and look at your answers. How many "agree" did you check? Do you feel confident about these skills? Some of the "agree" answers also tell you something about yourself. How might those answers affect your skills? How many "not sure" did you check? These are skills you are not quite sure about, so they need practice. How many "disagree" did you check? These are skills that you know you need to work on.

Engage in a Skill Survey Role-Play with a partner.

Recall what you learned in this chapter by completing the Chapter Review.

CHAPTER 6

Strategies of Intervention with Individuals, Groups, and Families

· ·

What Techniques Will You Need to Apply When Working with Different Groups of People?

20th Century Fox Film Corp/Everett Collection

While reading this chapter, actively engage yourself with the resources it provides. Watch the videos, check out the websites for the organizations, and think critically about the questions that are asked. Then prepare yourself to have a discussion with your classmates and Human Services instructor.

Did you ever see the movie *Bushwhacked* starring Daniel Stern? He pretends to be a scout leader and attempts to take a group of boys on a camping trip. The young boys are excited about their adventure and clearly need some guidance in learning about the out-of-doors. Their leader quickly discovers that he must possess organizational techniques and teaching strategies if he wants his boys to work as a team, develop self-discipline, and improve their survival skills. However, these are skills that he has not yet mastered! Wanting to be a good scout leader and having the knowledge and expertise to be a good leader are two different things. In this hilarious movie, Daniel Stern gets himself and the boys in one disaster after another because of his lack of specific strategies and techniques necessary to be a good leader. When he finally stops trying to impress the boys and actually begins to develop relationship with them, the trip takes on a more positive note. He finally earns the trust and respect of the boys after he enters into a partnership with them. This is exactly what happens when we work with individuals, groups, and families. When we are genuine and take the time to develop a relationship with our consumers, we begin to trust one another. Building a rapport is always the first step in our work in Human Services. Then we can continue offering services like intake, resource and referral, and case management. Let's take a look at these specific intervention strategies you would be using when you work with individuals, groups, and families in Human Services.

> **Watch a trailer of the movie _Bushwhacked_ at the IMDb
> website.**

What's It All About?

_Learn Professional Techniques to Work with Individuals, Groups, Families,
and the Community_

Implementing strategic interventions with clients involves learning professional techniques to work with individuals, groups, families, and the community. This is what students typically like the best because you are learning what to do when you meet with clients. First, let's take a look at what you need to learn in order to be effective in working with individuals of all ages. Then we will proceed with interventions for groups and families, and finally, interventions for working in the community.

Working with Individuals

_Learn How to Do Intakes, Assessments, Treatment Plans, Resource and Referral,
Case Management, Counseling, and Caregiving_

Intake

There are many roles we play as Human Services workers when we are employed to work with individuals. One of the most common types of jobs undergraduates are hired to do is that of an **intake worker**. Intake works have a very important role in the agency because they are usually the first person to see a client. They must use their skills to develop rapport and a trusting relationship with the client if they want any meaningful work to occur. An intake involves interviewing a person and gathering as much information as possible so that a determination can be made as to the nature of the problem. Most agencies have some kind of intake process, which involves the worker interviewing the client, asking questions, and obtaining information that is then recorded in an agency or data file. In addition to questions asked, sometimes workers require clients to bring in pay stubs to document their income if eligibility for service has to be determined. Programs like food stamps, housing and energy assistance, and child care are among those services that ask for income verification.

Intake workers usually see clients for one or two sessions, collect the data that is necessary, and then make a determination as to the type of service the client is requesting. They do not develop long-term relationships with clients, since when their work is done, the clients' service is established or they are referred to another worker in the agency for the service needed like counseling or case management. Intake workers gather mostly demographic data like name, address, telephone numbers, marital status, place of employment, salary, number and age of dependents, and type of service requested.

Maria approached the Department of Family and Children's Services very timidly. She never had to ask for assistance, but her husband, Juan, had been injured in an auto accident and was in critical condition in a local hospital. She had been a stay-at-home mom for several years, was not employed, and had two young children. Without Juan's paycheck, they could not pay the rent or buy groceries. Since Juan was not injured at work, she did not think they were eligible for workers' compensation. They did not have health insurance, and they had a high deductible on their auto insurance along with no collision insurance. She needed to find out what services she may be eligible for, but she was also frightened that the children would be taken away from her if she could not prove she could care for them. Although they were legal residents, she knew that many people had negative feelings about Mexicans. She promised herself she would be careful and give only the briefest of information in order to get food stamps or perhaps some other service temporarily. The first worker Maria met with was very busy and did not stand or greet her when she entered the office. At first she thought she was not seen when she came into the building. Then she realized the worker was on the phone and did not raise her head. She was finally told to take a seat and provide documentation of all her recent income. While Maria explained the situation and dug around in her purse for the pay stubs, the worker was busy and looked uninterested but dutifully completed the paperwork and asked Maria to sign the documents. The worker made copies of the pay stubs and told Maria the department would notify her sometime within the next two weeks if she was eligible for anything. Maria thanked her and left the building hoping she would receive something but thinking that she would never last two weeks without some help.

Interventions and Direct Services

Understanding and Mastery: Knowledge and skill development in intake interviewing

Critical Thinking Question: Was the worker helpful? What did she do that you liked/disliked? Would you have done anything differently? What are the cultural overtones to this case? Can you think of a time when you were afraid to give too much information about yourself? Is Maria justified in her thinking about Mexicans?

Intake Work is a very important job because intake workers are the first person to encounter the client in an agency. Read the two intake interviews with Maria, above and below, to get an idea of why the intake worker is such an important person.

Maria waited for two weeks but without any assistance she was desperate for help. She called the Department of Family and Children's Services to check on the status of her application. She was told it was pending, and Maria explained her situation to the telephone worker again. She was asked to come in a second time to meet with another worker who may be able to help with emergency assistance. Maria was relieved to hear this and made arrangements to take a bus to the agency, dropping the children off at an acquaintance's home on the way. She walked the last five blocks because she was out of money. It was very hot, but she was determined to keep her appointment. She prepared herself for another meeting like the last one but was surprised when this time she was greeted by a worker who introduced herself as Ms. Sara Collins. She walked into the waiting room to meet Maria, shook her hand, said "*hola, coma estas?*" and invited her to come back to her office. She smiled brightly as she offered Maria water or a cold beverage. Maria indicated that she spoke English as well and so the conversation continued in English. Ms. Collins offered an apology for the length of time the application process was taking. She asked how Juan was doing and even inquired where the children were today? Maria was surprised that Sara knew so much about her family, and she felt comfortable with this worker who seemed eager to help. She told Sara she had to pay a babysitter so that she could attend the meeting. Ms. Collins informed her that in the future if more meetings were needed, Maria should bring her children with her. A child care area with toys was right outside the worker's office, so a watchful eye could be kept on the children. Maria was so relieved that she began to cry. Sara immediately gave her some tissues and offered her a comfortable place to sit. "Why don't you tell me about what's been happening over the past few weeks?" Sara asked. "I can't imagine going through such a difficult situation with two small children." Maria began to tell Sara the whole story beginning with the accident, the lack of health care insurance, limited auto insurance, and no current paycheck coming into the family. She was willing to work, but she had no job prospects. Sara listened intently allowing Maria to tell her everything. Then she asked Maria questions about the type of procedures Juan was having at the hospital. She asked if there were any family members or friends who could help Maria with the children, give rides to the hospital, or offer support? She reviewed the file from the weeks before, confirming names and dates and then asked if Maria had spoken with anyone from Juan's place of employment to see if any help could be given. She asked about his physician and inquired whether Juan spoke fluent English so that he could understand the hospital workers. Sara then offered to help Maria find emergency food through the Salvation Army that day, give her a ride to pick up the food, and then pick up the children and take everyone home. Together they completed an application for Medicaid health care funding for the family. Sara also called the local Red Cross office to make a referral for Maria for emergency cash assistance. Then she agreed to find out about other resources like subsidized day care so that Maria could begin to search for employment. Together they developed a plan of services that both she and Maria thought was acceptable. She gave Maria some bus tokens so that she could ride the bus free for a few days when she traveled to the hospital to see Juan. Maria left the office feeling better than she had in weeks. Another appointment was set for the end of the week to review what other services Sara could find that might help Maria. Although the agency could not directly provide all the services Maria needed, Sara explained that referrals could be sent to other agencies for services on behalf of Maria. As an intake worker, Sara explained that she was willing to do this.

Engage with a partner to complete this <u>Intake Role Play</u>.

● ●

Interventions and Direct Services

Understanding and Mastery: Knowledge and skill development in intake interviewing and location and use of appropriate resources and referrals

Critical Thinking Question: Was this worker helpful? What did she do that you liked/disliked? Were you able to identify specific skills that she used? How does this worker differ from the worker in Case 1? How was culture handled in this example?

● ●

Although Sara was an intake worker, she was knowledgeable about resources and referral, another type of intervention that is used by Human Services workers. She was also beginning to build services around the family, which could be classified as the beginning of case management, another type of intervention in Human Services. Sometimes in Human Services, the interventions and techniques that we use overlap. You will read more about these services later.

View a sample Intake Form.

Assessment

An **assessment** is another type of strategy that is used by Human Services workers to determine what issues are affecting the client. It is important that problems be identified so that appropriate resources can be found for the client. A mutual working relationship is critical during the assessment process since the client needs to feel involved in identifying the problem and choosing a path for change. Depending on the agency, an intake worker may complete the assessment interview. However, in many clinical agencies, the worker must have enough experience or a master's degree in social sciences in order to complete the assessment. It is a more in-depth analysis of clients and their issues and involves a very thorough interview between the worker and the client.

Watch the video "Assessment" to see how the worker interviews the client to gather the information.

An assessment interview may take up to two hours and includes not only demographic information but personal and psychosocial data as well. The worker must be very skilled in developing the relationship so that the client feels comfortable giving background medical and psychological history, financial information, as well as data on substance abuse, criminal activity, family violence, or sexual issues. The worker and the client assess the problems together and prepare for the next part of the working relationship known as treatment planning or contracting. *Case assessments* may also include or even be called *psychosocial histories*. A very thorough analysis of the problem is needed so that an accurate plan of work can be established (Kuyken, Fothergill, Musa, & Chadwick, 2005). You will include things such as family history, risk factors, current life situations, and client strengths and resources. There are many different kinds of formal assessments that may be used, including the Description-Assessment-Contract (DAC) (Cournoyer, 2010), the *DSM-IV-TR* (American Psychiatric Association, 2000c), or the *PIE Classification System* (Karls & Wandrei, 1994a).

The DAC is a three-part, written assessment of the client's demographic information, the worker's perspective, and the mutual contract that is developed. This is a general tool that can be used in various agencies, but it is very thorough. Each area of this assessment includes information that is written as a narrative in paragraph style rather than as fill-in answers to specific questions. A complete DAC assessment may be eight to ten pages in length. Remember to use discretion when writing your reports. Record only information that is factual, not your impressions or thoughts. Case files can go to court so you must keep the information succinct and objective.

A shorter assessment that is used in many agencies is called *SOAP*, which stands for Subjective, Objective, Assessment, and Plan. Rather than lengthy narratives, the worker completes a short paragraph describing each area. If an identified problem requires an intervention, then a written plan must be used. In some agencies, a thorough treatment plan with measurable goals and objectives is used, but in other agencies the SOAP format is seen as sufficient. In this type of recording, a short description of the plan to be introduced is included in the case file.

View a sample SOAP assessment by reviewing the document Problem-Oriented Recording (POR) and the SOAP Format.

In mental health settings, the *DSM-IV-TR* is a diagnostic tool that is used to determine if clients exhibit symptoms indicative of psychiatric disorders. The *DSM* is a manual of disorders that are classified with codes that are used in the mental health system. This is an assessment tool you would become familiar with if you were interested in working in mental health settings. The PIE assessment, or Person-In-Environment, looks at the four dimensions: problems in social role functioning, environmental problems, mental health problems, and physical or medical conditions. Many social workers use the PIE assessment. In addition to these assessments, several scales or surveys may be used to determine if there are any other issues like drug or alcohol dependence, depression, or even learning disabilities.

CAGE is a screening test for alcohol, and several tests are available for drug dependency as well. Senior centers may use assessment scales specific to gerontology, and counseling centers may use depression inventories to test for bi-polar or other depressive disorders. Schools may use tools to test for attention deficit disorders (ADD or ADHD). So, depending on where you work, you may use screening tools that are specific to your agency to help determine the type of problem the client exhibits. These will be in addition to assessment questions that you and the client will work on together. Scores of tests and results of surveys and screenings are part of the case file. Some agencies, like state and federal programs, use assessments with specific questions that the worker asks and then completes as fill-in answers. Other agencies use assessments with specific content areas that the worker addresses and then records in a narrative format for the record.

It is important to evaluate the work you do with people to demonstrate how effective your interventions are in treating the problem. For example, Rapid Assessment Instruments or RAIs evaluate clinical interventions for a wide variety of problems. If you work with children or people in institutionalized settings, you may use assessments that are more visual or hands-on that employ *art* or *play* techniques, like *eco-maps*. Learn more about Rapid Assessment Instruments (RAIs) and why they are needed. We will talk more about behavioral techniques when working with children in Chapter 9.

Engage with a partner to complete this Assessment Role Play.

● ●

> ### Planning and Evaluation

Understanding and Mastery: Analysis and assessment of the needs of clients or client groups

Critical Thinking Question: If you were the client, did you feel comfortable with your worker? Were you able to relate personal information to them? If you were the worker, were you able to gather the data you needed? Did the gender of the client make a difference to the case?

● ●

Treatment Plans

Once an assessment determines the nature of the problem, and the client agrees with this analysis, then a **treatment plan** or contract can be developed to address these issues (Mehr & Kanwischer, 2011). A treatment plan includes a few measurable goals with a time frame indicating when these goals will be met. Goals are the projection of what both the client and the worker hope to accomplish. Becoming drug free, getting a job, or graduating from college are examples of goals. Now think of when it would be realistic for these goals to become a reality? Your goal may be to graduate from college in four years so that date would be included in your time frame. A few specific steps are then placed under each goal designating how that goal will be met. Those steps are called objectives and are also measurable.

In some contracts you would indicate who was doing what, when, and where. In this type of treatment plan you can easily evaluate if you are making progress. You can determine if an objective step is missed and know if it will lead to loss of a goal. The worker and the client work together to make sure the goals and objectives are measurable and attainable. Then follow-up proceeds so that the work can stay on track. Having dates for the attainment of each step makes the objective measurable. It's a good idea to work on about one or two goals at a time. If you have too many goals for the client it can get overwhelming. Your clients might feel like there is too much work to do or they don't see any progress. If they are successful at one or two goals, they are more likely to want to continue working on more goals.

Treatment Plan

Goal: To Become Drug/Alcohol Free by October 1st

Objective 1:	Enter Detox Unit at Memorial Hospital for 14 days beginning June 1st.
Objective 2:	Enter Residential Drug/Alcohol Program on June 15th for three-month program.
Objective 3:	Attend counseling and exercise sessions daily, nutritional information sessions bi-weekly, and groups weekly beginning June 15th.
Objective 4:	Participate in family group sessions once per month during treatment beginning June 15th.
Objective 5:	Receive support and guidance daily through Alcoholics Anonymous meetings beginning September 16th after release from Residential Drug/Alcohol Program.

● ●

You can make treatment plans or contracts for anyone with any issue. Even children are capable of developing plans to change their behavior. Sometimes rewards are given when people reach milestones. It can be a simple "Good job, you did it" acknowledgment or it can be a token. In residential programs, clients are often rewarded with some small award or token gift. This often works well with children who need to make significant changes to their attitude, school grades, or behavior.

Test your comprehension of <u>Working with Individuals:</u> <u>(Part 1)</u> by completing this quiz.

Resource and Referral

When we work with consumers who come to our agencies, sometimes they may not be eligible for our services, and they may not be aware of other community programs. We often refer them to services like food stamps, health care, employment, GED programs, transportation, meal on wheels, or other aging services. We can offer the service of our agency and then refer them to other resources in the community as well. This is called **resource and referral** work. It might involve giving them brochures or other handouts of the service, making a telephone call on their behalf, or sending a referral form to another agency. Human Services professionals must be knowledgeable about all that the

ZUMA Press, Inc./Alamy

Human service practitioners learn to assess client problems and help find solutions to issues. In this photo a counselor and a physician are assessing a patient chart at the Cancer Center in Albuquerque, New Mexico.

community has to offer. We are the people who know the programs, other social service workers, and often the eligibility guidelines for other programs (Woodside & McClam, 2011). Maintaining a file of all the services in our community is an essential part of being a Human Services worker. Most counties or regions have a directory of services with names, telephone numbers, and addresses of the agencies along with descriptions of the services they provide. A local agency like United Way is usually responsible for updating this directory. It is a good idea to purchase one of these directories that may resemble a small telephone book, for your area. Keep it handy so that you can look up services that your clients need. It is also a good idea to keep a personal file of your contacts at agencies with telephone numbers and information about services that may not be in the directory. Many larger communities have resource and referral agencies that hire Human Services workers to provide information to the community through online websites, telephone answering services, or walk-in programs.

Case Management

A *case manager* is a specific type of worker who arranges for the client to receive a number of services at the agency as well as other community agencies. Case managers work closely with a number of other workers ensuring that the needs of their client and their family members are met (Martin, 2014). Case managers may work with a network of other services and are aware of eligibility guidelines of various programs, and they stay abreast of current changes in policies and procedures for programs in their area. A case manager must work quickly to find services for the consumer and in some agencies may do the intake and assessment as well. In bigger agencies, the case manager works closely with the consumer after the intake and assessment are completed. The case manager must locate all of the services that are stated as requirements in the case assessment plan. For instance, if the plan calls for family counseling, a referral to a job training program for dad, a GED program for mom, and ADD testing for the oldest son, then the case manager is responsible for setting up all of these services. Then the case manager continues to work with consumers to make sure they are getting these services (NASW, 2012). When a worker meets regularly with a client to track what is happening with his or her services, or telephones a client or other agency to make sure everything is going well, we call this follow-up. This technique is very important in Human Services because we need to make sure clients are actually receiving the service once it is determined they are eligible and want the service.

In high-risk families, it is very important to build resources around people so that they have access to services like food stamps or meals on wheels for nutritional assistance, housing vouchers and rental assistance to prevent homelessness, Medicaid and other state health care programs to prevent acute illnesses from becoming chronic and to protect young children and the elderly from life threatening diseases. Counseling programs can also teach people how to cope with difficult situations, help parents learn appropriate discipline techniques, and offer better ways for marital couples to communicate. When we attempt to find many resources that can help and protect a single consumer or their family, we call this *wrap around services*. Oftentimes it is more effective and more cost-efficient to provide these services to an individual or family rather than removing a child from the home or placing someone in residential care. Most individuals are more comfortable living at home with familiar people who love and care for them. At times though, it is necessary to remove children, victims of domestic violence, or isolated seniors from their homes in order to make sure they are cared for by others who can protect them from harm. It is a more expensive alternative to provide out-of-home care and is often not the most beneficial to the client, so a thorough assessment of the situation must take place in order to determine if this step is necessary.

Counseling

Another technique used with clients is *counseling*. When a worker develops a relationship with a consumer and uses the skills we talked about in Chapter 5, counseling may take place even if the role of the worker is that of a case manager. Counselors listen effectively to what people have to say, assist them with looking at their problem, and work together with them to develop a treatment plan to help them cope with the difficulty. Counselors do not tell people what to do. Did you ever do anything someone told you to do? Parents will tell you that when they tell their children what to do, they usually have difficulty with compliance. Often the children will do just the opposite! No one likes to be told what to do. In counseling, we listen, review options, make suggestions, and then together with the client work toward a mutual agreement of what could be done. Professional counselors who are hired specifically for this role must have at least a master's degree and usually a license from the state where they reside. They have advanced training in skills and methods to assist people with stressful life events like divorce, death, and mental health disorders.

Watch Intervention for an example of an intensive case manager working with a client.

Caregiving

Human Services workers may be hired as caregivers who supervise others in group settings. Caregivers can be found in residential settings, group homes for the disabled, children, or seniors, or even in day care centers. Caregivers must have knowledge of stages of human growth and development so they understand what is appropriate behavior for the age group with which they are dealing. They usually have at least an associate's degree. These workers must have personal qualities of compassion and patience to deal with life issues that arise in these settings. They must also be knowledgeable about professional skills like interviewing, building trust and rapport, and listening effectively. Caregivers are usually given specific training by the agencies that employ them, so they know how to use techniques necessary for their agency. They may be trained in behavior modification, appropriate disciplinary techniques for children and adolescents, de-escalating maneuvers for crisis situations, and even self-defense to protect themselves from violent situations with acting out children, adults, or the mentally ill.

Watch the video Social and Emotional Competence from the Center on the Social and Emotional Foundations for Early Learning.

Explore Healthy Child Care America to get up-to-date research, best practices in child care, and links to numerous organizations.

Test your comprehension of Working with Individuals: (Part 2) by completing this quiz.

Working with Groups

What Are the Four Basic Types of Groups and How Do You Develop a Group Proposal?

All of the strategies and techniques previously talked about are used with groups and families. It is easier to learn first how to work with individuals and master the strategies and techniques to become competent in this area. Then you can begin to use your skills to work with a larger group of people. Human Services workers may use a variety of different strategies or techniques with larger groups and families. *Facilitation* is a skill that allows you to keep the conversation going in a group by making sure that everyone present has an opportunity to participate. You must be aware of what the purpose of the group is all about and then ensure that the *assessment plan* includes goals and objectives that move the group toward the purpose. You may be employed to facilitate a group in a school, mental health setting, hospital, drug and alcohol facility, or adolescent group home. Groups are very powerful because they have the strength of all the members to encourage or motivate other members to change their behavior. Most agencies offer some kind of group treatment since research demonstrates that groups are very effective and cost-efficient. Most insurance companies will reimburse agencies for group treatment for a patient. Workers will need a license or certification in their profession in order to get reimbursed for group therapy, which is a specific form of treatment.

Types of Groups

There are basically *four different types of groups* (Corey, Corey, & Corey, 2010). These include: task groups, psycho-educational groups, counseling groups, and psychotherapeutic groups. Just about every agency uses group work, so understanding how to facilitate a group is necessary in Human Services. Let's take a look at these groups to understand how they differ.

Task groups are formed to complete a task of some kind, and they can be organized by anyone. You don't need a college degree to be a task group leader, but you do need to understand how this type of group works. Task groups are organized as a team with a leader who helps the group work toward completion of its goal. Girl Scout leaders and their troops who work together to sell cookies during the campaign each year are an example of task groups. A book club is a task group, so is the local PTA or soccer team. A good leader is needed to run these meetings, organize events, or recruit members. A board meeting of a local nonprofit agency is also a task group. The president of the board of directors is the group leader who keeps the other directors on task to ensure that the agency is fiscally sound. So, anyone who is knowledgeable about group process and is a good leader can be a facilitator of a task group.

Psycho-educational groups are formed for educational purposes, and the leader teaches the group about some new activity or method. Members join these groups because they are interested in learning something new, so the group leaders are usually college graduates who have expertise in a given area. Workers with an associate's or bachelor's degree are eligible to teach these types of groups. Parent education classes at the local high school are a good example of this type of group. Foster parent training is another example of a psycho-educational group.

Counseling groups are formed for alleviating symptoms of distress of the members, so the leaders of these groups are formally educated. People who were recently divorced, suffered the loss of a loved one, or who are depressed are examples of the types of people who would join a counseling group. These people are well aware of their issues and want relief from the symptoms of anxiety or despair. The leader must be well trained, understand counseling theories and techniques, and is usually graduate level or beyond with a license or certification.

Psycho-therapeutic groups are for people with personality disorders or some other mental health issue. People in these groups are not aware of what their particular problem is since it is not a conscience issue. Examples of psycho-therapeutic groups are community mental health groups for people with schizophrenia or other psychotic disorders. Leaders of these groups have specialized training, a graduate or doctoral level degree, with a license for practicing in their state.

Test your comprehension of <u>Working with Groups</u> by completing this quiz.

Developing a Group Proposal

Every group has a purpose for its existence, and it is important that you establish the rationale for your group before you begin as a leader. If you have an established plan with goals and objectives and you know what you are planning for the group, it will be more successful than if you just decided to meet with a group of people and discuss some issues that were important to them. Planning a group before its inception is good practice. Some steps to consider when developing a proposal for a new group include the following (Corey, Corey, & Corey, 2010):

- Consider the Purpose for Your Group
  What is the reason you are organizing this new group? Have you been asked to develop a group for students who are at risk of failing out of school? Do you think that a pain management group will benefit the cancer treatment in your medical facility?
- Develop a Plan with Goals and Objectives
  Remember to keep your goals measurable with one or two specific goals and steps or objectives to meet the goals. For example, a measurable plan would be:

  Goal 1: The goal of the student achievement group is to graduate eight, at-risk, high school seniors by June 1.

  Objective: To meet daily after school with eight, at-risk seniors to ensure better study habits by the beginning of the spring semester to prevent them from failing classes.

- Organize Your Group
  You need to think about how many people you want in your group, what ages you want to include, whether your group will be mixed or single gender, where you will meet, how often and for how long you will meet. Will child care be provided? What about refreshments? You may need to get permission from a supervisor before you can begin to offer the group. Remember that if children are in a group, parental consent must be obtained beforehand.
- Plan Your Group Activity or Lesson
  Remember that each group you facilitate should be focusing on the group goal. There are many kinds of skills and techniques that can be used in each session. Many groups use verbal techniques where every member participates in a

discussion or engages in a verbal activity like a role-play. Psycho-therapeutic groups may learn how to cope with anxiety, discuss dreams and their meanings, or leaders may interpret behavior. Other groups focus on activities, and members may play games, do arts and crafts, watch videos, read and discuss books, learn study skills, practice math problems, cook food, take field trips, or plan group dinners. It depends on the type of group you are facilitating. The key is that for a group to be successful all members must actively participate and feel that they are getting something from attending the group. It is the expertise of the group leader that helps the members develop a trusting relationship and moves them toward completion of their goal. If the session activities are interesting and stimulating for the members, then they are likely to return for another session.

- Evaluate Your Group Sessions

How is it going? Evaluation can be done verbally or in writing at the end of each session. You may also want to survey people before the group begins to find out what the members expect from the group, what they hope to learn, or if they are in agreement with the group goal(s). When the group is over, you can survey them again to find out if they learned anything, if their expectations were met, and if they felt the group goal(s) were attained. In this way, you can demonstrate whether or not you have met your goals for the group. This may be an important factor if funding is needed to continue the group.

Putting Strategies to Work

Try Practicing Your Group Work Skills

It is a good idea to practice all the strategies, techniques, and skills you have learned to become a competent worker. Put yourselves into groups of eight to ten students. Choose one student to be the group leader. Now discuss the Human Services major for

Human Services professionals lead groups for seniors and provide assistance with a variety of aging issues.

vm/E+/Getty Images

ten minutes. Or you can choose to discuss the development of a Human Services club at your school, with volunteer and service learning opportunities. If you are the leader, you must facilitate the group conversation, keep it going. Try to get everyone to participate in the conversation. Try not to let any one person dominate the group conversation. As the leader, it is important that you get others to speak, rather than yourself. It will be easier if you are in a circle. Use your Human Services skills to facilitate this group discussion. Learn to focus, use eye contact, encourage people to talk, and ask open-ended questions.

What did you think of this exercise if you were the leader? Were you able to keep the group conversation going for ten minutes? How did it feel to be a member of this group? Did you participate? Did everyone participate?

Working with Families

Understanding Family Systems, Genograms, and Different Types of Interventions

When you work with an individual, you must keep in mind that people come attached to **family systems**. All families serve a purpose and can either support and encourage members and assist them in dealing with personal issues, or they can contribute to the ongoing problems individuals may experience. At the heart of most issues are interpersonal problems with others. It is important to see how family members cope with difficulties and to recognize what resources are available to assist others. Some families do not have the capacity to assist other members with issues like divorce, death, loss, incest, financial hardships, or medical incapacities. Mental health problems may prevent a family or members of a family from expressing empathy or knowing how to help their siblings, parents, or relatives. Some people struggle financially so they are not in a position to help others even if they want to help. Professional Human Services workers have to assess individuals in relation to their family and help the client make decisions to benefit themselves while at the same time understand how it may impact their family. I have counseled people who were afraid to take a positive step because of possible repercussions from their family.

> ### Self-Development
>
> *Understanding and Mastery: Conscious use of self; clarification of personal and professional values; reflection on professional self*
>
> **Critical Thinking Question:** Consider yourself as an example. What kind of support do you get for attending college? Is your family supportive? Does your family help you emotionally or financially? Do your family members offer to assist you in some way so that you can attend class or get your work done?

Over the years I have worked with students whose families have tried to sabotage their education in some way. They made it difficult for the student to attend class, care for children, do homework, keep employment, and attend to homemaking and meal preparation. Sometimes an assessment may reveal concerns that family members have about the student gaining an education. People may fear that an education will allow a person to become more independent, move away, or leave a spouse. In one family I worked with, the student was the first family member to receive a college education so other members were critical of her initiative, afraid of what that meant for them, and did not see the value in an education. It was important for the student to understand what was happening in her own family and to learn how to communicate her desire to learn. In this way her parents and siblings began to change their perspective of education. At her graduation, one of her siblings decided she also wanted to attend college.

An assessment used with families is called a **genogram**, a visual tool that depicts the structure and history of a family (McGoldrick & Gerson, 1985). Genogram is useful to go back about three generations to see if any patterns emerge such as drug or alcohol abuse, divorce, incest, early death of family members, critical events, or disruption of family relationships such as members who move long distances, children placed in foster care, family members who serve in the military for long deployments, or people who are incarcerated for long periods.

Learn how to complete a <u>Genogram</u>.

> **Human Systems**

Understanding and Mastery: Changing family structures and roles

Critical Thinking Question: Now that you have learned about a genogram and checked out the website, try to do your own genogram. See if you can go back three generations. Do you see any family patterns that emerge such as medical conditions, communication issues, or family structural similarities such as divorces or teenage births?

• •

When you work with families, you use all the same skills as in individual work, but you also have to understand family systems. Sometimes the client's biological, psychological, or social problem may be indicative of a family problem. So when we assess an individual, we also consider the family system (Martin, 2014). Several therapists have developed models and techniques for use with families. If you decide to obtain a graduate degree in a counseling field, you will be sure to study these models more closely. Let's learn about some of those models now.

Human Validation Therapy was developed by Virginia Satir (1988) and emphasized building self-esteem, understanding family roles and rules, and developing better communication through negotiation. She used techniques like *family sculpting* and *family reconstruction*. Learn more about <u>Virgina Satir's Theory of Family Therapy</u>.

Salvador Minuchin is the founder of **Structural Family Therapy**, a model that looks at the structural organization of the family (Sherman & Fredman, 1986). The goals of this therapy are to reduce the dysfunction in a family and bring about change through restructuring the family system. Techniques include *family mapping*, *reframing*, and conducting *enactments*. Learn more about the <u>Minuchin Family Center</u> in New Jersey where you can get certified in this method of treatment.

Read more about <u>Carol Gilligan</u>.

Feminist Family Systems Therapy addresses the issues of *power* and *gender* in family systems. Gender-based *roles* and *rules* are challenged, and problems of family violence, cultural discrimination, ageism, poverty, race, class, and sexual orientation are addressed (Howatt, 2000). Although there are several therapists with views on feminist theory, <u>Carol Gilligan</u> (1982) is a noted theorist who has produced many articles on this perspective.

Solution-Focused Therapy, developed by William O'Hanlon, Michelle Weiner-Davis, and Steve deShazer in the late 1970s, looks at goal driven solutions to family problems. Therapists guide the process and move quickly to the solution phase rather than dwelling on the source of the problem or the history of the family unit. Clients work toward goals that are attainable. Techniques include asking a series of specific questions called *miracle questions*, *exception-finding questions*, and *scaling questions*. It is often called Brief Therapy since in comparison to traditional models of therapy it takes less time for goals to be achieved. Read more about Solution-Focused Therapy at Good Therapy.

Murray Bowen's (1978) **Family Systems Therapy** is based on the belief that family members are connected to one another and influence each other's behavior. Bowen also believed that all family members are in a constant struggle between emotional connectedness and emotional distance from one another. Bowen's techniques include the use of *genograms*, *family questioning*, and the use of *eight forces*, which influence family functioning. Explore The Bowen Center for more details, examples, and opportunities for training in this model of family therapy.

Around the Globe

Bullying around the World

As Human Services workers, we have to deal with many issues that affect individuals, groups, and families. We need to use our knowledge of theories, models, therapies, strategies, and skills to listen effectively to our clients, make accurate assessments, and then develop mutual treatment plans with specific goals and objectives to help people resolve their difficulties. One issue that we are hearing more about each year is that of bullying. It is happening worldwide to school children, adults at work, and even college students because of how they look, their culture, race, sexual orientation, or gender. Rates of child and adolescent suicide are climbing higher, with 44% of attempted suicides successful in Great Britain each year. It is devastating to parents, friends, and teachers to find that such young children are in pain over difficult interpersonal relationships, which resulted in bullying.

In June of 2012, the YouTube video of the 68-year-old bus monitor, Karen Klein, in Greece, New York, went viral. Her job required her to sit near the back of the bus

bramgino/Fotolia

Here a young boy is being bullied by bigger older boys who use their size and strength to intimate those who are smaller.

and maintain control over an unruly group of middle school boys. Millions of viewers around the world watched as four boys taunted her in a ten-minute mobile phone video that they placed on YouTube in an ultimate act of humiliation. These seventh-grade boys used profanity to insult and threaten her until she cried. They jeered that her family all killed themselves because they didn't want to be near her. This statement was particularly difficult for Karen whose oldest son committed suicide ten years ago.

As people around the world watched this video they became enraged, not the result the bullies were expecting. Instead of sneering at Karen, the world supported her. One 25-year-old Canadian nutritionist, Max Sidorov, was so moved by the video that he decided to set up a website for donations to send Karen on a much deserved vacation. Southwest Airlines joined in the collection and donated a roundtrip flight for Karen and nine of her family members to Disneyland. She was shocked to learn that over $700,000 had been donated in her honor with suggestions that she retire early from her $15,000 a year job. She was interviewed on local, state, and national television stations and was humble in her disbelief that so many strangers from around the world would want to help her. She asked that people please stop calling and threatening the bullies who had been identified in her local community. Apparently they were receiving death threats. She indicated that the school district would discipline the boys, and she would not press charges. She was, however, considering the offer of retirement once she received the donation check. She and Max are also working together to stop bullying by setting up a foundation that will work with victims.

Watch the video about the bullied bus monitor, Karen Klein.

As Human Services workers these are the kinds of issues that we confront every day. Using our intervention strategies to help people learn how to communicate effectively with others and to develop appropriate lasting relationships is critical.

Think Human Services

How Would You Organize a Group for Young Children?

Think about the movie Bushwhacked. What could Daniel Stern have done differently to create a more organized, safer, and successful group camping trip for his scouts? Think about all the necessary group skills and techniques that could have helped him. If you wanted to start a group for children what type of group, of the four that you have learned about, would you want to develop? Consider a proposal with the five steps to group development. Write down each step in your proposal as you think about how you would organize each session.

Get some feedback on your proposals from classmates. Did you consider all the five steps? What did you forget? Do you think it would be fun to actually facilitate a group like this? Where can you get some experience in becoming a group leader? Can you volunteer for a local organization that does group work with children like the Girl Scouts or Boy Scouts, or YMCA? Perhaps your class can organize a group activity that can be presented at a local Girl's and Boy's Club or school.

Human Systems

Understanding and Mastery: How small groups are utilized, theories of group dynamics, and group facilitation skills

Critical Thinking Question: Now think about everything you have learned in family systems. If you were a school social worker who was asked to work with school bullies, what models or therapies that you read about would you use? Did you find any particular models useful?

Linking Skills to Practice

Developing a Community Resource Directory

Begin to develop a directory of services file for yourself. Include areas such as mental health programs, aging services, children's services, health care, parenting services, educational programs, employment services, drug and alcohol programs, disability programs, AIDS programs, transportation services, emergency services, food programs, homeless shelters, and other areas of service that you can think of. Create an electronic document of services with the name of the agency, address, telephone number, contact person, and a brief description of each service.

You also have the option of purchasing one that was already compiled for your community. It will give you access to many agencies in your area with information you may not have been aware of before.

How easy was it to get this information? What did you learn about the services in your community? Now make copies for everyone and put together your own directory of services.

Did You Know?

How Did Groupwork and Family Therapy Originate?

Groupwork is an effective treatment and intervention that is used today in a variety of settings. Did you know how it got started? During World War II, the mental health status of American soldiers was declining, and there were not enough psychiatrists, social workers, and other mental health workers to provide individual counseling. In an effort to provide more service, a counseling group for soldiers was developed with an amazing twist. Not only were more soldiers served at one time, it appeared that the group had a powerful impact on the mental health of the soldiers. They provided moral support and strength to one another. Mental health workers noted the group provided support and motivation to one another. More research was begun on the group method, which has become a popular form of treatment today. This strategy also has financial and policy implications because it is both cost-effective and cost-efficient. Most insurance companies approve of a limited number of group meetings as a qualified treatment technique.

Family therapy as a treatment modality can also be traced back to World War II. With the sudden reunification of families after the war, it became apparent that various issues were rooted in the rebuilding of the lives of these families. Long deployments meant that parents and their children had not spent much time together. Mothers had begun to work outside the home and so the traditional roles of homemaker and breadwinner were re-assigned. The idea of family systems therapy took hold, and by the 1950s it had gained respect as a counseling treatment (Howatt, 2000). The professional disciplines of psychiatry, psychology, social work, Human Services, and counseling all support the idea of treating families through a variety of approaches associated with family systems theory.

Other interventions that workers use may be more administrative in nature. In Chapter 7, we will look at the roles a worker plays when they develop budgets, write grants, assist in fund-raising, do research, or advocate for clients. Workers in these roles may also develop agency policy or complete evaluations on interventions to determine their effectiveness.

What Would You Do?

Imagine That You Are a School Human Services Worker

Sometimes we have to put strategies of intervention together as we work with people. Consider this case as if you were a school human services worker and this was a new issue for you.

Case Study	School Human Services Worker

Imagine that you are an elementary school human services worker in an urban area and you have several new Asian immigrant children who have moved into the neighborhood and are attending the school. There are Korean, Vietnamese, Chinese, and Indian students. These children are between the ages of eight and ten, and all speak English. You are concerned about their ability to transition into the school since there have been some bullying problems with new children in the past. You are also aware that parents are not involved in school activities or the Parent–Teacher Association. The children ride the bus to another part of town, and you have not seen the parents of any of these children yet.

Field Day is approaching, which is a popular activity in the school. All classes will be involved in a number of outdoor activities with all children participating in competitive games for prizes and awards. You are thinking this could be stressful for children who are not familiar with the types of games that will be played. There are many team sports, and you know that children may be embarrassed if they do not understand the rules of how to play the games. You sit down to think about how to involve the students and their families in this new school.

Consider what you have learned regarding group skills, family dynamics, assessments, and treatment plans. What types of interventions would you develop with these children and their families?

Recall what you learned in this chapter by completing the Chapter Review.

CHAPTER 7

Strategies of Intervention with Communities and Organizations

Mary Kent/Alamy

What Do We Need To Know About Working With Non-Profit. Profit, or Government Organizations?

While reading this chapter, actively engage yourself with the resources it provides. Watch the videos, check out the websites for the organizations, and think critically about the questions that are asked. Then prepare yourself to have a discussion with your classmates and Human Services instructor.

Did you ever wonder how much strategic planning goes into a presidential election? If you watched the events leading up to the 2012 election from the viewpoint of all the political parties, you probably realized what a complex mix of strategies was involved. People working for the candidates have a strategic goal in mind—to get their candidate elected. They want to win! They work together as a team conducting research to determine what the voting public thinks about the candidate, they collaborate with teams that are working in other regions, states, and local areas, and they evaluate what is working and what needs to change. You may have gotten a telephone call surveying your interest for a particular candidate or asking for your response on an issue. Workers want feedback from people so they know how to present their candidate publicly. Often policies are analyzed before the candidate gives his or her support for an issue. It is important that the candidates speak publicly about their ideas for the future of the country so they can demonstrate their leadership abilities. Efforts are put into mobilizing resources and conducting fund-raising so the candidate has enough money to purchase media advertisements, hire additional campaign staff, and travel to locations around the country, often with a cadre of campaign workers.

Read **A Day in the Life of a Political Campaign Worker** from the *Princeton Review* to learn more about this career.

Many people scoffed at the idea that President Obama had experience as a *community organizer* and thought that was inadequate and unprofessional experience to mention for a presidential candidate. When he won his first election, people started to reconsider this perspective. Now that he has been reelected perhaps people will have more respect for this role. What does it mean to be a community organizer anyway?

It certainly seemed those skills were very helpful in getting Barack Obama elected as the first African American President in U.S. history and then re-elected for a second term. Let's take a look at what techniques and strategies are necessary when you work with communities and organizations.

Read about **Campaign Management Tools from Aristotle**-a company that assists in organizing data systems, managing staff, and assisting with fundraising.

What's It All About?

What Are the Intervention Techniques That We Need to Know in Order to Work Effectively within Our Communities?

Many Human Services workers choose an indirect service job that is more administrative but still affects the services the client receives. They may like the challenge of *identifying needs in their community, speaking publicly* about the lack of services or the injustice to groups of citizens who lack the power to speak for themselves like children, immigrants, or the impoverished elderly. They might enjoy *developing new programs, organizing events to raise money for their agency, recruiting consumers* for the program, or *writing grants* to obtain funding. All of these strategies are necessary to maintain strong Human Services agencies. We must have well-trained professionals who not only enjoy working with the consumers, but who also want to participate in the growth of the program. Workers need to understand how to empower their clients and enlist the support of other Human Services agencies if they want change to occur in their programs or their regions. For this reason, we teach students how to work within their communities and how to organize and manage programs. This is as much a part of Human Services as the important roles of counselor, group facilitator, or family worker. Let's take a look at the role of a community organizer.

Community Organizing

What Are the Various Roles of a Community Organizer?

A Human Services worker who is considered a **community organizer** has several roles. First, community organizers must understand the dynamic network of agencies in their region and have the necessary *interpersonal skills* to *collaborate or network* with other professionals regarding the *coordination* of services for their clients (Neukrug, 2008). They may represent a particular agency and act on behalf of that program to make sure they receive their fair share of federal, state, or local funding.

They may also make sure that their agency knows about changes in social policy, coordinates services with other agencies, and makes agency officials aware of any pertinent changes to its government contracts that might impact the clients. They *speak on behalf of their agency,* or *advocate for it,* at meetings or public hearings. If you are interested in this type of work, you will learn about *needs assessments, research and evaluation, advocacy, public speaking, mobilizing resources, fund-raising, outreach strategies, policy analysis,* and *grantsmanship.*

Community organizers may also be employed by local planning councils like the United Way, which acts like an umbrella agency for all the Human Services agencies in that area (Morales, Sheafor, & Scott, 2010). In this role, the worker represents all the agencies and tries to improve services in his or her area by coordinating services so there is no duplication of services. In other words, no two agencies are receiving funding for doing exactly the same thing. The community organizer may notice gaps in service for clients and meets regularly with representatives of all the Human Services agencies to *identify service needs* and then determines how everyone will work together to solve the problem. Let's look at an example of an agency from my personal experience.

Search for the video by Mechelle Wallace, Community Engagement in the Early Years Helps Mississippi Vulnerable Children and Families Thrive on the W.K. Kellogg Foundation website.

In one area where I worked, Family Connection was the umbrella agency that provided networking opportunities for Human Services. The community organizer, who was the director of that agency, coordinated monthly meetings with representatives of all the local agencies like the Department of Family and Children's Services, Aging Services, Community Mental Health Program, Drug and Alcohol Services, Rape Crisis, Domestic Violence Center, Probation and Parole, Juvenile Justice, Health Department Services, and several other nonprofit agencies that served families. At one of these planning meetings, members discussed their most pressing concern for families. A needs assessment that was sent to all of the agencies revealed that child sexual abuse was on the rise, and diagnostic and treatment services for children was lacking in our community. Children had to be taken to another county for a forensic interview and medical evaluation. This was unacceptable, and the members of the Family Connection Group, under the leadership of the community organizer, worked together to write a grant to obtain funding for a new child advocacy center in our county. Members from all agencies worked together identifying what services they could provide, how they could participate in either writing the grant, obtaining a facility for the new program, providing training for new employees, or assisting with fund-raising. It took two years to complete the project but eventually the Children's Advocacy Center became a reality.

This demonstrates the effectiveness of a community organizer in identifying human needs and collaborating with others in the network of Human Services agencies to bring new and vital services to a region. Skills and techniques used in this process include developing needs assessments to determine what services are lacking in a community. This can be a survey that is sent to residents, Human Services agencies, and clients. *Research and evaluation* skills are important for a community organizer because they inform the worker of current services that are available and what needs to be changed. Knowing how to advocate for your clients and speak publicly about an issue is necessary to show your support. Workers must also mobilize their resources, knowing how to get everyone involved. They need to understand fund-raising strategies, which are often needed to

Human Services workers advocate for community issues and speak publicly about political concerns. Here a state representative talks with a community organization in Detroit.

Jim West/Alamy

keep a program from closing. They use outreach strategies to include people from rural areas, institutional settings, or other locales to broaden the issue at hand. The more people are involved in supporting an idea, the better. They must educate people on current and proposed policy changes for their state or region, and finally, they must understand how to write grants. Funding an existing program or developing a new one means that money must be obtained from a variety of sources. Community organizers must understand how to develop a diverse array of funds in order to sustain programs for their community (Burger, 2011).

Sometimes community organizers are also *community planners*. Human Services workers may sit on planning boards and help determine what new services should be provided in a community, where new schools should be built, or where neighborhood medical centers could be placed so that low-income families can access services. The idea is to help improve conditions for everyone, and the community organizer or planner may represent those residents who usually do not have a voice in the community like minorities, children, low-income people, immigrants, the disabled, homeless, or the chronically unemployed. It is important that everyone have a voice in planning or providing for new services. The purpose of a community organizer is to build a power base for his or her clients. Community organizers teach their consumers how to work together and use their group power to influence change. Workers educate the community about the social problems that exist and work with community groups to develop goals that will solve these problems. Community organizers and planners are advocates for the poor, the mentally ill, and the "invisible" people in a community who need representation. Community planners may interpret state and local research to determine what new or additional services are needed in a region. More schools, housing, public transportation, or health care may be necessary when populations increase or people move to the suburbs of a community. These community workers are often political activists who build support for their cause and often in the process teach their clients how to become involved in civic action and collective leadership (Stuart, 2004).

Human Services workers who act as community organizers are also called *change agents* because they use their skills to make the necessary changes in a system either by themselves or through collaboration with others (Mandell & Schram, 2010). They build trusting relationships with consumers, agency personnel, and community leaders. They educate others about the issue, speak publicly in a confident way about how change can occur, and they offer solutions to local problems. When they advocate for change, they encourage and empower the clients to begin to speak for themselves, helping them to take a more active role in determining their future (Woodside & McClam, 2011). Often they organize groups of people around an issue in order to gain public support for an idea. This is called a **change effort**, and when groups of people join together, we call this a **coalition**. Sometimes coalitions are needed to bring awareness about an issue to the community to see how much support is generated through the coalition of many Human Services agencies (Harris, Maloney, & Rother, 2004). We can often create a change by educating others, but we sometimes may need to be more persuasive if the desired change is not occurring.

Search for the video Poll Response: Norma Flores Lopez, Association of Farmworker Outreach Programs on the W.K. Kellogg Foundation website.

Engage with a partner in a Speech Writing Activity.

Test your comprehension of Community Organizing by completing this quiz.

Agency Management and Supervision

What Skills Does It Take to Be an Effective Agency Administrator?

After several years as a caseworker, then social service director, and later a home/school visitor, I was promoted to agency director of a child welfare program. I was knowledgeable about all the services we offered, was seen as a team player, initiated new ideas, and had supervised others for several years. It was a natural step to become an agency director and the pay and benefits were much better! At that time I had a master's degree in social work and several years of experience under my belt with the agency that had promoted me. Despite all of this preparation, after the first few weeks, I felt like I was drowning. Even though I had worked with my previous director, I had no idea of the depth and breadth of the job as an agency administrator. Although my background, education, and experience were solidly in the area of Human Services, I had no business or management background or skills, which would have been helpful in my role as an administrator. Some of my new responsibilities included:

- Working with a board of trustees
- Developing an annual budget of over $1 million
- Reviewing and updating our job descriptions
- Overseeing the hiring and firing of agency personnel
- Evaluating personnel
- Maintaining fiscal controls to stay within the annual budget

- Writing grants to increase our revenue
- Developing a plan for an annual fund-raising event
- Providing for staff training and development
- Creating both short and long range plans for the agency

It was also important that I understood how payroll worked since everyone wanted to be paid every two weeks! That meant that state and federal reports had to be filed on time each month and had to be accurate in order to draw down both our state and federal funds for the service that we provided. If we did not serve the contracted number of children and families, we could not ask for the contracted amount of money each month. It was extremely important that everyone did his or her part in writing reports, taking attendance at our child care facilities, and documenting what services were provided like counseling, in-home work with the families, transportation for children to our day care programs, and special services like speech therapy and medical care. That first year was an eye opening experience as I quickly learned how to complete each of these tasks. As the agency administrator, I was often the first one to come into the agency in the morning to begin my day and the last one out at night. Parent and staff complaints sometimes came my way, and often I was called to unexpected community meetings to represent my agency or to appeal for funds to some group. Let's take a look at some important strategies in managing people and agencies in Human Services.

If you are interested in agency management, be prepared to learn about *program planning, budgeting, fund-raising, working with boards of directors, grantsmanship, research and evaluation, and personnel management.*

Mission Statement

The first step is to become an administrator who understands his or her agency. Every organization has **a mission statement** with goals and objectives to guide the program. It is important to understand your mission statement because it tells you the purpose of the organization. If the mission is to provide quality, affordable child care, then you know what you are expected to do as the administrator. It is not necessary to hire counselors to provide marital therapy if that is not your mission. Some administrators make the mistake of providing services that are not in their mission simply because they received a grant to do so. Think carefully about your mission as you develop your short-term and long-range goals for the agency.

The mission statement is a written document that gives specific information about the agency's function. It is usually short but clear in its message of why the agency is in business. It can identify the intended population, goals of the organization, sources of funding, values that guide the program, and even the agency structure (Lewis, Lewis, Packard, & Souflee, 2006). The following is an example of a mission statement provided by the Council on Standards in Human Services Education, the national organization that accredits programs in Human Services:

The Council on Standards in Human Services Education is committed to assuring the quality, consistency, and relevance of human service education through research-based standards and a peer-review, accreditation process. Our vision is to promote excellence in human service education, provide quality assurance, and support standards of performance and practice through the accreditation process (Council for Standards in Human Services Education, 2011).

Mission statements usually appear in all the agency's documents and brochures or may be visible in the entrance to the facility. In one of our local Catholic hospitals, the mission statement can be clearly observed, written on a large plaque as you come through the door. It states that the facility will serve all people regardless of race, age, gender, disability, religion, or national origin.

Organizational Charts and Other Agency Documents

Agencies also have other written documents that explain their services, staff positions, funding sources, activities, fund-raising events, and long-range plans (Woodside & McClam, 2011). You can be asked to read *agency histories* that explain how the organization got started. This is also needed if you are writing a grant since funding sources will want this information. An **organizational chart** will allow you to see the structure of the organization and its chain of command. See the chart below to get a better understanding of how some human services agencies organize a chain of command (See Figure 7.1).

> ## Administrative
>
> *Understanding and Mastery: Managing organizations through leadership and strategic planning; planning and evaluating programs, services, and operational functions; supervision and human resource management*
>
> ───────────
>
> **Critical Thinking Question:** Imagine that you just opened a Human Services program for the homeless population in your community. Write a mission statement with goals and objectives that would explain the purpose of your program.

Job descriptions are also useful documents because they give specific duties that are required for each staff position. It is easier to do a job when you know what is expected of you. Often agencies will have *newsletters* that are placed at the entrance to the facility so visitors can read about activities the agency has engaged in like holiday programs, outreach services to new clients, or other special events. Approval of new grants or an upcoming fund-raising event can also be read about in a current issue of a newsletter.

Agency Auspices

There are many different types of Human Services agencies. If you think about your community, I will bet that you can name several programs that offer services to people. Some may be **private for-profit**. They are owned by one or more people, and they can charge what the going rate is for that service in your community. Any profits that are realized are divided among the owners. Examples of private, proprietary services include day care centers, counseling centers, some schools, even prisons. Another type of service is a **public or governmental agency**. They receive

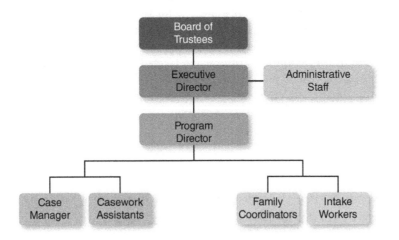

Figure 7.1

tax dollars to provide a service and this may be in the form of local, state, or federal monies. These agencies are usually very bureaucratic with a hierarchy of agency officials who implement policy and strict regulations based upon laws or governing bodies in the state. Some examples of these agencies are health departments, child welfare agencies, departments of juvenile justice, and state aging programs. The last type of agency is a **private nonprofit organization**. Agencies under this category are established as 501(c)(3) corporations with the Internal Revenue Service. This status exempts them from paying taxes and allows them to solicit tax-deductible donations to support their program. Nonprofit agencies are governed by a board of trustees, also called board of directors, usually made up of local members who develop policy for the program and who meet periodically to review the financial position of the agency. They hire the staff for the program and then appoint an agency director who manages the operation on a daily basis. The director reports to the board of trustees and keeps board members informed of agency activities, financial information, and changes to laws and regulations that govern the board's many programs.

Watch Creating a Business Plan for a Non-Profit Organization to learn how to start up a nonprofit organization.

Many Human Services agencies in the United States are considered private nonprofit; in addition to any local, state, or federal money they receive, they can also create annual fund-raising events. People who contribute money to those events can claim the amount as a tax-deductible contribution on their annual taxes. Examples of nonprofit organizations include programs like the United Way, the Red Cross, Girl Scouts of the USA, Boy Scouts of America, Second Harvest Food Bank, March of Dimes, and many other day care centers, community centers, mental health programs, or any church-affiliated services.

If you are employed in a private nonprofit organization, you will need to understand how to *conduct fund-raising, solicit donations, or write grants* since diversified funding is necessary to keep these organizations operating. Since they are not public programs, they are not guaranteed state or federal funds. Many people are surprised to learn that although the U.S. government provides many of the Human Services that are needed in America, like food stamps, Medicaid, housing and energy assistance, child care, community and economic development, youth development, and Social Security, the nonprofit sector is the primary vehicle the government uses to deliver most of the Human Services to Americans. It is more cost-effective for the government to deliver services by contracting with the nonprofit sector to provide services. However, many problems exist in this system. In a 2010 survey by the Urban Institute, it was found that although government contracted with nonprofit agencies to provide various social services, many problems occurred around underpayment, nonpayment, late payments, and reporting issues. The system appears to be so complex that agencies cannot easily navigate the system (Boris, deLeon, Roeger, & Nikolova, 2010).

Read Costs, Complexification, and Crisis from the National Council of Nonprofits to learn more about this issue.

Test your comprehension of Agency Management and Supervision (Part 1) by completing this quiz.

Strategic Planning

Every organization needs to have some direction. It needs a leader who has vision and can guide the growth and development of that program. Good leaders know how to reinforce responsibility, cultivate collaboration among the staff, allow for others to initiate new ideas, and inspire their workers to develop their individual potential as well as the potential of the organization (Kanter, 2006). Successful programs have people who want to be there, who look forward to coming to work, who think outside of the box with new ideas for services and programs for people. We all have worked in programs that were exciting, and the people were enthusiastic, and I'm sure you have worked in places that were not so inspiring. As an administrator, you have the responsibility to set the tone for your agency so the *development of short- and long-term goals* is important. What do you think you can realistically accomplish this year? What do others think? Learning how to collaborate as a team, and working together toward the agency's goals is important. Once the goals are in place then specific steps to meet those goals must be established. If your goal is to increase service to another county this year, how will you do it? The objectives are the specific steps you will take to meet your goal. Will you hire an additional staff person for that new county or will you add cases to your existing workers? Thinking through your goals and objectives and then discussing with your staff how the goals will be accomplished is necessary so that everyone is involved in the process.

Budgeting

Everyone has to live within a budget and it is no different in a Human Services agency. It is important that the director knows how to develop an operating budget and then maintains fiscal control of the agency. When you develop a budget, you list all of the income or revenue you anticipate coming into your agency. That might include federal, state, or local funding, money raised through fund-raising events if your organization is private nonprofit, client fees that are charged, and any grant money that you may receive. Then you list all of the expenses you anticipate including your staff salaries, fringe benefits, rent for your building, utilities, office supplies or service supplies like food if you have a kitchen, transportation charges, etc. Your budget needs to be balanced so if you have $150,000 in income, you must have the same in expenses.

Watch Harvard Human Services Summit Closing Remarks given by Jerry Friedman, Accenture's director of strategic initiatives.

A Human Services Summit was conducted at Harvard University in 2010. National, state, and local leaders of Human Services organizations came together to discuss their needs and addressed possible solutions. At this meeting, outcomes in Human Services that could be achieved through generative, integrative, and collaborative business models were discussed. Remember that Human Services is an interdisciplinary major. Understanding business principles can be worthwhile when it comes to managing an organization. This is especially important when it comes to fiscal matters like budgeting and financial planning. So gathering a cross section of professionals together to address solutions to community problems is advantageous.

Learn more about the annual summits.

Personnel and Program Management

In addition to understanding your agency and its mission, developing budgets and sound fiscal practices, and planning for strategic growth, leaders of organizations must be knowledgeable about how best to manage their programs. It is important to hire the right people for the right jobs. According to Bossidy & Charan (2009), not enough attention is given to this task by leaders of organizations. People selection seems to be the key in successful businesses. Hiring the right people and then developing their abilities leads to good planning and leadership development. This is a critical job in any organization and should be a key role of the agency administrator. You should spend as much time developing your people as you do on budgeting, planning, and overseeing finances.

Once an administrator has helped develop a vision for the organization, it is important that people feel empowered to implement that change. Sometimes that is not possible when structures, skills, systems, or supervisors impede that process (Kotter, 1996). It takes the entire staff working together to recognize what barriers exist that are preventing change from occurring. How can existing structures be changed? What kinds of training will people need in order to move the organization forward? Is everyone on board with these changes? If key people are opposed to a new vision or agency changes, they can prevent lower-level employees from taking action.

Leaders of successful organizations support *individual and system accountability*. They do this by holding themselves accountable and by communicating clearly with everyone in the organization what is expected of them. They make sure that individuals get the information they need to complete their job and that training is available where needed. People feel challenged and motivated when they are part of an organized effort to increase performance. Leaders need to make sure that mutual respect, communication, and collaboration is occurring (Kanter, 2004). That means that structures may need to be put into place so all workers can meet and discuss new ways of doing things, evaluate how change is taking place, and make adjustments when necessary. Weekly meetings may have to be put on the agenda with efforts made to include everyone in the process so there is balanced collaboration. Recognizing individual achievements is also important and leads to mutual respect among workers.

Recognizing the work we do in Human Services is important. At this annual awards programs for Extraordinary Science and Public Service, the award is huge!

Fund-raising and Grant Writing

Knowing how to raise money is an important part of an administrator's job in the nonprofit world. It can be done through an annual fund drive where money is collected to provide a service. Letters are sent to donors soliciting funds, and in return for a contribution, a receipt and thank-you note is given to the person for tax purposes. Sometimes events are organized around a particular theme or program and become annual fund-raisers that the community supports. In the area where I live, *dinners and auctions* are a popular form of fund-raising. A committee meets to determine how many items it wants to obtain for the auction. Some members are good at soliciting products from local businesses in return for a tax donation. Other members are good at planning the dinner and preparing the event itself. A date is chosen, tickets are sold, and the dinner and auction are held in the agency, at a local restaurant, or in a rented hall. All proceeds benefit the private nonprofit program. Other events that can produce income for a nonprofit include *creating a cookbook, organizing a formal charity ball, dances, carnivals, costume parties, telethons, walkathons, and marathons.*

Read about other creative fund-raising ideas for nonprofit organizations from The Fundraising Authority.

In addition to active fund-raising, agencies can receive money through **grants**. The idea of writing a grant may seem daunting, but if you get some training and a little experience, you can become successful at grantsmanship. Grants are monies that are provided through local, state and federal governments, private sources, and foundations or corporations. You do not need to repay grant money since it is not a loan. Once you are approved for funds, you can use them in your agency. Grants can be written for operating expenses that you have every day in your program. They can also be written for capital expenses like construction of a new building for a community center, or renovation of a kitchen in your nursing home, or purchase of a bus for your day care center. Although private, proprietary Human Services agencies and public programs may apply for some grants or foundation money, it is usually the private nonprofit agencies that are competing for the funds.

Writing a grant has several steps. First you must consider what you want the money for and then proceed to locate grants and foundations that offer money for what you need. It is not a good idea to write a grant simply because money is available. You must use the money for the intended purpose. If you apply for a $20,000 grant to hire a part-time caseworker so you can expand services, you cannot use the money to purchase new equipment for your agency. Grant money has only one purpose and that is very specifically explained in the grant criteria. The money usually must be kept separately, and an audit done at the end of the granting period to confirm compliance.

The next steps in the grant proposal usually include writing about the history of the organization, its mission statement and organizational chart, information on the board of trustees, goals and objectives of the program, program activities, annual budget, and plan for evaluation. Some grant applications are only a few pages in length, but federal grants can require very thorough information, including needs assessments of your community. Sometimes these grant applications can be over 50 pages, including appendices and other attachments. You can learn to write a grant by attending seminars at your local college or through continuing education programs.

Want to know what it's like to be a DRK Entrepreneur? Explore DRK Entrepreneurs to find out.

Social entrepreneurs are Human Services workers who create businesses to meet the needs of people. The Draper Richard Kaplan (DRK) Foundation offers a grant to develop or sustain your own Human Services agency. Are you up to the challenge?

Working with Boards of Directors

As an administrator of a private nonprofit agency, it is important that you have the skills to work with your **board of directors**. Each organization will have a set of bylaws establishing its governing rules and regulations. The bylaws are developed when the organization is created and the directors who write the bylaws agree upon various requirements for the organization. The directors identify the number of trustees they feel are required to oversee the agency, the number of meetings needed per year, and the set of officers who would oversee the agency along with their specific duties. It is important that you read the bylaws so you understand how your board of directors was created. Then you will need to create your schedule of meetings. Are you required to meet monthly, quarterly, or annually? What function does your board serve? Is it an advisory board or are there specific officers with responsibilities of a president, secretary, and treasurer? In my role as child welfare administrator, I had to prepare and submit monthly financial statements to the board treasurer who would approve or deny large purchases. He was also responsible, along with me, to sign payroll checks for the employees. So, you can see how important it is to have good working relationships with members of your board.

All nonprofit organizations are required to have an annual **audit** by a certified accounting agency. This financial evaluation is a very thorough appraisal of your agency and will determine the financial health of your organization. It will show whether you are in the red (You lost money and went over your budget.) or you are in the black (You didn't lose money and you are within your budget.). The audit then needs to be approved by the board of trustees since it is ultimately financially liable for the organization. It is the board of trustees that determines if the agency can continue to operate as usual or if more revenue is needed or expenses need to be cut.

You can see how basic courses in business could be very useful to a Human Services student. Consider adding some business electives if you have the space in your curriculum to do so, especially if you see yourself administering a Human Services agency in the future.

Research and Evaluation

All Human Services organizations need to demonstrate that they have *met their goals and objectives* for the year. Therefore, *research and evaluation* is an *essential* part of Human Services. If the administrator of a Meals-on-Wheels program says the program will provide in-home meals for 200 elderly clients each day, 5 days a week, for 52 weeks a year, the administrator must document that it was done. There are *several ways to evaluate your services*. All organizations are accountable for the service they provide in order for them to continue to get their funding. This means that records must be kept of meals served, counseling sessions held, number of people attending an event, or money spent on an agency activity for clients.

When you take your research courses, you will learn about the two methods of social research. One type is **quantitative research,** and it involves evaluating numeric data. You can collect information and analyze numbers to demonstrate this type of research. For instance, as the Meals-on-Wheels administrator, I can have my staff use daily delivery sheets to show that we distributed meals to 200 people each day. We collect the sheets daily and input the information so we have a database of what was delivered and where it was delivered. Now I have actual numeric data on the number of meals delivered each day.

How do I know that my customers like the meals that I delivered? How do I know that they even opened their doors and received the meals? A different type of research and evaluation will give me this information. **Qualitative research** is more descriptive and is not necessarily numeric. I may send my customers a survey of open-ended questions to complete. I put this in a return envelope and deliver it along with their daily meal, asking them to complete it and mail it back in the postage-paid envelope. I may ask them to rate the quality of their food or ask them to simply write about their meal. I may get 200 different responses and it may take me a lot longer to analyze my data with qualitative research. I may also have volunteers call each customer to get the information I want.

Now when I put my quantitative (numeric) research analysis together with my qualitative (descriptive) research analysis, I have a very strong picture of my Meals-on-Wheels service. I will know how many meals I served and if people like the food. I will also be able to tell if people actually got their meals. This information is then written up in a report that I will share with others. We will use this data in our agency to improve services, I will share it with my board of directors, and my funding sources will also want this information. Remember this when you take your research courses. Most students complain about these courses because they do not see their relevance to the work they want to do. They always ask me, "Why do I have to take research anyway, when all I want to do is counsel or work with people?" Well, now you know!

> **Administrative**

Understanding and Mastery: Developing budgets and monitoring expenditures; grant and contract negotiations; legal and regulatory issues and risk management; managing professional development of staff; recruiting and managing volunteers

Critical Thinking Question: Of all the strategies you have read about, what strategy do you think you would be good at right now?

. . . .

. **Test your comprehension of <u>Agency Management and</u>**
. **<u>(Part 2) by completing this quiz.</u>**

Around the Globe

Practicing Skills Learned in the Classroom in a Volunteer Setting

Many schools of social work and Human Services programs across the country are now offering students the opportunity to put into practice those skills, techniques, and values they have learned about in their classroom. It is no longer necessary to wait until you graduate to begin to help others. At Saint Leo University, where I teach, students can join S.E.R.V.E., Students Engaged in Rewarding Volunteer Experiences, for service learning challenges.

Watch Saint Leo University's <u>S.E.R.V.E.</u>, Service Learning Program, closing ceremony..

Students use their semester breaks to help others through mission trips to such places as an orphanage in San Jose, California, rebuilding efforts in the Gulf Coast through Habitat for Humanity in Mississippi and Georgia, working with disadvantaged youth in Costa Rica, Puerto Rico, Cuba, or by helping abused horses and other animals by working at an animal shelter in New York or other places. Each year the students choose different locations and projects that deserve their assistance. Sometimes they have to learn a new language, but they can always count on meeting new people, finding out about a different culture, and using the skills they have learned in the classroom. Service learning is available in many schools and is a great way to begin your Human Services career, although there is no pay and usually no credit given for the experience.

Putting Strategies to Work

Imagine That You Are an Agency Director

Now that you have an understanding of some strategies and techniques to use in managing Human Services agencies, let's have some fun and try them out. Let's assume that you are the new director of the United Cerebral Palsy agency in your area. You serve a two-county region with a staff of 12. Currently you have 65 families with service going to a center-based program in the city where people bring their children under the age of 5, three times a week for physical therapy and socialization. The program is from 9 a.m. to noon. Home services are provided for older children and adults after school and in the evening, within a 20-mile radius of the center. You employ two nurses, four Human Services workers/case managers, yourself (the director), an assistant director, two early education teachers, and two physical therapists. Although your funding is intact, your board of trustees would like you to develop an annual fund-raiser to support existing programs and possibly to begin offering more services in the rural areas of your counties.

Consider what type of fund-raiser you would develop. Who would you target to come to this event? What is your goal regarding how much you would like to raise in the first year? Think carefully about this event. Take out a sheet of paper and write down everything you will need for this event. Consider the date, number of expected participants, cost of attending, cost to organize the event, where the event will take place, and what you will need for the event. Now make a list of who will do what. Give yourself 15 minutes to plan this fabulous event and write down all the plans. Then put yourself into groups of four to discuss your events. Whose plan is the most realistic? Give each other some feedback on your planning.

Think Human Services

How Does Being Interdisciplinary Help Our Profession?

It is important that when we think Human Services, we also think about other disciplines and how they relate and interact with our own discipline. That is what makes Human Services so special. Our profession is unlike any other because it is made up of other professions. A true Human Services professional also understands perspectives from psychology, sociology, social work, political science, economics, criminal justice, or any of the other social sciences. Now, I'm telling you in this chapter that we need to recognize how business principles could also enlighten us and make us better Human Services administrators. We don't seek to close our borders, we seek to open them wider while learning from other professions. This is what makes our profession great. This open attitude will continue to broaden our perspectives and allow us to better understand and work with others in our agencies, our communities, our educational institutions, our nation, and our world. If we always think about how Human Services can learn something from another discipline, we can't help but move our profession forward. This is what I love about Human Services.

In the book *Good to Great*, Jim Collins describes a five-level hierarchy of leaders. He describes certain businesses that are good and the leadership model that was used to get them there. In order to move forward and become great, it is the leader of the organization who must have the capacity to do this. He goes on to give specific examples of how great businesses and organizations are grown by leaders who cultivate exceptional skills that are both business and interpersonally oriented. Great companies have leaders who demonstrate personal humility and ambition for their institution rather than for themselves (Collins, 2001). When we strive to build lasting Human Services programs that meet the needs of our communities, we can move our profession, our agencies, our nation, and our world from good to great.

According to Collins (2001), specific capabilities propel people toward Level 5 leadership. A Level 5 is the highest level of leader. Such leaders build greatness through personal humbleness and intense ambition for their institution. They are more concerned with their organization moving ahead than with any credit given to them for their sacrifices. Level 4 is right below Level 5. Level 4 leaders are still excellent leaders because they establish a vision and set high goals and standards for other workers to reach. The next step down is Level 3, with workers who are considered highly effective. They use resources wisely and utilize cost-efficient measures in meeting program goals for the organization. Level 2 leaders are lower-level leaders but are considered valuable members of the team because they make individual contributions based on their skills. They work well with the team to reach the group goals and objectives. Level 1 is the lowest level of workers who are very well trained and participate with their team using their knowledge, skills, talent, and good work ethics.

Linking Strategies to Practice

Think of Yourself as a Social Entrepreneur

Put yourselves into groups of three and imagine that all of you are social entrepreneurs in your local community. Now think of a social problem that lacks current services in your community, like homelessness, child abuse, teen pregnancy, domestic violence, drug and alcohol abuse, mental health issues, poor quality child care, juvenile delinquency, chronic unemployment, illiteracy, developmental disabilities, or poor health care. What services would help to meet the needs of one of these social issues? Now develop a program with services to meet the need you have described. Look at the requirements for the Kaplan proposal, which is about three pages long. Develop the proposal considering your mission statement, program goals and objectives, program activities or what you will actually provide (i.e., day care, employment, training, access to health care, etc.), how you will do it, an annual budget, and your plan of evaluation. Remember that you can request up to $300,000 over a three-year period, so you can be granted $100,000 in your first year. Have fun. Give yourselves at least 30–45 minutes to work on this exercise and then present your plan to the class. Get some feedback from them. Is this a good proposal? Is it competitive? Realistic? Could it help solve the problem? How can you sustain the program financially after three years when the grant is up?

Read the Draper Richard Kaplan Foundation's Our Grants to learn how they *partner with entrepreneurs to build strong, capable organizations.*

Did You Know?

Burnout Is a Real Condition in Human Services. Know How to Prevent It.

Working while in close personal contact with people to whom you are giving services can be stressful at times. Be prepared for consumers who are angry, disrespectful, hurt, or unappreciative. This can be difficult when we give so much of ourselves to others.

In Human Services we call this **burnout**. Sometimes it can manifest itself in physical symptoms causing the worker to experience headaches, sleeplessness, stomach problems, and anxiety. This can result in workers wanting desperately to leave the organization or the profession, vowing never to work with people again. While they are waiting to exit the agency, their work suffers, and they often are negative about their job and peers. Sometimes workers feel like they have no place else to go, and so they continue to work, but in a robotic fashion, doing only what is absolutely necessary and avoiding any complications. They maintain limited interactions with clients and other workers in the agency. Their work is rigid, and they come across as uncaring workers. This is known as **encapsulation** and is as damaging as the negative, burned-out worker who can't wait to leave Human Services for another job.

Did you know that when you feel burned-out in a Human Services job it is not your fault? It is not because you can't do the job or because you aren't good with people. Lots of researchers have found multiple reasons for this phenomenon called burnout (Mandell & Schram, 2010). Most of these reasons are related to the systems where we are employed. Some causes of burnout include:

- Sociological conflict known as alienation—when the structure of a organization effects people and they can't see the positive impact they are having on clients because the work is fragmented
- Psychological conflict—worker's unconscious conflicts are reactivated when the client has the same issue as the worker
- Personal values conflict with those of the agency—for example, working in an abortion clinic if you are a very religious person
- Low pay and few benefits, which prevent workers from paying their own bills, or they may struggle with working overtime to earn more money or taking on a second job
- Heavy caseload or expectation that everyone will work until the job is done
- Very bureaucratic organization with stiff rules and regulations
- Tight schedules with not enough time for all the appointments, meetings, and additional work
- Low work space or poor resources that prevent workers from doing effective work on behalf of the clients; not having a private office to meet with clients or having old computers or technology to store client data
- Agency apathy when it comes to helping workers or clients
- Resistant clients who do not want help from the agency
- Difficulty helping involuntary clients or not having enough resources to help them

It is suggested that as Human Services supervisors, we hold the key to preventing burnout in our workers. So, we want to make sure that as Human Services students you are prepared to become a good supervisor. There are a variety of things that we can do to help workers identify stresses of the job. Make time to discuss difficult cases with your workers when you become a supervisor. Hold weekly meetings with your staff to collaborate on cases and allow workers to share successful client stories with others. Everyone likes to hear about a job well done. How can it be repeated? Be careful not to overload your staff with work. Make sure people are taking their required time off and having time to refresh. If they work overtime, give people time off. Support salary increases and benefits so people feel appreciated. Set aside time for social gatherings at work so people can discuss something other than work. Celebrate special occasions like workers' birthdays. Listen to problems your workers bring to you and, in difficult cases, help them make decisions. Set up a support group for your workers so they can bring cases and client issues to the group for resolution.

As a worker, make sure you get enough sleep, exercise, and eat nutritious food each day. Working through lunch is not a healthy option since you need a break from the work and good food to finish your workday. Plan activities outside of work so that you are not always working, planning to work, or thinking about work. Make sure you have a group of friends outside of your workplace who can talk about other things. You are less likely to continuously talk about work if you are not with people you work with. Remember the reason that you took the job was to help people. Keep your attitude positive and practice getting enough time away from the agency to have a separate life outside of work.

If you can't get beyond your negative feelings and still don't feel that you are being rejuvenated, then you may need to consider different employment. It is not fair to you or to your clients if you remain in an unhealthy, unresponsive environment that is making you sick and unhappy.

What Would You Do?

Change the Way You Think, Feel, and Work Each Day

After learning about the strategies you would use to organize communities, plan change efforts, or manage Human Services programs, what would you do if you were employed in an agency where consumers came last, services were poor, the staff was not respected, and there was no collaboration? Suppose you were expected to begin work by 9 a.m. each day and work until 5 p.m. with a one-hour lunch break. However, there were so many clients that people often worked after 5 p.m. and lunch breaks were cut short to accommodate all the scheduled appointments. You were expected to determine a client's eligibility for a counseling service, but you were not told if the client ever received the service. You could see that the client needed more than just counseling since he or she also appeared depressed, agitated, and often angry. You did not have staff meetings to discuss what else could be done in your agency to help the client. You wondered about other community services that would benefit your client. You found yourself getting tired around 3 p.m. and you couldn't wait until 5 p.m. rolled around and you could go home. Some workers in the agency were especially negative, and you found yourself working in your office with the door closed so you could avoid other workers. You found yourself thinking that you only needed ten more years to have your retirement vested, but you didn't know if you could make it that long. What would you do? Make a list for yourself and then put yourself into a small group where you can discuss this example. What did you decide to do? What would others do? Is this realistic?

Recall what you learned in this chapter by completing the Chapter Review.

CHAPTER 8

Ed Andrieski/AP Images

Current Social Issues

What Are the Current Problems Facing Our Society Today? How Can Human Services Workers Help to Prevent or Work to Solve These Problems?

Where were you on July 20th, 2012, when the world learned of the incredible violence inflicted on 79 people from Colorado who attended the new Batman movie, *The Dark Knight Rises*? It seems impossible that a shooter entered the theatre and murdered 12 people and horribly injured 59 more at point-blank range. It seems more impossible still that the shooter was a young, neuroscience major who had recently dropped out of his Ph.D. program. What causes people to plan and carry out such devious acts of violence? This is difficult to understand how more and more of these incidents occur each year. How can Human Services professionals either help to prevent these senseless acts or help people cope with the outcome of these tragedies? Violence is just one of the many social issues Human Services workers deal with on a daily basis. We will look at many of these problems in this chapter. Do you think this violence could have been prevented? How so?

Read an article on the <u>Colorado shooting suspect, James Holmes</u>.

What's It All About?

Many Current Social Issues Require an Array of Human Services to Meet the Needs of the Client

The longer you live, the more likely you are to remember historic events in your own lifetime. Your impression of those events or the information you have heard from others can have a lasting impact. My grandparents often talked about the Great Depression and what they had to do to survive. It affected how they saved and spent money and where they hid the cache they compiled from years of working. My grandmother would put her earnings in the freezer where she was sure no one could steal it or even find it! Living during the Depression taught her to be extremely cautious with her funds. We of course thought it was funny when she came to visit and would immediately hide her cash under the ice cubes. We were not as affected by the same life events that had affected her. Clearly major happenings, both positive and negative, can have an imprint on our collective minds. My generation could remember where they were when President John F. Kennedy was assassinated. Your generation may remember 9/11 and the attack on the Twin Towers in New York. Often what is an important issue today may get trumped by a bigger issue tomorrow.

Although many events in our lifetime are memorable, some may stand out. In my lifetime, for instance, I can remember sitting in the living room with my family and watching astronaut John Glenn blast off into space for a journey around the earth. No one could believe it was possible in 1962 to orbit the earth, but everyone sat glued to their television to see if the space capsule would continue on its journey or fall backwards to the ground. I remember 1969, when American astronauts in *Apollo 11* first walked on the moon. Then in 1986, the unthinkable happened. A shuttle mission was scheduled to start a new program, Teacher in Space. Sharon Christa McAuliffe was chosen from 11,000 teacher applicants to be the first teacher to go into space. However, after only seconds into the mission the *Challenger* exploded, killing all crew members. It was shocking to absorb this information after so many successful NASA flights.

Learn more about the history of the US Space Program on the John F. Kennedy Presidential Library and Museum website.

I can also remember when we got our first color television in the late 1960s. It was a big deal to watch all the variety shows and sitcoms in color. Can you remember where you were when you heard about national or global events like the Columbine shootings, or the Virginia Tech shootings, or the 9/11 disaster in New York at the Twin Towers, or the earthquake in Haiti? Did you watch the royal wedding of Prince William and Kate Middleton? These are the events that mark the passing of time in our life and the history of our family, community, state, nation, and world. If you are from another country you probably remember significant events from other places where you might have been, like the earthquake and Tsunami in Japan. What are current events today quickly become historic events by next week. Just how do these events impact us as human beings? How do we react to such news? Do we respond by thinking about how we can be helpful or is it too painful to think about serious events and so we ignore the news or hope someone else is doing something useful? People react to events in a variety of ways, choosing to cope in whatever way they can. Human Services professionals are usually the people who step up and deal with the issues first themselves and then try to help others cope with the aftermath of the situation. Let's take a look at the many current social issues we are faced with today that require an array of Human Services to meet the needs of all human beings on earth.

Watch documentary footage of the 2011 Japan Earthquake and Tsunami showing the rushing waters.

Global issues have a lasting impact on us. Watch the video on the tsunami in Japan for real-life footage of its catastrophic damage. Be aware of how this video makes you think or feel. What would you do if you were in Japan at the time of the tsunami? How would you cope with such a disaster? How would you help others?

Poverty

Issues, Rising Rates, and Populations Affected

No issue is more pervasive in our time than poverty. It is unimaginable to many people that a country as rich as the United States has so many people who go to bed hungry each night. Do you know who the poorest people are in the United States? If you said children, you would be correct. According to the United States Census Bureau, the *younger you are in the United States, the more likely you are to be poor.* In fact, 26% of children under age 5 and 21% of those of ages 5 to 17 are currently living in poverty.

What does it mean to live in poverty anyway? There are two measures of poverty in the United States, which is sometimes confusing. These are the **Poverty Threshold** and the **Poverty Guideline**. Statistics from the United States Census are used to classify the number of people each year who live in poverty. This is called the poverty threshold. A simplified version of the threshold is used by the Department of Health and Human Services to determine who is eligible for federal poverty programs like food stamps, school lunch, and other federal programs. These are called poverty guidelines. The United States *defines poverty by establishing an income level below which you are considered poor and eligible for federal or state services.* Although the cost of living may vary from one state to another, the poverty guideline is a federal standard and may vary in the 48 contiguous states and the District of Columbia, as well as for Alaska and Hawaii.

Sociologists tell us there are different types of poverty (Carl, 2010). If you lose a job and have difficulty paying your bills for a short time until you are employed again, we call this **transitional poverty**. If your employment is unstable and you find that you have a job for a few months and then get laid off often, we call this **marginal poverty**. Families that are poor from one generation to the next and struggle with stable means to support their children live in **residual poverty**. Finally, **absolute poverty** exists when a person doesn't have enough to survive. Although many people in the United States may suffer from the first three types of poverty, not as many live in absolute poverty. People in undeveloped parts of the world that struggle to find food and water would be examples of absolute poverty. In the United States, programs like church soup kitchens, homeless shelters, and food stamps assist people with basic needs for survival. When we compare ourselves with others and their level of poverty we call this **relative poverty**. For example, if we think our car is too old to drive compared to our neighbor's, we may be relatively poor (Carl, 2010).

Who is living in poverty in the United States? Well, single women with children have a higher percentage of living in poverty. As a result, children are the largest group of those who are affected by poverty issues in the United States. One in five children is a victim of poverty. A woman who earns less than $19,090 a year and has children to support is living below the **poverty line**. If she earns less than $9,545, this is considered extreme poverty (Children's Defense Fund, 2012a). She is eligible for services if she lives in extreme poverty. So poverty is linked to low wages, which is often linked to lack of education and to family or marital structure. More single mothers live in poverty than women who are married or who live with a partner who shares expenses.

Not everyone realizes that he or she may be eligible for assistance on such meager wages. Programs like *Food Stamps* through the U.S. Department of Agriculture, cash assistance through *Temporary Assistance to Needy Families,* or *Medicaid* can help families. Human services workers are employed in all of these agencies and they inform people, often their family, friends, and neighbors, of services that are available. I had a student who would come to class and announce when the *federal energy assistance program (EOA)* would start taking applications for utility assistance in the winter. She knew that many of the Human Services students and their families were eligible for the subsidy! Interestingly enough, these students did not consider themselves poor. They were surprised when she announced one night in class what the income guidelines were. They never saw themselves as clients, but they did recognize how difficult it was to work, pay bills, and feed and clothe their children. Other nonprofit organizations like churches, shelters, and food programs such as the *Second Harvest Food Bank* all work together to provide services to low-income families as well.

Why do we even care about poverty anyway? Did you know that of all the industrialized countries on the earth, you are more likely to live in poverty if you reside in the United States? Many people are surprised by that fact. I say, "shame on us." How could we distribute our resources so unequally that in 2010, 16.4 million children were poor and 7.4 million lived in extreme poverty (Children's Defense Report, 2012b)? Poverty increases depending on where you reside in the United States. The poorest white children represent about 13% of the population and most likely live in states like West Virginia, Kentucky, Arkansas, Tennessee, and Mississippi. It's even worse for black children who have a poverty rate of 39% and may live in the top five states with the highest percentage of poverty for them. Places like Maine, Wisconsin, Nebraska, Iowa, and Oregon have this distinction. The five states with the highest rates for poverty for Hispanic children include South Carolina, North Carolina, Tennessee, Pennsylvania, and Georgia (Children's Defense Fund Report, 2012c). All in all, poverty costs the United States about $500 billion per year!

What are the outcomes that we can expect if children grow up in poverty? Put your thinking cap on and imagine what happens when you are poor. Why is it so important that we provide services to help children grow up in healthy, productive families? If you said that children who are poor don't eat as well and lack a healthy diet you are correct on that point. Poor families often live in areas where they cannot access affordable, quality foods like fresh fruits and vegetables, good sources of protein, and high-fiber carbohydrates. Often poor families take children to fast-food restaurants where they can get free or cheap children's meals they can afford. It may be filling, but those meals often contain high fat, sodium, and calories, with low protein. Children from low-income communities are often the same children who suffer with diabetes, obesity, and other health problems. *Poor health is definitely linked to poverty. Dropout rates are also higher in poor communities.* These children often do not complete high school, they have greater *difficulty finding jobs* without a diploma, *they receive lower wages*, and *work fewer hours* than those with more education. So *health, education,* and *employment* are three criteria that have *lower outcomes* for children growing up in poverty.

I hope that this disturbs you and motivates you to do something to stop this trend. We need Human Services workers who will talk about these issues, challenge our community leaders to develop new and better programs for families who live in poverty, and who voice their opinion to our elected officials. You need to *vote* and ask questions of the people who are running in your state and national elections. What do they plan to do in your area for people who need help? Do they realize this is costing the taxpayers a lot of money if nothing is done?

One person who has been very supportive of programs for all of our poor children is **Marian Wright Edelman.** An activist for children's rights, she began her career in the

1960s and is the founder and President of **The Children's Defense Fund** in Washington. Its mission is to *Leave No Child Behind*.

> **Read more about <u>Marian Wright Edelman</u>, her life and struggles as a graduate of Yale Law School and being the first black woman accepted to the Mississippi state bar.**

The Children's Defense Fund publishes an annual report of issues affecting children in the United States. Read all about poverty and the demographics that define it. You can look up information on your state as well. This is a great website to use for any research papers you are doing on poverty or child welfare. You simply can't be in Human Services and not be knowledgeable about Marian Wright Edelman and all that she has done and is still doing for our poorest members of society.

> **Explore the <u>Children's Defense Fund</u> to learn about what is happening in your state and the nation. Go to the main webpage, click on Research Library, and then scroll down to State Data on Children.**

Working with children and families who live in poverty is sure to occur if you work in Human Services. Since poverty is so pervasive you will see its influence if you work in child welfare agencies, schools, public health clinics, day care settings, hospitals, or residential care programs. If you want to work specifically with those who live in poverty, look for programs for the economically disadvantaged like Head Start, homeless shelters, federal housing programs like HUD, or Economic Opportunity Authorities. Review the website, <u>Innovations for Poverty Action</u>, for information on careers in this field.

Human Services Delivery Systems

Understanding and Mastery: Economic and social class systems including systemic causes of poverty

Critical Thinking Question: Why are you 2½ times more likely to live in poverty if you are a child than if you are a senior citizen in the United States? Consider your community. Where do the poorest members live? Are they getting the services that they need? What are some short-term and long-range goals that you think can help change that community?

> **Test your comprehension of <u>Poverty</u> by completing this quiz.**

Crime and Violence

Criminal Offenses, Domestic Violence, and Child Abuse and Neglect

I started this chapter by talking about some violent events that have occurred in the recent past. Over time people have become so used to these acts of violence and the periodic outbursts that even though no one likes to hear about a shooting, abduction, or a carjacking, they are not surprised. When the act loses its ability to shock people, we call this **desensitization**. Psychologists have found in their research that people who watch continual acts of violence on television are less affected by real or televised violence than people who have not watched acts of violence. People who are not desensitized to the senseless acts of horror are more upset when they engage in watching televised violence or see real violence (Mullin & Linz, 1995).

What is crime and violence? According to sociologists, when a person breaks a law a **crime** has been committed. A *crime is a violation of a written norm that has become a law* (Carl, 2010). Crimes can be *violent* and *nonviolent*. Stealing, shoplifting, and selling drugs are crimes because laws are broken, but they are not necessarily violent crimes. If during the sale of drugs a shooting takes place then the crime becomes violent. *White-collar crimes* for instance involve the *loss of property* but do not necessarily physically harm anyone. However, white-collar crimes committed by those in high-status jobs actually cost the United States about $500 billion a year, much more than *street crime* (Reiman & Leighton, 2012). Crimes like cheating Medicare, embezzling, evading income tax, and bribing officials are all considered white-collar crimes. Violent crimes, on the other hand, involve physically harming another person. Shootings, vehicular accidents, arson, and assaults are all considered violent crimes. Currently more people are in prison for non-violent crimes due to *zero tolerance* and *three-strikes laws*, which require automatic, mandatory sentences for three-time felons. Mandatory sentences can carry life imprisonment for crimes like selling drugs (Henslin, 2013). Although it may seem like more violent acts are being committed recently, there has actually been a decrease in violent crime (Blumstein & Wallman 2006). The FBI reports that violent crimes in the United States have fallen for the fifth straight year in a row. The use of media to extend the coverage of these events makes some people wonder if too much attention is being given to criminals who commit violent offenses.

Did you know that the *United States has the highest incarceration rate in the world*? Although we have less than 5% of the world's population, we have almost a quarter of the earth's prisoners. The United States represents about 4.6% of the total global population but holds the title for 26% of the world's incarcerated population! This rate is 6 times higher than countries like Canada and 13 times higher than Japan (Ferrante, 2011). If you consider that for every 100,000 people, 750 are in jail, you will get a better picture of our criminal justice system (Benokraitis, 2012). My guess is that you know someone who is in a local jail or sentenced to hard time in a state prison. Changes in state and federal laws make both violent and nonviolent actions felonies, which may require mandatory sentences.

If you have an interest in criminal justice, you are sure to find a place in this system, however it may not be in a rehabilitative position. Prisons today are overcrowded and contain many agitated, aggressive, and mentally ill prisoners. Assaults and rapes are common; there are limited freedoms, and no privacy. Although rehabilitation is proven to be a factor in helping inmates adjust to life on the outside after their release, not enough services exist. Human Services workers are needed to help them find jobs, housing, money for rent or food, a driver's license, counseling, or drug and alcohol treatment (Benokraitis, 2012). However, the employment positions that exist for workers are more likely to be in the area of correctional guards or jobs designed to help warehouse these individuals. The figures for incarceration in our prison system continue to rise

Test your comprehension of Crime and Violence by completing this quiz.

Overcrowding in prisons is common in many states. In California prison riots have been blamed on over-crowding. In this photo you can see how prison beds are lined-up dorm-style in the gym to accommodate as many prisoners as possible.

ZUMA Press, Inc./Alamy

along with the recidivism rates. About 50% of those who are released return within three years after committing another crime.

Domestic Violence

When we talk about crime and violence, we can't forget *gender violence*. What do you know about **domestic violence** against women? Most communities have an emergency shelter to protect women and their children from men who batter and abuse them. I have had several students over the years who did not recognize the damage done to them or their children until they were in a Human Services class and we discussed destructive relationships. Women with low self-esteem can be victimized and controlled by men who engage in *verbal abuse*. This can also eventually escalate to *physical abuse*. *Alcohol and drugs* don't help the situation either. Often, women feel like they can handle the situation. "Oh, he's just drunk tonight. He will be okay tomorrow." They tolerate a bad home life because they need his money to pay the bills, or they believe they are worthless and couldn't find anyone else. Did you know that research shows 11% of men who abuse their wives or girlfriends will actually kill them (Zastrow 2009)? It is difficult for workers to specialize in this area for long periods of time because there is such high turnover and burnout of professionals in this field. Do you know that in my professional experience I learned that a woman who comes to a shelter will most likely return home seven or eight more times before she finally leaves her abusing partner? This can be difficult to deal with when you see the same women returning again and again and choosing not to make a change in their situation.

Men can be victims of domestic violence as well but are less vocal about the abuse. They are ashamed of the situation and embarrassed of the fact that a woman has injured them. This makes identifying male victims difficult and providing services for them even more difficult, since they are usually not allowed to live in the shelter with victimized women and their children. If you know of someone who is in an abusive relationship, refer him or her to a counselor or shelter for help.

Psychologists and sociologists have attempted to explain why crime and violence exists. Both disciplines have their theories. Psychologists believe from their research and experience that some people display personality disorders that predispose them to criminal activity. A strong link exists between IQ and crime. Those with low IQ are more likely to commit crimes and may have "thinking errors." These people tend to blame others, are immature in their thinking, impulsive, do not think about consequences, and may engage in chronic lying (Samenow, 2004). These characteristics enable the unlawful and criminal behavior.

Sociologists, on the other hand, tend to look at social factors rather than the individual as the culprit. They see criminal behavior developing as a result of social interactions with others who you view as a role model in your life. A family member or close friend or neighbor may teach you the criminal role through gang membership. The idea that criminal behavior is learned is stressed by sociologists. Another interesting fact is that prison inmates tend *not* to be married and *do* have *low* levels of education. It would seem that two influencing factors in keeping people from committing crimes are *marital status* and *education*. What do you think? Are psychologists correct? Or sociologists?

If you are interested in working in this field, you will have many options but the burnout rate is high. It is difficult to work with people who may continually break the law and may not want to change. Dealing with domestic violence can be frustrating if you see victims who are unwilling to make necessary life changes and continually put themselves in harm's way. If you work in this field, you must have a strong sense of self and work to motivate others to change. Opportunities exist in federal and state agencies like police departments, prisons, probation offices, emergency shelters, and in nonprofit community agencies. Here is a website for jobs in probation.

History

Understanding and Mastery: Historical and current legislation effecting services delivery; how public and private attitudes influence legislation and the interpretation of policies related to Human Services

Critical Thinking Question: Since the United States has the highest incarceration rate in the world, do you believe that it is the safest country? What are the rates of crime and violence in your community? Go to your state government website to find out if you don't know. Who commits most of the crimes? What do you think are some reasons for this criminal activity?

Review Junvenile Probation Officer job opportunities available to you throughout the U.S. on Simply Hired.

Child Abuse and Neglect

Most of us probably have good memories of our childhood. Fun-filled family vacations, holidays with traditional foods and gifts, backyard barbecues, outdoor activities, and on and on. Not everyone is that lucky, however. In fact, some people are lucky just to get away from their family. It is hard to imagine a home filled with violence, fear, threats, or verbal and physical assaults. For many years I worked within the child welfare system and saw the damage that years of neglect and abuse could do to a human being. That child who was once shamed, belittled, and beaten will grow up to become a parent. What kind of skills have such children learned to become good parents?

Home can be a dangerous place for many people. The Children's Defense Fund (2012d) estimates that between 3 and 10 million children in the United States are involved in some type of *domestic abuse* either from a parent or from someone else in the home. Spouse abuse, child abuse, and even substance abuse are common in many households where children grow up. *Alcohol* and *drugs* add to existing problems and angry parents can turn violent when they are stressed or agitated. Over 13 million children live with a parent who has a substance abuse problem. As a result of drugs and alcohol, a person's parenting abilities may become diminished and as a result the child may come face to face with the mental health, child welfare, or correctional systems (Crosson-Tower, 2013).

What is the difference between abuse and neglect? Every state has laws to protect children who are considered minors until they reach the age of adulthood for their state. In some places it is 17 years of age and in others it is 18. Although every state has its own definition of what constitutes abuse, there is a general agreement that abuse occurs at different levels. There is physical, verbal, and sexual abuse. Physical neglect is also a different category of harm.

Neglect of a child occurs when a caregiver cannot meet the physical and emotional needs of his or her child. This would include such things as food, shelter, clothing, medical care, education, protection, supervision, and guidance. In my years in child welfare I would say I saw more cases of neglect than abuse. Oftentimes families that were poor were unable to provide for their children, although they loved them dearly. Sometimes foster care was needed because families did not have the money to pay for food, rent, or utilities. By law, children were required to be placed in a more stable environment until the parents could provide adequately for them. If the fees that were paid to the foster families were given to the biological families, the children would not need to be placed at all. However, this is not how our child welfare system works. Some agencies do have emergency monies available for low-income families but many do not.

Physical abuse occurs when an injury to a child is not an accident and causes disfigurement, impairment of physical health, loss of or impairment of a bodily organ, or risk of death (Crosson-Tower, 2013). In the state where I live, physical abuse is apparent if it leaves a mark. So, if you spank your child and it leaves a mark then it is considered physical abuse. Since some parents still believe that spanking is a reputable form of discipline, this definition is necessary. If bruising appears on a child after a spanking, it can be considered abusive. If a child is reported on suspicion of being harmed, it must be investigated in that state within a period of time depending on the age of the child. Usually the younger the child, the quicker the investigation must take place. Obviously younger children cannot protect themselves from angry, abusive adults.

Sexual abuse is another form of child abuse and refers to any type of sexual activity with a child who is being used for sexual stimulation of an adult (Crosson-Tower, 2013). A sexually abused child may be prodded for further activity with an adult and may be used for prostitution or pornography. The abuse may take the form of activity in the home as in incest or sexual exploitation by a family member. It can also take place with another trusted adult or even a peer. Children who have been sexually abused may become perpetrators and abuse other children as well. Sexually abused children may have been fondled, forced to touch the abuser in some way, or penetrated either vaginally or rectally. In the recent past, we have seen such trusted adults as teachers, priests, Boy Scout leaders, and football coaches accused of sexual abuse. Human Services workers must be aware that these abuses occur without regard to race, social class, or educational level of the child or family.

Verbal abuse is another form of violence against children, but it is difficult to prove. Parents or adults who berate a child, constantly putting the child down, blaming the child for household problems, or calling the child names, are guilty of this abuse. Verbal abuse affects children's self-esteem and their ability to cope with issues of daily living. Listen carefully the next time you are in a department store or buying groceries. How do people talk with their children? If they say insulting things to them in public, imagine what they say at home. Rule of thumb: Speak to your child with respect if you want respect in return. Speak to them like they are your best friend and with time they will be.

All types of abuse are destructive to children and adults. Children who grow up in violent homes often repeat the cycle of abuse because that is what they have learned. They need to work with a counselor to overcome their anger, fears, and anxieties about the abuse. Both children and adults can learn new ways of dealing with difficult situations and can stop the cycle of abuse.

> **Read a sample chapter of _Raised on Fear_ by Lee Cox for a firsthand account of life in an abusive home.**

There are many opportunities to work with child abuse and neglect both directly and indirectly. Every state has a child welfare agency that investigates cases of abuse and neglect as required by law. The names of the agencies vary from state to state. Some of these agencies may be in the Departments of Health and Human Services, some in the Departments of Family and Children's Services, or some may simply call their agency Child Welfare. You need to find your state agency and determine what the qualifications are for being hired. Most departments will have a unit that investigates abuse and neglect, and then they will also have a foster care unit. Smaller agencies may have one department that does it all. All agencies are charged with protecting children in their state, and so laws will exist that mandate under what circumstances children need to be removed from a home and placed in foster care under the protection of that state. You would look for jobs as a caseworker. Jobs will also be available in agencies for children in residential care. You may be hired as a counselor, caseworker, or caregiver in these facilities. You would also need to be aware of child abuse and neglect issues if you work with children in day care centers, Head Start Centers, schools, or counseling agencies.

When you work with vulnerable populations like children and the elderly, you will be considered a mandated reporter of child abuse, and you will receive training from your state agency so that you will be aware of what constitutes physical, sexual, and verbal abuse in your area. As a state worker, you may be required to investigate cases of reported abuse. Most states use some form of law enforcement to assist in that process. Visits to a family's home, a school, or other agency may be required to observe the child or elder, to determine if signs of physical or sexual assault are evident. This type of investigation requires extensive training in assessment and knowledge of state laws in your area.

> **Learn about careers working with children from Save the Children.**

Case Study   Child Welfare

After reading through the information about child abuse and neglect, let's consider the following case study. It is actually one of my old cases with names that have been changed for confidentiality purposes. My first job was in child welfare as a caseworker in a rural town in the Appalachian mountains in the northeast. As you read through the case with me, think about your reactions as if you were the caseworker.

Now that you know about the different types of abuse and neglect, think about this case and determine whether it is abuse or neglect. How would you feel going into the home? What would you do? I was 22 years old at the time and I'm sure I made a lot of mistakes. I would certainly do some things differently today.

Sharon and Harry were an unmarried couple with two small boys, Jeff age three and Donny age five. They came to the attention of the child welfare authorities because they lived in housing on the outskirts of town that was about to be condemned. We were notified about the property by the county supervisor who thought children lived in the home. My initial background investigation yielded some family information. The children did not attend any early childhood programs. The parents were not employed. My first visit was to determine if services were needed and to make an assessment of the situation. I traveled along a steep mountain road and crossed a rickety bridge to get to my destination. The mountain home was precariously built at the base of a hill, and sat lopsided facing a small creek, as if it were about to fall into the swirling waters. I felt dizzy when I approached the home and noticed that an old rug was being used as a door to the front of the house. Apparently the wooden door had fallen off and this was the replacement. I thought to myself, "ok, do I knock on the rug?" I didn't have to think long because a smiling, young woman appeared with two small children behind her. I introduced myself saying that I was from the local child welfare agency and I heard that their home was on a county list of facilities that may be condemned by the town and perhaps I could help with some services. She hesitated in her answer and then looked behind her. Harry, her partner, entered the front area with a look of distrust and caution. I held out my hand in greeting and introduced myself to him. He did not shake my hand, but instead shook his head and said his name was Harry and his partner's was Sharon. I proceeded to explain the reason for my call and offered to tell them about services that we could offer. Harry declined and said they had everything they needed and they would let us know if they required services. I knew I was expected to leave with that statement, but I needed to see more. I looked around their property and remarked on what a beautiful view they had of the mountains and the town below. That drew a smile from both of them. Harry wanted to show me the back of the property and invited me to come into their home so I could walk out the back door with them. I was horrified when I walked into what looked like an abandoned shell of a home with an obvious fire pit for a wood stove in the center of the main room, an obsolete kitchen, and a few open doors that led to bedrooms. Out the back door was an even more beautiful view of the mountains below. The back yard revealed an area for cleaning and skinning animals. Sharon explained that Harry was an excellent hunter and provided the family with plenty of deer meat, rabbit, and other small game. A small garden lay beyond the backdoor with what appeared as a variety of vines and perhaps some type of produce. Harry was quite proud of Sharon's announcement and proceeded to tell me about his days of hunting and fishing. About that time a small raccoon jumped upon the back porch and decided to take a sniff at my boots. I was paralyzed with fear since I had always heard that raccoons carried rabies, especially if you saw them during the day. The children were delighted to see the animal and squealed with delight while Sharon ran to get him some "vittles."

The animal was quickly distracted with the food and ran to the corner of the yard to eat his treat. "He's our pet raccoon, she reported, and he wouldn't hurt a fly." My heart was beating faster and my mind was racing, thinking about all the dangerous elements in this environment that was home to them. The children were warming up to me by then and were taking my hand, wanting me to see all the critters in the back yard, their tree swing, where they swam in the creek below, which was a good four feet below! As we walked back inside, I asked the parents what they would do if the house was condemned, since legally they could no longer live there. They indicated they had no plans to move and had no money, so they felt there were no options. I then began to explain the services that our agency offered and spoke about day care for the children to provide them with some socialization, housing assistance for a rental property in town, and perhaps eligibility for food stamps and medical care. Sharon was delighted since she thought the boys would like the child care facility they could see from their front yard. Harry was not as certain. He felt that he would be allowed to stay on his property since no one had bothered to tell him to fix up the place or leave. As we talked, the children swarmed around Sharon, sitting on her lap, grabbing her hand. She quietly led them to the kitchen area where she produced some cookies from a jar on the counter. They offered me some coffee and a place to sit on their one chair in the kitchen. I cautiously took the seat not wanting to offend them, but I declined the coffee. We talked about the type of home they would want to consider and I promised to pick Sharon up the following day so we could visit the children's day care center. We had a discussion about the open fire in their living room and Harry explained that it was exactly like camping except they had beds to sleep in and an iron grate around the "wood stove" to protect the children from getting too close. A huge opening in the roof allowed for the smoke and flames to travel right up the chimney. I left that night with conflicting feelings about leaving the children in that environment, even for a night. I called my supervisor and gave her a detailed description of the situation. Since the family was open to my interventions, she felt it was best if I made plans for services the next day and quickly removed them all from this environment. We did not make plans to remove them that night.

Human Systems

Understanding and Mastery: An understanding of the capacities, limitations, and resiliency of human systems

Critical Thinking Question: Would you consider this case study, Child Welfare, a case of child abuse or child neglect? What are the cultural elements that you need to consider? Think about services for this family. Would you do anything differently? Would you have left the children in that environment for the night? Why didn't I drink the coffee that was offered to me? How can you work with families that have values so different from your own?

Test your comprehension of <u>Domestic Violence also Child Abuse and Neglect</u> by completing these quizzes.

Drugs and Alcohol
Teen and Adult Use and Misuse

Review the Centers for Disease Control and Prevention to learn more about Adolescent and School Health in the United States.

There is probably no area of social services where you will not be impacted by drugs and alcohol. Teenagers experiment with drugs and alcohol and even middle school-age children report they have used alcohol or tried marijuana. Adults abuse both, mentally ill people are affected by the medications they take, people with chronic illnesses may overdose on their prescription drugs, and even Hollywood celebrities sensationalize their use of illegal drugs like cocaine. Young actors and actresses can be seen on the covers of tabloids for excessive partying, ruining their careers over the abuse of drugs and alcohol, and spending short stints of time in jail or rehab. Whether you agree with it or not, drugs and alcohol are a part of the fabric of American society.

In Human Services, we often find that serious, life-altering determinations are made based on drug or alcohol issues. Child welfare agencies serve parents who are found incapable of caring for their children because they are substance abusers, the school system has no choice but to expel students who bring marijuana to school, and counselors develop court mandated treatment plans for people who cannot cope with daily living, are homeless, cannot hold a job, or spend too much time in local bars. Mental health therapists write court reports for adolescents who have been arrested for driving after drinking and are on probation, and home health workers make referrals for residential care for their elderly clients who live alone and abuse their pain medications. It doesn't matter what age group you work with or what setting you work in, drug and alcohol issues will affect the work you do in Human Services.

What do the statistics tell us about alcohol and drug abuse? According to the National Institute on Drug Abuse (2013) a survey revealed that 52% of Americans had at least one drink in the 30 days before the survey was taken and about 42% of high school seniors had at least one drink in that time period. The Centers for Disease Control indicates that *alcohol abuse by minors is a serious public health concern*, although both alcohol and tobacco use by minors has decreased in the last few years. Consumption of alcohol by minors before the age of 15 increases the likelihood that long-term alcohol abuse will occur. Alcohol contributes to traffic accidents, relationship difficulties, family problems, school failures, participation in a crime, and a host of other issues for youth. Alcohol correlates with violence in the home and is also linked to adult traffic accidents, DUIs, and other related family problems.

If you scroll through the website from the Substance Abuse and Mental Health Services Administration (SAMHSA), you will see videos from various states that describe *policy changes* they have made in their area to *reduce underage drinking, alcohol dependence, and family problems related to alcohol*. Learn how Louisiana had to alter its policies in order to change its image in New Orleans. Mardi Gras and other events in the Big Easy were often seen as

Human Systems

Understanding and Mastery: Processes to effect social change through advocacy work at all levels of society including community development, community and grassroots organizing, and local and global activism

Critical Thinking Question: Watch the videos from SAMHSA and consider the implications of the policy changes that were made in Michigan, Louisiana, and Alaska. Do you think these changes will prevent youth from underage drinking? What were the unintended consequences of the policy changes in Alaska? What is being done in your community to prevent underage drinking?

family unfriendly and too lax in alcohol sales to minors. Watch the video on Alaska and learn the challenges of "wet," "dry," and "damp" communities.

In addition to alcohol, drug use by youth is a major concern. Although tobacco and alcohol use have declined somewhat, *marijuana use by high school teens has risen* 17% since 2007 (Centers for Disease Control, 2012). Marijuana appears to be the drug of choice with 61% of those under age 15, who receive treatment for drug abuse, ingesting this drug more frequently than any other. Derived from the Cannabis plant, marijuana is a psychoactive drug containing the compound THC. It is usually crushed, rolled in paper and smoked, much like tobacco in a cigarette. However, more creative uses have been found where the drug is inhaled through a variety of breathing pipes or water bongs. Comprehensive research on drug abuse shows that marijuana alters brain chemistry resulting in poor coordination, difficulty with memory and concentration, loss of motivation or ambition, increased hunger, a relaxed or "high" feeling, as well as the possibility of paranoia or panic attacks, depending on the potency of the drug. Marijuana is addictive and it can be difficult to stop. Reports of anxiety, irritability, and increased craving for the drug are common. Marijuana is seen as a gateway drug, often the first choice of teenagers who go on to try and use other more addictive and life threatening drugs like cocaine, crystal meth, LSD, or heroin. However, the perspective of teens is that marijuana is not a dangerous drug.

Review what the National Institute on Drug Abuse has to say about alcohol as well as other drug use in the United States.

The ten most popular drugs used in the United States can be classified as uppers, downers, or all arounders. Uppers stimulate the central nervous system and include drugs such as cocaine, amphetamines, caffeine, and nicotine. Downers are central nervous system depressants and include painkillers, morphine, and alcohol. All arounders are psychedelics or hallucinogens and include marijuana, LSD, and ecstasy.

New synthetic forms of marijuana called K2 and Spice are fashionable at the moment with teens believing this is a natural drug with few side effects. Until recently it was easy to obtain and could be purchased legally in gas stations and head shops. A herbal mixture of dried plant leaves and chemical additives, it is a psychoactive mind altering drug that has proven fatal to some teens. As a result it has been pulled from shelves and is now illegal to purchase, sell, or possess by the Drug Enforcement Administration.

In addition to problems with drugs and alcohol regarding teen use, adults' abuse of these substances continues. According to the Child Welfare League of America (2002), over 13 million children live with a parent who has used illegal and addictive drugs during the past year. This drug-using behavior complicates the parent–child relationship making adults *incapable of raising their children, making decisions, and handling daily responsibilities*. In her textbook *Exploring Child Welfare*, Crosson-Tower (2013) describes several situations where adults are ineffective in coping with children due to their own drug use. Those who work in child welfare agencies are often confronted with issues related to drug and alcohol use such as *physical and sexual abuse, violence in the home, neglect, abandonment,* and *poor parenting.*

Use of alcohol by pregnant, adult females increases the probability of **Fetal Alcohol Syndrome (FAS)** or **Fetal Alcohol Effects (FAE)**. Both of these conditions have been shown to cause physical and mental abnormalities like *low intelligence, hyperactivity, mental retardation, facial aberrations, and impaired development* (Golden, 2005; Zastrow, 2009). The statistics on the number of mothers who use drugs during pregnancy is staggering and so are the health problems associated with the infants born to them.

Zuckerman and other researchers conducted secondary analyses on a number of research studies involving drug use among pregnant women. Some studies included self-reporting of drug use by women, others contained results of urine analysis of pregnant women, and still others contained hospital records of drug addicted infants upon delivery. According to a review of the literature over 160,000 newborns were exposed to crack or cocaine while in utero, over 612,000 to marijuana, over 44,000 to hallucinogens, 93,000 to stimulants, 39,000 to sedatives, and over 2.6 million to alcohol (Zuckerman, Fitzgerald, & Lester, 2000). These babies suffered with low birth weight, high mortality rates, numerous health problems, and impaired emotional and mental issues. When born, crack addicted babies must go through withdrawal and are often emotionless and difficult to care for. Those in Human Services must educate both young people and adults about the harsh realities of drug and alcohol addictions both for themselves and for their children.

Students who are interested in working in the drug and alcohol field will find opportunities that exist in community mental health settings, as well as other nonprofit programs for adolescents and adults. Private programs are also available for those with the means to pay for residential care and expensive treatment options. Workers should be knowledgeable about dual diagnosis since many of those with drug and alcohol problems also have mental health issues. A working knowledge of the *DSM-5,* a diagnostic tool used in this field, is required (see Chapter 6). Human Services workers would counsel individuals, groups, and families who suffer with these issues as well as develop and teach prevention programs to students and young adults.

This area on drugs and alcohol may seem very real to you. Most of us can think of a friend, family member, or neighbor who has a substance abuse problem. Maybe some of you have struggled with your own issues. Recognizing that you have a problem is the first step; finding help is the next step. It is a difficult path to recovery that takes time, patience, self-forgiveness, forgiveness from others, support from others, and tons of self-control, which needs to be learned and practiced. Often these are the very characteristics that you didn't have in the beginning of your addiction. Organizations like Alcoholics Anonymous (AA), Narcotics Anonymous (NA), the Salvation Army, local churches, hospitals, and counseling agencies all offer support groups or treatment options. Here is a case I handled many years ago.

Case Study ▶ Neonatal Substance Abuse

I was teaching a group dynamics class several years ago, and during the break one of my students, Natasha, got a call from the local hospital, which was right next to our college. She was asked to come over right away for a short meeting with the director of nursing and the child welfare agency caseworker. She told me she would be back by the time the break ended. The meeting took longer than expected, and she arrived back at the college for the remaining 15 minutes of class. She was holding a very tiny infant girl who appeared to be premature. Natasha's sister had given birth to the baby the night before and the baby was born cocaine addicted. In fact, the hospital said it was the highest amount of cocaine they had ever seen in an infant. The authorities were called and the mother was tested for a variety of drugs. She was positive for alcohol, cocaine, and marijuana. The hospital could not by law allow the mother to care for the baby. The mother was charged with child endangerment and would be placed in jail with the possibility of rehab and treatment within 48 hours. The child welfare agency was forced with the decision to place the baby outside of the home since the biological mother was being charged in the case, the father was not in the area, and no other parents or grandparents of the mother were available. So, the sibling of the baby's mother was called as the next of kin to care for the infant. That was my student. Natasha was the baby's aunt and immediately moved to gain custody of the child, although she had one child of her own already and as a single parent her funds were limited. She brought the baby back to class where we all oohed and aahed over the precious bundle. What became very clear to all of us was the baby's demeanor. She was lifeless, like a rag doll. She was trancelike, making no sounds, and was not curled in a ball like most babies who prefer the fetal position. This baby lay flat and motionless, her limbs hanging limp, not moving a muscle. She appeared dead. I repeatedly asked if the hospital had discharged the baby in this condition. Natasha said "yes," indicating that her sister had no insurance, and so the hospital was looking to move the baby to a family member's home immediately. We all kept checking to make sure the baby was breathing and she was, very deeply. Although we did not normally have children attend our classes, I did make an exception that day so that Natasha could retrieve her niece, she could finish the last few minutes of the class, and we could discuss this situation. I felt this was an excellent learning opportunity for the entire class. Natasha was willing and eager to share this situation since she wanted the help and support of her Human Services classmates. Obviously confidentiality was an issue for Natasha, her family, the situation, and the class. The students had many questions, observations, and some excellent suggestions and resources for Natasha, which we discussed. Natasha was grateful for the exchange since it gave her an opportunity to think about what to do next. When the class was over she took her niece home, recognizing the challenges that lay ahead of her.

Planning and Evaluation

Understanding and Mastery: Analysis and assessment of the needs of clients or client groups; development of goals, design, and implementation of a plan of action

Critical Thinking Question: Neonatal Substance Abuse. What is your assessment of this situation as well as some of the ethical issues that we discussed that day? What are some of the concerns that you had for this baby? What does she need? How can the Human Services class be helpful in designing a plan of action for Natasha? Have you ever seen or worked with cocaine addicted babies or children? What was that like for you? How did they behave? Compare this with what you have learned about child growth and development. Is this normal development?

HIV/AIDS
Statistics, Symptoms, and Treatment Options

If you were born after 1980, you grew up hearing about HIV and AIDS. You may even remember when this disease first came on the scene. No one knew what to think of this insidious disease that was killing so many of U.S. residents, especially in the lesbian, gay, bisexual, and transgender (LGBT) communities. Famous dancers, artists, fashion designers, and actors were all learning of their fate with little hope in sight. The United States was not prepared for this virus that attacked the immune system and would not respond to the antibiotics and other medicine that were used to stop its rampage. It seemed to come out of nowhere with the Centers for Disease Control reporting 108 cases in 1981, but by 1986 the number of AIDS cases had risen to 16,458 (Martin, 2013).

Starting as a virus, the human immunodeficiency virus or HIV develops into AIDS (acquired immunodeficiency syndrome). HIV is *transmitted through sexual intercourse, by sharing unsanitary intravenous needles, through blood transfusions, or from infected mothers to their unborn children.* Originally it was believed that the disease was spread through homosexual contact, and so heterosexual partners were often not concerned with this disease. However, the World Health Organization (2013) now reports that worldwide the most prevalent transmission is through heterosexual contact.

Researchers have tracked the development of AIDS to West Africa where it began probably around the early part of the 20th century. As the virus spread worldwide, it became a pandemic, reaching nearly every corner of the globe. It has seen the most devastating effect on the sub-Saharan region of Africa where millions of children have become orphaned due to the loss of one or both parents.

Early *symptoms of the disease include flu-like symptoms* followed by a long period of no symptoms. Eventually the immune system is left weakened and unable to fight off infections or any illnesses. Initially attempts at treatment were futile, and confirmation of the HIV virus was a sure death sentence as the virus erupted into full-blown AIDS. Massive efforts by the LGBT community, health professionals, and other activists put treatment options on the national agenda. Research quickly revealed that prevention was necessary, especially in the homosexual and addiction communities. Nationally efforts were aimed at providing information on safe sex, use of clean needles for addicts, and early detection.

Review the latest statistics and treatment options for <u>HIV/ AIDS</u> at the Centers for Disease Control website.

With promising treatment available today, the virus is considered more of a chronic condition rather than a life-threatening one. New antiviral therapies are very effective at keeping the disease from progressing. Those infected with the HIV virus can now expect to live almost to a full life expectancy. However, the *treatments are expensive* and *may not be covered under all insurance* policies. So, those with no insurance or poor coverage are left with few options for treatment and therefore, inadequate care. Countries in Africa are still the most profoundly affected by this disease.

According to the Centers for Disease Control in Atlanta (2012), there are more than *one million people in the United States currently living with AIDS; about half a million people have already died from the illness* since the agency started tracking the virus. The CDC reports that the southern part of the country has been hit hardest. One-half of all new HIV and AIDS cases are in the South, and more deaths caused by AIDS are reported from this area as well.

One reason is that detection of the disease in the early stages is not occurring in this area as rapidly as it should, and treatment is either not available or not affordable for low-income populations. The South tends to be the poorest area of the United States with many rural communities in many states. AIDS is now being described as a disease of poverty. Mississippi, the poorest of the 50 states, has the highest rate of AIDS and the highest death rate from the disease as well. Those in the rural areas of the South are the least likely to receive early detection and treatment due to transportation issues and lack of medical care. Human Services workers in health care settings and prisons are most likely to encounter cases of HIV/AIDS.

For those students interested in working in this area of Human Services, educating others about the illness and methods of prevention is critical. The disease is spreading rapidly through the U.S. prison system due to rape and other intimate associations. After release from prison, some inmates may unknowingly bring the disease to their heterosexual partner. Others infected with the virus may not even be aware they have it. Employment would occur in public health settings as well as nonprofit agencies that work with poor, underserved populations, particularly in rural areas. Workers may counsel individuals and families who are infected with the virus, educating them on treatment options. Community health programs may also hire individuals to educate people about safe sex and other methods of protection. Skills in public speaking, grantsmanship, counseling, and teaching would be necessary.

> ## Client-Related Values and Attitudes
>
> *Understanding and Mastery: Confidentiality of information; integration of the ethical standards outlined by the National Organization for Human Services/Council for Standards in Human Service Education*
>
> Critical Thinking Question: It is estimated that one in five people with the HIV virus do not even realize they have the disease (Centers for Disease Control, 2013); how might this effect the general population? Do you think we should mandate that all residents receive an HIV/AIDS screening? What are the legal or ethical implications of this kind of policy?

> ## Review the AIDS Healthcare Foundation for information on careers in this field worldwide.

Problems of Cognitive Functioning

Mental Health, Mental Illness, and Developmental Issues

We all have good and bad days, highs and lows. However, if you find yourself having more bad days and more lows, an inability to get out of bed, a loss of desire for doing the things that once brought you happiness, then you know something is wrong. It is reported by the SAMHSA (2012) that one in five adults and one in ten children experience some mental health disorder each year. About 12% of Americans seek out professional help due to their inability to cope with some life event. Adolescent girls between the ages of 12 and 15 experience triple the amount of depression as younger girls (SAMHSA, 2012).

Mental health refers to our sense of well-being. We are in good mental health when we can cope with the events of daily living and balance school, work, and personal and family life. Life may become stressful, but we manage to use the resources and support personnel available to help us get through difficult times. This is normal, and we can expect to be happy and relaxed as well as busy and stressed out at times. It's how we manage all the components of a busy life that determine our mental health. Do you work hard, but then come home and relax, put your feet up and enjoy time alone or with your family? Or do you work hard, stay late, skip meals, and then come home exhausted and fall into bed without the enjoyment of a friendly conversation or the benefit of nourishing, healthy food? Mental and physical health go hand in hand. As we age, we learn that to deny ourselves the benefit of either good physical health or good mental health will certainly affect our ability to copy with daily living. When you are in good mental health, you think, feel, and behave appropriately.

Mental illness refers to a change in your cognitive, affective, or behavioral abilities. When you find that you can't think clearly, are overly emotional, or develop anxieties and phobias that interfere with your ability to enjoy life, then we say you are suffering with a mental illness. This means that your natural state of thinking, feeling, and behaving has changed. Professional help may be needed to get you back in good mental health. Psychiatrists, psychologists, social workers, and Human Services workers may all assist you in your efforts to get better.

Read more about the difference between mental health and mental illness at The International Society for the Psychological and Social Approaches to Psychosis.

If the *problems you exhibit in your daily living regarding how you think, feel, or behave are not new, but rather conditions that you have always had, then you most likely have a personality disorder.* This is part of who you are and not something that has recently changed. Personality disorders are more difficult to treat since medications may not alter an existing personality. The problem may be more developmental and requires a different kind of treatment. Treatment varies for mental illness, developmental issues, and maintenance of good mental health. Let's take a look at the three areas of *mental health, mental illness, and developmental issues*, and see what kinds of treatment would be needed for each one.

In order for our mental health to remain good, we must rest, exercise, eat wholesome food, refrain from drug or alcohol addictions, and spend as much time doing enjoyable things as we do working. This can be difficult for people who have high-pressure jobs and a multitude of tasks to complete each day as well as child and household responsibilities. They may begin to lose sleep and as a result don't think clearly. As they get overstressed and run down, their immune system may become weakened, and as a result they develop colds, infections, or viruses more easily. When they can't keep up their frenzied pace and work begins to slide, they may become irritable, frustrated, and angry. Relationship difficulties may then occur. At this point the person is not thinking, feeling, or behaving like himself or herself and is in poor mental health. Individuals in such a condition may need to adjust their schedule or take steps to get themselves back into good mental health. If they see a therapist, it may be recommended that they slow down, prioritize what absolutely needs to be done in a day, and save time for themselves. Usually when people begin to balance their work and other activities, their mental health is restored.

When people begin to sense that their thoughts, feelings, and behavior are not normal or not what they used to be, they may be suffering from a mental illness. A tool that is used to diagnose mental illness is called the *DSM-5* (2013) This stands for the *Diagnostic and Statistical Manual of Mental Disorders* and is used in mental health settings by psychiatrists, psychologists, social workers, and Human Services workers. This book helps classify the symptoms a person is experiencing to determine what the mental illness may be. It gives names, definitions, and symptoms of mental disorders. Some types of mental illnesses include anxieties, phobias, depression, dissociative disorders, eating or sleeping disorders, impulse control disorders, organic mental disorders like Alzheimer's disease, addictions, and schizophrenia. Treatment may include medications that alter the chemicals in the brain and can help a person to think more clearly, sleep better, or become less depressed. Medications may be necessary to stop auditory and visual hallucinations, as in schizophrenia. Some people may take the medications for a short period of time and feel as good as new with relief from their anxiety or panic attacks, in which cases the medication may be stopped. Other people, such as those who hear voices or have hallucinations, may need to take medication for longer periods or for a lifetime. Along with medications, psychotherapy is often necessary since the ability to talk through your problems with a therapist can be just as meaningful as taking medications. Individual and group therapy can be recommended for a client who has a mental illness.

People who have personality disorders or developmental issues have always experienced some difficulty in their thinking, feeling, or behavior. Paranoid and antisocial personality types fall into this category. Disorders that are evident from infancy or early childhood like mental retardation, attention deficit disorder, autism, and hyperactivity can also be placed here. Some medications may be useful as with hyperactivity and attention deficit disorders. However, behavioral therapies have also proven effective with some of these populations. Behavior modification programs that are established with a reward system are useful for people with mental retardation and low IQ. Working with a therapist with whom you can develop an interpersonal bond is also important to treatment, which can be either individual or group.

You would think that jobs would be plentiful in this field since we see evidence of mental health problems and developmental issues in the United States every day. You cannot talk about crime, violence, addictions, or child abuse without talking about the overlap of mental health issues. Every national act of violence that Americans have seen from the shootings in Colorado, to the shootings at Virginia Tech, to the shootings in Arizona, all revolved around an individual who had mental illness. By now you would think America would have excellent prevention and assessment measures. It is not so. It is hard to predict when a person will stop taking his or her medications or go on a violent rampage. We do not have adequate mental health facilities in our communities for all the people who need the service. So, jobs are available but are not as plentiful as they should be. Funds for mental health services have continually diminished over the years. Many states have not put additional dollars into these programs, so many are run on limited budgets. Many people who are mentally ill end up in the prison system, so they may receive some kind of services there.

> ## Interventions and Direct Services
>
> *Understanding and Mastery: Theory and knowledge bases of prevention, intervention, and maintenance strategies to achieve maximum autonomy and functioning; skills to facilitate appropriate direct services and interventions related to specific client or client group goals*
>
> **Critical Thinking Question:** What types of services do you think cost more: prevention services for maintenance of good mental health or intervention services for mental illnesses or developmental issues? What kinds of mental health services are available in your community? Are they effective?

Explore The Social Service Job Site to lean about mental health or other social services throughout the United States.

Homelessness

A Growing Trend among Youth

There probably aren't many communities in America that are not affected by **homelessness** in some way. Travel around the country from urban cities, to the suburbs, to rural towns and you will find plenty of shelters for homeless men, women, and children.

Agencies, like the Salvation Army, that have traditionally provided shelter for people who were struggling on the fringes are full to capacity most nights. Churches and other nonprofit organizations also provide help with shelters when the larger community programs are full. There seems to be an endless supply of people wanting or needing a place to sleep. Tent cities have also sprung up in places where shelters didn't exist, accommodating families that have lost their home in the mortgage crisis.

According to the National Law Center on Homelessness and Poverty (2012), globally it is estimated that between 20 million and 40 million urban households are homeless and 1.3 billion live in inadequate shelters. About 2 million people are homeless each night in the United States, sleeping in parks, shelters, or on the streets. Twenty-four states have had an increase in homelessness in the past year. Men represent about 44% of the homeless population, women about 13%, and families about 36%. What is most startling is the increasing number of youth who are homeless. It is our biggest problem in homelessness right now. *About 1.5 million children are considered homeless, with 39% of those under the age of 18 and 42% of that figure children under the age of 5.* As Human Services providers, we have to ask ourselves what are we doing if we can't help young children find a place to sleep at night?

> **Read more about national initiatives and what is happening in your state at the <u>National Law Center on Homelessness and Poverty</u>.**

What causes homelessness? There are many reasons people are left without a permanent place to live. Families cite unemployment, poverty, and lack of affordable housing as reasons for their situation. Many families move back into homes with their parents, friends, or other relatives. However, when the living situations become too small for everyone to share, or when families are unable to find employment to pay their way, they may be asked to leave. Many single mothers and their children may move from one house to another, choosing not to overstay their welcome in one area. This may make it difficult for children to attend the same school for any length of time if they are constantly on the move. So, disruption in school and social activities are issues for homeless children.

Single people who are homeless are more likely to suffer from drug and alcohol abuse, mental illness, as well as unemployment. About 44% of the men who are homeless are military veterans, often older, unemployed, and with possible mental illness as well as substance abuse problems.

> **Search the Safe <u>Horizon</u> website to learn more about its Streetwork Project.**

The growing number of youth who are homeless are often runaways with histories of physical abuse (46%) and sexual abuse (17%). According to Safe Horizons (2012), many of these youth grew up in families with substance abuse and mental health issues. There is a concern for these youth since many are targets for prostitution, human trafficking, pornography, and other criminal activity. Safe Horizons, a shelter program in New York, is a good example of an outreach youth homeless shelter.

A study by Barbara Ehrenreich (2001) revealed that working full-time, at a minimum-wage job would not earn enough to pay for the housing that was available in several different parts of the country where she lived during her research. Her conclusion was that it was impossible for many people to afford housing in America since wages were too low to support the rents or mortgage costs. She asked Congress to provide for more affordable housing for families. However, since her book was published, more Americans are now homeless due to the mortgage crisis, making it a continued concern for Human Services workers who try to meet the needs of low-income people every day.

Read about Barbara Ehrenreich's social experiment and the resulting book: _Nickel and Dimed: On (Not) Getting By in America_.

Legislation passed in 1987, the McKinney-Vento Act, has provided for shelter housing and emergency services for the homeless population for more than two decades. Despite efforts aimed at helping this group, their numbers have soared making homelessness in America a national concern. New initiatives are being developed to treat the homeless situation. President Obama's administration is trying not only to provide services for the homeless, but to eliminate the term "homelessness" altogether. The **Hearth Act** was passed in May of 2009 as an amendment to the McKinney Act and provides _prevention services for families before homelessness occurs, has a rapid transition program for women and children who are victims of domestic violence, consolidates several of the Housing and Urban Development's competitive grant programs, and creates a rural housing stability program._

Explore the programs that HUD has to offer for Homeless Assistance.

You can also read about best practices in working with the homeless as well as a radical new program called _Pathways to Housing._ This innovative program actually provides individual housing for the chronically homeless population, many are also mentally ill and/or substance abusers. It is reported that the program is actually less expensive than allowing people to sleep on the streets where emergency vehicles are often called several times a week to break up fights, take people to the hospitals, or retrieve people during inclement weather.

According to the PBS video, Home at Last, providing housing for the chronically homeless population is not only humane, it is a good business decision since housing costs are approximately $22,000 per year while the cost of emergency medical care due to living on the streets costs about $100,000 per year.

Watch Home at Last? to follow Foote, the homeless man, in this radical new approach to helping the homeless.

There are many opportunities to work with the homeless population in many types of Human Services positions. Entry level _intake workers_ meet clients upon entry to a shelter, _case managers_ assist them in locating services they need like jobs, medicine, mental health counseling, schools for children, food stamps, social security etc. _Job coaches_ help people write resumes, prepare for job interviews, and assist in finding jobs. _Grant writers_ can help agencies find the money they need to fund their agency and also to plan fund-raising events. The salaries may vary depending on the size of the agency and the position, but the rewards are plentiful when you can help someone change their life.

Client-Related Values and Attitudes

Understanding and Mastery: The least intrusive intervention in the least restrictive environment; client self-determination; belief that individuals, service systems, and society can change

Critical Thinking Question: Do you think it is a good idea to provide a home, no strings attached, to the homeless population? Why or why not. What are the results of the Pathways program if you watched the video?

Watch the featured video on the website for the Coalition for the Homeless in New York City, one of the largest programs for the homeless in America.

Around the Globe

How Does Military Life Affect the Family?

We can't forget about military families when we discuss current social issues. At no time in American history has the resiliency of the military family been more challenged that it has been with this war in the Middle East. With both men and women serving in the volunteer military, it has been necessary for the government to call upon units for deployment three and four times within the span of this decade. Of the 200,000 women who have been deployed, over half have been mothers.

How does military life affect children? We do know that traditionally families have been very flexible and responded well to the deployments that change their daily routines and send them moving across the country or the world. This means that military families can expect to spend time in more than a few places as they raise their children. This can be difficult on children who have to make new friends, learn new cultures, and respond to new school systems. However, the war in Iraq and Afghanistan has been different. Rapid deployments mean that families are not moving together and often both mom and dad are gone at the same time leaving the children in the care of grandparents, friends, or other relatives. The use of Army Reservists and National Guardsmen to assist the military in Iraq and Afghanistan has been a policy change as well. In the past both the National Guard and the Army Reserves have remained in the states for national and state emergencies. The loss of these adults for such long periods of time is unprecedented. It was unexpected for both the soldiers and their families who did not have the same training as military spouses and their children. So, they were not prepared emotionally for the separation. Time will tell how this has impacted the social, emotional, and developmental growth of the children they left behind.

What kinds of services are provided for military families? Each branch of the military has an array of services to meet the needs of the soldiers and their family members. So whether it is the army, navy, air force, or Marines, a type of community services is

Families arrive in Fort Hood, Texas, to greet their loved ones after the veterans return home from the Iraq war.

provided that includes family services, counseling, parent education, programs for disabled family members, school programs, day care, mental health services, medical care, housing assistance, recreational programs, and many other services to help families as they move in and out of military installations across the world (Kinsella, 2011). However, those who serve in the National Guard or Army Reserves most likely do not live on military bases and so the services available for families who live on or near a military base may not be accessible to these military units and their families.

Other concerns for military families right now are the number of returning soldiers who are suffering with **posttraumatic stress disorder (PTSD)**. This is a disorder that has affected large numbers in the military and includes generalized anxiety, the inability to sleep, flashbacks or reoccurring nightmares of war and the violence and terrorism witnessed while stationed in war zones. The disorder prevents soldiers from conducting normal activities and interferes with daily living.

Listen to an NPR interview, Military Moms: How Wars Affect Families, regarding her deployments to the Middle East.

Putting Theories to Work
Psychological and Sociological Theories for Some Social Issues

Have you ever talked with someone about a social issue and found his or her opinion was totally different from your own? Perhaps you thought that teenage mothers needed help and assistance with parenting, medical care, and training for a job so they could support themselves and their children. You might have thought this was especially important if they had dropped out of school, were under the age of 18, and were single mothers. Someone else might have thought services like that would encourage teens to have babies and if they got themselves into that predicament, it was their own fault. Well, there are many theories that attempt to explain why a current problem exists in the first place. Let's take a look at some current issues and the theories that sociologists and psychologists use to explain them.

Why Does Poverty Exist?

According to sociologists Mooney, Knox, and Schacht (2007), three perspectives attempt to explain why poverty exists: the structural-functional, conflict, and symbolic interactionist perspectives.

Structural-Functionalists believe that poverty results from a breakdown in societal institutions like employment, education, family structure and too little government support for social service programs. As a result of the breakdown of these institutions, a culture of poverty develops where people feel helpless and dependent and have no expectations for the future. Often people in this situation are single parents, females with little education and poor employment opportunities.

Those who agree with the **Conflict Perspective** would best explain their position by the often-quoted words, "the rich get richer and the poor get poorer." In this perspective, we often refer to *Karl Marx's theory of economic equality* where he compared the owner of the means of production (the bourgeoisie) with the worker (the proletariat). In his theory, Marx contends there will always be a struggle for scarce resources, and those at the top will always be favored over those at the bottom. Laws and policies are written to protect and benefit the rich while those at the bottom pay higher taxes, higher prices for goods, and receive lower wages. Conflict theories support the idea that worldwide economic reforms to solve poverty have actually benefited the rich.

The **Symbolic Interactionist Perspective** looks at how symbols and labels are attached to meanings. People who receive social services, food stamps, or some kind of cash assistance are often considered to be poor, undeserving, or lazy. They may begin to see themselves in this way as well. People who do not receive any assistance at all may see themselves as independent, responsible, or wealthy. They begin to see themselves in this way and so their self-esteem is positively affected by their label. The poor people are negatively affected. They may feel shame or powerless. These labels affect how people perceive themselves, how they obtain jobs, get educated, and even prepare for the future.

Why Do Some People Get Drug or Alcohol Addicted?

Psychologists would say some people get addicted to drugs and alcohol for a combination of social, psychological, and biological reasons. **Psychological theories** suggest that some people may have a tendency to use drugs or alcohol due to certain personality traits like shyness, anxiety, or introversion. People may feel more relaxed and are better able to talk to others or develop interpersonal relationships when they use either alcohol or drugs. **Social theories** indicate that young adults or even teens who experiment with drugs or alcohol may do so because of peer pressure, initiation in a gang, or the feeling that it is acceptable to do so. Two of the most abused and unhealthy substances Americans use are alcohol and tobacco, although both are legal and culturally acceptable. **Biological theories** teach us that many people have a genetic predisposition to addictions for either alcohol or drugs. This is because the experience that some people derive from drugs or alcohol is more pleasurable than the experience for others, making the likelihood of craving alcohol or drugs more intense for some people.

Why Do Crime and Violence Exist?

Some psychological, sociological, and biological theories explain why crime and violence exist. According to psychological theories, some offenders suffer with mental illness, unhealthy relationships with parents, or a psychopathic personality disorder that may lead to crime and violence. Several sociological theories attempt to explain crime and violence as well. Robert Merton (1957) developed the concept of Strain Theory to explain how people may want the same things that he calls goals. These goals may include a good job, money to buy houses, cars, etcetera, but often the means to get these things is offered to only the privileged who can obtain education, training, or job referrals. As a result, people get creative in how they adjust the means to acquire the end result. Conformists accept the traditional way of reaching goals by achieving the means, so they go to school to get good jobs. Innovators adjust the means to get to the goals. They may need to commit street crimes in order to achieve wealth and power because education does not work for them. Ritualists accept the means of culturally accepted hard work but reject the goal of reward or money. Retreatists, on the other hand, reject both the means and the goals and become socially unacceptable like drug addicts or homeless people. Rebels may replace society's goals with new goals, and so they reject both society's means and goals in place of their own. Biological theories suggest that central nervous system malfunctioning, an overabundance of stress hormones, vitamin and mineral deficiencies, chromosomal abnormalities, plus heightened levels of testosterone can all elevate levels of aggression, which can lead to crime and violence.

What Are Some Social Issues Regarding Teen Pregnancy?

Although teenage pregnancy is a concern in the United States, its rates have been declining in the past decade. Of all the industrialized countries, America has the highest rates of teen pregnancies, births, and abortions. Most other industrialized countries have better prevention programs and availability of contraceptive measures.

According to the website Teen Help (2013), about three quarters of a million girls become pregnant each year resulting in about 500,000 births. Although pregnant teens may finish high school or get their GED, they are less likely to continue with their college education. It is estimated that one out of every ten births is to a teen mother who will struggle with independence, poverty, and job-related issues for a lifetime. By age 30, only about 1.5% of those who were teen mothers have gone on for college degrees. It is estimated that teen pregnancy costs the United States about $7 billion per year in the form of entitlement benefits and health care, so developing prevention programs is certainly necessary. Most teen mothers who give birth also choose to keep their babies since unwed teen motherhood is more acceptable today than it was decades ago.

About one third of all births in the United States are to unwed mothers as compared to one half of all births in countries like Sweden or Norway. However, unlike the Scandinavian countries, the United States does not have family allowances, universal health care for mothers and their children, free-or low-cost quality day care, paid maternity leaves, or any of the other family-friendly services offered to citizens of Sweden, Denmark, and Norway. In the U.S. women are unlikely to receive medical care unless they are eligible for Medicaid or work full-time and have a generous employer who sponsors a health care plan for employees and dependents. In the United States, rents and/or mortgages are high, there are no family allowances, day care can be very expensive depending on where it is located, and medicines for children's illnesses are expensive.

In addition to concerns for the mother, there are numerous concerns for the newborn baby. Teenage girls who do not receive prenatal care are more likely to have complications with their pregnancy, low birth weight babies, and greater chances of infant mortality. Mississippi leads the United States with the number of infant deaths before the first year. According to a report by CBS News (2013), cuts in state Medicaid programs have made access to health care more restrictive for many people. This has been especially difficult for young, African American teenagers whose infant mortality rates have soared.

Watch the video, <u>Mississippi's Rising Infant Mortality Rate from CBS</u>, to learn more about the sudden surge of babies dying in Mississippi.

Do you know of a teenage girl who is pregnant? What information could be helpful to her right now? What services do you think she should be receiving in order to give birth to a healthy baby? How can we be sure these girls all receive the services they need? What if they do not receive any services? <u>Teen Help</u> has statistics on teen pregnancy as well as information and resources on prevention.

Watch the video from the <u>Children's Aid Society</u> on Dr. Carrera's Adolescent Pregnancy Prevention Program.

Critical Thinking Question: What issues are teenagers dealing with developmentally at this stage of life? How does being pregnant effect the developmental stage for both boys and girls when they find out they are about to become parents? How might this effect the newborn?

Linking Theory to Practice

Teaching Stress Management Techniques to Soldiers with PTSD

PTSD is a mental health disorder that is affecting many of American returning military troops. Characterized by generalized anxiety, panic attacks, inability to sleep, and recurring thoughts or dreams of the violent situations witnessed in battle, it is the most prevalent disorder being treated in our military hospitals and veteran centers.

Treatment includes antianxiety medication, individual and group psychotherapy to discuss the thoughts, issues, and problems the soldier is experiencing. Behavioral techniques are also important in treating this illness. People experiencing PTSD may work individually with a mental health professional or be treated in a group with others who are suffering from the same condition.

Some techniques used to help with this disorder may include relaxation techniques that aid in reducing the stress levels of the patient. Professionals teach people how to use visualization to imagine they are somewhere, in less stressful situations like lying down on the beach, walking in the mountains, or sleeping on a hammock somewhere. They learn how to control their thoughts and use deep breathing to become relaxed. Other techniques involve stretching and exercise, and use of good nutrition and supplements to make sure the body is healthy and not running on empty. Patients may be taught how to use yoga, tai chi, or transcendental meditation.

If you enjoy helping others but also enjoy learning about how other disciplines can work together to solve problems that are social, biological, or psychological, you may be interested in this field. Learning how to work with people who suffer from mental illnesses like PTSD involves understanding how the mind and the body work together. You need to study how nutrition affects both our mind and our body and how adding vitamins, minerals, and other supplements to our daily routines can help our organs function properly, reduce stress, and prevent an overload on our immune system. The importance of daily exercise and stretching is important for our muscles and aids in alleviating stress. Learning how to open up and talk with others about how we are feeling is also important to good mental health. We need the support of other people in order to cope with difficult situations. So, you can see how nutrition, psychology, sociology, and kinesiology are all fields that would be important for Human Services professionals to study if they wanted to work in mental health, particularly with PTSD patients.

Did You Know?

Communities Are Finding Creative Ways to Feed, House, Train, and Employ People.

There are so many social issues that individuals, groups, and families are trying to cope with, that Human Services agencies are in demand. Nonprofit organizations, public programs, and private for-profit agencies all offer services that provide individual counseling, day care, drug and alcohol rehabilitation, mental health group counseling, parent education, housing assistance, food stamps, health care, support services, probation and parole, victim's assistance, rape crisis, emergency housing, homeless shelters, foster care, adoption, nursing home care, home health care, hospice, as well as a multitude of services for disabilities.

Some communities are finding creative ways to fund housing and provide services for homeless individuals and families and also to train them for jobs. One program, Interfaith Hospitality Network, is available in 41 states and the District of Columbia and is very effective in getting local churches of all faiths to collaborate. Churches, representing a cross section of faiths, provide lodging for families for a short period of time. Church buildings may be used for volunteer meetings or case assessment and intake for the homeless. Each church takes turns being the host to a family for a short period of time while volunteers and professional workers assist the homeless individual or family with job training or employment searches. Day care centers provide the daily care of the children when needed, and church volunteers provide the meals while the homeless are located at their churches. This service has reduced the cost of providing for the homeless population by two thirds the cost of other shelter programs (Family Promise, 2012).

Communities have found creative ways to assist people with job training and employment as residents struggle to find jobs and more people move in and out of areas looking for work. It is estimated that one out of every four homeless people is a child. This has become more of a family issue in the last few years as unemployment has risen and people across America have lost their homes due to the mortgage crisis. Collaboration among agencies is more important than ever. One such program, the Starfish Cafe, in Savannah, Georgia, has gotten national attention. Organized under the umbrella of Union Mission, an organization serving the low-income and homeless populations in the area, it has partnered with the Savannah Technical College's Culinary Arts Program to provide training to local homeless folks. While living in a shelter, students attend the training program. The cafe is open six days a week and provides the final internship setting for homeless students who have completed the classroom portion of the culinary training. Lunch is offered for local residents in the cafe who come to buy the good food as well as the opportunity to help the students. Upon graduation from the program, caseworkers from Union Mission assist students in finding real restaurant employment in local establishments. It is a wonderful example of agencies collaborating to help homeless people get training and find jobs.

Read about the national attention <u>Union Mission and the Starfish Cafe</u> received when Al Roker and the *Today Show* came to visit.

What Would You Do?

Autism Is a Growing Concern among Parents.

There is an alarming rise in autism rates in the United States with 700,000 children now diagnosed with the illness. One in every 110 children will have autism, with rates for boys higher at 1 in 70 (Dr. Oz, 2013). Autism is a neurological disorder that affects the social and emotional development of a child. Issues of impulse control, difficulty with interpersonal relationships, and behavior disorders are all part of the illness. Communication for an autistic child is almost impossible. Autistic children see the world as a very complex and confusing place, and their emotional foundation is not developed enough for them to handle daily living. Dealing with a child with autism is stressful for the parent, siblings, teachers, and other family members. Knowing how to handle daily living situations before they get out of control is important. So educating caregivers, teachers, and other community members would help everyone learn how to deal with the growing number of autistic people.

If you watch the *Dr. Oz* seven-part television series <u>What Causes Autism?</u> you are sure to learn some new information, which could be helpful if you work in a Human Services agency where you deal with autistic people. Part 1 of the series is devoted to introducing you to three families who struggle with their autistic children. Watch Part 1 and choose one family to answer the critical thinking questions below. The series has seven parts that address various aspects of the illness.

Part 1—What causes autism?, Part 2—Are vaccines to blame?, Part 3—Pediatricians discuss where they stand on vaccines, Part 4—Dr. Oz reveals what he did for his own children, Part 5—The role of environmental risk factors, Part 6—Older mothers and autism—is there a link?, and Part 7—Warning signs every parent should know. The series will help build your knowledge base about autism, its challenges, and some ideas to help in your work with this population. After watching Part 1—What causes autism?—choose one case to answer the following questions.

Case Study

FAMILY ONE
Eileen is a single-parent mother with three autistic children. Gianna is eight years old, Marz is six, and Vincent is six.

FAMILY TWO
Alison Singer is the mother of Jodie who is 13 years of age. Alison is also the president of the Autism Science Foundation that funds research on autism.

FAMILY THREE
Charles is a married father of Malik who is six years of age.

CHOOSE A FAMILY AND ANSWER THE FOLLOWING QUESTIONS

FAMILY ONE
How would you define Autism? Is it a mental health, mental illness, or developmental issue? What are the challenges that Eileen faces with her children? What behaviors did you see in the video that would indicate Autism was present in her children? Who was the "guardian angel" that she spoke about in the video? Why is this resource important for her son? Do you think being a single parent is an issue for her? How so?

FAMILY TWO
How would you define autism? Is it a mental health, mental illness, or developmental issue? What are the challenges that Alison faces with Jodie? Did you see any unusual behaviors in the video that you would recognize as autistic? What are Alison's fears?

Do you think her role as president of the Autism Science Foundation effects her ability to care for Jodie in any way?

FAMILY THREE
How would you define autism? Is it a mental health, mental illness, or developmental issue? Charles spoke on behalf of his family. What are some of the challenges they face with Malik? Did you see any of his behaviors that you would recognize as autistic? Does Charles have any advantages or disadvantages in caring for his son as a married, adult male?

Recall what you learned in this chapter by completing the Chapter Review.

CHAPTER 9

Working with Children and Adolescents

· ·

Human Services Involves Working with Children and Adolescents in a Variety of Settings Using Specific Skills and Strategies

20th Century Fox Film corp/Everett Collection

Chapter Outline

Did you ever watch the movie *Home Alone*? If you did, you can probably remember Macaulay Culkin as the eight-year-old boy, Kevin, who accidentally gets left home when his family goes on a Christmas vacation. Antics abound when he is faced with a pair of idiotic burglars who attempt to rob the houses in his neighborhood. At first Kevin is afraid of being alone in his house and then realizes the *power that comes with independence*. He must fend for himself, make his own meals, and guard his home from attacks. Kevin becomes empowered and quickly learns how to purchase necessary items, becomes adept at avoiding the police and even faces his fears when he confronts the neighbor next door whom he believes is a murderer. *Home Alone* is a fine example of the fears, mistakes, and challenges children encounter as they grow up.

Unfortunately, in many families being left home to fend for yourself or to supervise younger siblings is not at all uncommon. In a real story from the *Detroit Free Press*, a robbery took place in the house where a ten-year-old boy was left home alone with his infant sister. The boy rushed to his neighbors for help and was not harmed in the break-in, but the thieves managed to get away with televisions and other electronics. The Detroit police were called and when it was discovered that the children were indeed home alone, the child protective authorities were called. The mother came home later in the day wondering where her children had gone. At what age do you think children are old enough to stay at home alone and care for other siblings?

Watch the video Detroit Kids Left Alone While House Is Robbed from the Detroit Free Press.

Why Do Children Need Services and What Programs Are Available?

Do you enjoy working with children and adolescents? Many of us may have grown up caring for younger siblings or assisting a neighbor or older family member with their children. I was an aunt at an early age and had the distinction of helping my sisters care for their children. I enjoyed organizing birthday parties and summer activities, but I was not left totally unsupervised until I was an older teen. Apparently my family realized there was the potential for too many dangerous or emergency situations to occur. I still had the opportunity to learn how to deal with childhood squabbles, teach the youngsters how to share, and feel good about my ability as the authority figure.

This chapter will explore the work Human Services workers do with children and adolescents who are under the age of 20. Age 17 or 18 is recognized in most states as the beginning of adulthood, even though age 16 is usually the age adolescents begin to drive legally. What is interesting is that **Erikson's Eight Stages of Psychosocial Development** lists adolescence as lasting into the early 20s. Psychologists today would even add a stage to Erikson's model. *Emerging adulthood* is the new stage, which describes the 20s as a time when young adults are still trying to figure out who they are and where they are going. Since today those in their 20s are still attending college, trying to get jobs, and may still live in their parent's home, some theorists say that the stage of Early adulthood may now not begin until the early 30s (Arnett, 2004). Sociologists tell us that those who marry tend to do so later than in years past (Goldstein & Kenney, 2001). Let's begin by talking about working specifically with children under the age of 12.

Working with Children

There are so many jobs that involve working with children of various ages. My first job was in a day care center, and I was a toddler teacher so I needed to know something about developmental stages. It is very important that you understand what constitutes appropriate development. Many of the parents that I worked with did not understand developmental stages because many of them had not finished high school and were not aware that even babies had tasks they had to master. That meant that in addition to working with my babies to ensure that they were walking, talking, and developing fine and gross motor skills, I also had to educate their parents. For example, new parents may believe that infants and toddlers will be fine resting in a crib or playpen all day while they clean the house, make dinner, watch TV, or do chores. Infant stimulation is extremely important to brain and physical development. We now realize that holding babies, making eye contact, reading to them, playing music, and exercising their growing limbs is an essential part of their development. So as Human Services workers, we not only work with children, but we also work with their parents, teachers, or other caregivers who may be in the home or in a day care center.

What are the stages of development for children? According to Erikson's Eight Stages of Psychosocial Development, human beings go through stages during their lifetime, mastering tasks along the way as they move from one stage to another. Some children go through stages faster than others, especially if they are provided with the right stimulation and nurturing from caregivers who allow them to grow and develop.

The task at hand for infants is learning how to develop trust. Babies learn this from their caregivers. If you provide food, a clean diaper, love and attention when a baby cries,

Table 9.1	Erikson's Stages of Psychosocial Development (Erikson, 1963)	
Age	**Developmental Stage**	**Task to Master**
Infancy (birth to 1 year)	Trust vs. Mistrust	Babies learn to trust when their needs are met.
Toddler (1–2 years)	Autonomy vs. Shame & Doubt	Toddlers master independence by doing things for themselves, or they are doubtful of themselves.
Preschool Age (3–5 years)	Initiative vs. Guilt	Preschoolers learn to initiate their own activities and take responsibility, or they become irresponsible.
Elementary School (6–12 years)	Industry vs. Inferiority	Children feel competent about learning new skills or they feel inferior to others.
Adolescence (13–early 20s)	Identity vs. Role Confusion	Adolescents develop good self-esteem and know who they are, or they become confused.

warmth, and a comfortable place to rest, a baby will learn that caregivers are there for him or her. When they cry, which is their way of communicating, someone should be there to make sure their needs are met. When these needs are met consistently, a baby develops trust. If no one attempts to ever comfort the crying baby, food is not given when the baby is hungry, and love, support, clean diapers, clothes, or bedding is never available, then the baby learns *not* to trust because no one is there to trust. So, as workers we need to teach those with infants and toddlers why it is important to meet their needs. This is especially important if we work with teen mothers who are adolescents themselves and may not understand the role of the caregiver.

Review Table 9.1 for some of the stages of development for children and adolescents.

Explore the eHow website for numerous parenting tips and advice for new moms.

Do you see yourself working with infants, toddlers, or parents of these youngsters?

Why Do Children Need Services?

Can you think of some of the reasons why Human Services professionals would work with children? Think of all the possible issues affecting children and families and that will give you some ideas. Human Services workers are employed in child welfare agencies, day care centers, camps, schools, residential group facilities, Head Start, churches, hospitals, mental health centers, YMCAs, community centers, recreational programs, organizations like the Girl Scouts and Boy Scouts, Salvation Army, Good Will, and in disability centers like United Cerebral Palsy, or Easter Seals.

Some issues affect a child's growth, and so workers assist to make sure services are provided so the child can *develop appropriately*. Some examples of these issues would be family *violence, physical abuse and neglect, homelessness, or lack of basic needs like food, clothing, or medicine*. Workers may help families find homes, apply for food stamps, or get medical care through Medicaid or a state health insurance. Sometimes workers collect clothing for families that can be distributed at schools or other locations. Human Services workers may also assist parents in finding jobs so they have the money to afford basic necessities for their children. Sometimes children have to be removed from homes because it is *not safe* for a child to remain in the custody of their parents. Foster parents may be recruited so children can spend some time away from home while their parents get counseling, attend a drug and alcohol program, find a job and prepare to buy the necessary items needed for the child, or attend anger management classes. All of these programs are organized and a follow-up provided by the Human Services worker.

Even when children are developing normally, they still need appropriate **role models** and activities to enhance their learning. Programs like the Girl Scouts, Boy Scouts, community recreational programs, YMCAs, day camps, day care centers, and Head Start are all examples of programs that enhance a child's development. Human Services workers may be employed as *child care supervisors, teachers, or group workers*. In this role, the worker has to plan activities and games that are age-appropriate and fun! You need to teach children how to take turns, participate in a group, work independently and also as a team, learn to separate from their parents and family members, and learn how to work with new leaders. This can be especially difficult for young children who may not have had the opportunity to attend programs away from their parents. **Separation anxiety** may occur, which causes great distress for the child and oftentimes for the parent(s) as well. One way to deal with this anxiety is for the child and parent to attend a *pre-visit* to the center, camp, or facility where the child can meet the staff and other children while the parent is in attendance. The program can be explained to both the parent and the child, and then some time should be used for the child to begin to play with others while the parent watches. The child will begin to feel comfortable with the staff and other children, and the parent can see that the child is happy and the program is safe. Now when the first day of the program comes, it won't be such a shock for the child to come into the building. The child and the parent are now familiar with the surroundings. Make sure the person who met with the child and parent at the pre-visit is there to greet them both on their first day. Consistency is important. Remind them of the fun that is occurring that day and then allow the child to say goodbye to the parent. Move the child into the play area so the child can begin the day.

> **Human Systems**

Understanding and Mastery: Theories of human development; changing family structures and roles

Critical Thinking Question: Thinking about Erikson's theories, how can Human Services workers assist children with their development if they are struggling to deal with their parents' divorce, death of a parent or sibling, sickness, violence in the home, or inability of their mentally ill parent to care for them?

• •

According to professional standards, Human Services students must be prepared to work with individuals, groups, and families and have an understanding of the theories of human development if they are to work with various populations. Our curriculum must include the knowledge and theory of the interaction of human systems and how they all work together. Think of all the connections that a child needs in order to develop successfully. These would include individual, group, family, organizations, community, and societal networks. Take a minute and reflect about the kinds of issues children would have with any of these systems if they were not functioning properly.

By now you have probably thought of a thousand reasons why children may need services. You would be correct if you said children are effected by *divorce, death of a family member, moving, drugs and alcohol in the home, family violence, unemployment of the parent, homelessness, gang influence in the neighborhood, medical problems with a parent or the child, mental health issues with a parent, self-esteem issues, juvenile delinquency, poor school performance, anger management*

Test your comprehension of Working with Children and Why Do Children Need Services? by completing this quiz.

issues, adoption, foster care, military deployments of parents, peer pressure, inability to make friends, or problems adjusting to new situations like schools or new communities.

What Types of Programs Are Available?

Children need all types of programming to help them develop, and we have a continuum of these services available from prevention through crisis services. **Family support services** are those efforts that are designed to *prevent* problems from occurring in family life, whereas **family preservation services** are put into place after a family *crisis* has occurred (Crosson-Tower, 2013).

Family support services offer programs that all children can take advantage of, and they provide a mix of activities, information, and support services on a voluntary basis. Workers provide these services in early childhood or Head Start Centers, schools, or organizations like the YMCA, Girl Scouts or Boy Scouts. Community and recreational programming falls into this category. You may work in a neighborhood center that provides day care, summer camp, or weekend activities, as well as periodic events that give children information they need to make good decisions. One of our community centers teaches children about "good touch and bad touch," a prevention program for child sexual abuse. Children learn where people can and cannot touch them, and whom to tell if they are touched inappropriately. Some recreational centers provide drug and alcohol information to children as young as elementary school age because we know that in some neighborhoods, children are approached to buy drugs at an early age. Human Services workers are employed in these centers and provide support and guidance to children, supervise their activities, and often make referrals to other services that a child may need like medical care, or personal counseling. Workers may identify a child who appears to have been abused, left unsupervised in the home, or allowed to run freely in the streets late at night. This type of behavior can lead to criminal arrests and delinquent charges. So workers may refer these children for services from the local child welfare agencies before they get into serious trouble. For the most part though these programs are voluntary and the children and families who attend want to be there. You will have a mix of children with appropriate developmental skill levels and those who need some assistance, support, or intervention. Human Services workers are sure to find enjoyable jobs working with the day care center, teen zone, or adult counseling program. These community programs with activities available for all ages are the services of the future.

If you enjoy working with young children, have a lot of energy, and an abundance of patience, then you would love working in these types of programs. Get ready to supervise large groups of children, go on field trips to local places of interest, and learn to develop games and activities for small and large groups. If you have an ability like *singing, dancing,* or *playing an instrument,* you can easily use these *skills* in your professional work with children. Do you like *art?* You use plenty of imagination, paste, glue, crayons, and paint when you work with small children.

Explore the Brea Community Center in California for activities it offers for children and families.

Watch the video on The Importance of Play produced by the Gesell Institute of Human Development at Yale University and Kaboom Play, a national nonprofit organization dedicated to building a great place to play for every child in America.

Family Preservation Services of the Department of Family and Children's Services in the United States comes into play when a crisis has occurred in a family and local authorities must step in to protect a child who is in danger. These services are not voluntary, and so the skill of the worker is important in developing relationships with families that are sometimes resistant. Often families do not see the critical nature of the event and do not want the service that is required. Remember my case with Sharon and Harry in Chapter 8? Clearly Harry did not want my services in the beginning and saw no need for the county to step in and offer day care or a home for his family. It was necessary for me to develop a working relationship with him in order for both him and Sharon to cooperate with my agency. Insisting that people do something is not the best way to handle family situations. Although, at times it is the last resort when families simply cannot agree with the court system or other agencies. In the beginning if workers develop good relationships with their consumers, it benefits everyone. If people feel that you are really there to provide assistance and you follow through and do what you say you will do, families will learn to trust you. It is much easier to work with a family on *mutual goals* that everyone can agree on, than to insist they do something. That is why learning how to develop your interpersonal skills is so important.

Family preservation services are crisis services and include programs like child welfare agencies that provide *foster care, residential group care for children, and adoptions.* Services may also include *juvenile probation and parole, youth detention facilities, domestic violence shelters, mandatory individual or family counseling, child advocacy centers, rape crisis programs, drug and alcohol treatment, or classes in parenting or anger management.* Workers in these facilities are dealing with children who have been victimized or traumatized by an event they have witnessed. These children may have been exposed to murder, beatings, incest, and events beyond your wildest imagination. Children are often exploited by adults because they are powerless both physically and emotionally. Young children trust adults who may take advantage of them. Human Services workers then have to use their skills to develop appropriate relationships with these children and teach them to trust adults again. This can be a difficult and lengthy process. Be prepared for children who are angry, do not respond, are sassy, critical, or violent.

Family preservation services also include intensive work with biological families that may need help with parenting skills, appropriate discipline, and housekeeping. Imagine that some people grow up never learning why it is important to keep a clean house, assist a child with homework, or have consequences when rules are not followed at home. As a Human Services worker, you may be teaching your families these life skills. Remember the case of Sharon and Harry in Chapter 8? The children had never been in a bathtub or slept in a real bed before moving into the apartment that I acquired for them. That may seem impossible to believe, but that is the reality of what we sometimes deal with in Human Services.

Learning how to use **behavioral techniques** will help you in working with these children. You may have to take small steps in your relationship, develop realistic goals they can achieve, listen to what they have to say, and provide the type of service you think they need. You may feel that working with them on an individual basis is what the child needs right now. Perhaps some children would benefit from a group with other children who have similar issues. Remember that small children often cannot identify their emotions and they are sometimes confused by what they are thinking or feeling. Children learn through play and so it is natural for children to express themselves and deal with their problems through play. Young children would have difficulty sitting in a group therapy session and "talking" about what they see as the problem. They would quickly tell you the group is boring and would want to know what activities you had planned for them. So, workers in these settings have to establish games and exercises that children can play to help them work through their issues and assist them with developing the skills they need to cope with difficult situations. Art and play therapy can be useful treatment modalities to learn in working with these children. Allowing the children to express themselves through an art activity can free the child from pent up feelings of anger, loss, or sadness. Then the worker can discuss the artwork with the child to listen, lend support, or use their skills of reflection to help the child become aware of how he or she is feeling.

Another type of programming is available for children with disabilities and involves providing them with the tools they need to develop both physically and mentally. Some children may have congenital abnormalities that challenge their cognitive and physical abilities. Workers with state health departments, United Cerebral Palsy, or programs like Babies Can't Wait will deal with children who struggle to walk or gain control of their muscles, have hearing and speech impediments, have visual disorders, have great difficulty with other fine or gross motor skills, developmental delays, autism, or emotional disturbances. Human Services workers in these programs must

Watch the video to learn more about Play Therapy from the Association for Play Therapy.

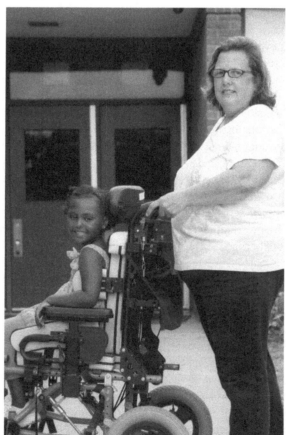

Kim Gunkel/E+/getty images

Human Services practitioners may work with special needs children in schools, day care centers, rehab programs, or hospitals.

be knowledgeable about appropriate stages of development as well as the illnesses and developmental delays affecting these children. Additional training is sometimes offered by the agency, and workers are expected to have a level of experience in working with children with disabilities. Employment for workers includes such jobs as *case managers*, *intake workers*, *child care supervisors, or group workers*. Children in these facilities may attend full- or part-time and additional supportive services may be needed in the home. Working with the parents is necessary, and the Human Services workers may coordinate all the services the child needs as well as work to involve the parents in the treatment plan.

Preservation services are crisis oriented and are the most expensive programs to operate because they often involve removing a child from the home and placing them in a foster home, group home, or residential treatment facility. Child welfare services are costly because court services are usually mandated, and other programs like juvenile probation and parole may be involved. In addition, court-mandated drug and alcohol treatment programs are expensive. Supportive services are less costly and are voluntary. These services offer appropriate activities, supervision, and role models for youth. However, these programs, because they are preventive in nature, are not seen as necessary and often struggle for funding. Head Start, the federally funded early childhood program for the economically disadvantaged, is threatened with either cuts or closings every budget year. Do you think we should put more money into supportive services that are preventive than we do for preservation services, which are crisis oriented? What is a good solution for this problem? Write down your thoughts and then discuss with your peers in a small group.

When we work with children, we have to be prepared to offer a variety of services as well as techniques to different age groups. As a home and school visitor, I often had to work with young children in the day care center, do screenings and assessments, meet with parents to discuss the results of testing, and then either make referrals to agencies or create services for the children in our program. I conducted parent education training programs, facilitated single-parent groups, learned how to conduct early childhood screenings, and counseled young children. One of the most effective ways to help children with their emotional and behavioral issues is through a type of counseling called play therapy. Children learn through play, and since they often cannot express verbally what they feel, play is the best medium for them to work through their issues. In the following case, I worked with a few children who were exhibiting social and emotional problems in the day care center. The case is specifically about Amy, a four-year-old cancer survivor who attended the children's center, but who was reluctant to engage in activities with other children and did not seem happy in her interactions with others. I was asked to intervene by her teacher who was concerned for Amy's development.

Test your comprehension of <u>What Types of Programs Are Available?</u> by completing this quiz.

Case Study ▸ Child Counselor

When I was a caseworker/home and school visitor/counselor, I worked in a comprehensive child development program and often wore many hats. We provided educational day care, protective services to children who were in foster care but attended our day program, speech therapy, testing and screening services, transportation for children who lived in isolated areas of the county, medical care, counseling services for children and their parents, and a single-parent support group. I often worked with individual children who were having difficulty with the loss of a parent through divorce or death, transition to school, separation anxiety, and medical problems.

Amy was four years old and had suffered with leukemia for three years. Her cancer was currently in remission, and her prognosis was excellent. Her parents were delighted. She was still quite thin with short, wispy blond hair that was growing in after her treatments. She was referred to me by her teacher because after four months in the center, she was still seen as introverted, shy, reluctant to participate, and did not make friends easily. Her attendance was sporadic, and although she did not suffer from separation anxiety in the morning, it was clear that she did not appear happy to be there. She never smiled, and her whole demeanor was one of sadness and hesitancy. I observed Amy over a few days in different areas of the center and noticed that she enjoyed the art corner the best. So, I proceeded to develop a plan for her and developed both an individual and group curriculum, which I shared with her parents. They agreed with the plan of activities, signed the consent forms, and we began our work together which lasted for nine sessions. The treatment plan included one-hour activities on Monday, Wednesday, and Friday for three weeks. There was no fee for the service since her parents had already paid for the program, and I was a full-time staff member.

I also developed similar, individual plans with three other children who were having difficulties. Ethan had recently had an eye surgery for a cancerous tumor and was adjusting to his glass eye. He was five years old and had recently returned to the center after being absent for six months due to his surgery and rehabilitation. He returned with a glass eye that other children had not seen. Josh, age five, was having difficulties with his parents' separation and was usually a happy, active child. Recently he was having some tantrums followed by periods of silence and inactivity. Ginny, age four, was a happy child who was born with a visual impairment that left her blind in one eye and with the ability to see with the other, but with glasses so thick it was a wonder that she could see anything. She was often teased by a few of the other children who were frequently reprimanded by the teachers for this behavior. She would get physical, hitting other children when they teased her and this just seemed to spark more teasing. My plans included work with all four children individually for the first week and then weeks 2 and 3 would involve group work with all four children. I would evaluate the children's behavior at that point to determine if more sessions were needed. All the children had been referred to me by their teachers who were concerned about their lack of participation (Amy, Ethan) or acting out behavior (Josh, Ginny). Self-esteem was a concern for all the children. I will focus on Amy for this case, but I wanted you to have a description of the other children in my group. Here is an excerpt from one of my sessions with Amy.

***

Week One: The first day that I met with Amy, I explained that I was a counselor in the center. I knew that she was aware of me, but I was not sure she was clear of my role that was different than a teacher's. We talked about what I did, and I allowed her to visit my office and walk around looking at all the toys and games I used with the children. She was curious about each doll, puppet, or teddy bear, and we played a game naming each toy. I suggested we use names of the children from the center, and she eagerly did this demonstrating to me that she did know the names of her classmates. I smiled often and complimented her on her ability to remember the names of the children. She giggled and gave a slight smile. After about ten minutes of this game, I asked if she liked to draw. She said she did, so I asked if she would like to draw a picture of herself. She thought about this for a few seconds and then nodded yes. I proceeded to gather the necessary items and asked her to help me retrieve the butcher-block roll of paper, crayons, markers, glue, yarn, fabric, glue stick, and scissors. She followed me to a private corner of the art room, which was empty. It was naptime, and she was given special privileges to meet with me instead of sleeping. She quietly asked if I was taking her back to her cot. When I told her she was free of naps for a few afternoons while we played together, she smiled. "Will the other kids have to take naps?" "Yes, today they will. Although next week, Ethan, Josh, and Ginny will join us for some games, and they won't have to nap either. We will all play together." She was quiet as she thought about this and then asked what we were going to do today. I asked her to help me roll out the butcher-block paper on the floor. This was a chore because it was quite heavy. We both laughed as we managed to get the block of paper to roll just right. Finally the paper was spread out in a large area of the art corner. "What are we going to do with this?" she asked wide eyed. "Lie down with your back on the paper and I will draw an outline of your body all around the paper," I said. She looked puzzled but did as I asked. I took the large black marker and proceeded to draw her outline on the paper while she lay perfectly still. She giggled when I came too close with the marker and it tickled her ear. When I was done, she got up and looked at the outline. "Well, that is a big body, but it looks nothing like me," she announced. "That is your job," I said. "Use any of the materials that we have and draw your image inside the outline. Make your face with the crayons or markers, put on the hair with yarn, use the fabric to make clothes, draw in your hands and feet with paint, color your shoes, whatever you want to draw. Here is a mirror if you want to look at yourself while you are drawing. Use the scissors to cut up whatever you want and then paste everything on the Amy body." She looked doubtful, hesitated, but then started slowly and began drawing in her features. She stopped, looked in the mirror, waited, and thought about her next step. Then she began to draw again. I was impressed with the detail she provided as she obviously took this job so seriously. I realized then what a pensive child Amy was and how that played into her behavior at school. She thought about things carefully before she did them, unlike the impulsive nature of the other four year olds that we dealt with at the center. This was a very mature child who was forced to deal with an adult medical illness in her early years. No doubt her parents were always serious, careful in their deliberations about what course of treatment to obtain for their daughter. She was used to adults and careful, logical, serious considerations. She was not used to noisy, impulsive, raucous children who played with abandon and didn't have a care in the world. She was probably put off by this behavior and a little timid about how to get into this type of play. She was also an only child and did not have the benefit of a sibling to play with or observe. I sat nearby and watched her work, commenting on what she was doing. "You look very serious Amy. I can tell this is important to you. You are a very good artist. Those really look like your beautiful, blue eyes." She carefully cut fabric to make a shirt and pants and then glued them into place. I thought her fine motor skills were excellent as I noticed how well she cut with the safety scissors, how she managed to get the shirt and pants glued on the body just right. I wondered if her illness had forced her to sit quietly with coloring books and crayons for long periods of time, rather than exerting herself running and jumping like other young children. When she finished, she stood back and observed her artwork. "Amy it is beautiful, and you worked so hard on it. I think you are a wonderful artist. What do you think?" I said. "Can I take it home for my mother to see," she asked proudly? "Of course, but I do have one question," I remarked. "You colored in your eyes, your shoes, gave yourself some clothes, and even painted your fingernails, but I notice that you didn't give yourself much hair," I said. "That is because I don't have much. It all fell out when I was sick. I had beautiful, long blond curls and they all fell out. Now my hair is ugly," she said matter-of-factly. She said this with such frankness that I was taken aback. "Amy, your hair is not ugly. It did fall out when you were sick, but it has grown back. It is thicker now and although it is short, it will continue to grow. If you want it long, it will grow long again." I said. "It will?" she said with a look of astonishment. "Amy, look in the mirror. What do you see?" We both looked in the mirror at the beautiful child with the short, golden hair and smiled. I knew that I had a lot of work to do on self-esteem with Amy. I also knew that we had a wonderful beginning.

Answer these critical thinking questions for the <u>**Case Study: Child Counselor**</u>**.**

Would you like this type of work? You can be very creative in developing curriculum for a child. The expressive arts can be very helpful when you are working with people who are not verbal. Consider art, music, dance, poetry, play, drama, even cooking to help people express their thoughts and feelings. This is the first step to changing behavior, feeling better, and becoming happier and healthier individuals.

I used many skills and treatment techniques when I worked with children in the center. However, I had to present them as games since children's play is work. Unlike adults who may answer direct questions or know how they are feeling, children get more out of play.

Games and Activities for Children

When you work with children, you often feel like Mary Poppins because you need a bagful of activities, games, songs, and fun. Keep a file of all of your "tools" and add to them as your professional life goes on. I have worked with children for many years as a day care teacher, home school visitor, counselor, child welfare caseworker, social worker, Human Services worker, trainer, Girls Scout leader, Boy Scout den mother, soccer mom, school chaperone, and college professor. I started keeping a file of games, songs, and activities years ago, and I still have it. I used it with my own children and the neighborhood gang when all the kids would come to our home to finger paint with pudding, make peanut butter play dough, have art parties, or dinosaur digs. I really enjoy playing with children, and as a worker you really do have to get down on their level and *play with them*. Children are not inhibited so it takes adults a while to learn how to play without feeling foolish. If you see yourself working with children under age 12, you may enjoy some of these games and activities.

BIBLIOTHERAPY   Books are a wonderful way to connect with a child, so reading together can be a useful activity. After the book is read, discuss the meaning of the book, what the child understood, or the message you want the child to learn. Some good books are *The Giving Tree*, *There's a Nightmare in My Closet*, and *Where the Wild Things Are*. Dr. Seuss's books are a wonderful way to teach children to read and build self-esteem at the same time. The *Goose Bumps* series is mildly scary and teaches children how to handle some basic emotions like fear, frustration, and anger.

The Harry Potter series is for older children who can handle scary, magical type stories. Any book that can be read and discussed with themes that impact the child is important. Consider books about divorce or death, moving to a new home/location, living in a military family, adjusting to a new sibling/baby in the home, coping with foster care, adoption, incarcerated parents, drugs or alcohol in the home, family violence, running away or basic issues of growing up.

MOVIES OR VIDEOS   These can also be useful in teaching a child how to cope with an issue. Watch a movie together and then discuss its implications. Disney movies are family friendly, and most contain themes that can be discussed like divorce, death, moving, acceptance, self-identity, making friends, growing up, making good decisions, or a variety of relationship and family issues. Movies like *Shrek*, *Toy Story*, *Lion King*, *Home Alone*, ET, and *Mrs. Doubtfire* are all good examples of movies that deal with issues that affect children.

ARTS AND CRAFTS   If you work with children consider using all types of art medium: paints, clay, sand, markers, crayons, ceramics, drawing materials, and scraps of paper, fabric, carpet, or textiles for crafts. Allow children to use their imagination to make puppets, create their own dialogue for shows, and make puppet theaters so they can give shows to other children. Let them mix paints, do finger painting with foods like pudding, create sand tables, draw pictures of themselves and others, make memory books, tee shirts, and create objects from clay. Imagination is a wonderful tool that children need to use to feel better about themselves and to develop competence and self-esteem.

MUSIC AND MOVEMENT   Allow children to sing, dance, play instruments, and enjoy music and movement. This release is important to children who may have been sitting in classrooms for eight hours a day. After-school programs and day care centers need to have plenty of music and movement activities. If you don't play an instrument turn on your MP3 player so children will have the benefit of happy melodies. Create areas where children can enjoy this activity and encourage song, dance, and music, which can also be combined with other areas like art. It is beneficial for children to attend programs that offer music in the background of the center activities. It also helps maintain control because if children like the music, they will listen to it and be less likely to engage in yelling, fighting, or other attention-getting behavior.

> **Explore the PBS website and select Elmo; browse the videos for Sesame Street to find Choreographer-Melissa McCarthy & Elmo.**

SPORTS AND OUTDOOR ACTIVITIES   Many children today are obese, spending their days in school and their time at home on the computer. If you work with children, get them outside. Organize a softball game, play basketball, teach them to swim, take them hiking or on a picnic, or show them how to row a boat. Any outdoor activity is wonderful for exercise, sunshine, and fun! Children need to participate in team activities, learn to ride a bike, play soccer, or just run around. Many children today come from families where money is not available for extra curricular activities like team sports, camps, or lessons of any kind. Many single-parent families headed by females do not have males who can take a boy fishing, teach boys how to throw a ball, or provide the guidance that young boys need. If you work with single-parent females with sons, make sure that you find appropriate, adult males who can mentor these boys.

Human Systems

Understanding and Mastery: How small groups are used in Human Services settings; group facilitation skills

Critical Thinking Question: How comfortable are you facilitating groups for children where you play games, perform puppet shows, or sing and dance? These are skills we need when we work with children.

Working with Adolescents

If you enjoy working with adolescents you have your work cut out for you. This is probably one of the most tumultuous stages of development and can be very trying for the adolescent as well as the parents, caregivers, teachers, and coaches who attempt to guide the youngster toward adulthood. *Adolescence is the transition between childhood and an emerging adult* and can last for many years, although it is traditionally marked as the time between ages 12 and about 20. As children grow and develop, their bodies change physically, their brains develop and mature effecting reasoning abilities, and their emotions take a roller-coaster ride. If you have ever worked with children who are entering puberty, you know how difficult it can be with happy, cooperative people one moment and sobbing, obstinate ones the next. Adolescents are often embarrassed by their physical changes in height, weight, or growth of breasts, facial hair, or the deepening of a male voice. As the reproductive organs develop, girls begin **menarche** or their first menstruation. This can be a frightening time for girls who are prepared for this change or who have not been instructed as to what is happening to their bodies. **Spermarche** is the term for a boy's first ejaculation. This can be a difficult time for boys who live in female, single-parent households if no male is available to guide the young man and answer his questions. The average age for the onset of puberty in girls is now 10 in North America and about 12 for boys, much younger than in previous centuries. This is most likely due to our diet and decreasing childhood diseases (Baird, 2012).

According to Erikson, adolescents enter a stage of development called *Identity vs. Role Confusion.* In this stage they become self-aware and begin to understand what they like and don't like, examine their values, and determine career goals. Adolescents choose their peers and are conscious of any imperfections that will draw attention to themselves like weight issues, braces, acne, or poor choices in clothing. They try hard to fit in but also want to be acknowledged for their individuality. When I look back at my junior high school pictures, all the girls look alike! We all have straight hair, parted down the middle, with pierced ears and similar clothing. The boys resemble one another as well with the same long hairstyle, jeans and tee shirts. During adolescence **cliques** often develop and allow only certain people to enter into their circle of friends. This makes it extremely difficult for the adolescent who wants to be part of the clique but is not invited to join. The pressure of fitting in to a particular peer group can be daunting for adolescents but also helps them form a sense of identity. At times the identity they develop may come in conflict with the identity parents want their children to assume.

Joining a gothic group and wearing all black and having multiple body piercings may stimulate disagreements and arguments at home if parents are not supportive of this identity. Many adolescents are in constant struggles with their parents over clothing, make-up, curfews, and other house rules. As adolescents demand their independence, parents fear that their children are not making good choices and may get into trouble with drugs, alcohol, unprotected sex, or break the law. The pressure of developing a sense of identity coupled with the fear of not fitting in with your peers as well as conflicts at home can be cause for emotional turmoil in adolescence.

Explore _The Humanity Project_ where they use music and the arts to teach kids about issues like self-esteem, bullying, and helping others.

Why Do Adolescents Need Services?

What are some of the reasons that adolescents would need Human Services? Consider that workers may be employed in schools, hospitals, drug and alcohol treatment facilities, mental health centers, counseling centers, runaway shelters, recreational programs, career oriented services, teen pregnancy programs, residential treatment programs, foster homes, or organization like the Boys and Girls Clubs, Boy Scouts and Girl Scouts, and local community centers or recreational programs.

Like children with the same issues, adolescents suffer from _divorce, death of a loved one, family violence, drug and alcohol in the home, homelessness, poverty, unemployment of a parent, or anger issues._ Adolescents also have additional pressures because they are still developing emotionally and cognitively, and their judgment is often impaired. At the same time, they are physically capable of doing things that a child cannot. We often see adolescents who _drop out of school, run away from home, are able to acquire drugs and alcohol, drive cars while under the influence of substances, or get pregnant after casual sexual encounters._ Teens who run away from home usually do so because of sexual abuse or violence in the home. They often become the target of exploitation by adults who lure them into pornography or prostitution. Workers then must be ready to address the needs of adolescents, be patient, listen to them, treat them with the respect they desire but also with the understanding that they still need assistance in good decision-making. Adolescents may more readily accept the help of a school counselor or Human Services worker at a Boys and Girls Club or recreational center than they would of their own parents. Workers must know how to use their skills to negotiate contracts and treatment plans with both the adolescent and their caregiver/parent. Until the age of adulthood, which is usually 17 or 18 in most states, treatment can only be given with parental consent. Most agencies will require the parents or guardians to agree with and sign treatment plans.

Explore the HBO website for information on Adolescent Addiction.

Test your comprehension of Working with Adolescents and Why Do Adolescents Need Services? by completing this quiz.

What Types of Programs Are Available?

what to expect regarding their physical changes and sexuality. Both boys and girls need to understand the role of *hormones* in their development and how to avoid risky and irresponsible behavior. These discussions are necessary but often disregarded by adolescents who don't believe anything will happen to them. It is very sobering when friends and relatives they know become pregnant, overdose on drugs, or receive DUIs for excessive drinking. As a worker you may teach courses on drug and alcohol awareness and prevention, sexual activity and teenage pregnancy, or mental health issues.

Deciding what career path to follow is also a part of growing older. You may be working in a school setting in a guidance department and assisting students with their college applications, SATs, or college visitations. You may be scheduling speakers for a career day where local professionals can present information on their industry or how to pursue such a job. Part of self-identity involves knowing who you are and what you want to become.

Family preservation services include programs like child welfare, family and children's services, juvenile probation and parole, sheriff youth camps, residential group homes, foster care, domestic violence shelters, rape crisis centers, homeless shelters, runaway centers, drug and alcohol programs, and mental health services. They typically come into play when a family support system breaks down and a young person is left unsupervised with little guidance, often in dangerous or desperate circumstances. If you work in these facilities you will be providing treatment rather than preventive services and activities.

Drug and alcohol issues in the home can escalate into family violence, often involving adolescents who may try to protect other family members or themselves. Foster homes may be provided for adolescents who are not able to remain in their own homes. When adolescents choose friends that engage in drinking, drugs, or unlawful acts like theft, burglary, or selling drugs they are likely to get arrested and spend time in a juvenile correctional facility. Obtaining legal representation and attending court can be an uncomfortable experience for a family that has not suffered such problems in the past. Financial burdens may make it difficult to pay for proper legal representation and the adolescent may spend more time in a correctional facility than he or she had planned. All this may be happening at a time when an adolescent is developing self-identity. Human Services workers have to encourage their young clients to finish their treatment plans, make better decisions, and get on with their life. The difficulty is in ensuring that the adolescent does not identify with a life of crime or see that this lifestyle is somehow adventurous. This is where appropriate adult role models can help a young person to envision a better life through education, hard work, and good decision-making. Adolescents in these programs have already suffered abuse, rapes, beatings, stabbings, gun-shot wounds, drug and alcohol addictions, or have been arrested for crimes.

It is much easier to help a healthy child develop a positive, self-identity through preventive services than it is to help an abused, angry, emotionally damaged child develop a positive self-image once a crisis has occurred. We need all kinds of programming to help our youth and many Human Service workers to assist our children and families at each stage of development so that family crisis is the exception. Consider this case when I was a recreational worker with children and adolescents. Developmental issues, drugs, gangs, peer pressure, and juvenile delinquency were all part of what I saw in one summer.

When I was a student, I was hired as a community recreation worker for the county where I lived. During the summer, the elementary schools were used as recreation sites, and workers were employed to plan daily activities and supervise groups of neighborhood children from preschool age to adolescence. This was a common practice in the northeast at that time and allowed a diverse group of neighborhood children to attend a program close to their home. Boys and girls of all ages and ethnic and racial backgrounds would spend their summers at the recreation program. We were allowed to use certain rooms in the school as well as the playground area, and we were open from 9 a.m. to 5 p.m., Monday through Friday.

The particular school where my recreation program was based was in a low-income, disadvantaged neighborhood in a school that had limited resources to use and a playground that was old and in disrepair. I had requested the county evaluate our resources, but was told that some playgrounds were better than others and ours had been updated two years earlier. Apparently the equipment had been broken during that time, and the county did not have money in the budget to repair the playground again. I had access to whatever mobile resources the county had in its storeroom downtown. I visited there frequently to collect arts and crafts materials, musical equipment, jump ropes, basketballs, softballs, and snacks for our program.

I was hired along with another coworker, and our task was to stimulate and enrich the environment of the neighborhood for the summer. I was delighted with my summer job as it gave me a chance to use the skills I was learning in child and adolescent development, community outreach, and program planning. It turned out my partner was not as thrilled with the job and spent his time playing basketball alone on the playground, leaving me to organize the day's activities and deal with the task of supervising about 50 children and adolescents. I had no idea of the challenges I would face with this employment.

Planning the daily activities was very rewarding. I had a list of games that was provided by the county, and I had created my own list of games I remembered from my Girl Scout days. I had also taken classes in early childhood and had a file of activities and games useful for different age groups. I arrived early each morning to set up the playground area with volleyballs and nets, basketballs in the designated area, hung the swings that we took in each night, and turned on the water for a small cement wading pool for the young children who often came to the playground with their mothers. I created new areas for hopscotch, jump rope, and another area for Chinese jump rope, with a rope I had designed myself out of rubber bands. I also set up an arts and crafts area along with different activities each day to make it more interesting for the children, so they didn't get bored with the same games. I would put out various materials to make pot holders, lanyards, puppets, and a space for play dough and clay modeling, painting, or a sewing project where the older children could make purses, ties, or colorful headbands, badges, tee shirts, or jewelry with sparkles, paint, yarn, or whatever else we had to decorate their item. We also had a small kiln so participants could create some pottery out of clay, and it could be baked in the oven later in the afternoon. I kept the inside of the building for snack time or whenever it got too hot for everyone to be outside. On rainy days, I would bring games from home and set up battleship, monopoly, twister, candyland, checkers, clue, scrabble and card games like old maid, fish, and rummy. Picnic tables lined the inside of the basement that we were allowed to use. We were not to go beyond this room into the classrooms, which were on the upper floors. The basement door that led to the upstairs was locked so as not to tempt anyone from disobeying this rule. There was certainly plenty to do both inside and out of the building so having access to the classrooms was not necessary and was a big no-no as far as the county recreation program was concerned. "Stay out of the classrooms" was the constant mantra we heard from our supervisors.

I enjoyed planning the day's activities and seeing the smiles on the faces of the children and teens as they arrived. Many had never played the games that I provided and were in constant awe of some board game or activity that was totally new to them. As a result, we had a banner year at the playground! Both boys and girls enjoyed the games, and the boys were often the ones who wanted to try Chinese jump rope because they had never seen it before. We had more participants that summer than the county had ever registered before in that playground. Supervisors would stop by to see how we were doing and they would check the registration sheet to make sure the addresses of the participants were local. Some days the playground was so full people were waiting in line to play both indoor and outdoor games.

I was pleased there was so much enthusiasm for the program, but it was difficult supervising so many children, making sure adults were in the pool with small children, teaching youngsters how to play the games and follow the rules appropriately, and also listening to problems and arguments that had to be negotiated. It was amazing how many children had never learned to share, or how to wait to take their turn, or how to participate as a team member in a group sport. Older children bullied the younger ones, and young children were often impulsive and would lash out and hit or bite other children, or their siblings who would attend with them. Our job was to supervise and make sure that no one would get injured. After only a few days on the job, I learned that rules had to be posted. If they were not followed, it was important that consequences be activated. Some children were not allowed to attend playground activities for a day if they were sent home due to aggression or the breaking of some rules. Since they all wanted to participate, it was not hard to get everyone to start following the rules.

They enjoyed the activities I provided, and the snacks were a big hit since many of them indicated they had no food at home to eat. It was hard for me to imagine not having enough food to eat or not having snack food at home. The children ate heartily as if it were the only meal they would get that day. It might have been. On Fridays the county provided pizza, and everyone came to the playground on Fridays, including the mothers who would stay for the noon meal with their babies and young children. Obviously this program was important to the people of this community, and they frequently told me what a great summer program it was for them.

I was invited to the homes of some of the teenage girls. When I had my afternoon break, they would all encourage me to come to their homes to see their new kittens or puppies, new babies, or meet their grandmas. I loved being involved in their lives, and I spent time each day listening to their problems, teaching them how to French braid their hair, or allowing them to give manicures to each other in the basement of the school. They clearly enjoyed this "girl time," and we discussed boys, school, and their life goals and plans. I was exhausted when I went home each day but felt rewarded for the work that was done. I wanted to provide something new and exciting each day for the neighborhood since it seemed like they were enjoying it so much. After about three weeks, the climate changed as new participants emerged on the scene.

It was challenging to supervise both children and adolescents at the community center. I felt like I was getting pretty good at providing games and activities for all the different age groups that attended, and for the most part the days were busy and there were few incidents and only minor injuries like small cuts and bruises. Then one day when I arrived for work, I noticed a small group of older males rough housing on the playground equipment. They were much too big for the merry-go-round, and I was afraid they would break it. I walked over and introduced myself and asked them to please stop jumping on the equipment so hard, as it was sure to break. When I got up close, I saw that these were not older youth; they were men older than I was, perhaps between 21 and 24 years of age. They sneered at me and said, "hey teach, this is our play yard. We've been here long before you, and we'll be here long after you're gone. It's a free country; we can sit wherever we want." I asked them if they intended to stay for the day and what was their purpose? There were four of them, and they clearly looked to the tall, blond man with severe acne who was obviously their leader. I later learned his name was Nick. He responded by saying they had nothing to do that day so they might as well hang around. I told them I had to start setting up the games for the day and if they needed me I would be around the playground. Clearly this group of young men intimidated me, and I needed help. I found my partner playing basketball on the other side of the playground and told him about our newcomers. He said, "They have been here awhile. I heard there was a gang on this side of town, but since I don't live here I never saw them. Guess this is them." I wondered what we should do, and I asked for his opinion. "Nothing we can do right now. Let's just ignore them and maybe they will go away. Why would they want to hang around a children's playground anyway?" he said.

We did ignore them that day, but their presence seemed to be making everyone nervous. No longer did the mothers bring their babies and small children to the pool area. The boys who attended were not as cooperative and refused to play the games or activities saying they were stupid, sissy games. They argued loudly with their siblings or other children and started bullying the smaller children calling them names. When I suggested one boy go home for awhile and come back when he could cooperate, he sneered at me and dared me saying, "oh yeah, and who is gonna make me go home?" It was surprising to hear this retort since this boy had been so agreeable on other days. As he was talking back to me, I caught him glimpsing at the gang in the corner of the playground. It was obvious he was trying to impress them. The presence of this gang of older males had clearly affected the attendance and behavior of the participants of our program. At the end of each day, the boys would make their way to the corner of the playground where they would spend some time with this group of men. I saw those boys taking cigarettes from them, and I suspected there were probably other substances that might have changed hands, although I never saw it. I'm sure there was plenty of activity on this playground after hours.

Late one afternoon it started to rain and the children came into the building. I had games laid out on the tables and music playing for them. It was always easier to keep control of the group by using music since everyone would be quiet to listen to their favorite songs. Along with the children, in marched Nick and the gang who promptly sat on top of the picnic table forcing the children to move their games to a small corner of the room. I explained that the children wanted to play games and they would have to move. One of them said, "it's raining, and we don't want to get wet." They just sat there teasing the children, making fun of their art ability if they were drawing, or pushing the checkers around on the board and disrupting the game of two players. "You can help me supervise a group of children if you like," I said. I also suggested they play a game if they wanted to and they just laughed. I grew tired of their bullying and antics and asked them to leave since this was a program for children and adolescents and although they could sit on the playground, they really had no need to be in the building. One spoke up and said, "We're listening to the music." I don't know why I did this next thing, but I was so tired of all of them I walked to the radio and pulled the plug. "Now there is no music, please leave," I said firmly. They looked stunned but reluctantly got up and left. I was shaking after they left the building. One of the teen girls said, "You're brave, but you probably shouldn't have done that. That might come back and kill you. You can't believe the things they do." Another girl said, "That is not true. Johnny is the oldest and he's my cousin. He acts tuff but he isn't. Everyone thinks they are so bad, but my mom says they are just pathetic. They all failed out or dropped out of high school, have been in and out of jail, can't find or hold a job, and are always in some kind of trouble. Johnny started hanging with this group when his daddy died. He was the only one around here with a father, not many have daddies. He was close to his dad too." Although she was giving me a glimpse into the lives of these individuals, I still felt very uncomfortable and inadequate dealing with this gang of men. I was 19 at the time and all of these individuals were older than I was, and I was very intimidated by their presence each day, since I saw them as a threat to the younger children.

After work that day, I drove to the county office building and reported to my supervisor about the gang of men who had started hanging out on the playground. "Did they destroy anything?" she asked. "Not that I am aware of," I replied. "Did they hurt anyone or threaten someone?" "No," I said knowing what her answer would be before she spoke. "Well, they might be just looking for something to do, and we can't stop them from just sitting in the playground unless they are destroying something or hurting someone," she said. "Well they did jump on the equipment and I thought they would break it. They seem to be affecting both the attendance and the behavior of the children who do attend," I said. She thought about this for a minute and suggested I go back to planning activities and focus my energy on that, instead of on the uninvited group hanging out in the playground. She said she would look into the issue. The city was planning a parade for the bicentennial celebration of the city, and she wanted all the community centers to participate by making something that could be displayed on a float in the parade, which would be held at the end of the summer. All playground participants could ride on the float if they wanted to do so. I left the meeting feeling like my request for help was ignored, but I took her advice and started thinking about what I do best, planning activities.

The next day I circled the children and adolescents and told them about the parade that would take place downtown in August. They were excited about the prospect of riding on the float but some asked how they would get there? They had no car and their mothers worked during the day and no one was home to provide a ride. We decided we could all take public transportation together so that everyone could participate. It also made me realize that some of these children were left alone at home and the community center was being used as a free day care center for the summer. No wonder everyone was so hungry at snack time.

For the next few weeks, the community center was busy as everyone worked together to decide what to make that would represent our program for the parade. I let them make the decision as to what they wanted to do and a few teens had the idea of making a huge, paper-mache birthday cake for the city. Everyone agreed and the cake was formed, the paper-mache put into place, then it was painted and decorated with paper-mache candles. It was a messy job but everyone enjoyed doing it. They left each day excited about what they were doing and how the cake was coming along. Some of the children spoke to the men who still sat in the corner of the playground and they cheerfully told them about the beautiful cake they were making and how they were learning to use paper-mache. It took several weeks to complete and one of the teens, who knew how to do calligraphy, drew a beautiful script across the top that read "Happy Birthday to the City." Everyone was excited about the result, and we left the building that last evening with the cake drying on the picnic table in the basement. I locked the door and looked forward to the parade the next day. When I returned in the morning and opened the door, the cake was smashed into a million pieces and the lock to the upstairs classrooms was broken.

When the children arrived that morning and saw the damage, they were shaken, angry, and some started to cry. I felt defeated but had to keep my enthusiasm up for the group. They were all looking forward to participating in the parade, and I wondered how we could still do this. It was obvious to everyone who had done the damage, and someone indicated that Nick and two of his friends had been arrested the night before on a drunk and disorderly charge when they caused a disturbance down the street. A fight had broken out and the police were called. They were in the county jail at the moment.

I notified my supervisor as well as the police about the damage to our property as well as any vandalism that might have occurred in the school. We all decided to keep our plans of participating in the parade. I asked them to go home and get the items they had made during the summer and we would put them on display on a table on the float. So they all ran home and got headbands, puppets, potholders, lanyards, jewelry, and pottery. We packed everything up, got on the bus and went to the parade and had a wonderful time.

The summer came to an end without anymore incidents. I learned later that year that Johnny had been found dead, hanging from a rope in the playground. It was not determined if it was a suicide or a homicide.

As you think about the tasks of a community recreation worker, you can imagine how helpful it is to understand human growth and development. Do you think the behavior that I observed with the playground participants was expected for their age and developmental stage? My "girl time" with the neighborhood teen girls was very important as it provided them an opportunity to develop a relationship with an adult female who was attending college. This demographic was not available in their area. They asked me many questions about college, what I was studying, and what my future plans included. I hope I was a role model for them as I encouraged each of them to stay in school, get good grades, and then choose a college to attend. A difficulty I did encounter was with my work partner. It was impossible to interest this young man in his summer duties. He saw his role as a participant, rather than as a leader. He spent his days playing basketball. Have you ever worked with a colleague who was not helpful? How could he have been more useful to the neighborhood adolescent boys who attended the play-

Planning and Evaluation

Understanding and Mastery: Program design; program implementation; program evaluation

Critical Thinking Question: Did my knowledge of child growth and development prove useful in planning the summer recreation program? Would you have implemented something different? How would you evaluate the program I designed?

ground each day? Although Nick and his friends were adult men, their behavior was more like that of adolescents. I have often thought about what Nick and his friends were lacking in their development. What kind of services could have been useful for them? Human Services workers can fill a huge void in an adolescent's life when they work in recreation programs like the YMCA, YWCA, or Boys and Girls Clubs.

Crime, Punishment, and Juvenile Offenders

Adolescents who have been victimized are placed in the protective custody of the state and reside in a group home or foster care. They may be receiving individual, group, or family therapy. Some may also be receiving medical care or mental health services where medication is prescribed. These young people may be asked to testify in court as to their injuries and those of others. These events may make it difficult to attend school, participate in athletic events, or develop healthy interpersonal relationships with others. If they are allowed to remain in their home, the family will be affected by the crisis and will most likely be receiving services as well.

Youth who are perpetrators will be arrested, charged with a crime, and held in juvenile correctional facilities, and depending on their crime, may be housed with adults. A court hearing will determine the sentence, and perpetrators may have to complete months or years of residential lockup. In these juvenile facilities they will be allowed to attend school, but their daily activities will be limited, and their freedom will be curtailed. It is difficult to develop a positive self-image once you are imprisoned for an unlawful activity and labeled a criminal. Spending long periods of time in these facilities will only enhance your identity as a criminal as well. According to sociologists Glaze and Maruschak (2008), about half of the prison inmates in the United States have a family member who has also spent time in jail. It would seem that children and adolescents who grow up in families where crimes and arrests are an acceptable way of life are also likely to develop a criminal tendency.

Human Services workers in these facilities would most likely be facilitating some groups or doing individual counseling with these youth. It would be important at this stage of development for workers to help the adolescent develop a positive self-image and an identity that does not include criminal activity. If adolescents have the possibility of probation or parole, appropriate adult role models would be necessary. Connecting the adolescent to positive community activities and a different peer group upon release would be necessary if a life of crime is to be avoided.

> ## Explore a different approach for helping youth at <u>Outback Therapeutic Expeditions</u>.

Punishment for juveniles is often controversial. Physical punishment or "spanking," has been proven by many child care experts to be ineffective in changing behavior and may in fact model more violent behavior for the child. In adolescence, many would agree that it is no longer acceptable to physically spank or strike a person who is growing into adulthood and who has developed reasoning abilities. Many parents feel that those reasoning abilities are often inadequate and poor decisions lead to school failure, arrests, substance abuse, even death. Risky behavior in teens is nothing new, but the types and amounts of crimes that young people commit is alarming. It has also been found that disadvantaged youth are at high risk for adult crime and substance abuse problems, so early intervention is necessary to help these youth avoid a life of crime and incarceration (see <u>Science Daily</u> to learn more).

As more juveniles commit serious crimes, they are often sentenced as adults and may serve time in an adult facility depending on the crime and the state they live in. A controversy exists over whether to treat young offenders as juveniles or adults. In 19 states, juveniles between the ages of 16 and 17 can be tried and sentenced as adults and executed if found guilty when the crime constitutes a sentence worthy of the death penalty (Juvenile Crime and Issues, 2012). The U.S. Supreme Court outlawed the death penalty for juveniles age 15 and under. What do you think about this issue? How should adolescents be held accountable for their behavior?

Around the Globe

SOS Children's Villages Work With Children Worldwide

When you are raised in a middle-class home with good food, love, support, clothes, toys, and the expectation that you will go to school, it is difficult to believe that millions of young children around the world are alone, living on the streets at a very young age. *Poverty* is prevalent in so many countries that it is not unusual for parents to abandon a small child so they can try to survive themselves. Children are left to fend for themselves without food, water, or shelter. Poverty, crime, drug addiction, and HIV/AIDS are responsible for making millions of children around the world orphans. Children learn to survive by begging, stealing, joining gangs, and engaging in criminal activities. They do not attend school, but instead spend their days attempting to find food or earn some money. Perhaps they sell something they have made or stolen. They sleep on the streets or wherever they find a safe spot to rest. They learn at an

Werii Francois/Alamy

These homeless street children from Nepal are left to their own devices when it comes to survival. Abandoned children are common in some countries where poverty is great.

early age how to protect and defend themselves although they are still vulnerable and are often exploited by older children and adults. In some countries, they are used as drug runners and are beaten or punished by the authorities unless they offer money or a bribe to stay alive. They are sold into slavery or prostitution and are wise beyond their years—by the time a child of the same age in the United States is entering first grade. Children in many countries are not seen as family assets and are left to die, which many do before their fourth birthday.

You can read all about these street children and the countries they come from at the website for SOS Children's Villages, an international organization founded by Hermann Gmeiner in Imst, Austria, that provides help for children around the globe. This children's program was founded in 1949 and is now serving over 1 million children and their families in 125 countries through 518 children's villages and 383 youth homes. They offer health, education, and community outreach to children through medical centers, schools, nurseries, and a family strengthening program (SOS, 2013). In countries where families exist, services are offered to support the family and keep it intact so children are not abandoned. In areas where children are already alone, SOS mothers are recruited and trained to care for these children providing a loving and nurturing environment. Women and often men are paid to act as surrogate family members for children who would otherwise have no appropriate caring and loving adults to raise them. This model provides the basic nurturing, food, shelter, and clothing a child needs and also offers adults the opportunity to get paid for a job in areas where poverty and unemployment exist. The organization is extremely successful and has opportunities for sponsorship of a child, fund-raising partnerships, and employment possibilities.

Read the article "SOS Children in South America: Family Strengthening and Street Children."

Putting Theories to Work

Anthropologists, Psychologists, and Sociologists Help Us Understand Why Families Are So Important

No matter what discipline you study you will find that no matter the culture, the family is a very important institution. *Psychologists, sociologists,* and *anthropologists* have all studied the family with the same conclusions. The family is the primary unit of socializing a human being into its culture. It is the best institution we have for teaching cultural values to our youth and for passing our traditions and other cultural mores to the next generation.

Psychologists tell us that from birth, an infant develops a **bond** with his or her caregiver and will begin to recognize the face, voice, and touch of the person with whom he or she forms an **attachment** (Bowlby, 1969). At about 8 months of age, babies develop **stranger anxiety**, preferring to be near their caregiver than someone new. Harlow (1958) through his research on rhesus monkeys demonstrated that *physical and body contact* with a warm and nurturing caregiver was an important criterion for infant attachment and development. In his work with primates, Harlow found that infant monkeys were drawn to the surrogate wire monkeys that were covered with soft cloth rather than to the wire monkeys with no cloth padding, even though both types of surrogates delivered nourishment. Psychological research is important to understanding our role as infant caregivers. The family is usually the first caregiver for the infant, and its importance in the emotional and physical development of the child cannot be underestimated. Children who do not develop an attachment to a significant other or who do not have their needs met at an early age may develop emotional or mental issues as they grow up.

Sociologists study the family and tell us that we develop our sense of self, our identity, and an idea of our culture from our family. As *agents of socialization*, families pass on to the next generation values, mores, attitudes, and beliefs about society and their culture (Henslin, 2013). Other agents of socialization are our schools, churches, and peer groups, but families are the first agents of socialization in a child's life. Gender roles are taught in our families, and we learn what is acceptable and not acceptable when we live within this institution. Cooley (1902) developed a theory called the Looking Glass Self, referring to the development of our identity, which is shaped by others' views of us. In a family, we begin to see ourselves as big or little, fat or thin, beautiful or ugly. These concepts are often taught or at least reinforced by our families.

Another sociologist, George Herbert Mead (1934), studied the role of play in a child's life. He recognized that play is child's work and through it they learn to take on the role of another person. Often the first people that children imitate are family members. I remember when my two young sons would watch their father shaving. Afterward they would climb onto the bathroom counter with their plastic shavers, look in the mirror and pretend to be shaving. Family members are usually the significant others that children imitate. In his theory, Mead stressed that young children first learn how to imitate or mimic others, then learn how to play the role of others. My younger son at this stage wore his cowboy boots and a cape off and on for months choosing to dress up whenever possible as either a superhero or a cowboy! Children playing in a dress-up corner can be observed rocking a baby, or pretending they are a police officer or fireman. Once they learn how to put themselves into someone else's shoes, they are capable of organized play and can move into learning team games. As a team member, children must be able to play multiple roles. For instance in some games children have to decide who will hide or who will be it, or who will be a runner or who will protect the goal. Sociologists would agree that families are important in socializing and teaching humans how to become members of a society. Children who are not socialized properly may not adhere to the values or mores of society, and by the time they are adolescents they may be headed for a life of crime or considered outcasts because of their unusual or deviant beliefs. In a look at criminal justice statistics, it is startling to see that at least half of all the prison inmates in this country also have a relative who has been imprisoned. This statistic points to the fact that people involved in crime may socialize others to this activity as well, demonstrating the significance of agents of socialization.

Anthropology is the study of humans, past and present. There are four areas of study including *sociocultural, biological, archaeological*, and *linguistic anthropology*. As researchers look for similarities between the past and the present, they also study cultural patterns. Studies on family yield information on kin and *kinship patterns* revolving around race, social class, gender, and marriage. The family is an integral part of research studies, as anthropologists understand the significance of the interrelationships among biology, kinship, and marriage.

You can learn more about the study of anthropology at the American Anthropological Association.

Think Human Services

What Issues Affect Children and Adolescents in Your Community

You have learned a lot about child and adolescent growth and development. Think about what group you see yourself working with in your community. Are there programs that you think provide *excellent services*? Ask your instructor to invite a representative from these agencies to come speak to your class. Perhaps you can have a panel discussion with a few agency representatives. What do they see as the *primary issues* affecting adolescents in your community? What *gaps in service* exist? What needs to be done to deliver better services? How can individuals or groups (like your class) be helpful? Perhaps you can plan a field trip to one of these agencies. It is interesting to see a residential facility for adolescents, attend a court hearing for juveniles, or assist a local Boy or Girl Scout troop with an activity. These are all useful ways to get some experience with adolescents.

Linking Theory to Practice

Think Critically about What You Have Learned. How Does It Relate to Human Development?

You can probably think of why it is important for Human Services workers to understand the psychological, sociological, and anthropological research on families. What did you learn from your own family regarding your cultural or ethnic background? Make a list of what they taught you and who in the family was important to your socialization.

Did you ever hear of the psychological term *bonding* or *attachment*? Have you ever witnessed an infant who is bonding with his or her caregiver? If you have your own children, you can probably remember what an intense experience it was when you bonded with your own babies. You fall in love with those little infants and their downy hair and velvety skin. How do you know if the infants are bonding? What do they do to tell you they feel loved and comforted?

Erikson's Stages of Development start with Trust vs. Mistrust. Do you think that Bowlby's theory of bonding and attachment are related to trust? How does this theory relate to adolescents who join gangs? When you read about my work as a community recreation worker, what did you think about Nick and his friends? What benefits did they provide each other in their male group? Was it an effective group for them? Today, young men with criminal records would not be allowed to hang around playgrounds. Laws also prevent adults from selling drugs or cigarettes to youth. Did you ever feel intimidated or frightened in a job? How did you handle it? What could I have done differently with Nick and his gang?

Cooley's theory of the *Looking Glass Self* describes the development of the self-concept as something that is external as much as internal. If the external environment influences our self-concept, why is it important for Human Services workers to understand this perspective? Are adolescents affected by this theory or only young children? What must Human Services workers do to help develop the self-concept in adolescents?

Anthropologists study the family, cultures, and kinship to determine if there are any similar patterns in the past or the present. Has your family of origin changed over time due to interracial marriages or emigration? Does your family speak the native language of your ancestors? Do you have many similar patterns in your family history regarding your culture or traditions? Do you have any family patterns that have changed regarding your culture or traditions?

Did You Know?

Child Care Requires the Use of Knowledge, Values, and Skills with the Child and Parents

When day care or child care workers are hired, it is usually required by law that a criminal background check be completed. It is necessary for the welfare of the children that workers be free of drug or alcohol issues, felonies, or any charges related to domestic violence, assault, or battery. In addition, many agencies also have a probationary period for workers to ensure they are a good fit with the program.

If you work with infants and toddlers, it is important that you understand Erikson's Stages of Development, psychological theories of bonding and attachment, and sociological theories of socialization. Workers often spend more time with a child during the day than parents who work seven to eight hours. So, we know that infants need to be held and comforted, fed regularly, changed often, and provided with plenty of rest and safe, comfortable bedding every day. It is important that the same caregiver(s) be available each day in order for the infant to develop an attachment to that person(s). Workers who are not interested in child development or who do not enjoy holding, feeding, or touching an infant are not the appropriate caregivers for young babies. Day care centers that continually hire part-time workers who pass through the agency on their way to a higher-paying job may be putting the development of young children at risk. Child care workers need to understand child development and encourage imitation, role play, and organized games as the child ages. They need to be positive in their discipline and help develop a child's self-concept and confidence. If you become a child care agency director, think about the importance of the theories you have learned and how you can put them into practice.

What Would You Do?

Apply Your Knowledge of Developmental Stages

According to Erikson's theory, adolescents are dealing with the stage of Identity vs. Role Confusion. Assume you are working in a school setting with an adolescent female,

Tiffany, who is failing some of her classes and not attending school regularly. Another student tells you that Tiffany has been hanging around with some older boys who have dropped out of school and who sell drugs on the street corner. She has come to your attention because of her repeated absences. You make an appointment to visit her home to talk with Tiffany and her parents. During the visit, you discover that her mother has recently left the home due to marital problems. The father appears concerned about his daughter and quite protective, hesitating before he answers your questions. You suspect he does not want to get his daughter into trouble with school policies regarding absences. He indicates that she has been sick, and he was aware she was not attending classes. You inquire about Tiffany's grades, but she shrugs it off saying she is almost 16 and can quit anytime after that. Her father says nothing to encourage her to attend school and finish her degree. You notice that Tiffany's attire is promiscuous, and you are concerned that her behavior and attitude will get her into sexual trouble as well. As far as you know she is not expecting, but you see her as a high risk for pregnancy.

Think about what you have learned about the Stages of Development and adolescence. What is the problem as you see it? What are some goals that you have for Tiffany? How will you get her and her father to cooperate with you? What does she need at this stage of her life? Write down you answers and then get into a group of three and share your answers with your classmates. Do they have different goals for Tiffany? Did they see the problem the same way that you did? After working in a group, would you change any of your ideas or goals? Did you combine your ideas and goals?

If your discussion included content on the developmental stage of Identity vs. Role Confusion, you were all right on track. As a young woman, Tiffany is in need of an appropriate female role model. The absence of her mother is significant. You would need to find out if the mother is still playing a role in Tiffany's life. If she is, then a meeting between the parents to discuss your concerns is appropriate. If Tiffany's mother is not available, then you need to discuss with her father the need for Tiffany to have contact with an adult female. Is there a grandmother or aunt who can step in and provide the necessary supervision and female guidance at this time? If the father indicates there is no one, then suggest a Big Sister program where Tiffany can begin to develop a relationship with another female who can meet her emotional needs. Your relationship with Tiffany is also critical. Discuss your concerns with her about her style of dress and the adult males she has befriended. As your relationship develops, she may tell you more about her feelings of loss regarding her mother. It is difficult for children to understand why a mother would leave home without them. She is also losing her class standing as she fails classes and misses school. No doubt her relationships with peers at school are also in jeopardy. Since this is a girl who may feel abandoned, it is important that you maintain your relationship with her and not close the case or transfer her to another worker. With supportive teachers, parent(s), and other female adults, you will be able to assist her with the transition from adolescent to young adulthood.

Recall what you learned in this chapter by completing the <u>Chapter Review</u>.

CHAPTER 10

Peter "Hopper" Stone/Disney ABC
Television Group/Getty Images

Working with Adults and the Elderly

Demographics in America Are Changing as the Baby Boomers Age. How Will These Changes Effect Human Services?

Chapter Outline

The Emmy award–winning situation comedy *Modern Family* has captured the attention of America's television viewers. It is a humorous look at families today with their configurations of stepparents, blended unions, and adopted children. Despite a high divorce rate in the United States, people still like the idea of living in a family, and the remarriage rate in America confirms this. In the sitcom, generations of adults have transitioned to the idea of marriage and divorce, remarriage, homosexual marriage, and biracial marriage. Jay, the eldest adult, has divorced and remarried Gloria, a Colombian beauty who brings her precocious adolescent son into the blended family. Jay's homosexual son and his partner adopt a Vietnamese baby. Jay's daughter, Claire, is married to an eccentric realtor, and they have three children, a free-spirit teen, an A+ nerdy adolescent, and an unusual, somewhat weird preteen. This is not your typical '50s *Leave It to Beaver* family. However, despite the obvious changes in family composition, this modern-day family resembles the traditional, nuclear family of decades past as the members struggle with the age-old issues of work, school, and raising children. It is a charming presentation on an old television favorite, *The Family*. This show has captured the attention of the family-loving U.S. population. We remember the fun of growing up in our own family, vacations, holidays, and neighborhood friends. For those who do not have such good memories of childhood, it makes them believe that good times do exist when we gather with parents, siblings, and children. Despite squabbles, sibling rivalry, and family competition, the idea of a loving family is still the norm in America, and the show, _Modern Family_, is a snapshot of what we believe a family should resemble. Watch just one episode, and you'll be hooked as you marvel at the real-life issues concerning gender, ethnicity, sexual orientation, and age that these adults are challenged to face.

What's It All About?

Working with Adults and the Elderly in a Variety of Settings

Many people enjoy working with adults rather than children or adolescents because they have already matured and the tumultuous hormonal years are over. Even though most states recognize 18 as the _legal age for beginning adulthood_, many people would agree that developmentally teens may not be ready for this responsibility or for the consequences of their actions at this benchmark. Many people prefer working with older adults who are past this transitional stage of development from adolescence to maturity. Although 18 is the legal voting age and the acceptable time when the military begins recruitment, controversy still exists over the legal drinking age, which is set at 21. Many car rental companies will not rent cars to anyone under the age of 25, and insurance companies charge higher rates for young adult males below 25 or 26. They are considered high risk for accidents, and their rates are considerably higher than those for other age groups. Ages between 18 and 26 can still be difficult as young adults try to identify who they are, what they want to become, and struggle with issues of maturity and independence. Some Human Services Workers prefer working with older adults past this stage of development since less physical energy is required than in working with children or adolescents. However, it is just as challenging since adult issues are varied and may require employment in agencies dealing with people who have both mental and physical disabilities, medical problems, or drug and alcohol concerns. Adults are more likely to respond to verbal therapies so individual and group counseling is popular with this age group. For the most part, adults can articulate what symptoms they are experiencing and why they have come for assistance. Unless they are in the protective custody of the state or under the guardianship of some other family member, adults can sign their own consent forms for treatment.

Recall the discussion of Erikson's Stages of Development.

Although Erikson grouped adults into three or four categories of developmental stages, some modifications have been made to his original theory with psychologists today calling the young adult an _emerging adult_ and the older adult moving into several other categories where people are more mature and living independently. The emerging adult will eventually grow into _early adulthood_, but it may take some time (Arnett, 2004). Unlike years past, when young adults could find work easily, marry, and begin family life, today's young adult often postpones family life in lieu of a career, travel, college, or military duty. Even though the recession has receded, it has created more delays in reaching full early adulthood for this age group as they discover the difficulty of finding full-time employment with benefits. Even a college degree does not guarantee a place in the labor market, and young adults today are faced with the challenge of trying to match their skills with prospective jobs. So, living at home with mom and dad may be a reality until they are able to land that job that allows them to pay all of their own bills and live independently. Today, the young adult, from 21 to the early 30s, may still be living at home with parents, finishing college, or completing military duty.

Erikson's Theory of Psychosocial Development describes the *early adult* as a person who must master the tasks associated with *intimacy vs. isolation*. Because of present conditions, then, people could well be in their early 40s and still be in the early adult stage (Baird, 2010). They must learn independence and find a life partner who is willing to share in their daily trials and tribulations. An adult who has successfully mastered this stage will have developed the necessary interpersonal skills to maintain relationships at work and in personal situations. Those who are unable to master this stage of development will have great difficulty coping with job responsibilities, work roles, and other people in the workplace. They lack the skills to sustain friendships or intimate relationships with others and often find themselves isolated and alone. This situation can lead to depression, alcoholism, and eventually becomes the reason they seek treatment for a variety of symptoms.

Middle adulthood is that period of life from about our 40s to our 60s (Baird, 2010). This life stage requires adults to recognize the task of guiding the younger generation. It is usually the time when adults focus on raising their children, developing their career, volunteering time in their church, coaching children and teens in sports or other activities, and helping their communities become better places to live and work. Psychologists call this developmental challenge *generativity vs. stagnation* since failure to give back to others often results in feeling a lack of purpose. People who are not successful in this stage of development are critical of others, their accomplishments, and are often negative and unhappy with their own life and experiences (Baird, 2010).

Late adulthood emerges around the late 60s and is becoming one of our longest life stages, as people are aging up and living longer. Traditionally older people who have successfully mastered this stage have felt rewarded by a life of wonderful experiences, work opportunities, and family life. Those who have felt less than satisfied are often left feeling that their life has been a failure and they become depressed and disengaged. This stage is referred to as *integrity vs. despair* (Baird, 2010).

Working with adults can be a very rewarding experience when together you negotiate plans to change behavior or address life-threatening situations that require professional services.

Read about the Community Mental Health Center, Inc. in Southeastern Indiana where they provide a variety of services to adults and the elderly.

Why Do Adults Need Services?

Both young and older adults require a variety of services to cope with the problems of daily living. Some adults require assistance in learning how to develop *better interpersonal skills* so they may be better able to obtain and maintain employment as well as intimate relationships with others. Counseling in an individual or group setting may meet this need and is often provided in both public community mental health centers as well as private counseling settings.

Addictive behaviors are often seen in adults, and symptoms can include excessive *drinking* or taking *illegal substances* like marijuana, meth, or cocaine. Addictions can also include gambling, eating, and other excessive habits, even working. A variety of programs exist that offer adults the opportunity to learn about addictive behaviors and how the brain is affected. Treatment is offered along with information on the importance of nutrition, physical exercise, and life balance. Working in the addictions field may bring you in contact with both male and female adults who suffer from *anorexia nervosa* or *bulimia nervosa*. These eating disorders distort individuals' perception of their body image, and as a result they see themselves as too fat and begin to starve themselves, or they binge eat and then purge the food from their system. Both conditions are life-threatening and require treatment to recover a person's sense of self.

Gambling is another addictive behavior that is often seen in the adult who can't stay away from the slot machines, poker games, or even the purchasing of excessive lottery tickets. It is a social concern because many people whittle away their life savings, college funds, and retirement savings on their gambling debt. Substance abuse and addictions is an interesting field and offers opportunities in residential facilities as well as in community centers.

Read the article on gambling addictions from HELPGUIDE.org.

Adults are also treated for a variety of other issues that require assistance from Human Services professionals, including *physical disabilities* due to accidents; long-term *health problems; mental illnesses* like depression, anxiety, bipolar disorder, and schizophrenia; *homelessness; PTSD (post-traumatic stress disorder); incarceration; domestic violence; rape; poverty; divorce; death* of a loved one; and *parenting issues* to name just a few. Many adults also decide to *change careers*, and they return to school after raising their children or after completing a military career or retirement. Human Services workers assist these adults as they transition from one job to the next. Working with adults gives you plenty of opportunities to use your knowledge, values, and skills in Human Services.

Explore Talk Therapy Television's website and select the Mental Health tab to watch videos that interest you.

Test your comprehension of <u>What's It All About? and Why Do Adults Need Services?</u> by completing this quiz.

Adrian Sherratt/Alamy

Human services workers care for seniors in this shelter program. Mental health services, senior day care, and independent living programs are all needed by our elderly population.

What Types of Programs Are Available for Adults?

There are many services available for adults in a variety of settings. Hospitals offer **support groups** for cancer patients and their families. Often the patient is taught pain management techniques to cope with chemotherapy or other treatment modalities. Prisons offer individual and group counseling for incarcerated individuals. Attendance may be mandatory depending on the sentence of the individual and the facility. Inmates may attend sessions involuntarily and may be *resistant* to changing their behavior. However, adherence to prison rules is required since it establishes organizational control, so inmates may not have a choice. The counselor has to use skills to overcome resistance as well as deal with a host of other issues that brought the individual into the criminal justice system. This may include mental illnesses, substance abuse, and defiant disorders. Many facilities offer assessment and job training skills so that upon release from prison an inmate may gain employment. It is estimated that only 65% of adults in prison have a high school degree (National Reentry Resource Center, 2012). Assisting prisoners to obtain a GED while incarcerated becomes a goal of most correctional facilities.

> Read about <u>The National Reentry Resource Center</u> to watch the video featuring Roberta Peeples on helping incarcerated adults regain employment after release.

Other agencies that offer adult services for a variety of other issues include *community mental health centers, private counselors, child welfare agencies* that are working toward reunification of the children with their parents, *colleges, home health agencies, drug and alcohol programs, homeless shelters, military services, food stamp and food distribution programs, domestic violence centers, rape crisis programs, wellness programs* through the department of health, and other state and federal Human Services agencies.

Some adults are mandated to receive services, and their attitude about attending is often reflected in their behavior. They may miss meetings, show no interest in the topic, or they may become very involved if they want change to occur. Many new techniques and programs are created every day as technology offers us the opportunity to work with people who have not requested services in the past. People who live in rural areas where services are limited might be interested in working with a counselor online who may be located in a different state. Webcams and audio technology allow us to network with people who might not have considered services previously. Working with adults is a very rewarding and challenging field and the skills of the Human Services worker can be utilized in a variety of settings.

Information Management

Understanding and Mastery: Using technology for word processing, sending e-mail, and locating and evaluating information; using technology to create and manage spreadsheets and databases

Critical Thinking Question: Can you think of any services that might be offered online?

Forty million Americans suffer with anxiety disorders that prevent them from enjoying life (Brain & Behavior Research Foundation, 2012). Panic disorders, generalized anxiety, PTSD, obsessive-compulsive disorder (OCD) and phobias can prevent people from working, going outside of their home, traveling, attending school to obtain a degree, or even socializing or meeting new people. Can you imagine not being able to take a vacation, visit a new destination, finish your Human Services degree, or even go to the movies because of your anxiety? Many people have irrational fears of failing a test, falling off of a bridge, getting laughed at in public, being humiliated by others, and the list goes on and on. As a result they have a physical reaction in certain situations that is most uncomfortable. There are over 100 symptoms of anxiety that may affect each individual in a different way (Anxiety Centre, 2012). Some common symptoms include a racing heartbeat, dizziness, sweating, inability to sleep, headaches, or difficulty breathing. Since these symptoms mimic the onset of a stroke or heart attack, the anxiety only increases as the person believes he or she is suffering from a more serious condition. In PTSD a patient may experience flashbacks or relive a critical life event. This increases the level of anxiety, and the person suffers with such discomfort that it may paralyze him or her with fear, worry, or dread. Many in the U.S. military have been diagnosed with PTSD after repeated deployments to the Middle East.

> **Explore MedicineNet.com to watch the slide shows on phobias, generalized anxiety, and more.**

The good news is that there are treatments for anxiety. Psychotherapies include cognitive behavior therapy (CBT) and systematic desensitization. CBT involves assessing the individual and developing a treatment plan that reduces irrational thoughts and behaviors. Systematic desensitization is a step-by-step introduction of the stress inducing stimulus accompanied by controlled relaxation techniques. The goal is to increase relaxation and eventually enable the patient to cope with the stressful situation. Many medications are also available that increase the ability of the brain to deal with anxiety. Some natural supplements are also available that may help the condition as well. Both medications and psychotherapy combined have proven to be the most effective in dealing with a variety of anxieties (Medicine.NetCom, 2012).

Interventions and Direct Services

Understanding and Mastery: Theory and knowledge bases of prevention, intervention, and maintenance strategies to achieve maximum autonomy and functioning; skills to facilitate appropriate direct services and interventions related to specific client or client group goals

Critical Thinking Question: Have you ever been affected by anxiety or a phobia? What worried you? Did you realize it was an irrational fear? How did you learn to cope with this anxiety? What treatments worked for you?

> **Read about the latest research in mental health and the brain at the Brain and Behavior Research Foundation.**

Why Do Elderly Adults Need Services?

The demographics of the United States, and many other countries as well, are changing. Only 3% of the U.S. population was over the age of 65 years in 1900, and by 1990, 29.6% of the population was in that age category. By 2010, that figure had risen to 38.6% of the population, and it will continue to rise as the baby boomer generation ages (U.S. Census, 2012). Many of us still have parents or grandparents who are living healthy, productive lives. My grandmother lived to be 96 years old and was quite energetic until the last few months of her life. My husband's parents, who are in their 80s, still drive to visit us for vacations! People are living *longer, healthier lives*, and we can now expect that upon retirement many more constructive years may be available to us. What we do with this time is up to us. Today people are choosing to travel, spend time with their families, volunteer in their communities, or take up a new interest or hobby like gardening, painting, or joining a book club. For people who have saved for their retirement or who worked in organizations with established benefit programs, life in the later years can be enjoyable. However, the recent recession has had a negative impact on retirement programs and many elders can no longer take advantage of early retirement. In fact, many are still working

Watch the AARP video Recession Hurts Older Workers.

full-time, engaged in raising their grandchildren, or worried about their lack of savings. In a recent study of baby boomers, many were anxious over the loss of jobs, lack of long-term savings, and the fact that they own homes they can neither afford nor sell (American Association of Retired People, 2012).

As we age, there are more health complications to be considered. Some issues affecting our elders include heart disease, cancer, arthritis, osteoporosis, falls, breathing difficulties, depression, and chronic diseases like Parkinson's, Alzheimer's, or dementias. If you enjoy working with the older population, you need to be knowledgeable about the risks associated with aging. Maintaining good health becomes a critical issue as we age. It is important to eat nutritious, well-balanced meals, exercise, keep busy, and enjoy a positive outlook by engaging in both indoor and outdoor activities with friends, family, and neighbors. Most communities offer a variety of activities for older folks through the Office of Aging or senior citizens centers. People can take advantage of most programs at low or no cost.

Since the population of elderly adults is growing, it is reasonable to assume there will be more jobs available in Human Services for this age group.

> **Explore current issues affecting the elderly at the <u>AARP</u> magazine website.**

Do you see yourself working with this population?

What Types of Programs Are Available for Seniors?

Imagine yourself as an older adult. What would you want your life to look like? Do you see yourself working, volunteering, traveling, or enjoying home life? These are considerations we must face as we age. Sometimes things don't turn out they way we had planned. Spouses die, poor health forces us to use life savings to pay for medicine or care for a loved one. Many programs, both public and private, exist to assist us as we age. Most communities have funding from the **U.S. Department of Aging** for **senior citizen centers** that are open Monday to Friday and offer elders a hot lunch, snacks, arts and crafts activities, holiday programs, and the chance to socialize with others their own age. Transportation may be available to get people to the programs if they do not drive. **Adult day care** may be offered as well for family members who need extra care and supervision and who do not do as well independently in their own homes. Many private nonprofit organizations also exist that offer similar services as well as *enrichment activities* for elders who want more advanced programs like book clubs, trips to various points of interest, or visits to museums or music programs like symphonies or local concerts. In Hilton Head, South Carolina, an octogenarian club offers elders the opportunity to take yoga classes, join book clubs or walking and exercise groups, travel, participate in college seminars, and learn a variety of new skills in computer technology. You must be in your 80s to join, however, no youngsters allowed! It is marvelous to think we can still enjoy life at this age. Wouldn't we all love to age so gracefully and anticipate our golden years in a positive way?

For many, however, aging can be a difficult process. As my mother-in-law says, "aging isn't for sissies!" Although you may feel the same, look in the mirror and you may not recognize the person you see. Our bodies change, movement becomes difficult, and bones are more fragile and break easily. Heredity plays a huge part in the aging process. Long-term illnesses are passed down from one generation to the next. Conditions like diabetes, cancer, heart disease, arthritis, even Alzheimer's disease can be genetic, so not everyone is lucky enough to live a long and healthy life. Services like *home health care* can provide medical assistance so elders can remain in their home as long as possible, adult day care is an option for families who work but have an older adult who lives in their home. **Respite care** offers caregivers the chance to get a break to go shopping, rest, or just get out of the house for a while. Apartments for the elderly now have many options from independent living to skilled care. Medical personnel may be available in the facility to provide immediate care if someone falls or needs assistance. If their health declines, they may be moved to skilled care in their complex.

Residential nursing homes also provide care for many of our seniors, especially those who suffer with dementia or Alzheimer's disease. These facilities offer safeguards so patients cannot wander off the property, a condition common to those with this illness. Locked floors or wards for this population are not uncommon and should not be viewed as punitive. It is often necessary for the safety of the patients. Human Services workers who are employed in these facilities sometimes spend as much time with the family members as they do with the patients explaining services, encouraging relatives to visit the program, and developing holiday or themed activities to which family are invited. Workers *spend time individually with patients, organize groups* for socialization, and conduct *case management* to ensure that everyone has the medical and health services that they need.

Emotional and psychological changes occur as we age as well. Spouses and children sometimes die before the elder member, making the latter's life lonely and isolated. Poor health can make each day a challenge as people struggle to walk, hear, or see. It may be impossible to participate in activities that were once enjoyable. You can no longer swing a golf club, or see well enough to do your sewing, or even handle the heavy skillet to make breakfast. People become depressed, stop eating, lose energy, and become apathetic. *Mental health services* are extremely important for this age group, but we know that many who suffer with emotional and psychological issues do not receive the services they need. Did you know that suicide ranks the highest in our elderly population? At 21%, it is the age group with the highest percentage of suicide (Mental Health & Advocacy Project, 2012). It is estimated that 18–25% of the elderly population needs some type of mental health service for conditions like depression, schizophrenia, psychosomatic illnesses, or anxiety; yet only a small percentage are receiving services.

There is no doubt that Human Services workers will be called upon to deal with aging issues in their community. Although we have numerous programs that currently exist, many more are needed as our population continues to age up.

> **Read about some of the most common issues of aging at AgingCare.com.**

Human Systems

Understanding and Mastery: Processes to effect social change through advocacy work at all levels of society including community development, community and grassroots organizing, and local and global activism; processes to analyze, interpret, and effect policies and laws at local, state, and national levels that influence service delivery systems

Critical Thinking Question: Why do you think that so few elders are receiving the mental health services that they need? What can we do as Human Services workers to change this statistic?

> **Read <u>Overlooked and Underserved: Elders in Need of Mental Health Care</u> to know all about mental health and aging issues as described by the Mental Health and Advocacy Project.**

Our senior population is increasing worldwide as people live longer. Here Chinese men spend time socializing in the town square in Qinghai Province.

Tom Salyer/Alamy

As Human Services workers, think about all the possible services your community needs for its older citizens. Develop a list with two columns. In one column list all the services that currently exist. This will probably require you to do some research. You can look online for a directory of services for your community. Oftentimes the United Way organization will publish a listing of social services for a county, so you may need to contact your local United Way Agency to determine what programs exist in your community for elders. In the second column, list all the services that you think need to be provided but currently are not provided. This list provides an opportunity for Human Services workers to think about developing new and innovative programs in their communities. Consider an action plan for a service that you would like to see initiated. Do you see yourself working with the aging population in your community? What type of program would you like to work with locally? Would you consider developing your own program?

Test your comprehension of <u>Why Do Elderly Adults Need Services?</u> and <u>What Types of Programs Are Available for Seniors?</u> by completing this quiz.

Around the Globe

People Are Living Longer in All Parts of the World

Read all about <u>World Health Day</u>.

What a wonderful time to be growing older. At no time in our world's history have so many elderly people been alive and in such good health. Lower fertility rates with smaller families in most countries coupled with better health care for everyone has meant that demographics are changing around the globe. According to the World Health Organization (2012), the world's population is aging up with the proportion of those over age 60 expected to double to 22% by the year 2050. A total population of 1 billion elderly is anticipated by that time. Japan already has 30% of its population over age 60. Currently it has the world's largest population of elderly.

Listen to <u>what people in Japan have to say about what they are doing to have a healthy old age.</u>

The Hindu (2012), an Indian newspaper, indicates that by 2050, 64 countries will have an elderly population that exceeds 30%, with 80% of the world's older population living in developing countries. It is estimated that in India one out of every six people would be an elder, and China will have even larger numbers. Today 90 million seniors live in India, and 90% of those still do some type of work to support themselves! Worldwide women are living longer than men, and India is no exception. Three out of five single, older women in India live alone and are very poor.

Read *The Hindu* to learn more about Concerns over an Aging India

A report from the Department of Economic and Social Affairs of the United Nations (2013) indicates that by 2045 the world's population of elderly will exceed the number of children under the age of 15. This will happen in developed countries faster than in countries with lower levels of development. The interesting fact is that these changing demographics are happening worldwide with population growth for the elderly occurring in industrialized countries faster among those people with a higher socio-economic status. However, it is occurring in developing countries at a faster pace among the poor elderly. The fastest growing population growth in all countries is with those over the age of 80. They represent a growth of 4% a year globally. Do you know anyone who is over the age of 80? My in-laws are over 85 and still drive, participate in a classic car club, enjoy dancing, and still socialize with friends.

What are some of the implications for a growing older population? Concerns for *health care* are a priority. One reason for the growing elderly age group is improved health care worldwide, the eradication and control of chronic and fatal diseases like smallpox, diphtheria, polio, tuberculosis, and others. However, aging populations need continued health care and access to services. Labor markets and the economy are also affected when people retire and a pool of younger workers is not available to fill the positions. Elders who live alone are at a disadvantage when they have no support systems or younger family members who can assist them. Lower fertility rates and smaller families with younger members mean that fewer family members will be available to help their elders. This means that expanded social services need to consider services for the elderly. Pensions and retirement benefits also mean that those with higher incomes can retire while those with no benefits will have to remain employed for longer periods of time. In developing countries, illiteracy is a common problem, and among the elderly this is a concern if employment is a factor to be considered. Read <u>what the UN says about the world's growing elderly population</u> and the challenges Japan faces. (CTV News, 2012).

Human Services Delivery Systems

Understanding and Mastery: The range and characteristics of Human Services delivery systems and organizations; the range of populations served and needs addressed by Human Services professionals

Critical Thinking Question: Compare the article from CTV News regarding the UN's position on protecting our elderly population worldwide with the article from Aljazeera news regarding Japan's struggle with its aging residents. What do you think should be done?

Watch <u>Aging Japan</u>, a video of aging Japanese people and the struggles they face, on Aljazeera news, 101 East.

Germany was one of the first countries to develop a comprehensive welfare system late in the 19th century. State social insurance for accident, health, and old age were developed first with the addition of unemployment and long-term care added in the 20th century. Today tax-financed family allowances, tax concessions, pensions for the elderly, funds for the disabled, universal health care for everyone, accident, long-term

Watch the video of Johanna Quaas, the oldest active gymnast in Germany at age 86. She is fabulous!

care, and unemployment insurance means that poverty in old age is less likely than in any other age group. Currently 27% of their country's spending is devoted to public welfare for all of its citizens. This is in direct contrast to the United States where provisions for all citizens is not a priority, but rather spending on public welfare programs for specific eligible participants is about 16% of our country's spending. Germany is the country with the third largest proportion of elderly after Japan and Italy. Low birth rates and increasing life expectancy make reform of their welfare system necessary so that it can be available for future generations.

Test your comprehension of <u>Around the Globe: People Are Living Longer in All Parts of the World</u> by completing this quiz.

Putting Theories to Work

Understanding Developmental Theories Is Necessary When Working with Adults and Seniors

According to Erikson, adulthood has several stages. Early adulthood (20s to early 40s), middle adulthood (40s to 60s), and late adulthood (late 60s and up) indicate that adults need to master life tasks at each stage (Erikson, 1963). Young adults must learn how to *develop intimate relationships* with others. They have close relationships with friends, family, colleagues, and life partners. At this stage they may marry, move in with someone, or decide they want to engage in long-term relationships with another person. Acceptance by other adults is important during this life stage, or you may feel *isolated* and alone. In middle adulthood, people focus on raising their children, assisting their family, or helping the future generation by guiding or advising them. During this stage, adults may offer to volunteer their services at schools, churches, or in their community. They are rewarded when their expertise and guidance is valued and requested by others. Erikson called this *generativity* or giving back *vs. stagnation* or self-absorption. By late adulthood, people are generally satisfied with their lives and reflect happily on their family, life choices, and career goals. Those who have not mastered the developmental tasks at each stage may be left feeling lonely, empty, or with a sense of failure. We call this stage of development *integrity vs. despair*. As Human Services workers, we can assist adults at each stage of their development to ensure that essential life tasks are completed.

Read the following scenarios and decide what you would do as the Human Services worker in each case. How would you assess the problem? What is happening to the adult in the scenario? How can understanding Erikson's developmental life stages be helpful to these workers?

Jason is 21 years old and is quite shy. He is a student in a large university that he has attended for two years. He knows few people and spends most of his time studying for his major classes in genetics. Jason loves his classes but finds he must spend considerable time reading, studying, doing online assignments, and writing reports in order to get the grades he needs to get into medical school. He spends most weekends in the library and has few friends at the university. He did meet a few people in his first year when he lived in the dormitory, but it was much too noisy for studying so he moved into his own apartment during his sophomore year. Lately he has not been sleeping well, he is anxious, feels depressed, and isn't interested in eating. He has decided to take advantage of the university's mental health clinic to see if he may need some medicine. You are the Human Services worker in the mental health clinic who completes the intakes on all new consumers.

How would you assess Jason's situation?
What would you want to know to help you make a determination about services for him?
What might you consider in terms of goals and objectives for Jason?

Tameka is a 45-year-old divorced mother whose two children are now older, married, and living in another state. Tameka has worked two jobs for years while she put her two daughters through a private high school in her community. Both daughters were good students and took advantage of Tameka's guidance and assistance as she mentored them into early adulthood. They love their mother and were grateful for her ability to help them select colleges and later employment opportunities. The oldest daughter is now married and working for Comcast and has recently been promoted to a position in North Carolina, nine hours from her mother's home. The youngest daughter was married last month and has moved to Colorado with her new husband. For the first time in 24 years, Tameka finds herself alone at home. She is not sure what to do with herself. She has decided to come to the women's transitional center in her community. She has heard good things about what they do and hopes she will learn about some service that will give her life more meaning.

You are the Human Services worker in the women's transitional center. What do you see as the issue effecting Tameka?
What would you include in her assessment?
What might be some goals and objectives for her?

Gloria is a 75-year-old single, elderly woman who lives in an apartment complex in Fort Lauderdale. She worked for 50 years as an accountant and is still sharp with numbers. She finally retired last year from her accounting company and decided to have some fun and move to Florida. Much to her surprise, her apartment complex is filled with elderly couples who are still active. She was hoping there would be more single men and women whom she could befriend. Although she has met several people, she feels uncomfortable because they all talk about their children, grandchildren, and other family members. Gloria has no family members who are still living, was never married, and has no children or grandchildren. She never felt left out because she had no children, but now she is feeling that perhaps she should have considered marriage and children. When she was younger she was always so busy with work, her agency, and moving around the country to accept promotions, that she didn't want the responsibility of a family. Now she is starting to think she made a mistake. She is wondering if maybe she should move back to Ohio where she had lived for some years. Lately she has been feeling unhappy, apathetic, and tired. She came to the senior citizens center today because she was passing it on her way to the grocery store, and she wondered what services were provided here.

You are the Human Services worker in the senior center. How would you assess Gloria's problem?

What else would you want to know about her?

What questions would you ask?

Can you think of goals and objectives that might be helpful to her?

Linking Theory to Practice

How Do Different Theorists View the Aging Process?

If we apply different theories of aging, we begin to understand the behavior of our elders. According to **disengagement theory** (Cumming & Henry, 1961), older people withdraw themselves from active social life as they prepare for their impending death. They often see themselves as not needed and become preoccupied with their own feelings or memories. After retirement, they gradually transfer their power to the younger generation by disengaging with others, allowing younger people to gain control of work or social situations. The **activity theory of aging** is quite different. It says that older people are happiest when they stay involved and not disengaged (Schulz & Rockwood, 2006). Productive elders, who work, volunteer their time, give back to the younger generation, and enjoy hobbies like gardening, golf, or travel are good examples of this theory. Did you watch the video featuring Germany's Johanna Quaas, in the section Around the Globe? Wasn't it amazing to watch this 86-year-old woman swinging around the parallel bars in her gymnastic activities? I'm certain Johanna would agree with the activity theory of aging.

More recent research on aging suggests that seniors like to stay busy but are selective in their activities. The **socioemotional selectivity theory of aging** (Carstensen, 1991) suggests that older people decide who they want to spend time with in their remaining years. Children, family, close friends, and marriage partners become the focus of their time. If they continue to work, it is for social relationships or economic reasons rather than career goals.

Concerns of aging seem to point toward economic insecurities, physical limitations, loss of friends and family, and **ageism** or prejudice toward those who are older. Despite these negative aspects of aging, research shows that seniors today are more satisfied with their life than those of middle age, who also report more satisfaction with life than young adults (Mroczek, 2001). As some seniors demonstrate, the aging process can be an enjoyable time of life if we are surrounded by people we love and value.

Did You Know?

Many Seniors Are Active in Volunteering, Which Is Important for Their Well-Being

Adults and the elderly can give back to their community by volunteering their services to help others. Volunteering improves lives and allows you to become socially active in your community so you can become a part of the solution to local problems. You have read about Erikson's Developmental Learning Theory. How does volunteering support this theory? By giving back to others, you can help yourself since you are mastering the task of generativity rather than becoming consumed with your own issues. When you help someone else, you often realize how insignificant your own problems are in comparison. So volunteering is a great way to help yourself and your community.

Volunteers of America is a national faith-based organization that has been assisting people with their needs since 1896. It is one of the largest charities and nonprofit organizations in America that offers services in 46 states, the District of Columbia, and Puerto Rico. Through community centers and a mobile outreach center, it offers affordable housing to homeless individuals, the elderly, disabled people and veterans. Its branches serve 2 million people annually in 400 nationwide centers where they work to improve health services, find affordable housing for people, and increase employment opportunities. Full-time professional Human Services staff use their skills to mobilize volunteers in their community to do a variety of activities for different populations. Programs for the elderly include shopping assistance, minor home repairs, yard work, medication management, and any service that would allow seniors to remain living independently longer. Community centers are also funded so seniors can get a daily meal, transportation, medical care, prescription drug fulfillment, or resource and referrals. Case management services are provided to coordinate services. Elders who cannot get to a community center can receive Meals on Wheels. The RSVP (retired senior volunteer program) recruits retired elders to become volunteers who may take part in a foster grandparent program, companion services, or other volunteer activities. Volunteers of America also offers skilled nursing care and assisted living centers in many communities. It offers programs for youth and families and receives some of the largest federal grants to end homelessness in America. Go to the website for Volunteers of America to learn about its services for children, adults, families, seniors, the disabled, and veterans.

What Would You Do?

Apply Your Knowledge to These Cases Dealing with Adults

Read the following cases and decide what types of services should be provided for these adults or seniors. What stage of development and issues are they dealing with at this time in their life?

Mario has just been released from prison for a felony conviction for selling drugs in his neighborhood. He served three years of a five-year sentence and has been released early in a special program in his state for first time convictions for nonviolent offenses. Mario is 22 years old, did not complete high school, and now has a felony on his record which makes finding employment difficult. You are a Human Services worker in a county probation and parole office, and you have been assigned to work with Mario.

What are some concerns that you have for him, and what services do you think would be beneficial?

What might be some of Mario's developmental issues?

Janet is a 41-year-old military veteran who did two tours in Iraq and one tour in Afghanistan. She is married and the mother of a 13-year-old son, Edward. Her husband, Robert, is a retired military as well and was the primary caregiver for Edward while she served time in the *Middle East*. Both Janet and Robert receive military pensions. Robert is also responsible for two teenage children from a previous marriage. He sends child support to his ex-wife on a regular basis. Since she has returned home from Afghanistan, Janet has been having difficulty with Edward. He is sassy, doesn't do his homework when she asks, and in general seems disinterested in listening to her. Janet is also experiencing PTSD, with periods of anxiety and flashbacks to her time in Afghanistan where she suffered injuries from a roadside attack. She is trying to deal with her own issues, but she is so tired and not able to sleep. The problems with Edward are just additional burdens on her, and she finds herself screaming at him after school. Robert does not have the same issues with Edward, and although he has spoken with Edward about his disobedience, he has also spoken with Janet indicating that her personal problems are an issue. She calls to make an appointment at the mental health center where you are the Human Services worker. She indicates in the call that she wants some counseling for her son because he is out of control. During the conversation, she mentions that she thinks she may have a touch of PTSD and this is making it difficult for her to handle her teenage son.

What services would you suggest for her?

What developmental issues is she dealing with currently?

Recall what you learned in this chapter by completing the Chapter Review.

CHAPTER 11

Spirituality and Faith-Based Practice

Personal Beliefs Are a Catalyst for Change and Human Services Workers Respect the Religious and Spiritual Aspects of Helping

Saint Leo University

Christmas is the time of year when Christians celebrate the birth of their Lord and Savior Jesus Christ. It is common to see indicators of the season: Christmas decorations, trees, and festive lights. For many people, however, the signs of Christmas are a reminder that not all Americans are Christians. From its beginnings as a small colony, America has celebrated its holidays by giving thanks to God. As a multicultural society, the United States recognizes that different religious groups pay homage to their own God, which may not be Jesus Christ. In the more recent past, the notion that Christians could expect to display their symbols in public places has been challenged in the courts. Today religious decorations depicting the Christmas holiday can be seen in churches or other private religious institutions like schools or universities, but not in public places. In the chapter opening photo you can see the beautiful Nativity Scene displayed on the campus of Saint Leo University during the Christmas season. Saint Leo is a private, Catholic university founded by the order of the Benedictine monks in 1889. Every year students, faculty, staff, and administrators gather for Christmas carols, goodwill, and treats after the traditional Christmas concert. The outdoor Nativity or *Creche* depicts the baby Jesus and His parents, Mary and Joseph, along with the shepherds, angels, and wise men who followed the star to find their God. This is a beautiful, lighted evening program that gives everyone a chance to participate and feel good about the season. It is an anticipated annual event on campus, which highlights another successful semester, a time to give thanks to God, and to share fellowship with our university community before leaving campus for the holiday break.

People are free to practice whatever religion they would like in America, a nation that is considered to be the most religiously diverse and the most tolerant of religious differences. The First Amendment gives people freedom of speech but also separates church and state, thus disallowing displays of religious symbols in public places. Some consider this fair since it follows the basic tenets of our constitution and the Bill of Rights. Others feel that Christmas has become a commercial, rather than a religious, holiday with decorations depicting a Santa Claus, and public signs reading generic messages of *Happy Holidays to All*. The idea that Christmas is a time of giving is still a belief, and merchants are rewarded with hefty profits from sales during the holiday season, which officially kicks off on Black Friday, the day after Thanksgiving, and continues until December 25th, Christmas Day. Orthodox Christians from central and eastern Europe follow the Gregorian calendar, according to which Christmas falls on January 7th.

In addition to Christmas, other religious and ethnic holidays are celebrated during the month of December. Those of the Jewish faith celebrate Hanukkah for eight days from December 8th to 16th, also known as the Festival of Lights. This holiday celebrates the rededication of the Holy Temple in Jerusalem. Muslims commemorate Ashura, a day of mourning for the martyrdom of Husayn ibn Ali, the grandson of the Prophet Muhammad, on December 5th. Buddhists honor Buddha's enlightenment on Bodhi Day, December 8th. The international holiday of St. Nicholas Day is celebrated on December 6th as children around the world put out their shoes in the evening so they can be filled with candy and small toys. On December 12th, Mexico remembers the Virgin of Guadalupe, the Virgin Mary, mother of God. Those of Scandinavian ancestry celebrate Santa Lucia Day in honor of Saint Lucy on December 13th. Las Posadas is a nine-day Mexican Christmas celebration, which lasts from the 16th to the 25th of December. The journey of Mary and Joseph is reenacted as a procession of people, carrying a small doll to commemorate Jesus, travels from house to house in their community looking for a place to stay before Mary gives birth to Jesus. When people reach their final destination, the host family provides a holiday party for the travelers and their friends. The holiday has its roots in Catholicism. Canadians and those from the United Kingdom look forward to Boxing Day on December 26th when gifts are exchanged among family and friends who visit each other's homes. Kwanzaa, from December 26th to January 1st, is an African American holiday that was started in 1966 by Dr. Maulana Ron Karenga and promotes three areas, which include a strong family, history of the African American people, as well as unity of their people.

These religious and spiritual holidays all represent a belief system practiced by millions of people worldwide. Did you ever consider how many holidays are celebrated based on a religion? Imagine if there were no religions or spiritual beliefs. Many of the holidays just described would disappear. How important are your beliefs to the holidays you celebrate? Does your family prepare for Easter, Passover, Ramadan, Dia de los Muertos, Vesak, or Holi? Individuals' belief systems impact their lifestyle, what is important to them, and how they celebrate or enjoy personal holidays or days off with family and friends. Even people who do not necessarily believe in all the tenets of a religion may still participate in holiday gatherings with family and friends. Some Christians only go to church once or twice a year to attend a service on Christmas or Easter. They still enjoy the celebration of giving gifts, decorating a tree, and having dinner with family. So holidays have special meanings for people, and their beliefs may be reawakened during a seasonal ceremony.

This chapter will highlight the importance of our diverse beliefs, explain the difference between religion and spirituality, and help us understand why we need to practice tolerance and acceptance of another's point of view. The foundation of a personal belief system is often the strength that a person brings to a relationship. In Human Services, we understand that our ability to help others is enhanced when we understand and value their belief system. Our profession teaches people how to respect and collaborate with others whose beliefs are different yet equal to our own.

> ## Human Systems
>
> *Understanding and Mastery: Emphasis on context and the role of diversity (including, but not limited to ethnicity, culture, gender, sexual orientation, learning styles, ability, and socio-economic status) in determining and meeting human needs*
>
> **Critical Thinking Question:** Do you think that by observing or participating in a religious service different from your own, you may begin to appreciate another culture?

Review the <u>Diversity Calendar</u> at the University of Kansas Medical Center's website to learn more about these holidays and the customs and traditions that accompany them.

What's It All About?

What Is the Difference between Religion and Spirituality?

Since the beginning of mankind, humans have been asking the age-old questions of where did I come from, why I am here, and what is the meaning of life? This has led to our belief in a higher being, in someone or something that is larger and more powerful than us, which has led us to try to discover the truth of our existence. This truth or belief is personal and relates to our own experiences, values, culture, and that which has been taught or passed down from one generation to the next. The search for the answers to these questions has led us to the beliefs, which form the basis of either our spirituality or our religious convictions.

What does it mean to be spiritual or religious? What is the difference? According to author and academician Norris Chumley (2011), both terms relate to a belief in a higher power, with spirituality being a more modern version of one's values and perhaps diverse connections of religious beliefs. For example, some people claim to be "Jew-Bu's" referring to their religious background in Judaism along with new beliefs in Buddhism. Other people claim to be Christians but also follow the teachings of Eastern Yogi's. On the other hand, when we speak about religion, we can also say the person is spiritual, but **religion** refers to *systematic beliefs* with organized rituals and formal traditions that usually take place in a church, temple or mosque. There are rules, ceremonies, and literature that denote their belief system (Carl, 2010). Christians follow the Bible, members of the Jewish faith read the Torah, and Muslims adhere to the Quran. Christianity is the largest of all world religions with Islam the fastest growing religion. Judaism is one of the oldest with Taoism, Buddhism, and Hinduism all considered ancient religions. All organized religions use some form of prayer, which may occur in a place of worship, at home, or in the case of Islam, outside with members dropping to their knees in prayer while they face east toward Mecca. By contrast **spirituality** is more personal and found within one's self. It is *not organized* nor is it found in a specific church or house of worship. It is individual rather than communal. Being spiritual implies that you are self-reflective and relate to your own God and the world around you in your own way and in your own space.

Religion is *cultural* and gives us the *traditions* that we associate with many of our holidays. If you are a member of a religion, what are some of the traditions that you expect from your community? Most churches have a choir, and music is a central element in the daily or weekly service. Many gospel singers got their start in their church choirs. Whitney Houston was famous for her beautiful voice in her church in Newark, New Jersey, long before the rest of America knew her. Your church may also provide the food that you remember on religious holidays. Many families prepare elaborate meals for their church and family members with special foods and recipes being passed down from one generation to the next. Do you decorate a tree at Christmas, light your menorah at Hanukkah, or enjoy the sweet dessert Sheer khurma during the holiday Eid al Fitr, if you are a Muslim? Religions offer us the wonderful traditions that blend with the culture of our country. So even if you do not practice a religion, you may still uphold the traditions of your culture which started with your religion in your church.

Listen to a powerful Gospel featuring Whitney Houston and her friend Cece Winans.

Not everyone is religious or spiritual. **Atheists** do not believe in any God and in fact would argue that governments, schools, and other public institutions benefit when religion is not part of their program or policies. **Agnostics** on the other hand are not convinced that a God does or does not exist. They often look for scientific proof that a God exists. **Theists** believe that one or more Gods exist, and these are the people who attest to be religious or perhaps spiritual if they do not belong to any organized religion (Kline, 2012). Christianity and Judaism are **monotheistic** believing in one God while Muslims believe that Muhammad was God's prophet. Hinduism is **polytheistic**, believing in many gods, while Buddhism is neither monotheistic nor polytheistic since it focuses on practical ways of living that can lead humans to enlightenment.

All religions teach nonviolence and peaceful means of living with others. They value help to the poor, strength by prayers, and respect for others. *Beliefs*, *rituals*, and *morals* are the three elements that Henslin (2013) uses to describe any religion. Morals are inherent in all religions, and it is through our religions that we become socialized at an early age. Can you remember going to church as a youngster and listening to your priest, minister, rabbi, or Imam? Did their preachings include lessons on the sinfulness of killing, lying, or stealing? Regardless of our religious background most religions teach us that all humanity is united.

Read more about the Geneva Spiritual Appeal of 1999 at the Canadian website for religious tolerance.

If religions teach *tolerance* why are so many wars created around religious issues? It is difficult to imagine how or why so many people distort the teachings of their religion to justify their actions. Extreme religious Islamic groups are responsible for terrorists attacks in the Middle East, Ireland is separated by the Protestants in the North and Catholics in the South, civil wars in the Sudan cause Muslims, Christians, and Animists to clash, and in Bosnia Orthodox Serbians tried to eradicate Muslims through acts of genocide. In 1999 a group of religious leaders including Buddhists, Protestants, Catholics, Orthodox Christians, Jews, Muslims, and other faiths gathered in Geneva, Switzerland, to develop the *Geneva Spiritual Appeal*. This proposal calls on world political and religious leaders to denounce future violence by any group that uses religion to justify its actions. Although this doctrine has been seen as somewhat effective, according to Canadian newspaper and website

Church choirs are a common tradition of churches in America. Seen here is the adult choir of St. Martin's Lutheran Church in Austin.

Religious Tolerance (2001), 26 countries from around the world have been involved in wars during the last ten years, which involve a blend of racial, ethnic, religious, and economic conflicts.

Client-Related Values and Attitudes

Understanding and Mastery: The worth and uniqueness of individuals including culture, ethnicity, race, class, gender, religion, ability, sexual orientation, and other expressions of diversity

Critical Thinking Question: If all religions teach nonviolence and yet many countries engage in wars created by religious beliefs, do you think that sanctions and consequences by religious organizations would be more effective than political sanctions in stopping the violence?

Watch the video from the <u>Huffington Post</u> on the American pastor who received eight years in an Iranian prison for his religious beliefs.

Test your comprehension of <u>What's It All About? What Is the Difference between Religion and Spirituality?</u>

Around the Globe

People May Respond with Violence When Their Belief Systems Are Ridiculed

When people's values and belief systems are ridiculed, they may respond with anger and violence. If people believe they are being publicly humiliated or insulted, their reaction

This photo is from Kuala Lumpur during the uprising in the fall of 2012 when an Internet movie sparked a debate over the portrayal of the Prophet Muhammad. Here Muslims protest as they march toward the U.S. embassy.

can be harsh and immediate. In September of 2012, demonstrations and riots broke out in at least nine Middle Eastern countries to protest an Internet film, which negatively depicted the Prophet Muhammad. Seventy-five people were killed and thousands were injured in violence that led to days of terror that rocked the Middle East, with Muslims lighting fires, tearing down American flags, and attacking schools. Muslims across the region were outraged about the video and scenes of attacks on U.S. embassies were prevalent. A fire was set at the embassy in Tunisia not long after the attack in Libya, which killed the U.S. ambassador Chris Stevens. It was believed that Americans were to blame for a rogue film that portrayed the Prophet Muhammad in a disrespectful manner.

The 13-minute English film created by Nakoula Basseley, an Egyptian-born Coptic Christian from Los Angeles, mocked the Prophet Muhammad in the anti-Islamic film, *Innocence of Muslims*. In the film trailer apparently the Prophet Muhammed is depicted as a fool and a religious fake who engages in sexual acts. The video begins with a persecution of Coptic Christians and references to poor human rights in Egypt, which set off immediate demonstrations in the Muslim world. The film's producer, Basseley, also known as Sam Bacili, was arrested by the FBI after an investigation turned up multiple parole violations dating back to his 2010 charges of identity theft and stealing of $800,000 from six financial organizations. His questionable background also includes a prison sentence in the 1990s for the manufacturing of methamphetamines. His more recent theft of multiple Social Security numbers and the opening of fraudulent credit cards earned him another arrest in 2010. Basseley spent over a year in jail and was then given a five-year parole sentence in California. He was released in June of 2011 and started working on the film soon afterward by recruiting investors, despite his lack of film making experience. In addition to money supplied by his wife's family in Egypt, he indicated that several Jewish investors were financing the film. This sparked additional protests at the Israeli and American embassies abroad. This turned out to be a myth and although no Americans were charged in the case, Muslims in the Middle East blamed the United States for the depiction of the Prophet Muhammed. Taking to the streets to protest the film, their view of Americans was one of outrage as they believed their prophet was mocked and belittled by a country that was intolerant (*Wall Street Journal*, 2012). A Pakistani minister put out a bounty for the death of the filmmaker who is now serving a one-year prison sentence in California with four years of supervised release time to follow. President Obama has asked YouTube to consider blocking the video but YouTube has instead voluntarily blocked the video in several Muslim countries. It feels it is within its constitutional rights to show the video in other places since the film is not against Muslims and therefore does not count as hate speech.

Watch a video of student protestors in Afghanistan.

Putting Theories to Work

How Does Religion Affect Our Moral Behavior?

According to sociologist Emile Durkheim, religious beliefs unite people into *moral* communities. It is expected that those who value religion also respect life, treat others with dignity, and believe that lying, stealing, and cheating are wrong. When we *socialize* young children, it often includes introducing them to a religious community of elders who preach about the difference between right and wrong. Moral communities care about their members and reach out to assist others. Most religious groups and churches offer services to their parishioners, like food pantries, marriage and/or bereavement counseling, bible study, youth groups, parenting classes, or emergency cash assistance. Usually members of the church community volunteer their time and offer donations of food, clothing, money, or other resources to their church. Why do people offer to help others? Some theories suggest that when we help others we feel better ourselves. Some may feel they have an abundance of resources that they wish to share. This moral commitment to assisting others is consistent with early religious beliefs that God would want you to share your resources with others. In fact some believe that by helping others in this lifetime they are guaranteed a lifetime of eternal bliss when they die. Whatever the reason, religious organizations and churches provide a multitude of social services nationwide. We are dependent upon our churches to continue providing the services they offer to the poor, sick, homeless, elderly, and disabled populations.

The Influence of Religious Leaders

Most religions have an international or national leader who works within their organization to develop policy and extend the religion's mission throughout the world. The Roman Catholic Church elected a new pope in March of 2013. Archbishop Jorge Bergoglio from Argentina was elected as the 266th leader for the worldwide Catholic Church. A champion of the poor and a believer in a new and perhaps more radical change for the church, he accepted the name of Pope Francis, a throwback to Saint Francis whose challenge by God was to change the church during the 13th century. Saint Francis recalled a vision from God telling him to rebuild the church because it was going to ruin. As a follower of Saint Francis, the new Pope agreed to follow the teachings of our Lord Jesus Christ and walk in his footsteps. Pope Francis is known as a humble priest whose work with the poor and downtrodden earned him recognition in South America. He has called on women and youth to spread the good teachings of their faith to others. Many are watching to see if he will be an effective leader and if he will make changes that will impact the role of women in the church.

Read <u>The Catholic Herald</u> for up-to-date news on Pope Francis.

Another religious leader of international fame is renowned American Christian Evangelist Billy Graham, whose media presence brought him into homes beginning in 1949, with his radio programs and later with television. He is an ordained Southern Baptist minister who preaches to the ordinary people as well as being an advisor to many presidents. Several of his broadcasts can still be heard and his message is the same, "let the gospel of the Lord Jesus Christ prepare you for the life you live." Billy Graham's Rapid Response Team has assisted with national and international relief efforts for hurricanes, earthquakes, and other disasters. In this <u>video</u> watch as his team prays with the residents of West Texas to remember one of their own after the explosion of the fertilizer plant in April 2013.

Although Hindus do not have one human leader or a hierarchical authority structure, many leaders have preached Hinduism throughout history. In this religion, God himself is considered the true leader while the scriptures guide people. One famous Hindu leader during the 20th century was <u>Mahatma Gandhi</u>, an Indian lawyer who worked to end British rule in both South Africa as well as India. He fought for social justice through peaceful noncooperation and advocated for Indians during the Independence Movement. He was killed in 1948 by a radical Hindu fanatic. His message of nonviolent civil disobedience and his simple lifestyle of a vegetarian diet and fasting were symbols of hope to the oppressed and impoverished around the world.

His Holiness the 14th Dalai Lama, Tenzin Gyatso, is the head monk of the Gelugpa lineage of Tibetan Buddhism. In his role as global leader for Buddhist monks, he preaches tolerance, compassion, and nonviolence. He brings an awareness about poverty, global conflict, and hunger, reminding people not to forget to help those in need and to begin moral ethics in early education. His speeches about the "culture of compassion" teach us about the need for warm heartedness, a key factor for healthy individuals, healthy families, and healthy communities.

Watch a rare appearance of the <u>Dalai Lama</u> during his stay in Northern Ireland.

The Jewish faith has no single body with a leadership position. Various branches of Judaism around the world appoint their own governing bodies. Local leadership in religious congregations or Synagogues is held by the Rabbi who has religious training. In Israel there is a Chief Rabbi, but in the United States local congregations choose their own Rabbi, with additional assistance provided during the prayer service by the Cantor. Read about the story of the <u>Jewish people</u> in the 20th century.

Today 1.6 billion of the world's population are Muslims who adhere to the teachings of Islam. The Prophet in this religion is Muhammad and their holy text is the Quran, which was developed in the 7th century. There are two main denominations of Islam, the Sunni and Shia sects. Most of the world's Muslim population belongs to the Sunni sect. The worship leader is called an Imam and works in a local mosque to lead services.

Explore articles and videos by scrolling through the Religion of Islam website.

Test your comprehension of Putting Theories to Work and The Influence of Religious Leaders by completing this quiz.

Religious Groups and the Provision of Social Services

The establishment of the *White House Office of Faith Based and Community Initiatives* in 2001 under President Bush's direction was a step in acknowledging the importance of our religious groups to the provision of social welfare services. The new office under President Obama is the *Council on Faith Based and Neighborhood Partnerships*. Many people think that federal dollars should not be used to assist religious groups with providing social services, since that would be a violation of the separation of church and state.

How does religion affect our behavior? The Pew Charitable Trust, a national research organization, has studied the topic of religion and public social services. According to the Pew Forum on Religion and Public Life (2012), state prison chaplains believe that organized religion is essential to the rehabilitation of prisoners. In a survey of 50 state prisons, chaplains indicated that the number of inmates enrolling in religious services and activities has increased in recent years. They say the enrollments of prisoners in religious groups are up and they contribute to a more civilized and orderly community of inmates. They also indicated that religious groups are important to the overall rehabilitation of the prisoner as well as to their aftercare and community support upon release.

Read more about Pew Charitable Trust and their work.

Other research also indicates how religion correlates with behavior. Early studies by Durkheim revealed that religion affected suicide rates. After studying several European countries, he found that Catholics and Jews commit suicide less than Protestants. In fact men commit more suicide than women and unmarried folks more than married. He concluded that those who were closely tied to their social group were less likely to kill themselves because they were well connected. He called this theory *Social Integration* (Henslin, 2013). Some religious groups, like Catholics and Jews, believe that only God can take a life and that man is doomed to hell if he attempts to take his own life. This is how Durkheim explains his theory of social integration.

Churches and religious groups are important partners in providing Human Services in the United States. They provide an array of social services often free of charge. Here clothing is given to homeless people by volunteers from United Christians in Christ Church in Michigan.

Jim West/Alamy

Self-Development

Understanding and Mastery: Conscious use of self; clarification of personal and professional values; awareness of diversity

Critical Thinking Question: Do you think that your religious or spiritual beliefs helped to develop your personal sense of self?

The more connected we are to our social group and believe in and agree with its values, the less likely we are to take our own life. This theory is still valid today. When we work with people who exhibit high-risk behaviors, we often make sure they have good social supports like family, friends, professional helpers, a church, neighbors, or even concerned co-workers. **Integration** is a key concept when we look at developing treatment plans for our consumers.

Test your comprehension of <u>Religious Groups and Providing Social Services</u>.

Think Human Services

How Do Your Religious and Spiritual Beliefs Affect Your Health?

The idea that patient care should be more integrative and less one-dimensional is a progressive way of thinking. It makes sense that the mind and body influence each other and yet scientific thinking in the 20th century was geared toward methods that could be empirically tested. Current research now allows us to test theories and analyze patient results related to a variety of categories including patients' physical health and symptoms, their social support systems, their levels of stress and condition of their mental health, their religious and spiritual beliefs, and the environment where they live, work, and recreate.

A more comprehensive picture emerges of the patient in their life space, which indicates their daily habits, cultural and spiritual values and beliefs, their diet, family life, housing situation, neighborhood environment, economic level, and occupation.

Surveys report that 95% of Americans believe in a God and 71% consider themselves to be spiritual. A study by Maugans and Wadland (1991) looked at religion and family medicine by surveying physicians and their patients. Results indicated that patients thought physicians should consider the *religious* and *spiritual beliefs* of a patient when medical issues were discussed such as diagnoses, treatments, and end of life concerns. Studies also demonstrate that prayer has a positive effect on health outcomes as well as being a powerful tool for prevention of such problems as depression or substance abuse issues.

Spiritual Assessments are now part of many medical assessment packages with specific questions geared toward a patient's religious or spiritual beliefs and how they feel this will impact their health, medical decisions, or treatment. This is important in the Human Services profession since practitioners in the helping professions are usually involved in gathering this data during assessment interviews in hospitals, clinics, health departments, or other medical programs. It is important for a thorough assessment to be conducted before an accurate diagnosis can be given to the patient. Physicians, nurses, Human Services workers, social workers, and any other professionals on the team need to ensure that individualized assessments accurately depict the patient and his or her complex mix of symptoms, needs, and issues before treatment can begin.

> **Explore Spirituality and Medical Practice: Using the HOPE Questions as a Practical Tool for Spiritual Assessment from the American Academy of Family Physicians.**

Linking Theory to Practice

Integrated Medicine Now Has a Religious or Spiritual Component

How do religion and spirituality effect our health and state of well-being? Current research into the mind and body connection reveals that our physical health can be effected by our emotions and mental condition. Stress can make us sick and hope and positive emotions can help us get well. According to the Bravewell Collaborative (2012), integrative medicine attempts to put the patient at the center of the treatment and assesses their *physical, emotional, mental, social, spiritual* and *environmental* well-being. How a person deals with a physical illness or news of a chronic disease is often dependent upon his or her values and belief system. Some people turn to their religion for *support* and *relief*; others use their spiritual sense to guide them in making treatment decisions. In the past, scientists were slow to admit prayer had any real validity in treating diseases. Current research is now testing our belief systems to determine how effective religious and spiritual practices are in the healing process. Many people give credit for their recoveries to their God, their prayer, or a miracle. Some physicians are even perplexed as to the recuperative powers of some people who are in the final stages of a chronic illness. When people revert to healthy lives there is often little evidence to support what happened. The idea that a person's belief system could prevent illness or assist a person in recovering from an illness is no longer an unusual concept. As you saw from the HOPE questionnaire that is used in a medical assessment, the power of a person's religious or spiritual practice can have a lasting impact on the type of treatment that is provided to a patient.

> **Watch the three-part video series "The New Medicine" from Bravewell Collaborative.**

Hope is a powerful tool in fighting illness as you heard from Dana Reeve, wife of Christopher Reeve and spokesperson for The New Medicine PBS Special. Although both Dana and her husband, Christopher Reeve, are now deceased, they endured many years of physical and emotional stress after Chris's spinal cord injury. Many people thought that Christopher Reeve was a real *Superman* for his ability to withstand the treatments and procedures after his accident.

Did You Know?

Both Eastern and Western Cultures Have Religious and Spiritual Practices
That Have Health Benefits

Human Services practitioners need to know a variety of skill sets in their work with individuals, groups, families, and communities. We need to understand how to *interview* people using appropriate *questioning*, how to *network* with agencies to find services for our consumers if we are case managers, and how to *analyze* a situation if we are doing *case assessment and treatment planning*. Each case requires us to think carefully about the individual, his or her problem, possible solutions, and an *action plan* that can be negotiated with the client. How does the person think about the situation? How does the person feel about the issue? How has it affected both the person and his or her family? Are they willing to take steps to make a change? Can you develop a *trusting relationship* with this person? What are the *values and beliefs* this person has regarding you, the agency, and the treatment plan? These are all important questions.

Often people rely on a *higher power* to help them make decisions. Some people pray daily asking for guidance in doing the "right thing." A therapist who persists with reasoning that is scientific may not be relating to the client who is more intuitive and spiritual. Eastern cultures may be better suited to meet the needs of people who value their spiritual senses rather than scientific data. Western culture is more suited to scientific data and understanding religious doctrine whose ideology has been formatted with ritual traditions like Sunday Catholic masses, Protestant Church services, and Saturday Jewish Temple services. Westerners are becoming more familiar with the Islamic religion and are learning about the Eastern spiritual practices of Buddhists, Hindus, and Muslims. Since they are so different than our own religious practices, some people are reluctant to try anything that appears strange or cannot be empirically validated. However, research today is pointing to the *health benefits that can be attributed to practices that are spiritual and religious in both eastern and western countries.* For instance, the Zen sitting *meditation*, which is similar to prayer, can calm you down and lower your heart rate. The Islamic use of *prayer beads* is very similar to Catholic rosary beads and can be a great way to focus your thoughts on a more peaceful activity than constant worry or anxiety over an issue. The Hindu practice of continually *repeating a mantra* has the same effect of helping us to forget persistent negative thoughts, even if it is just for a short time. Research has demonstrated that the Buddhist practice of *yoga*, which stretches and relaxes our muscles, can *reduce stress and alleviate heart and lung disease, as well as improve musculoskeletal strength.* The *martial arts*, t'ai chi and jujutsu, are also examples of both spiritual and religious philosophies that include *body exercise and self-discipline* that tone and *strengthen the muscles as well as develop cognitive skills*. Both Eastern and Western religions have some similar practices that are considered healthy for both the mind and the body such as *fasting, reading and studying the holy book, reciting prayers, chanting, singing, celebrating traditions through fellowship, learning how to use silence, and giving back to others through hospitality or acts of charity*. Some eastern religions also practice *vegetarianism*. Buddhism stresses the *importance* and *beauty of nature* and *uses the spiritual tools of meditation, the writing of poetry, painting, calligraphy, flower ar-ranging*, and *the development of Zen gardens* in its teachings. The Japanese and Korean *tea ceremonies* have also been described as spiritual in nature since they evoke ancient rituals blended with Zen religious philosophies. Participants move very slowly and are silent and deliberate in their focused movements. It is a beautiful experience that is considered an art form.

Watch the video of the <u>Kyoto Japanese Tea Ceremony</u> to appreciate the beauty of this tradition.

What Would You Do?

What Religious or Spiritual Techniques Could Be Used in These Exercises?

Consider the following scenarios and think about how a person's religion or spirituality might be helpful in dealing with the situation. Even if you are not a religious or spiritual person, how can your knowledge of someone else's beliefs inform your practice? What have you learned about both eastern and western religions and spiritual practices that can benefit someone's physical and mental health?

1. You are working in a medical clinic in a low-income neighborhood and a young African American woman has just suffered a miscarriage in her third trimester. What would you say to her to bring comfort? Is there anything you could do to bring her peace of mind?
2. You are employed at St. Mary's Assisted Living Facility run by the Catholic diocese in your city. You enjoy working with the residents who are anywhere from 65 years of age to 100. Most of them are in great physical and mental condition, except for Mrs. Fowler who has fallen recently and broken her hip. It is apparent that she needs surgery and will require full care rather than assisted living, so she will be moving to another facility after her hospital stay. You know this will be difficult for her because she had many friends at St. Mary's and she loved all the daily activi-ties. You go to visit her and you consider what you will say to her. How would you handle this interaction?
3. Your best friend, who is an Orthodox Jew, is getting ready to run her first Boston Marathon. She has been in training for a year and has been practicing every day. You notice that her confidence is dipping as she says, "What was I thinking? I can't run the big marathon in Boston yet. I must be crazy!" What might you say to her that could help build her self-confidence?

Recall what you learned in this chapter by completing the Chapter Review.

4. You are employed at the local hospital as a life coach. Your patient, Tom Hayes, had a heart attack and then an open heart surgery last week. His recovery has been slow, although he is forcing himself to do all the same things he used to do. He has always been a type A personality, does everything at a fast pace, and eats all kinds of fast foods. How might his spirituality help guide him toward a different life style that you know he must begin or else he will be destined for another heart attack. How can you help him develop an integrative plan that will include assessing his physical, emotional, social, and spiritual self and then developing a treatment plan to meet those needs?

CHAPTER 12

Developing Your Professional Self

Human Services Professionals Are Most Effective When They Take Care of Themselves by Practicing Stress Management, Becoming Aware of Burnout Issues, and Planning for Career Development

AF archive/Alamy

We all enjoy working with people but sometimes our passion for helping gets us so excited about providing services for others that we become overwhelmed. We want to help our consumers so much that we give everything we have to providing help, even if it means working overtime, calling everyone we know to get resources, and spending our free time mobilizing assistance from friends, family, other agencies, and co-workers. When we finally get everything we think the consumer needs, we are exhausted and they may be less than satisfied, hoping we could have obtained more or done it faster. How would this make you feel? Many workers begin to feel unappreciated and actually start to resent the clients. Now we have a serious situation because if you are tired, bitter, feel unappreciated, and underpaid you will not be satisfied or happy when you come to work. This is a situation in the professional world of Human Services we call *burnout*. It is a condition we hope to avoid, but sometime in our career we most likely will experience this phenomenon.

Did you ever watch the television show *30 Rock*, written by Tina Fey? In the show Tina plays a frustrated supervisor, Liz Lemon, who is constantly battling with her coworkers and boss, Alec Baldwin. She tries very hard to make everyone happy and to get her team members to collaborate, despite their differences.

Have you ever gone out of your way to do something for someone and you didn't feel appreciated for it? I can remember feeling that way when I had first started working as a caseworker in a child welfare agency. I wanted to prove that I could do the job plus I did enjoy helping others.

Chapter Outline

Even though I arrived at work early, I felt compelled to stay late if a parent called to say he or she needed to speak to me. I would take my work home so that I could complete the necessary agency forms and narratives. That meant that after working all day, I would go home, eat a quick dinner, and then sit down and begin writing in my case files. I was on the road to burnout and I didn't even realize it. In addition, I was taking classes toward my graduate degree two nights a week. After a year of this type of schedule, I felt sick, underpaid, not appreciated, and tired. When I finally learned about burnout in one my classes, I realized I could be the textbook example! No one can continue on a rigorous schedule of work without having it affect their health and personal life. So, now I teach my students that you must have a balance in everything that you do. You need to please yourself first before you can give anything back to another person.

Explore the **NBC** website for videos, photos, and blogs of *30 Rock*.

What's It All About?

Developing a Personal Stress Management Plan, Knowing the Causes and Symptoms of Burnout, and Learning Methods to Cope

In a study I conducted in Florida some years ago, I found that Human Services and Social Work students were very different in their motivation for choosing their major than other students who chose their majors. In a study of several schools statewide, I found that education majors were often prompted to become teachers by their parents or relatives who were also educators. Business and marketing majors were motivated by economic rewards; they wanted to make money. However, social work and Human Services students *wanted to help others*. Many students indicated they had worked through problems themselves and now wanted to give back to others. They indicated that issues of substance abuse, death of a loved one, poverty, domestic violence, child abuse, homelessness, and low self-esteem all challenged them to seek assistance, work on treatment plans, and recover. Now they wanted to help others who were going through the same thing (Kinsella, 1997). This idea of using our skills to help others make a better life for themselves is the motivating factor in why we choose Human Services. Now we need to make sure that we are helping others as well as helping ourselves.

Human Services practitioners give a lot of themselves. *Compassion* for others is a quality that makes Human Services practitioners different from workers in other professions. You don't have to be compassionate to be a computer scientist, or an historian, or an economist. Human Services practitioners, however, really want to make a difference in helping others change their lives. This is the heart of why we do what we do. We are *challenged* by the work and *rewarded* by the outcomes for our clients. Often Human Services practitioners have worked through a difficult issue in their own lives and now they are ready to *help others* go through the same process. We need to be able to identify personal and professional issues, which affect our work, be prepared to handle these situations, and know how to advance our career in the Human Services field. Let's take a look at one of the most common complaints in Human Services.

Avoiding Burnout

Our compassion and empathy for others makes us different in this profession. We want to help others. However, research tells us that those in the helping professions like counselors, teachers, and social workers suffer more stress-related job problems due to the nature of their work, and it can last many years (Reed, 1979). It is difficult when people accept our services without saying "thank you," expect that we will "solve their problem," or become upset when things did not turn out the way they had hoped. It is disappointing for workers as well. When we can't find the resources that others need, we don't have the time to devote to just one case, or we are unhappy with the judge's decision to return a child to a family that we know will re-abuse him or her, we become disillusioned. When this happens, we may become tired, dismayed with our position, angry with the system, our coworkers, our agency, and sometimes with ourselves. We call this condition **burnout**. When workers feel like this, they become negative, have less energy to devote to new ideas in the agency, are tired, may call in sick, and are not productive members of the treatment team.

Physical changes in health are also symptomatic of burnout. Human Services practitioners may not sleep well, may have a change in eating habits, may experience headaches or migraines, muscle aches or pains, or develop stomach problems (Sweitzer, 1999). This is when changes have to be made if good consumer service is going to be provided and the practitioner is going to remain in the profession and be healthy.

Staying Healthy

So what do you do if you are feeling burned-out at work? First you need to identify the reasons for your feelings. Some practitioners are more vulnerable than others to burnout. One group is the new and inexperienced workers who are ready to set the world on fire with their enthusiasm and ideas. They are wonderful for agencies that have fallen victim to *laissez-faire*, business as usual, practices that have not had any new ideas or strategies in years. However, these workers could run into massive resistance from other workers who may not be interested or willing to change. So new practitioners continually push for change and try to convince everyone that change is needed. After a while

Staying fit, eating nutritious foods, getting enough sleep, and exercise are all important elements of avoiding burnout. Take time for yourself and stay healthy.

they become tired of fighting for change, and they wear themselves out, finally giving up and feeling sick and disheartened in the process. Some agencies may allow these enthusiastic beginners to *make changes by themselves*. They may end up doing all the work, staying late to complete a project, coming in on weekends to make that necessary change, and become physically ill and mentally exhausted. Another vulnerable group to the condition of burnout is the Human Services practitioner who has been doing the same job for years and is nearing retirement. Many people love what they do, but for workers who are tired of dealing with a bureaucratic system and who have never rejuvenated themselves, retirement is the solution they are waiting for in angst. They may want to leave and work elsewhere, but if they have a pension plan that requires them to remain in the agency for a period of time, they may feel that their options are slim so they remain in a job they don't enjoy until they can collect their retirement check. Over the years I have worked with some of these folks, and they will tell you frequently how many years, months, weeks, days, and hours they have until they can leave. These people can make it difficult for practitioners who want to enjoy their work. So what can you do to avoid burnout and the negative symptoms that accompany it?

Knowing that burnout can occur when you *are overwhelmed with your job responsibilities, feel unappreciated, underpaid, or have little authority to make change happen* can help you assess the situation. Be aware of how you feel, what mood you find yourself in after work, and what you think about when you are home. Consider your health. Are you sleeping through the night, eating nutritious meals daily, and getting exercise? Skipping meals to get all of your work done and working late into the night to complete reports will only make you more tired and less healthy to continue helping others in your agency. *Nutrition* is very important when you work in Human Services where we make decisions that effect people's lives everyday. You need to think clearly and be focused, so eating good sources of protein, carbohydrates, vegetables, fruits, and grains is necessary. Snacking on foods from the vending machine in the lobby will not satisfy your hunger or your need for nutrients.

You also need to make sure you *keep time for yourself* and have a personal life, which includes friends, family, and people who are not your coworkers. It is important that you spend time doing enjoyable things outside of work with people who know little about your work situation and will not be prompted to talk about your job. Spend time reading, going to the movies, exercising, or being outside in pleasant surroundings that make you feel good. There is nothing better to lift your mood than a walk on a sunny day, or a visit to a friend's home, or some other outdoor adventure. *Exercise* is a wonderful way to release stress so think about what works for you: walking, hiking, riding a bike, a workout at the gym, or a yoga or martial arts class, like t'ai chi. What makes you relaxed and happy? Do you have a talent for singing, art, woodworking, cooking, or playing an instrument? You don't need to give up your interests because you are employed in Human Services. Oftentimes combining your love of one thing with your passion for helping others can become a harmonious blend, allowing you to pursue your interests and perhaps sharing it with your consumers. When I facilitated groups for children, I often used my love of music to create activities that I enjoyed developing as much as they enjoyed participating. The idea is to keep growing personally as well as professionally so that you are happy with yourself and the work you do with others.

It is also important to realize that systems have an impact on people and often practitioners become tired and experience burnout working in faulty systems where they are expected to work for long hours with little pay and with large caseloads. It is up to us as professionals to advocate for better working conditions and to express our concerns to administrators when the workload becomes too large and impossible to produce quality results.

If you become a supervisor, know that you can reduce the stress on your workers by considering some *best practices* that will prevent them from burnout. When people have the opportunity to *express their feelings* and *give their points of view*, they feel they are valued as employees. Some prevention measures include *meeting regularly with your team members* and *allowing everyone to partici-pate in decision-making*. Give people *reasonable caseloads* and *adequate time to complete their work*. Advocate for *pay raises* for your employees and offer them *time off* if they work beyond their normal hours. Make sure workers are taking their *vacation days* and encourage people to *stay home if they are sick*. In one agency where I worked, we had an exercise class during the lunch hour so people could enjoy some stretching. You can also arrange for a walking group after lunch if the weather permits. That is a great way to spend time socializing with your coworkers and getting some fresh air and exercise. Arrange for time during the work-day to *relax and socialize periodically with your workers*, perhaps for a holiday party or a celebration of a job well done or for employees' birthdays. Having supervisors who recognize the difficulty of the job and appreciate the work that is done will help practitioners avoid burnout.

> **Test your comprehension of <u>What's It All About?</u> by completing this quiz.**

Career Development

Plan on Developing Yourself Professionally and Practice Lifelong Learning

It is very important in Human Services that you *stay informed of current changes* in the profession. You should also *confirm the competencies* you have learned in working with individuals, groups, and families by taking the certification examination for Human Services that is offered by the **Center for Credentialing and Education (CCE)**. This is a voluntary exam at most schools, so you may not be required to take this test. However, passing this national exam demonstrates to others that you are rec-ognized as a *certified* Human Services professional. You have learned specific competencies in *case management, assessment, treatment planning, administra-tion, community organizing, group facilitation,* and *cultural diversity* to name just a few of the practices you have been taught. You will become a **Human Services Board Certified Practitioner**, or an **HS-BCP**. When you see these letters after someone's name you will know what they mean.

> **Explore the <u>Center for Credentialing and Education</u> website for more information.**

Once you graduate from an undergraduate program and decide to take your certi-fication examination, you may then decide if you want to continue your education or get a job. As you saw in Chapter 1, there are many opportunities for Human Services graduates. A good starting place would be your local department of labor. You should develop a professional **résumé** of your work experience, including your *field placement*. Be sure to indicate the skills that you learned and what specific job titles or roles you had if you were employed in a social service agency either full- or part-time. Case man-ager, resource and referral specialist, child caregiver, or mental health aid are some roles that you should list if you had these types of jobs. List your volunteer activities and the courses you have taken as well. Provide the names of about three professional references including college instructors and your field placement supervisor. Always ask permission to list these people as references to make sure they will write you a letter or provide a telephone reference if necessary. When developing your résumé, you may refer many professional templates available online or through the Career Planning Office of your school. Your resume should have no typos, misspellings, or inaccurate information. Make sure you have someone edit your resume before you make a final copy. You might want to make several copies that you can distribute to local agencies or through your United Way. Many agencies offer the opportunity for you to apply online and upload your resume.

Watch the video on How to Write a Noticeable Resume for tips.

Apply to several agencies and be prepared if you receive a telephone call to answer questions or attend a job interview. Always look professional when you go to the interview. Dress for success. If you don't have professional clothes, buy a new dress or suit. If you can't afford to buy anything new, borrow some from a friend or ask your Career Planning Office if they can be helpful. Many college offices keep suits and dresses on hand so students can prepare for interviews and look their professional best. Bring an extra copy of your resume with you to the interview just to be sure they have a copy on hand. Be positive and outline your strengths and what you can do for the agency. It is not necessary to explain or defend what you see as weaknesses in your resume. That "C" that you received in the group dynamics class may not even be mentioned. Let the interviewer ask the questions and then respond without offering information that could be damaging. In my role as an administrator, I found that many young graduates often exposed their weaknesses in interviews when they were not asked for such information. You can practice for a job interview by role-playing with a friend. In this way you can anticipate what questions may be asked. Always put your best foot forward. Why should the agency hire you? What can you do for the agency? Be ready to negotiate a salary, ask about travel money or professional development funds, and health care and pension benefits. If you are doing home visits or traveling from one center to the next, will they reimburse your travel expenses? Remember that some agencies may not have the highest salaries, but their benefits package may exceed the agency that offers more money but has no health care plan. Let them know why you want to be hired. Read about the agency before the interview. Ask questions about their services, long-term goals, or fund-raising efforts. Then provide them with information as to how you can assist them with these goals. Have you done fund-raising for your church or the PTA? Are their service goals consistent with your career goals?

Keep in mind that your first job may not be the highest paying and may not be exactly what you thought you would be doing after graduation. All Human Services jobs provide the opportunity to put into practice the skills that you have learned. You will also begin to network and learn about other agencies in your community, which can help you make a change after you gain some experience in the work world. Waiting around for the perfect job to come your way may be a mistake. My first job was as a Toddler Teacher in a day care center, not the job I was planning to get. However, I found I loved working with the children and within a few months a position opened up for a home/school caseworker in a different agency that was affiliated with the day care center. I was hired because of my ability to work with young children and their families and because I was also known to the administrator of the day care program who provided me with an excellent reference for my next job. Never underestimate where one job can take you.

If you decide to continue with graduate school, you have several options. You can continue with a degree in the helping professions like Human Services or Social Work, or you may see yourself in the role of an administrator and pursue a degree in public administration or even business administration. Some students like the idea of mental health, marriage and family, or professional Counseling. Others decide to go into law or medicine and may need to make up additional credits before they can begin these graduate programs. Human Services is a good match for several master's degrees. You need to do your research to determine if the school has financial aid, offers internships, provides traditional or online classes or a blended format. Find out if the program you are interested in is accredited by any national organization and if the degree will lead to any certification or license. If you are interested in professional counseling, this is especially important because some degrees do not offer licensing, which can effect whether or not insurance companies will reimburse you for any services you provide. Make sure you check out your options carefully considering part-time and full-time classes.

Remember that Human Services professional organizations like the National Organization for Human Services (NOHS) or your regional Human Services organizations offer annual conferences in different locations around the country. By joining these organizations and attending these conferences you can learn more about the profession and advance your career in Human Services.

Become a member of NOHS.

> **Test your comprehension of Career Development: Plan on Developing Yourself Professionally and Practice Lifelong Learning by completing this quiz.**

Around the Globe

International Human Services

Did you ever consider working in another country for part of your Human Services career? Many people do just that. A variety of international organizations exist to assist people in developing countries with issues like poverty, violence, lack of education, unsafe drinking water, health care problems, HIV/AIDS, and homelessness.

> **Read about the International Services of the American Red Cross and their initiatives including immunization programs worldwide, HIV/AIDS education and prevention, and providing technical support and supplies to millions of people around the globe.**

As you have read in other chapters, people around the world are impacted by the number of aging seniors and the problems they face, the increasing numbers of homeless children who are left to fend for themselves, the epidemic of HIV/AIDS in Africa, and the devastating effects of the 2010 earthquake in Haiti which killed 250,000 people and left 630,000 living in makeshift shelters (*The New York Times*,

2012). As the poorest and least developed nation, Haiti was already facing massive health care and poverty issues before the earthquake. International workers from many organizations are still trying to bring a humane standard of living to this country.

> Explore <u>news, commentary and articles</u> about the earthquake and efforts to rebuild Haiti.

What organizations offer international Human Services positions? Action Against Hunger works to end hunger in many countries in Asia, Africa, and the Middle East. It also assists in providing clean drinking water.

> Explore the <u>Action Against Hunger</u> website for more information.

If you are interested in learning about volunteering, internship, or employment opportunities, check out <u>Virginia Tech's Career Services webpage</u>, which is a wonderful resource of a variety of agencies both in the United States and abroad that provide students with volunteer activities, paid and unpaid internships, as well as employment opportunities upon graduation.

Putting Theories to Work

Psychological and Sociological Theories of Burnout

When we talk about developing our professional self, our Human Services agencies are as much responsible as we are in guiding us toward career building opportunities. Some

International Human Services workers may choose to work in agencies around the globe. Here a German worker chooses a handicapped school for children in sub-Saharan Africa.

@Painet Inc./Alamy

systems do a wonderful job of this, providing funding for Human Services staff to attend continuing education programs and conferences. Each year the Human Services organizations like NOHS and the regional affiliates offer conferences regionally and nationally. There are also many online webinars and other educational workshops that can build skills in Human Services.

Other organizations don't do as good a job and often overwhelm practitioners with an excessive workload, low pay, and long hours. Many people feel that workers are not to blame for the condition of burnout, but rather the systems they work in fail to adequately support them, which leads to burnout. Some sociologists would go even further to describe the working condition as the problem. Karger (1981) found that people are often *distanced from the work they do, don't recognize the contribution they make to the organization, and may not be connected to other workers.* He called this **alienation** and referred to more systemic problems than individual problems, indicating that the worker was not at fault for burnout but rather the *structure of the organization* was at fault. Workers who don't see how the role they play in the agency can assist in change for the client may become uninspired to continue. For instance, the practitioner who completes the Intake for each new patient and then passes it off to the counselor for treatment may not see what gains the patient is making. This may affect the practitioner's sense of accomplishment because he or she sees the patient only upon entering the office and is not aware of the final outcomes. Therefore, burnout can also refer to the emotional and physical exhaustion that practitioners experience due to their working relationships with others (Sweitzer, 1999).

Psychologists would say that burnout may occur not only because of the structure of the agency, but also because of the *values and goals of the practitioner.* If a worker is uncomfortable refusing services to a homeless man because he is still drug addicted, or if he or she must counsel a pregnant teen to consider abortion as one option, the worker may suffer with personal *value conflicts.* The practitioner who is deeply religious and does not agree with abortion may have a problem with this aspect of his or her job. People in this position should consider a job change because all the prevention measures for burnout will not help this practitioner change his or her values or beliefs, and it is not the system that needs to change its policies in these situations.

Test your comprehension of <u>Putting Theories to Work: Psychological and Sociological Theories of Burnout</u> by completing this quiz.

Think Human Services

Analyzing Case Studies of Burnout

Consider what you have learned about burnout and read the following scenarios. Imagine that you have just been hired to work in these agencies. Working in a child welfare agency is a very stressful job and so a case like this is very realistic.

You have been hired as a caseworker in the Department of Family and Children's Services in your state. Your job is to assess each report of child abuse and neglect to determine if indeed it is a founded case, which means that it is true. If it is an unfounded case, it means that enough evidence is not available to determine that abuse or neglect has taken place. Records of the investigation will then be expunged in these situations. You have a very serious and responsible job. You don't ever want to make a mistake because you realize that a child's life can be at risk. You started out with 5 case files, but you have been at the agency for three months and you now have 15 open cases with court dates pending. You barely have enough time to finish one case when a report comes in on another child. You try to get as many done in one day as you possibly can, but often that means skipping lunch or dinner or both. You read your files thoroughly before you do your home visit, but often there is only a telephone call from a neighbor or relative and so you have little to go on. If there is indication of violence or drug abuse in the home, then law enforcement will accompany you on your visit. You interview the parents or guardians, see the child separately in a bedroom or bathroom to check for marks, and also do a quick observation of the home to determine if there is adequate and clean living space, appropriate-aged toys, enough separate sleeping space, and enough food for the family. If the case is founded, then you have protection from law enforcement if you have to remove the child. Then you need to find an immediate emergency placement in either a foster home or emergency child care shelter. All of this takes time and you may be involved with one case for many late evenings. Sometimes you have to accompany the child to a hospital or child advocacy center where a physical examination and forensic interview will confirm the physical or sexual abuse. You may need to complete additional paperwork for law enforcement if a criminal act has occurred. Many times you may go alone to a home if there is suspicion of neglect and not physical abuse. You still have to talk with the parents and see the child, but the situation may be linked to poverty and not violence. You may find that you use your case management skills as you refer the family for food stamps, Medicaid, mental health services, or Section VIII Housing for rental assistance. After you do your assessment in any case, you need to thoroughly write up a report in your online reporting program. Your reports have to be factual and objective since they will go to court for review by the judge and district attorney. You attend court every week to either advocate for the return of children to their biological parents or to prevent children from that fate. What reports you haven't been able to get done at work, you take home and complete in the evening. You usually fall into bed exhausted but unable to sleep.

You have been feeling tired lately and you have no energy, but you can't sleep. You have started taking medication for headaches and your stomach has been bothering you, so you aren't eating well either. You find that you can't wait until Friday comes, but this week you are on call as the emergency worker. That means that it is your turn to wear the beeper and you will be called if an emergency occurs.

What do you think is the problem with this worker?
What are the physical and mental symptoms she is experiencing?

Apply the techniques you have learned to make her healthy again. What treatment methods would you suggest in this situation? How would you assess whether or not burnout has occurred?

When you work with children, you need a lot of energy, and so you can become tired or physically burned out if you work in day care. Imagine what it would be like if you were hired to be the new Lead Teacher in this scenario.

Case Study ▶ Lead Teacher

You have been hired as the Lead Teacher in a day care center. You are very excited about your new position since it recognizes your Human Services degree and is a supervisory position so you are earning more money. On the first day you notice that the teachers in your team all seem tired, not very energetic, and they use loud and intimidating voices to discipline the children. You introduce yourself, and they tell you that you won't last long. You are apparently the third Lead Teacher they have hired in two months. "This place is a zoo and these kids are like animals!" one assistant teacher replies. "They expect us to watch too many kids and then those older ones come off the bus and it's crazy by 3 o'clock." You do some checking and notice that the assistant teachers haven't been given a pay raise in three years. The teachers have not used their vacation time because they get paid out instead. Each year they have chosen to just keep their vacation money since they don't get raises. All the staff eat lunch with the children as well. You are already thinking about what you have learned in your Human Services classes. Use the information you have learned about burnout and decide what changes you would make for your staff.

What is happening in this center that is causing stress?
What are the symptoms that the workers are experiencing?
How might this affect the children in the center?
If you were the new Lead Teacher what would you do?

Linking Theory to Practice

Can Understanding Theories Help Us in Our Assessments?

Sociologist Karger (1981) says that when a system is structured in a way that prevents people from seeing their work as part of the big picture of the organization, a process called **alienation** may develop. Think about the work of Thad, a Human Services student, as you read his story. Then consider if this job is a good starting point for a Human Services student. Why or why not? Does gender make a difference?

Case Study ▶ THAD

Thad was a Human Services student who attended the local community college. He lacked the funds he needed to stay in school, and so he went to his advisor for some guidance. She told him he was eligible for work/study and suggested that he contact the Early Childhood Center on campus because they were currently hiring, and work/study students were always accepted if help was needed in a department. Thad walked over to the Center and saw all the children running around outside on the playground. They sure looked like they were having a good time. He enjoyed children and was eager to meet the director and find out about the position. He was greeted inside the building by an Early Childhood teacher. When she heard his request for a work/study position, she quickly took him to the office to meet the director who was a middle-aged woman with kind eyes and a quick smile. She offered Thad a seat and had him complete an application for the position of child care assistant. She indicated that the center did indeed need help in the afternoons from 2:00–5:00 p.m. He would get paid every two weeks and could adjust his schedule when final exams or other coursework made it difficult to attend. He would receive $1.00 more than minimum wage plus a book stipend offered by the school. Thad thought that was a generous offer and accepted the position. He started work the following week and after the first day was baffled.

When he arrived for work all the teachers and the director went into a room in the back of the building. He was not invited to participate but instead was asked to remain in the room with about 30 sleeping children. He did not understand the point of sitting around and watching children sleep. Perhaps they did not expect him to stay today. He saw a woman in the kitchen preparing some snack foods, and he approached her and asked if he was supposed to be doing anything. She informed him that he was to sit quietly and watch the children until they woke up from their naps. She was preparing snack food for the afternoon rush when the older children would arrive from the public school. He went back and sat quietly until the children started to wake up. One by one they came over to him to find out who he was, if he would tie their shoes, read them a book, or play outside with them. He enjoyed his time with the children, but he felt that he must be missing something. In his Human Services classes, he learned all about case management, assessment, and treatment planning. This was babysitting. His advisor must not have understood what his degree was all about. He didn't see how this job would help him in his career. It bothered him that the educational staff did not include him in whatever they were doing. They obviously did not see him as a pre-professional.

Thad came to work for the next three days hoping that something would change or that someone would give him some professional role to play. Each day when he arrived, the teaching staff and director would say hello and then head for the office in the back of the room. Thad would sit quietly for about an hour and then the children would begin to rise. He really enjoyed playing with the children and getting to know their parents when they arrived at the end of the day. Still he couldn't help feeling like he was wasting his time. At the end of the week, he submitted his resignation to the center director and told her it would be his last day. He had gotten a higher-paying job in a nearby restaurant cleaning tables and washing dishes.

Intervention and Direct Services

Understanding and Mastery: Knowledge and skill development in the use of consultation

Critical Thinking Question: Have you ever worked in an agency where you didn't feel that the work you did was very useful because you couldn't see the final product? How did you resolve the issue? Did you have a supervisor you could talk with about your concerns?

You might have wondered, like Thad, what was happening in this agency. Does Karger's theory of alienation fit this situation? Consistent with the theory, Thad was feeling distanced from the work and could not recognize the contribution he was making to the program. He certainly was not connected to the other workers, which heightened his anxiety. He believed that his efforts were not considered professional and therefore people were excluding him. Of course that was not the case. Nevertheless, *that is what he perceived.*

Sometimes when we are first learning about Human Services, we assume that our work will always be very high tech or theoretical and that it will follow a professional pattern of assessment, treatment planning, and contracting. Actually a lot of the work that we do with others involves listening, observing, and guiding people. For example, I had a student, Jamie, some years ago who graduated with her Human Services degree and was hired as a Family Preservation Caseworker with her local Department of Family and Children's Services. After about a week she called me in frustration to say that she was quitting because the job was a joke, and they just wanted her to wash dishes. I asked her for some additional information, and we talked about what she was really doing. She had been hired to work with a young mother of two who had been a teen mom with her first child. Now at age 20, she had two children, few parenting skills, and no sense of how to handle the responsibilities of a home. Her children had been removed on a neglect petition and were in foster care for six months, but now both her four-year-old and two-year-old were back living with her. As a former child welfare worker myself, I knew immediately what was happening. Jamie was hired to be a role model for this young woman. Her job was to teach her how to be a mother, how to use appropriate discipline, and how to establish a safe, clean, and comfortable home. As a Family Preservation Worker, you assist the client with tasks in the home, showing her how to change sheets, wash dishes, sweep floors, and clean bathrooms. You are explaining the importance of this work and why it needs to be done and how often. For those of us who grew up in families where we had clean homes, clean clothes, and good food, we may misunderstand our role working with a family like this one. Remember that behavior is learned. If no one ever teaches you to how to make your bed, wash your clothes, or vacuum the carpet, you may not know how or understand its importance. Sometimes we do some very basic teaching in our role as a professional Human Services worker.

Now let's apply that thinking to Thad. He didn't realize the significance of his job. He saw himself as a babysitter, watching children sleep. He didn't value what he was doing, much like my student who believed she was hired to wash dishes. In reality both of these students had a very important role to play with their clients. My student had a wonderful opportunity to develop rapport and trust while she was teaching her client how to manage a household with two small children. She could teach the client all kinds of things about cleaning, cooking, budgeting, shopping, and parenting. All of these skills could be very useful to a young mother who may not have learned these things if she had no appropriate role model in her life. Likewise, Thad was serving a very important role with these young children who may wake up in a day care center feeling scared and lonely. Naptime can be a stressful time for children who don't want to sleep. They may look for their mothers or begin to feel homesick. New children in a day care center may have difficulty with naptime. Having a caring adult in the situation can be very soothing. Perhaps Thad could have walked around checking the children to make sure they were comfortable. If a child woke early, he could be there to reassure the child that naptime would be over soon and then it would be time to play. Maybe he could read a book to children who were not sleepy. For children who do not have a father who is available, a male role model in a day care center is priceless. Developing rapport and trust with a child who is suffering the loss of a parent is extremely important. He could fill a void in a child's life just by being there, listening to a child, and playing with the child. Sometimes Human Services students are surprised to learn that something so simple can be very therapeutic. Of course, if a supervisor had explained these things to Thad, he may have felt differently about what he was doing. His sense of self and his perception of the job would no doubt change. Since this did not occur, he unfortunately left the position feeling that his work there was useless.

Do you think that something could have been done differently to prevent Thad from leaving and to explain to him what could be learned in this situation? Can you think of anything that Thad could have done instead of resigning? If you said, "speak with his supervisor or the director," good for you! As workers we must take responsibility for our own issues and concerns. Instead of waiting for someone to explain something to us, we need to ask questions if we do not understand. Our training includes developing skills in interpersonal communication. That means that we need to learn how to communicate with others as well as teaching our clients the same skills.

Now let's look at this case from the director's point of view.

Case Study   Director

When Thad came into the building looking for a work/study job the director was delighted. What luck that a Human Services student would be eligible for work/study in the Early Childhood Center on campus. Thad's application was impressive, his grades indicated that he cared about school, and he was a male! Most of their children came from single-parent families with mothers who struggled to make ends meet. The director knew that many of the mothers attended school on campus and that many of the fathers were not available or not interested in seeing their children. In fact some of the fathers were in prison so she knew the children had limited contact with adult men. What a wonderful opportunity for the children to have an appropriate, male role model like Thad. It would also be good experience for him to learn how to develop his interpersonal skills with small children as well as their parents. Her staff would be delighted that the afternoons could be used for staff meetings and program planning while Thad watched over the children in the sleeping room. She knew that a responsible person had to be hired for that position. Often the children woke up crying after a bad dream, or they needed assistance going to the bathroom, and they always had to make sure that no one wandered outside during naptime. She was excited about her new hire because she just felt he was the right student for the job. Perhaps they could even include him in planning the Parent Night that would occur next month. She would have to talk to her staff about that to see what role he could play. She wanted the parents to meet Thad because a male child care assistant was a wonderful addition for the children. They only had one male child care assistant many years ago. She knew her parents would welcome the addition of Thad to the center. The Director was stunned when Thad turned in his resignation on Friday after only one week in the center. He looked like he was enjoying the children. She had no idea what had happened.

After reading the director's point of view were you surprised? Obviously she was delighted with Thad and what he could offer the children. What do you think she could have done differently? If you said she contributed to Thad's feelings of alienation, you would be correct. When people feel alienated or burned out, we must always consider the system within which they are working. Remember that if you become a supervisor, communication skills are just as important for you to use with your employees as they are with your clients. People need to understand their value in the agency. If this director had spent some time with Thad in the beginning and explained why his role with the children during naptime was so important, he may not have resigned his position. Even a debriefing after a few days on the job would have helped Thad. She could have asked how he was doing and what concerns he had at that time. Thad was also not aware that she had any plans to include him in a Parent Night. So both Thad and the director missed the mark by not communicating with each other.

Isn't it interesting to see this case from two different perspectives? Now you know how important good communication skills are in an agency.

> ## Interpersonal Communication

Understanding and Mastery: Clarifying expectations, dealing effectively with conflict, and establishing rapport with clients

Critical Thinking Question: What could the director have done differently that might have prevented Thad from leaving? How might he have been included so that he would see his role as important?

Did You Know?

Career Planning Offices Can Assist with Employment

Every college or university has a **Career Planning Office**. These professionals help students compose resumes, look for jobs, and learn to interview for a job. Most schools offer a Career Day where they invite companies to campus to recruit new workers. This is a wonderful opportunity to find out what jobs are available in your field of study. Sometimes the office will provide direct assistance for writing resumes or they may have an online template or video to watch. Career services are usually provided along with other programs your school offers so additional fees are usually not required. This is a wonderful service that you should become familiar with at your school. Many students never use the services of their Career Planning Office. This is a mistake. Take advantage of whatever professional help you can find when it comes to learning about volunteer placements, internships, and paid employment. The professionals in these offices have already done the research to know how and where to find jobs in your area. They also are a great resource for finding out what agencies offer placements for volunteers or internships. They may also offer professional clothing that you can rent or borrow for your interview.

Put yourselves into groups of two and role-play a job interview. This will give you the opportunity to practice answering the questions that will be asked of you in a real interview. You can be the student who is looking for a Human Services job, part- or full-time, and your partner can be the prospective employer. Talk first about the kind of job you want, what type of agency this is, and then allow yourself to think about the types of questions you want to ask, before you begin the role-play. You might consider the kind of services you will provide, what age group you will serve, if you drive a car, if you have a license, if you have experience with this population, why you should be hired for the job, and what you can do for the agency. Then proceed with the role-play for about ten minutes. Then evaluate what you did together. Give your partner some feedback. Did your partner have good communication skills, have good eye contact, shake hands with the you, and was he or she dressed appropriately? Could he or she have answered the questions in a different manner? Did he or she express interest in the job? If you give each other some good feedback it will help you prepare for the actual interviews.

If you were the employer, give your partner some feedback. Did he or she interview well? Would you offer him or her the job? Why or why not? Consider such questions as was he or she prepared for the interview, did he or she seem interested in the job, ask good questions, and have good posture and eye contact? Was he or she self-assured and confident?

Now switch roles so that you both have the opportunity to role play-the employer and the interviewee. It is always a good idea to role-play an interview so you can anticipate the questions and be prepared with good answers.

What Would You Do?

Develop a Professional Plan for Yourself

Now you know something about what to expect in Human Services when you work with people. You can also start to think about your professional self and how to develop your skills in a work setting or develop your career by advancing through graduate education. Sit down and develop a plan for yourself.

Recall what you learned in this chapter by completing the Chapter Review.

If you are planning on advancing your career through graduate school, it is not too early to begin investigating what field of study you will pursue. Where will you go to school? For what degree? Part- or full-time? Who will pay for this degree? Start researching the schools you are interested in attending because they may have undergraduate prerequisites you need to complete, so that information will be helpful now. Are you interested in a counseling type degree? Does the graduate program allow you to become licensed or certified?

References for Chapter 1

American Public Health Association. Retrieved 11/10/2012, www.apha.org/advocacy/Health+Reform/ACAbasics/

Catholic Charities USA. Retrieved 11/10/2012, Council for Standards in Human Services Education. www.CSHSE.org

DiNitto, D. (2011). *Social Welfare Politics and Public Policy*, 7th edition, Boston, MA: Pearson Education, Inc., Chapters 2–3.

Kinsella, S. (2009). The Social Welfare System, Services to the Military. In B. Mandell, & B. Schram (Eds.), *An Introduction to Human Services: Policy and Practice*, 7th edition, (pp. 208–212), Boston, MA: Pearson Education, Inc.

Kinsella, S. (2010). *Thinking about a Career in Human Services*, online book, Boston, MA: Pearson Education, Inc., Chapters 2–3.

Mandell, B., & Schram, B. (2012). *An Introduction to Human Services: Policy and Practice*, 7th edition, Boston, MA: Pearson Education, Inc., Chapters 1, 11, 36.

Martin, M. (2014). *Introduction to Human Services: Through the Eyes of Practice Settings*, Upper Saddle River, NJ: Pearson Education, Inc., Chapters 1, 3, 13, 15.

Mehr, J., & Kanwischer, R. (2011). *Human Services Concepts and Intervention Strategies*, 10th edition, Boston, MA: Pearson Education, Inc., Chapters 10–12.

National Organization for Human Services. www.nationalhumanservices.org

Neukrug, E. (2002). *Skills and Techniques for Human Service Professionals*, Pacific Grove, CA: Brooks/Cole.

Patient Protection and Affordable Care Act. (2010). Retrieved 11/12/2012, www.gpo.gov/fdsys/pkg/BILLS-111hr3590enr/pdf/BILLS-111hr3590enr.pdf

White House Office of Faith-Based and Neighborhood Partnerships. Retrieved 11/10/2012, en.wikipedia.org/wiki/White_House_Office_of_Faith-Based_and_Neighborhood_Partnerships

Woodside, M., & McClam, T. (2011). *An Introduction to Human Services*, Belmont, CA: Thomson/Brooks Cole, pp. 61–64, 116–121.

References for Chapter 2

Baird, Abigail (2012). *THINK Psychology*, New Jersey: Prentice Hall, Chapter 6.

Crosson-Tower, C. (2013). *Exploring Child Welfare; A Practice Perspective*, 5th edition, Boston, MA: Pearson Education, Inc., Chapter 15.

Chenault, J., & Burnford, F. (1978). *Human Services Professional Education: Future Directions*, New York: McGraw Hill.

DiNitto, D., & Cummins, L. (2007). *Social Welfare Politics and Public Policy*, 6th edition, Boston, MA: Pearson, Inc.

Erikson, E. H. (1963). *Childhood and Society*, New York: W.W. Norton & Company, Inc.

Gillon, Steve (2004). *Boomer Nation: The Largest and Richest Generation Ever, and How It Changed America*, New York: Free Press, "Introduction," ISBN 0-7432-2947-9.

Henslin, J. (2012). *Essentials of Sociology: A Down-to-Earth Approach,* 10th edition, Boston, MA: Pearson Education, Inc., Chapter 3.

Kinsella, S. (2010) Human Services Career FAQ, Media Assests, Boston, MA: Pearson Education, Inc., Chapter 2–3. https://docs.google.com/folderview?pli=1&docId=0B1UYBjObFHzEbmF1LWw4akd2dk0&id=0B1UYBjObFH zEeU1tSjJhYkl5TG8&tid=0B1UYBjObFHzENmdIdVhXRWE2V00

Kunz, J. (2011). *THINK Marriages and Families*, Boston, MA: Pearson Education, Inc., pp. 208–220.

Korpi, B. M. (2007). The Politics of Preschool: Intentions and Decisions Underlying the Emergence and Growth of the Swedish Preschool. Stockholm: Government of Sweden. Ministry of Education and Research.

Lagerberg, R. "Sweden—Where Children Count," Sweden. SE, Swedish Institute, created 06/2012. Retrieved 11/4/2012 http://www.sweden.se

Maslow, A. (1971). *The Farther Reaches of Human Nature*. New York: Viking.

Mandell, B., & Schram, B. (2012). *An Introduction to Human Services: Policy and Practice*, 8th *edition,* Boston, MA: Pearson Education, Inc., Chapters 1, 11, 36.

Martin, M. (2013). *Introduction to Human Services through the Eyes of Practice Settings*, 3rd edition, Boston, MA: Pearson, Inc., Chapters 1, 3, 13, 15.

Mehr, J., & Kanwischer , R. (2011). *Human Services Concepts and Intervention Strategies*, 11th edition, Boston, MA: Pearson Education, Inc., Chapters 10–12.

National Organization for Human Services. Ethical Standards for Human Services Professionals. Retrieved 10/4/2013 http://www.nationalhumanservices.org/ethical-standards-for-hs-professionals

National Organization for Human Services. What is Human Services. Retrieved 10/4/2013 http://www .nationalhumanservices.org/what-is-human-services

National Organization for Human Services. Generic Human Services Professional Competencies. In *What is Human Services*. Retrieved 10/4/2013 http://www.nationalhumanservices.org/what-is-human-services

Neukrug, E. (1994). *Skills and Techniques for Human Service Professionals*, Brooks/Cole

Springfield College School of Human Services (2010), www.spfldcol.edu SHS viewbook

Freden, J. "No Spanking, Please!" Sweden. SE, Swedish Institute, Retrieved 5/22/2011, http://www.sweden.se

Sweden. SE, Swedish Institute, "Fact Sheet," created 06/2012. Retrieved 11/4/2012, http://www.sweden.se

Teixeira Moffat, Colleen, "Helping Those in Need: Human Services Workers," *Occupational Outlook Quarterly,* Fall 2011, Vol. 55, Number 3. Retrieved Nov. 4, 2012,

The State of the World's Children 2009: *UNICEF Report*

Toseland, R., & Rivas, R. (2011). *An Introduction to Group Work Practice*, 7th edition, Boston, MA: Pearson Education, Inc. 35–40.

Wade & Tavris (2011). *Psychology,* 10th edition, Boston, MA: Pearson Education, Inc. Chapters 10–15.

Woodside, M., and McClam, T. (2011). *An Introduction to Human Services*, Belmont, CA: Thomson/Brooks Cole, pp. 61–64, 116–121.

References for Chapter 3

Addams, Jane. (1981). *Twenty Years at Hull-House,* New York: Signet. First published in 1910.

Cashin, Edward, J. (2001). *Beloved Bethesda: A History of George Whitefield's Home for Boys 1740–2000,* Macon, GA: University Press.

Crosson-Tower, C. (2013). *Exploring Child Welfare: A Practice Perspective,* 6th edition, Boston, MA: Pearson Education, Inc, 5, 175–180.

Day, Phyllis, J. (2012). *A New History of Social Welfare,* 7th edition, Boston, MA: Allyn & Bacon, pp. 103–114, 128–142.

Eccles, Jacquelynne, & Appleton-Gootman, Jennifer. (2002). *Community Programs to Promote Youth Development,* Washington, DC: National Academy Press, pp. 297–314.

Ferrante, Joan. (2011). *Seeing Sociology,* Belmont, CA: Wadsworth Cengage Learning, pp. 93–94.

Henslin, James. (2013). *Essentials of Sociology: A Down-To-Earth Approach,* 10th edition, Boston, MA: Allyn & Bacon, pp. 6–19, 64–66.

Hinding, A. (2001). *Proud Heritage: A History in Pictures of the YMCA in the United States,* Virginia Beach, VA: The Donning Company Publisher, pp. 15–20.

Jane Addams Hull House Museum.(2009). "About Hull House." Retrieved 10/6/2013 from http://www.uic.edu /jaddams/hull/_learn/_abouthullhouse/abouthullhouse.html

Kanel, K. (2008). *An Overview of the Human Services,* Boston: Houghton Mifflin.

Leeson, P. (2006, October). "Cooperation and Conflict: Evidence of Self-Enforcing Arrangements and Heterogeneous Groups," *American Journal of Economics and Sociology,* 65, 891–907.

Nye Lavalle and Associates (1996). The Charities Americans Like Most And Least, *The Chronicle of Philanthropy,* December 13

Parten, M. (1932). "Social Participation among Preschool Children," *Journal of Abnormal and Social Psychology,* 28, 136–147.

Piven, F. (2008, February). "Can Power from Below Change the World?" *American Sociological Review,* 73, 1–14.

Sigalas, Mike. (2009, February). "Orphanage Band Instrumental in Jenkins' Past and Future," *SCIWAY News, South Carolina Newsletter,* 63. Retrieved 1/5/2013 from http://www.sciway.net/south-carolina/jenkins-orphanage.html

Trattner, W. (1998). *From Poor Law to Welfare State. A History of Social Welfare in America,* 6th edition, New York: Free Press.

Woodside, M., & McClam, T. (2011). *An Introduction to Human Services,* Belmont, CA: Thomson/Brooks Cole, p. 40.

Zimbalist, S. E. (1977). *Historic Themes and Landmarks in Social Welfare Research.* New York: Harper & Row.

References for Chapter 4

Council for Standards in Human Service Education. (n.d.). "Overview of the CSHSE National Standards." Retrieved 03/25/2011,www.cshse.org/overivew.html

Europa Press Releases RAPID. "EU Pupils Are Learning Foreign Languages at an Earlier Age," Brussels, Nov. 21, 2008, IP/08/1754.

Henslin, James. (2011). *Essentials of Sociology: A Down-to-Earth Approach,* 9th edition, Boston, MA: Allyn & Bacon, pp. 218–219. Retrieved 10/24/2012, www.techknowlogia.org/TKL_Articles/PDF/345.pdf

Lum, D. (2004). *Selections from Social Work Practice and People of Color, A Process Stage Approach*, 5th edition, Belmont, CA: Wadsworth, Thomson Learning, pp. 8–11.

Mehr, J., & Kanwischer, R. (2004). *Human Services Concepts and Intervention Strategies*, 9th edition, Boston, MA: Allyn & Bacon, pp. 46–47.

National Association of Social Workers. (2001). "Standards for Cultural Competence in Social Work Practice." Retrieved 03/24/2012, www.naswdc.org/code.htm

Neukrug, E. (2008). *Theory Practice & Trends in Human Services, An Introduction,* 4th edition, Belmont, CA: Brooks/Cole, Thomson Learning, pp. 204–205.

PBS website Hidden Korea www.pbs.org/hiddenkorea/culture.htm

Pierce, R. L., & Pierce, L. H. (1996). "Moving Toward Cultural Competence in the Child Welfare System," *Children and Youth Services Review*, 18. pp. 713–731.

Pufahl, I., Rhodes, N., & Christian, D. (2001, November/December). *Foreign Language Teaching in 19 Countries.* Washington, DC: Center for Applied Linguistics, Knowledge Enterprise Inc.

Rothman, J. (2008). *Cultural Competence in Process and Practice, Building Bridges.* Boston, MA: Pearson, Allyn & Bacon, pp. 7–11.

Taylor, M., Bradley, V., & Warren, R. (Eds.). (1996). *The Community Support Skills Standards: Tools for Managing Change and Achieving Outcomes: Skill Standards for Direct Service Workers in the Human Services*, Cambridge, MA: Human Services Research Institute, pp. 7–11.

Videos of Travel China Guide website video.travelchinaguide.com/000604.htm

Woodside, M., & McClam, T. (2011). *An Introduction to Human Services*, 7th edition, Belmont, CA: Thomson/ Brooks Cole, pp. 253–254.

References for Chapter 5

Burger, William. (2011). *Human Services in Contemporary America,* Belmont, CA: Brooks/Cole, pp. 197–206.

Council for Standards in Human Service Education. Retrieved 11/1/2012, http://www.cshse.org

Cournoyer, Barry. (2010). *The Social Work Skills Workbook*, Belmont, CA: Brooks/Cole, pp. 155–168.

Howatt, William. (2000). *The Human Services Counseling Toolbox,* Belmont, CA: Wadsworth/Thomson Learning, pp. 14–18.

Ivey, A., Gluckstern, N., & Bradford, M. (2006). *Basic Interviewing Skills*, 4th edition, N. Amherst, MA: Microtraining Associates.

Mandell, B., & Schram, B. (2012). *An Introduction to Human Services: Policy & Practice*, Boston, MA: Pearson Education Inc., pp. 134–140.

Neukrug, E. (2002). *Skills and Techniques for Human Service Professionals*, Pacific Grove, CA: Brooks/Cole, pp. 81–90.

Study Abroad AIFS website.

Woodside, M., & McClam, T. (2011). *An Introduction to Human Services*, 7th edition, Belmont, CA: Thomson /Brooks Cole, pp. 201–208. Retrieved 4/2/2013, http://www.studyabroad.com/

References for Chapter 6

American Psychiatric Association. (2000). *Diagnostic and Statistical Manual,* 4th edition, text revision, (Electronic version), Washington, DC: Author. Retrieved 06/26/2012, http://online.statref.com

Bowen, M. (1978). *Family Therapy in Clinical Practice,* New York and London: Jason Aronson, pp. 60–75.

Corey, M., Corey, G., & Corey, C. (2010). *Groups Process and Practice,* 8th edition, Belmont, CA: Brooks/Cole, pp. 110–112.

Cournoyer, B. (2010). *The Social Work Skills Workbook,* 6th edition, Belmont, CA: Brooks/Cole, pp. 249–287.

Gilligan, C. (1982). *In a Different Voice,* Boston, MA: Harvard University Press.

Howatt, W. (2000). *The Human Services Counseling Toolbox,* Belmont, CA: Brooks/Cole, pp. 167–179.

Karls, J. M., & Wandrei, K. E. (1994). *PIE Manual: Person-in-environment system: The PIE Classification System for Social Functioning Problems.* Washington, DC: NASW Press.

Kuyken, W., Fothergill, C. D., Musa, M., & Chadwick, P. (2005). "The Reliability and Quality of Cognitive Case Formulation," *Behaviour Research and Therapy,* 43(9), 1187–1201.

Martin, M. (2014). *Introduction to Human Services: Through the Eyes of Practice Settings,* Boston, MA: Pearson Education, Inc., pp. 60–65.

McGoldrick, M., & Gerson, R. (1985). *Genograms: Assessment and Intervention,* 2nd edition, New York: W.W. Norton.

Mehr, J., & Kanwischer, R. (2011). *Human Services Concepts and Intervention Strategies.* Boston, MA: Pearson Education, Inc.

National Association of Social Workers. (2012). "NASW Standards for Social Work Case Management." Retrieved 06/26/2012, http://www.naswdc.org/practice/standards/sw_case_mgmt.asp#

O'Hanlon, W., & Weiner-Davis, M. (1989). *In Search of Solutions: A New Direction in Psychotherapy,* New York: W. W. Norton.

Satir, V. (1988). *The New Peoplemaking.* Mountain View, CA: Science and Behavior.

Sherman, R., & Fredman, N. (1986). *Handbook of Structured Techniques in Marriage and Family Therapy,* New York: Brunner/Mazel.

Woodside, M., & McClam, T. (2011). *An Introduction to Human Services,* Belmont, CA: Thomson/Brooks Cole, pp. 233–234.

References for Chapter 7

Boris, E., deLeon, E., Roeger, K., & Nikolova, M. (2010). Human Service Nonprofits and Government Collaboration: Findings from the 2010 National Survey of Nonprofit Government Contracting and Grants, Washington, DC: Urban Institute.

Bossidy, L., & Charan, R. *(2009). Execution: The Discipline of Getting Things Done*, New York: Crown Business, pp. 109–120.

Burger, W. (2011). *Human Services in Contemporary America*, Belmont, CA: Brooks/Cole, pp. 222–225.

Collins, J. (2001). *Good to Great*, New York: HarperCollins Publishers, Inc., pp. 17–35.

Council for Standards in Human Services Education (2011). Retrieved 11/1/2012, http://www.cshse.org/about.html

Kanter, R. M. (2004). *Confidence*, New York: Three Rivers Press, pp. 331–350.

Kanter, R. (2006). *Confidence*, New York: Three Rivers Press, pp. 182–256.

Kotter, J. (1996). *Leading Change*, Boston, MA: Harvard Business Review Press.

Lewis, J. A., Lewis, M. D., Packard, T., & Souflee, F. (2006). *Management of Human Service Programs*, 3rd edition, Belmont, CA: Brooks/Cole.

Mandell, B., & Schram, B. (2010). *An Introduction to Human Services: Policy and Practice*, Boston, MA: Allyn & Bacon, pp. 471–505, 539–559.

Morales, A., Sheafor, B., & Scott, M. (2010). *Social Work: A Profession of Many Faces*, Boston, MA: Allyn & Bacon, pp. 101–102.

Neukrug, E. (2008). *Theory, Practice & Trends in Human Services*, 4th edition, Belmont, CA: Brooks/Cole.

Stuart, L. (2004). *Community Organizing as Human Services*. In H. S. Harris, D. C. Maloney, & F. M. Rother (Eds.), Human Services Contemporary Issues and Trends, (pp. 267–274), Boston, MA: Allyn & Bacon.

Woodside, M., & McClam, T. (2011). *An Introduction to Human Services*, 7th edition, Belmont, CA: Thomson /Brooks Cole, pp. 227–240, 253–254.

References for Chapter 8

Benokraitis, Nijole. (2012). *SOC,* Belmont, CA: Cengage, pp. 134–135.

Blumstein, A., & Wallman, J. (2006). "The Crime Drop and Beyond," *Annual Review of Law and Social Science,* December, 125–146.

Carl, J. (2010). *THINK Sociology,* Upper Saddle River, NJ: Pearson Education, Inc., pp. 122–123, 140–144.

CBS News. (2013). "Mississippi's Rising Infant Mortality Rate." Retrieved 10/7/2013, http://www.cbsnews.com/2100-18563_162-2878184.html

Centers for Disease Control. (2012). "Adolescent & School Health." Retrieved 07/30/2012, http://www.cdc.gov/healthyyouth/alcoholdrug/index.htm

Centers for Disease Control and Prevention. (2013). *HIV/BASICS,* Atlanta, GA: Author. Retrieved 10/7/2013, http://www.cdc.gov/hiv/basics/index.html

Centers for Disease Control and Prevention. (2012). *Fact Sheets—Underage Drinking,* Atlanta, GA: Author. Retrieved 10/7/2013, http://www.cdc.gov/alcohol/fact-sheets/underage-drinking.htm

Child Welfare League of America. (2002). "Alcohol, Other Drugs and Child Welfare." Retrieved from www.cwla.org/programs/chemical/

Children's Defense Fund. (2012a). *The State of America's Children 2012 Handbook: Child Poverty,* Washington, DC: Author. Retrieved 10/7/2013, http://www.childrensdefense.org/child-research-data-publications/state-of-americas-children-2011/poverty.html

Children's Defense Fund. (2012b). *Research Library,* Washington, DC: Author. Retrieved 10/7/2013, http://www.childrensdefense.org/child-research-data-publications/data/trends-in-the-levels-and.html

Children's Defense Fund. (2012c). *Policy Priorities: Child Abuse and Neglect,* Washington, DC: Author. Retrieved 10/7/2013, http://www.childrensdefense.org/policy-priorities/child-welfare/child-abuse-neglect/

Children's Defense Fund Report. (2012d). *Children in the States Factsheets,* Washington, DC: Author. Retrieved 10/7/2013, http://www.childrensdefense.org/child-research-data-publications/data/state-data-repository/children-in-the-states.html

Crosson-Tower, C. (2013). *Exploring Child Welfare: A Practice Perspective,* Boston, MA: Pearson Education, Inc., pp. 90–97.

Diagnostic and Statistical Manual of Mental Disorders (2013) 5th edition, American Psychiatric Association, Arlington, VA: American Psychiatric Publishing, Inc.

Dr. Oz Show. (2013). "What Causes Autism? Part 1." http://www.doctoroz.com/videos/what-causes-autism-pt-1

Ehrenreich, Barbara. (2012). "Nickeled and Dimed: On (Not) Getting by in America." Retrieved 08/2/2012, http://www.barbaraehrenreich.com/nickelanddimed.htm

Examiner. (2012). "Fox News Exclusive: Colorado Shooter Sent Notebook to Psychiatrist." Retrieved 07/25/2012, http://www.examiner.com/article/foxnews-com-exclusive-colorado-shooting-suspect-sent-notebook-to-psychiatrist

Family Promise. (2012). Retrieved 08/18/2012, http://www.familypromise.org/program/interfaith-hospitality-network

Ferrante, J. (2011). *Seeing Sociology,* Belmont, CA: Wadsworth Cengage Learning, pp. 213–215.

Golden, J. (2005). *Message in a Bottle: The Making of Fetal Alcohol Syndrome,* Cambridge, MA: Harvard University Press.

Henslin, J. (2013). *Sociology: A Down-to-Earth-Approach.* 12th edition, Boston MA: Pearson Higher Ed.

Huffington Post. "Magic Johnson Still Beating HIV 20 Years Later." http://www.huffingtonpost.com/2011/11/08/magic-johnson-hiv-20-years-later_n_1081752.html

Kinsella, S. (2011). The Social Welfare System, Services to the Military. In B. Mandell, & B. Schram (Eds.), *An Introduction to Human Services: Policy and Practice*, 8th edition, (pp. 208–212), Boston, MA: Pearson Education, Inc.,

Martin, M. (2013). *Introduction to Human Services: Through the Eyes of Practice Settings*, 3rd edition Boston, MA: Pearson Education Inc., pp. 200–205.

Merton, Robert, K. (1957). Social Theory and Social Structure, Revised edition. Glencoe, IL: Free Press.

Mooney, L., Knox, D., & Schacht, C. (2007). *Understanding Social Problems*, Belmont, CA: Thomson/Wadsworth, pp. 188–190.

Mullin, Charles, R., & Linz, Daniel. (1995). "Desensitization and Re-sensitization to Violence against Women: Effects of Exposure to Sexually Violent Films on Judgments of Domestic Violence Victims," *Journal of Personality and Social Psychology*, 69(3), 449–459.

National Institute on Drug Abuse. (2013). *The Science of Drug Abuse and Addiction*, Bethesda: Maryland. Retrieved 10/7/2013, http://www.drugabuse.gov/

National Law Center on Homelessness and Poverty. (2012). "Program: Housing." Retrieved 08/01/2012, http://www.nlchp.org/program.cfm?prog=5

Reiman., & Leighton, (2012), *The Rich Get Richer and The Poor Get Prison*, 10th edition; Boston, MA: Pearson Higher Ed.

Safe Horizons. (2012). "Homeless Youth." Retrieved 08/02/2012, http://www.safehorizon.org/index/what-we-do-2/helping-youth-14/streetwork-homeless-youth-facts-220.html?gclid=CPzn9dfUybECFQP0nAodPyYAcQ

Samenow, S. (2004). *Inside the Criminal Mind: Revised and Updated Edition*, New York: Crown Publishers.

Save the Children. (2012). "Careers." Retrieved 07/31/2012, http://www.savethechildren.org/site/c.8rKLIXMGIpI4E/b.6226565/k.BA72/Careers.htm?msource=wexggcar0611&gclid=CPfw3LjwxrECFYOc7QodllMAOA

Substance Abuse and Mental Health Services Administration. 2012 "Depression Triples Between the Ages of 12 and 15 for Adolescent Girls." Retrieved 07/31/2012, http://www.samhsa.gov/data/

Substance Abuse and Mental Health Services Administration. 2012 "Underage Drinking (Michigan)." State/Territory Prevention Videos Retrieved 07/30/2012, http://www.samhsa.gov/

Teen Help. (2013). "Teen Pregnancy." Retrieved 10/7/2013, http://www.teenhelp.com/teen-pregnancy/

US Census Bureau. (2011). "Child Poverty in the United States 2009 and 2010: Selected Race Groups and Hispanic Origin." Retrieved 07/30/2012, http://www.census.gov/prod/2011pubs/acsbr10-05.pdf

World Health Organization. (2013). *HIV/AIDS*, Geneva, Switzerland: Author. Retrieved 10/7/2013, http://www.who.int/topics/hiv_aids/en/

Zastrow, C., (2009). *Introduction to Social Work and Social Welfare*, 10th edition, Pacific Grove, CA: Brooks/Cole.

Zuckerman, B. S., Fitzgerald, H. E., & Lester, B. M. (2000). *Children of Addiction*, New York: Taylor and Francis.

References for Chapter 9

About.com. "Juvenile Crime and Issues." Retrieved 09/12/2012, http://crime.about.com/od/juvenile/i/juvenile_death.htm

Arnett, Jeffrey. (2004). "Emerging Adulthood: Books and Articles." http://www.jeffreyarnett.com/articles.htm

Baird, A. (2012). *THINK Psychology*, Upper Saddle River, NJ: Prentice Hall, pp. 84–86.

Bowlby, J. (1969). *Attachment and Loss: Vol. 1. Attachment.* London: Hogarth.

Cooley, C. (1902), *Human Nature and the Social Order*, New York: Charles Scribner's Sons, revised edition 1922.

Crosson-Tower, C. (2013). *Exploring Child Welfare: A Practice Perspective*, 6th edition, Boston, MA: Pearson Education, Inc., pp. 230–233.

Erikson, E. H. (1963). *Childhood and Society.* New York. Norton.

Goldstein, J., & Kenney, C. (2001). "Marriage Delayed or Marriage Forgone?" *American Sociological Review, 66,* August, 506–519. Retrieved 4/16/2013, http://www.asanet.org/images/members/docs/pdf/featured/goldstein.pdf

Harlow, H. (1958). "The Nature of Love," *American Psychologist*, 13, 573–685.

Henslin, J. (2013). *Essentials of Sociology, A Down To Earth Approach,* 10th edition, Boston, MA: Pearson Education, Inc., 64–76.

Glaze, L., & Maruschak, L. (2008). "Parents in Prison and Their Minor Children," *Bureau of Justice Statistics Special Report*, August, 1–25.

Mead, George, Herbert. (1934). *Mind, Self and Society*, Chicago: University of Chicago Press.

SOS Children's Villages. Retrieved 09/30/2013, "SOS Children in South America: Family Strengthening and Street Children." http://www.street-children.org.uk/samericanstreetchildren

References for Chapter 10

American Association of Retired People. "Boomers and the Great Recession." Retrieved 09/21/2012, http://www
.aarp.org/work/job-hunting/info-09-2012/boomers-and-the-great-recession-struggling-to-recover-AARP-ppi
-econ-sec.html

Anxiety Centre, 2012, Retrieved 9/30/2012, http://www.anxietycentre.com/anxiety-videos.shtml

Arnett, Jeffrey. (2004). "Emerging Adulthood: Books and Articles." http://www.jeffreyarnett.com/articles.htm

Baird, A. (2010). *THINK Psychology*, Upper Saddle River, NJ: Prentice Hall, p. 110.

Brain & Behavior Research Foundation. Retrieved 10/02/2012, http://bbrfoundation.org/about

Carstensen, L. L. (1991). "Selectivity Theory: Social-Activity in Life-Span Context," *Annual Review of Gerontology and Geriatrics*, 11, 195–217.

CTV. "UN Urges Protection for the World's Growing Elderly." Retrieved 10/7/2012, http://www.ctvnews.ca/world
/un-urges-protection-for-the-world-s-growing-elderly-population-1.978330

Cumming E., & Henry, W. (1961) *Growing Old: The Process of Disengagement*. Basic Books, New York: New York. (Reprint: Arno, New York, 1979).

Department of Economic and Social Affairs of the United Nations, Retrieved 9/30/2013, http://undesadspd.org
/Ageing/DataonOlderPersons.aspx

Erikson, E. H. (1963). *Childhood and Society*, New York: Norton. *The Hindu*. "Concerns over an Aging India."
Retrieved 10/07/2012, http://www.thehindu.com/news/national/concerns-over-an-aging-india/article3972671.ece

MedicineNet.com. "What Is a Phobia?" Retrieved 09/21/2012, http://www.medicinenet.com/phobias_picture_
slideshow/article.htm

Mental Health and Advocacy Project. Retrieved 09/24/2012, http://www.mhaging.org/info/olus.html

Mroczek, D. K. (2001). "Age and Emotion in Adulthood," *Current Directions in Psychological Science*, 10, 87–90.

The National Reentry Resource Center. Retrieved 10/2/2012, http://www.nationalreentryresourcecenter.org/faqs
/employment-and-education

Schulz, R., & Rockwood, K. (2006). *Activity Theory: The Encyclopedia of Aging*, 4th edition, Springer Publishing Company, pp. 9–10.

United States Census Bureau, The 2012 Statistical Abstract, National Data Book. Retrieved 09/24/2012, http://
www.census.gov/compendia/statab/

World Health Organization. "Aging and the Life Course." Retrieved 10/07/2012, http://www.who.int/ageing/en/

References for Chapter 11

Bravewell Collaborative. "The New Medicine PBS Special." Retrieved 10/24/2012, http://www.bravewell.org/integrative_medicine/new_medicine/

Carl, John. (2010). *THINK Sociology*, Boston, MA: Prentice Hall, Pearson Higher Education, p. 270.

Chumley, Norris. (2011). *Mysteries of the Jesus Prayer: Experiencing the Presence of God and a Pilgrimage to the Heart of an Ancient Spirituality*, New York: HarperCollins.

Chumley, Norris. "Religious Versus Spirituality?" Retrieved 10/13/2012, http://www.huffingtonpost.com/norris-j-chumley-phd/exactly-what-is-religious_b_509871.html

Henslin, James. (2013). *Essentials of Sociology: A Down-to-Earth Approach*, 9th edition, Boston, MA: Allyn & Bacon, pp. 397–412

Huffingtonpost.com (2011), Huffpost Video, HPMG News, Retrieved 10/8/2013.

Kline, Austin. (2012). "Agnosticism/Atheism." Retrieved 10/13/2012, http://atheism.about.com/bio/Austin-Cline-5577.htm

Maugans, T. A., & Wadland, W. C. (1991). "Religion and Family Medicine: A Survey of Physicians and Patients," *Journal of Family Practice,* 32, 210–213.

Pew Forum on Religion and Public Life. (2012, March 22). "Religion in Prisons: A 50-State Survey of Prison Chaplains."

Religious Tolerance. (2001). "The Geneva Spiritual Appeal of 1999-October, Ontario." Retrieved 10/8/2013, http://www.religioustolerance.org/rel_prom.htm

The Wall Street Journal. "Unrest Over Anti Muslim Films Spreads." Retrieved 10/9/2012, http://blogs.marketwatch.com/thetell/2012/09/14/unrest-over-anti-muslim-films-spreads-in-middle-east/

References for Chapter 12

Karger, H. (1981). "Burnout as Alienation," *Social Service Review,* 55, 271–283.

Kinsella, S. (1997) *"A Comparative Cross-Discipline Study of Traditional and Nontraditional College Students,"* *The Journal of College Students,* Winter 1998, 32 (4), pp. 532–538.

The New York Times. "World." Retrieved 11/1/2012, http://topics.nytimes.com/top/news/international/countriesandterritories/haiti/index.html

Reed, S. (1979, January 7). "Teacher Burnout Is Growing Hazard," *The New York Times,* p. L12.

Sweitzer, H. F. (1999). Burnout: Avoiding the Trap. In H. S. Harriet & D. C. Maloney (Eds.), *Human Services: Contemporary Issues and Trends,* 2nd Edition, Boston, MA: Allyn & Bacon. pp. 339–356.

Index